AFRICAN POLITICAL, ECONOMIC, AND SECURITY ISSUES SERIES

POVERTY IN AFRICA

AFRICAN POLITICAL, ECONOMIC, AND SECURITY ISSUES SERIES

Focus on Zimbabwe
Alfred J. Cartage (Editor)
2009. ISBN: 978-1-60692-186-9

**State Building and Democracy in Africa:
A Comparative and Developmental Approach**
John W. Forje
2009. ISBN: 978-1-60741-371-4

The Land and Maritime Boundary Disputes of Africa
Rongxing Guo
2009. ISBN: 978-1-60741-637-1

**The Challenges in Administrative Political and
Developmental Renewal in Africa: Emerging Issues**
John W. Forje
2009. ISBN: 978-1-60741-265-6

**The Challenges of Administrative Political and Developmental Renewal in Africa:
Essays on Rethinking Government and Reorganization**
John W. Forje
2009. ISBN: 978-1-60741-266-3

**South Africa's Truth and Reconciliation Commission:
An Annotated Bibliography [Circa 1993-2008]**
Muhammed Haron
2009. ISBN 978-1-60741-229-8

Poverty in Africa
Thomas W. Beasley (Editor)
2009. ISBN: 978-1-60741-737-8

AFRICAN POLITICAL, ECONOMIC, AND SECURITY ISSUES SERIES

POVERTY IN AFRICA

THOMAS W. BEASLEY
EDITOR

Nova Science Publishers, Inc.
New York

Copyright © 2009 by Nova Science Publishers, Inc.

All rights reserved. No part of this book may be reproduced, stored in a retrieval system or transmitted in any form or by any means: electronic, electrostatic, magnetic, tape, mechanical photocopying, recording or otherwise without the written permission of the Publisher.

For permission to use material from this book please contact us:
Telephone 631-231-7269; Fax 631-231-8175
Web Site: http://www.novapublishers.com

NOTICE TO THE READER

The Publisher has taken reasonable care in the preparation of this book, but makes no expressed or implied warranty of any kind and assumes no responsibility for any errors or omissions. No liability is assumed for incidental or consequential damages in connection with or arising out of information contained in this book. The Publisher shall not be liable for any special, consequential, or exemplary damages resulting, in whole or in part, from the readers' use of, or reliance upon, this material. Any parts of this book based on government reports are so indicated and copyright is claimed for those parts to the extent applicable to compilations of such works.

Independent verification should be sought for any data, advice or recommendations contained in this book. In addition, no responsibility is assumed by the publisher for any injury and/or damage to persons or property arising from any methods, products, instructions, ideas or otherwise contained in this publication.

This publication is designed to provide accurate and authoritative information with regard to the subject matter covered herein. It is sold with the clear understanding that the Publisher is not engaged in rendering legal or any other professional services. If legal or any other expert assistance is required, the services of a competent person should be sought. FROM A DECLARATION OF PARTICIPANTS JOINTLY ADOPTED BY A COMMITTEE OF THE AMERICAN BAR ASSOCIATION AND A COMMITTEE OF PUBLISHERS.

LIBRARY OF CONGRESS CATALOGING-IN-PUBLICATION DATA

Beasley, Thomas W.
  Poverty in Africa / Thomas W. Beasley.
     p. cm.
  Includes index.
  ISBN 978-1-60741-737-8 (hardcover)
  1. Poor--Africa. 2. Africa--Economic conditions--21st century. 3. Africa--Social conditions--21st century. I. Title.
  HC800.P6B43 2009
  339.4'6096--dc22
                                                                                    2009024614

Published by Nova Science Publishers, Inc. ✢ New York

CONTENTS

Preface   vii

Chapter 1   The Impact of Road Infrastructure on Poverty Reduction in Africa   1
John C. Anyanwu and Andrew E. O. Erhijakpor

Chapter 2   We are the First Doctors Here at Home: Women's Perspectives on Sanitary Conditions in Mozambique   41
Maja Söderbäck and Malin Udén

Chapter 3   Livelihood Diversification, De-Agrarianisation and Social Differentiation: Comparative Analysis of Rural Livelihoods from South Africa and Kenya   75
Miyuki Iiyama

Chapter 4   Poverty and Maternal Health in Malawi   105
C.P. Maliwichi-Nyirenda and L.L. Maliwichi

Chapter 5   Oyster Mushroom Cultivation For Resource-Poor Farmers in Southern Africa   133
E.C. Kunjeku and L.L. Maliwichi

Chapter 6   Chinese Policies towards Africa: Poverty Alleviating or Poverty Promoting?   157
Jacqueline M. Musiitwa

Chapter 7   The Evolution and Dynamics of Urban Poverty in Zambia   177
Danny Simatele and Munacinga Simatele

Chapter 8   The Role of Small Scale Survivalist Enterprises in Generation of Household Incomes in Vhembe District of Limpopo Province, South Africa   193
Maliwichi, L.L., Oni S.A. and Sifumba, L.

Chapter 9   Gender Inequality and Poverty: The Kenyan Case   209
Tabitha W. Kiriti and K. C. Roy

| **Chapter 10** | The Globalization-AIDS-Poverty Syndrome in Africa
Pádraig Carmody and Glen Elder | **235** |

Index   **257**

PREFACE

Over the past few decades poverty has emerged as a global problem and a global agenda item in need of action. For that reason, the United Nations made its eradication the first Millennium Development Goal (MDG). The MDG's plan is for extreme poverty to be eliminated by 2015. Poverty is more of a concern on the African continent than elsewhere. Three fourths of poor people in Western and Middle Africa — an estimated 90 million people — live in rural areas and depend on agriculture for their livelihoods. One in five lives in a country affected by warfare. In conflict-torn countries such as Angola, Burundi, Mozambique and Uganda, the capacity of rural people to make a livelihood has been dramatically curtailed by warfare, and per capita food production has plummeted. A child dies every three seconds from AIDS and extreme poverty, often before their fifth birthday and more than one billion people do not have access to clean water. Every year six million children die from malnutrition before their fifth birthday. This book brings together new research on programs and policies from around the globe related to poverty in Africa and its elimination or alleviation.

Chapter 1 - There is general acceptance that economic infrastructure is critical for economic growth and poverty reduction, given its pivotal role in improving competitiveness, facilitating both domestic and international trade, and integration of the continent to the global economy. However, there is a large infrastructure deficit, both in terms of access and quality, to be filled in all the sectors (transport, energy, ICT and water). For instance, the level of access to electricity in Africa is only about 30 percent, compared to over 75 percent for other Less Developed Countries (LDCs). Access to water and sanitation is about 65 percent compared to 80 percent for other LDCs; the penetration rate for telecommunication is less than 13 percent compared to 40 percent in other LDCs; while access to roads is 34 percent compared to 50 percent for other LDCs. This situation has resulted, among others, in Africa's low rates of economic growth, low poverty reduction, reduced share of world trade and lack of international competitiveness. The high transaction costs arising from poor road infrastructure, for example, adversely affects development of African economies, hinders private sector development, and the flow of foreign direct investment (FDI). However, studies on the impact of road infrastructure had been confined mostly to developed economies and other developing economies, where road infrastructure developments swamp those in Africa. Indeed, few studies have examined the impact of road infrastructure on poverty in a broad panel of African (Sub-Saharan and North African) countries. This paper tries to fill this lacuna by constructing a panel data set on poverty and road infrastructure for African countries. It essentially examines the impact of road infrastructure on poverty reduction in African countries using panel data of 33 countries over the period 1990-2005.

The authors find that road infrastructure – proxied by paved roads (as percentage of total roads) – reduces the level, depth, and severity of poverty in Africa. But the size of the poverty reduction depends on how poverty is being measured. The author find that a 10 percent increase in road infrastructure leads to a 5.16 percent decline in the poverty headcount or the share of people living in poverty. Also, the more sensitive poverty measures – the poverty gap (poverty depth) and squared poverty gap (poverty severity) – suggest that road infrastructure will have a similar impact on poverty reduction. The point estimates for the poverty gap and squared poverty gap suggest that a 10 percent increase in the share of road infrastructure will lead to a 6.14 percent and 6.91 percent decline, respectively, in the depth and severity of poverty in African countries. In conformity with most theoretical and empirical literature, education significantly reduces the poverty headcount and severity in the continent. Regardless of the measure of poverty used as the dependent variable, income inequality (Gini index) has a positive and significant coefficient, indicating that greater inequality is associated with higher poverty in African countries, much in conformity with the literature. Similar results are obtained for trade openness. In the same vein, per capita income has a negative and significant effect on each measure of poverty used in the study. The author results also show that inflation rates positively and significantly affect poverty incidence, depth and severity in Africa. In all three poverty measures, the dummy variable for Sub-Saharan Africa is strongly positive – and strongly negative for North Africa. The policy implications of these results are discussed in the paper.

Chapter 2 - Lack of sanitation is an important public health issue in low-income countries. Globally, the lack of sanitation affects some 2.8 billion people, mainly the poor, women and children. The people affected are deprived of their dignity and at risk for several severe diarrheal diseases. However, improvements are often hindered by the fact that human excrement is a sensitive issue, and feasible solutions fail to consider cultural and gender issues.

With this background, this chapter focuses on women's sanitary conditions in a rural African village (Mozambique). An ethnographic approach was used to investigate the everyday sanitary conditions, understood through a theoretical framework of equity in health, and gender was used for understanding. During a two-month stay in the village, women in three households were followed and observed in their everyday work to explore the sanitary prerequisites. Furthermore, official and traditional leaders in the village were interviewed about their perceptions of the women's sanitary situation.

The findings show that every woman and her family members are obligated to deal with their human waste on an individual basis, creating solutions mostly from what could be obtained free within the confinements of their yard. This unhygienic situation rendered the women fearful of disease and accidents, especially for their children, resulting in both psychological and physiological discomfort. Maintaining sanitation was female work. However, only men were allowed to build new latrines, causing difficulties for the many women without husbands. Several positive forces also existed: openness, interest, knowledge and an already existing net of community development. Improvements are instead held back by poverty and gender disparities, depriving women of control over their own home and health.

Chapter 4 - Livelihood diversification, de-agrarianisation and social differentiation along differential access to off-farm incomes and non-agrarian assets turn out to be dominant features of rural poverty in contemporary Africa. They pose methodological challenges for researchers to conceptualise sociological typologies of rural African populations in the processes of de-agrarianisation and increasing social differentiation, while the existent development theories apparently underestimate their considerable implications on rural development. In response to the increased recognition of these features, the livelihood study has emerged to lead the focus of rural poverty analysis from an agriculture-centred, sector-level viewpoint to a household or individual-level viewpoint. The livelihood study, through synthesising empirical evidence across, should contribute to facilitating the analysis of social changes from the perspective of households/individuals and to refining existent development theories and policies.

This study attempts to search for effective criteria to identify typologies of rural Africans that reflect heterogeneities in livelihood diversification portfolios of farm and off-farm activities within and between communities, and to apply them to case studies from South Africa and Kenya. The South African case describes heterogeneous reactions by rural sub-populations to cope with social transitions (unemployment) and secure rural livelihoods. The Kenyan case examines heterogeneous reactions by rural sub-populations to de-agrarianisation over agricultural intensification.

The case studies reveal that de-agrarianisation processes, i.e., their causes, directions, extents and impacts on rural development and agricultural intensification, have shown considerable variations between South Africa and Kenya, depending on the local experiences of colonial histories, state policies, demographic and agro-ecological conditions, i.e., under-farming in South Africa and governance issues in Kenya. Nevertheless, it has also been found that de-agrarianisation and livelihood diversification in South Africa and Kenya have been similarly accompanied by the increasing social differentiation with differential accesses to non-agrarian assets. Synthesising the analytical results can contribute to deriving theoretical and policy implications on agrarian change in the era of globalisation.

Chapter 5 - A large proportion of Malawi's population is poor and unable to meet their basic needs. The country has not experienced a significant economic growth over the years to help eradicate extreme poverty and hunger. Poverty is one of the main contributing factors towards maternal mortality because women cannot afford conventional medical care. Malawi is the 13th poorest country with high maternal mortality rate of 984 maternal deaths per 100,000 live births. Although the government has made investment in health sector, most health facilities, which provide free services, lack essential drugs and equipment. Better services are provided by district and central hospitals but these are few and not readily accessible. People from rural areas are only attended to by district and central hospitals if they have a referral letter from health centres. In addition, private hospitals, which are fully equipped and readily accessible, charge exorbitant fees.

This study investigated, through participatory rural appraisal and questionnaire interviews, how maternal problems are managed in rural areas of Mulanje District in Malawi. Thirty three diseases were documented. There were mixed responses towards the causes of maternal mortality. Uterine rupture however seemed to be the major cause of maternal deaths. According to Ministry of Health and Population, uterine ruptures are caused by use of medicinal plants hence bans use of medicinal plants by pregnant women. Despite the ban, the study found that people still use medicinal plants. Trained traditional birth attendants, who are prohibited by the Ministry of Health and Population from using medicinal plants, were also found using medicinal plants. Thirty-two ailments prevalent among pregnant women were documented. Ten medicinal plant species used for six commonly prevalent maternity cases were also documented. Continued use of medicinal plants was attributed to inaccessibility of conventional health facilities, cultural reasons and poor reception at conventional hospitals. Despite being resource-limited, traditional medical practitioners especially traditional birth attendants, undertake substantial amount of child deliveries (at least 1,100 per month).

It is anticipated that for as long as the problems facing modern maternal healthcare delivery services prevail, people shall continue to use medicinal plants. There is there fore, a need to investigate if there is any link between medicinal plant use and maternal deaths so as to facilitate the safe consumption of these medicinal plants.

Chapter 6 - Oyster mushrooms of the genus *Pleurotus* are cultivated widely in the world, and are being cultivated on a large scale in most developing countries. However this mushroom cultivation technology has not been widely adopted and developed in most of tropical Africa. It has been neglected in spite of the advantages it has for the resource-poor farmers. Subsistence farmers often do not have enough land to produce crops on an economic scale, and often lack capital to initiate projects that require expensive infrastructure and investment. Oyster mushroom cultivation has the potential to provide food and also alleviate poverty from the sale of excess production. There is no requirement for land, and investment in mushroom house construction is minimal. Oyster mushrooms are primarily wood decomposing fungi, growing mostly in forest situations on tree trunks and wood detritus. However, they can be grown artificially in all kinds of environments and on various cellulosic waste products. The cultivation is done in built-up structures, and therefore the mushroom cultivation does not compete with field crops for space. The investment on infrastructure is minimal. Resource-poor families in Zimbabwe trained in this technology are cultivating oyster mushrooms as a source of food and also as an income-generating venture. Markets for the mushrooms range from boarding schools and hospitals to hotels. The other attraction for growing oyster mushrooms is that they utilize agricultural waste as a substrate.

Oyster mushrooms have a lot of similarities with wild mushroom which are a delicacy for most rural populations in Africa. They are a rich source of protein and vitamins, and are often used as a substitute for meat. In most of tropical Africa, wild mushrooms are picked during the summer season. They therefore tend to be a food source for only a limited time in the year, unlike the commercially grown mushrooms which are available throughout the year. Cultivation of *Agaricus* mushrooms requires large capital investment and specialized skills, and is not suitable for poor farmers. Wild mushrooms differ from the *Agaricus* species in their texture and taste. Like the tropical wild mushrooms, oyster mushrooms tend to be chewy, closely approximating meat texture. Oyster mushrooms are a rich source of protein, comparing favourably with meat and eggs. They are also a source of carbohydrates, minerals (such as calcium, phosphorus and iron), and vitamins such as thiamin, riboflavin and niacin. Various studies have put the protein content of oyster mushrooms from 15% up to 30% of their dry weight, depending on the substrate on which they are grown. They contain amino acids and enzymes that have been said to boost the immune system. They have also been shown to contain anti-oxidants that boost the immune system by acting as free radical scavengers. They are easily digestible, an essential component especially for sick people with sensitive digestive systems. They are therefore an ideal food for immunocompromised individuals such as people living with HIV/AIDS, as they improve the nutritional status as well as boosting the immune system.

Chapter 7 - Over the past few decades poverty has emerged as a global problem and a global agenda item in need of action. For that reason, the United Nations made its eradication the first Millennium Development Goal (MDG). The MDGs' plan is for extreme poverty to be eliminated by 2015. Poverty is more of a concern on the African continent than elsewhere. As China's involvement in Africa increases, China has been forced to deal with the issue of poverty. Although China's interest in Africa started with its interest in acquiring natural resources and extending its geopolical influence, due to poverty and other development issues that end up affecting trade, China has since developed a donor-recipient relationship with Africa. Despite China's involvement in development and poverty alleviation, there is a strong argument that China's assistance acts as a double-edged sword because on the one hand China participates in poverty alleviation and on the other hand it engages in practices that create and promote poverty, such as violating labor laws, trading in illegal timber and supporting governments that perpetuate human rights violations against their citizens.

Chapter 8 - Urban poverty has become a characteristic feature of urban living in Zambia. Statistical evidence suggests that of the 4.3 million people resident in urban areas of Zambia, 34 % live in extreme poverty while 18 % are moderately poor (CSO, 2005). These figures are indicative that more than half (i.e. 53 %) of the urban population in Zambia live in poverty (CSO, 2004, 2005). Despite these high figures in urban poverty, Zambia as a country has not yet developed an explicit policy framework with which to address the increase in urban poverty and vulnerability. Indeed the failure to formulate urban food policies at the national and municipal levels have played a significant role in the increase of contemporary food problems being faced by many urban residents in the country. This chapter reviews the history of urban development and welfare in Zambia and discusses the nature, roots and dynamics of urban poverty and the coping mechanisms employed by urban residents in Zambia. Institutions form a major part of the discussion throughout the chapter.

Chapter 9 - Most families in developing countries are resorting to small-scale businesses as a response to economic hardships resulting from inflation and economic changes. The families' role in small scale businesses is carried out under conditions of hardship that include limited economic resources, low levels of technology, lack of adequate knowledge and lack of appropriate skills. Self-employment in South Africa using a variety of skills has become an alternative source of employment for many low income households.

The main purpose of this study was to assess the ability of small scale income generating activities to create employment and generate household income. A total of 85 households were purposely selected using the snow-balling methodology. A set of both closed and open-ended questionnaires was used to collect data on household income generating activities from heads of households.

Results for household income generating activities showed no evidence of employment creation except that the activities were used to generate income and reduce household food insecurity. According to the results a mean income of R873.15 per month was generated by these activities. Although the income was not adequate to support a mean number of 8 dependants in a household, the income was higher than the pension grant of R700 which rural people depend on. The main constraints facing household income generating activities were: lack of working capital, lack of management skills, and marketing related problems. Financial support and skills training were identified as necessary strategies to overcome lack of working capital, lack of management skills and marketing constraints.

Chapter 10 - Socio-economic conditions in Kenya are deteriorating, and poverty rates are on the rise. This article finds that a significant and rising incidence of absolute poverty exists in Kenya and women suffer from poverty more often than men. This is more pronounced in female-headed households. The high poverty rates among women can be linked to their unequal situation in the labour market, their lack of voice and participation in decision-making in the family/household and other institutions and because gender disparities persist in access and control of human, economic and social reforms.

The female/male ratios in Kenyan decision-making institutions are highly skewed against women and they experience unfavourable enrolment ratios in primary, secondary and tertiary institutions. The share of income earned by women is much lower than men's share. The GDI and GEM, their weaknesses not withstanding, also show that gender inequality exists in Kenya.

Chapter 11 - The author seek to extend the framework proposed by Cradock (2000) who has argued that vulnerability to disease must be seen as "historically situated, structured by institutions, households and nations, and shaped by an ever shifting and relentlessly demanding global economy. But it must also be recognized that these structures and economies mesh inextricably with the social ideologies and cultural codes of particular times and places" (p. 164). The author are most interested in highlighting how risk is produced through time at multiple scales of analysis that include but also extend way beyond the body and include the household, place, region, nation, and the globe. The author argue that neoliberal logics have discounted larger scale processes, privileging sexual agency and so prevention efforts have remained fixated on question of personal responsibility and agency. The author attention to larger scale processes is driven by a desire to intervene in tragically failed HIV prevention efforts that remain fixated on question of individual sexual behavioural modification.

In: Poverty in Africa
Editor: Thomas W. Beasley

ISBN: 978-1-60741-737-8
© 2009 Nova Science Publishers, Inc.

Chapter 1

THE IMPACT OF ROAD INFRASTRUCTURE ON POVERTY REDUCTION IN AFRICA[*]

John C. Anyanwu[1†] *and Andrew E. O. Erhijakpor*[2]

[1] Development Research Department, African Development Bank,
Temporary Relocation Agency, BP 323, 1002 Tunis Tunisia
[2] Department of Accounting, Banking And Finance
Delta State University, Asaba Campus, Asaba Nigeria

ABSTRACT

There is general acceptance that economic infrastructure is critical for economic growth and poverty reduction, given its pivotal role in improving competitiveness, facilitating both domestic and international trade, and integration of the continent to the global economy. However, there is a large infrastructure deficit, both in terms of access and quality, to be filled in all the sectors (transport, energy, ICT and water). For instance, the level of access to electricity in Africa is only about 30 percent, compared to over 75 percent for other Less Developed Countries (LDCs). Access to water and sanitation is about 65 percent compared to 80 percent for other LDCs; the penetration rate for telecommunication is less than 13 percent compared to 40 percent in other LDCs; while access to roads is 34 percent compared to 50 percent for other LDCs. This situation has resulted, among others, in Africa's low rates of economic growth, low poverty reduction, reduced share of world trade and lack of international competitiveness. The high transaction costs arising from poor road infrastructure, for example, adversely affects development of African economies, hinders private sector development, and the flow of foreign direct investment (FDI). However, studies on the impact of road infrastructure had been confined mostly to developed economies and other developing economies, where road infrastructure developments swamp those in Africa. Indeed, few studies have examined the impact of road infrastructure on poverty in a broad panel of African (Sub-Saharan and North African) countries. This paper tries to fill this lacuna by constructing a panel data set on poverty and road infrastructure for African countries. It essentially

---

[*] The views expressed in this paper are those of the authors and in no way represent those of their respective employers.
[†] Corresponding Authors: E-Mail: J.ANYANWU@AFDB.ORG, E-Mail: erhijakpor@yahoo.com

examines the impact of road infrastructure on poverty reduction in African countries using panel data of 33 countries over the period 1990-2005.

We find that road infrastructure – proxied by paved roads (as percentage of total roads) – reduces the level, depth, and severity of poverty in Africa. But the size of the poverty reduction depends on how poverty is being measured. We find that a 10 percent increase in road infrastructure leads to a 5.16 percent decline in the poverty headcount or the share of people living in poverty. Also, the more sensitive poverty measures – the poverty gap (poverty depth) and squared poverty gap (poverty severity) – suggest that road infrastructure will have a similar impact on poverty reduction. The point estimates for the poverty gap and squared poverty gap suggest that a 10 percent increase in the share of road infrastructure will lead to a 6.14 percent and 6.91 percent decline, respectively, in the depth and severity of poverty in African countries. In conformity with most theoretical and empirical literature, education significantly reduces the poverty headcount and severity in the continent. Regardless of the measure of poverty used as the dependent variable, income inequality (Gini index) has a positive and significant coefficient, indicating that greater inequality is associated with higher poverty in African countries, much in conformity with the literature. Similar results are obtained for trade openness. In the same vein, per capita income has a negative and significant effect on each measure of poverty used in the study. Our results also show that inflation rates positively and significantly affect poverty incidence, depth and severity in Africa. In all three poverty measures, the dummy variable for Sub-Saharan Africa is strongly positive – and strongly negative for North Africa. The policy implications of these results are discussed in the paper.

I. INTRODUCTION

There is general acceptance that economic infrastructure is critical for economic growth and poverty reduction, given its pivotal role in improving competitiveness, facilitating both domestic and international trade, and integration of the continent to the global economy. However, there is a large infrastructure deficit, both in terms of access and quality, to be filled in all the sectors (transport, energy, ICT and water). For instance, the level of access to electricity in Africa is only about 30 percent, compared to over 75 percent for other Less Developed Countries (LDCs). Access to water and sanitation is about 65 percent compared to 80 percent for other LDCs; the penetration rate for telecommunication is less than 13 percent compared to 40 percent in other LDCs; while access to roads is 34 percent compared to 50 percent for other LDCs. This situation has resulted, among others, in Africa's low rates of economic growth, low poverty reduction, reduced share of world trade and lack of international competitiveness. The high transaction costs arising from poor road infrastructure, for example, adversely affects development of African economies, hinders private sector development, and the flow of foreign direct investment (FDI).

However, studies on the impact of road infrastructure had been confined mostly to developed economies and other developing economies, where road infrastructure developments swamp those in Africa. Indeed, few studies have examined the impact of road infrastructure on poverty in a broad panel of African (Sub-Saharan and North African) countries. This paper tries to fill this lacuna by constructing a panel data set on poverty and road infrastructure for African countries. It essentially examines the impact of road infrastructure on poverty reduction in African countries using panel data of African countries over the period 1990-2005.

As a result of the dearth of such studies, a host of key policy questions remain unanswered. Exactly what is the impact of road infrastructure on poverty in Africa? This question has become very crucial given that preliminary assessments of progress towards the Millennium Development Goals (MDGs) suggest that while a few African countries are on track to achieving the MDGs, the majority are either off track or slipping back. For instance, estimates have shown that at current trends, with the exception of North Africa and South Africa, few countries are likely to meet the goal of reducing the number of people living in poverty by half by 2015 (Table 1).

Table 1. Africa - Selected Social Indicators for MDG Monitoring

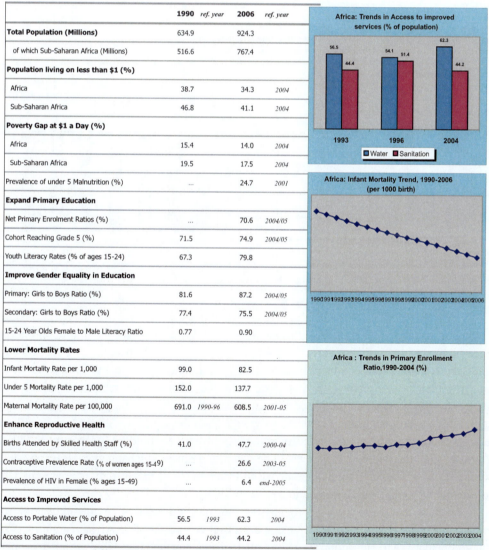

Sources: ADB Statistics Department, Poverty Indicators are from the world Bank, PovcalNet Database

Table 1: Africa - Poverty Trends 1990 - 2007

	1990	1996	1999	2002	2004	2006[4]	2007[4]
Total Population (millions) *							
North Africa	118.2	132.6	139.5	146.7	151.8	156.9	159.5
Sub-Saharan Africa	516.6	606.9	653.8	701.4	733.9	767.4	784.6
Total Africa	634.9	739.5	793.3	848.1	885.6	924.3	944.2
Population living on less than $1 (% of total population)							
North Africa [1]	3.4	2.7	2.5	1.9	1.7	1.5	1.4
Sub-Saharan Africa [2]	46.8	47.8	45.9	42.6	41.1	39.6	38.9
Total Africa [3]	38.7	39.7	38.3	35.6	34.3	33.1	32.6
Estimated number of Poor - population living on less than 1$ (million)							
North Africa	4.1	3.6	3.5	2.8	2.6	2.4	2.3
Sub-Saharan Africa	241.6	290.2	300.3	299.0	301.5	303.9	305.1
Total Africa	245.7	293.8	303.8	301.8	304.1	306.3	307.4

[1] : World Bank, POVCAL estimates based on data available for for 4 countries in North Africa
[2] : World Bank POVCAL estimates based on data available for for 30 countries in Sub Saharan Africa
[3] : ADB estimates based on the estimated number of poor for North Africa and for Sub-Saharan Africa
[4] : A DB estimates based on the assumption that the delining trend in poverty observed in 2002-2004 is maintained over the projection period of 2006-2007.
* Source: UN Population Division, 2004 Revision

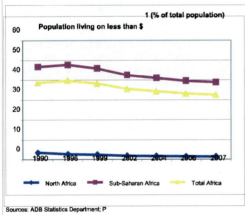
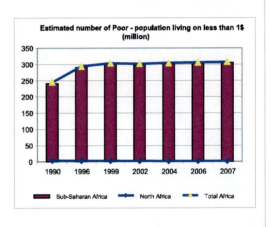

Sources: ADB Statistics Department; Poverty Indicators are from the World Bank, PovcalNet Database

One of the targets for reducing extreme poverty in Africa involves halving the proportion of people living in absolute poverty from 48 percent in 1990 to 24 percent by 2015. So far, it is only the North African countries of Algeria, Egypt, Libya, Morocco and Tunisia as well as Mauritius that have already met this target. On the African continent as a whole, little progress has been made, as the proportion of people living below the poverty line of $1 per day in Africa is currently high (Table 1) – the highest in the world. If current trend continues, the proportion of people living in extreme poverty in Africa would be 39 percent by 2015 – far greater than the targeted 24 percent. The situation remains unchanged even when we use 2005 prices from the International Comparison Program (ICP) recently re-estimated by Chen and Ravallion (2008) (see Tables 2 and 3).

This paper therefore proposes to answer the question relating to the impact of road infrastructure on poverty in Africa by using a data set composed of 33 African countries. This data set includes African countries (Sub-Saharan and North Africa) for which reasonable information on poverty, inequality road infrastructure could be assembled.

Table 2: Regional Breakdown of Headcount Index for International Poverty Line of $1.00 a Day Over 1981-2005

Region	1981	1984	1987	1990	1993	1996	1999	2002	2005
East Asia and Pacific	68.7	51.9	39.4	40.6	36.1	24.7	23.7	19.7	9.5
Of which China	73.5	52.9	38.0	44.0	37.7	23.7	24.1	19.1	8.1
Eastern Europe and Central Asia	0.7	0.5	0.4	0.8	2.1	2.5	3.4	3.7	3.4
Latin America and Caribbean	7.4	9.1	8.4	7.1	7.3	7.9	7.9	6.6	5.0
Middle East and North Africa	3.6	2.7	2.9	2.3	2.2	2.3	2.6	2.0	2.0
South Asia	41.9	38.0	36.6	33.6	28.6	28.9	26.9	26.5	23.7
Of which India	42.1	37.6	35.7	33.3	31.1	28.6	27.0	26.3	24.3
Sub-Saharan Africa	39.5	43.6	42.8	45.9	44.3	47.1	45.6	41.6	39.2
Total	41.7	35.0	29.9	29.8	27.0	23.6	22.8	20.7	16.1

Source: Chen and Ravallion (2008).

Table 3: Regional Breakdown of Number of Poor (Millions) for International Poverty Line of $1.00 a Day over 1981-2005

Region	1981	1984	1987	1990	1993	1996	1999	2002	2005
East Asia and Pacific	947.5	751.1	598.4	648.1	600.3	4275	424.6	361.9	179.8
Of which China	730.4	548.5	412.4	499.1	444.4	288.7	302.4	244.7	106.1
Eastern Europe and Central Asia	2.9	2.2	2.0	3.5	9.8	12.0	16.2	17.6	16.0
Latin America and Caribbean	27.2	35.7	34.6	31.2	33.7	38.2	40.2	34.7	27.6
Middle East and North Africa	6.3	5.2	6.0	5.2	5.4	6.1	7.2	5.8	6.2
South Asia	387.2	274.2	384.4	376.6	340.7	365.5	359.0	372.5	350.3
Of which India	296.1	282.2	285.3	282.5	280.1	271.3	270.1	276.1	266.5
Sub-Saharan Africa	157.3	189.1	202.4	236.9	247.4	285.0	298.8	294.4	299.1
Total	1528.8	1357.5	1227.8	1301.5	1237.3	1134.2	1146.1	1087.0	879.0

Source: Chen and Ravallion (2008).

The remaining parts of this paper are organized as follows. Section II sets the stage by examining the state of road infrastructure in African countries. Section III reviews the findings of recent empirical studies on the relationship between road infrastructure and poverty. Section IV then presents the method and data set. Section V describes the main econometric findings on the relationship between road infrastructure and poverty. The final section concludes with policy implications, including suggestions on how to increase investment and the quality of infrastructure in Africa for greater poverty reduction.

II. ROAD TRANSPORT IN AFRICA

Infrastructure's importance for growth, poverty and the Millennium Development Goals (MDGs) has been recognized at several major donor meetings, including the International Conference on Financing for Development (Monterrey, 2002) and World Summit on Sustainable Development (Johannesburg, 2002). Building on these efforts, in 2003, the DAC chose infrastructure as a major area of analysis for its Network on Poverty Reduction (POVNET). The Task Team on Infrastructure for Poverty Reduction (InfraPoor) was created to guide efforts by DAC members to enhance infrastructure's contribution to poverty reduction and economic growth.

Africa's major development challenges are the acceleration of economic growth and the reduction of poverty. The potential significance of transport infrastructure (TI) for investment, trade, growth and poverty alleviation has long been recognized. Not only does TI facilitate the direct provision of services to consumers, but it provides intermediate inputs that enter into the production of other sectors and raise factor productivity. By lowering the cost and reducing the time of moving goods and services to where they can be used more efficiently and/or fetch a higher price, TI adds value and spurs growth. Over time this process results in increasing the size of markets which is a precondition for realizing economies of scale at the level of the enterprise. This, in turn, attracts private investment, fostering private sector development. Well-designed TI projects clearly contribute to poverty reduction by improving the living conditions of people and by augmenting the opportunities available for trade and employment.

Transport is involved in the various spheres of the socio-economic life of our nations. Indeed, transport services are vital for the mobility of persons, capital and goods both to and within production units as well as towards market centers; hence the importance and urgency the African Union Commission attaches to this sector.

Transport contributes to the achievement of the wealth of Member States and, as such, is a real lever through which governments should work to boost socio-economic development thereby contributing to poverty reduction as asserted by the Heads of State and Government of the African Union meeting in Sirte in July 2005 by deciding to include within the framework of the Millennium Development Goals (MDGs) transport targets and indicators adopted in April 2005 by the African Ministers responsible for Transport and Infrastructure with a view to speeding up poverty reduction, a fundamental objectives of the international community.

Transport is an indispensable tool in facilitating the creation of a single socio-economic space that would lead to free movement of goods and persons in Africa. Transport services in the continent are by and large inefficient as manifested by high vehicle prices, poor routine maintenance, poor knowledge of operating costs, poor operating practices, poor routine maintenance, etc. These problems result into high transport costs in the region. In addition, Africa has 15 landlocked countries and their transportation needs to the seaports have to be adequately provided for.

Cumbersome administrative procedures and poor facilities within the transit countries are detrimental to the development of the international trade of these landlocked countries. Three areas are considered essential to achieve adequate transport efficiency and growth that would lead to the region's desired integration levels. They are: connectivity of the transport network; cost of transport; and quality of transport services.

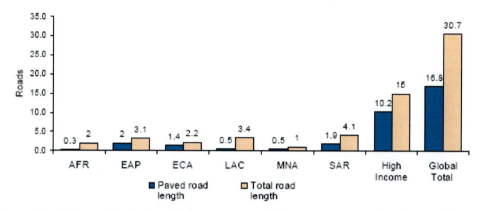

Note. AFR: Africa (Sub-Saharan); EAP: East Asia and Pacific; ECA: Europe and Central Asia; LAC: Latin America and the Caribbean; MNA: Middle East and North Africa; SAR: South Asia.
Source: World Bank (2008).

Figure 1. Length of the Road Network, by Region, 2005

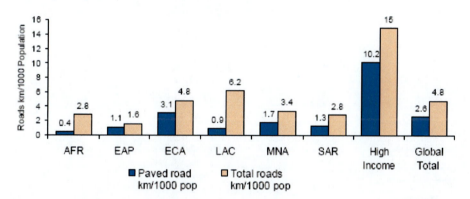

Note. AFR: Africa (Sub-Saharan); EAP: East Asia and Pacific; ECA: Europe and Central Asia; LAC: Latin America and the Caribbean; MNA: Middle East and North Africa; SAR: South Asia.
Source: World Bank (2008).

Figure 2. Ratio of Road Network to Population, by Region, 2005

With the advent of the internal combustion engine and improvements in road-building methods, roads have now come to dominate land transport between settlements and regions in most countries. This is because roads are multifunctional and can be readily accessed by a wide range of users. Roads provide the infrastructure used by private passenger transport (cars and motorcycles), buses, trams, taxis, para-transit services, own-account goods transport, commercial road haulage services, emergency services (ambulances, police vehicles, fire vehicles), utility vehicles (such as for refuse collection), and a variety of personal and freight transport functions carried out on foot, by bicycle, or by animal-drawn vehicles. They also frequently provide convenient rights of way for electricity, gas, telecommunications, water, and drainage systems. It is because of their high and diverse functionality and wide range of beneficiaries that roads have become such an essential component of all national transport systems, usually consuming the greatest proportion of public and private investment resources in both infrastructure and services (World Bank, 2008).

About 60 percent of the world's paved road length is currently in high- income countries; if this were measured in road lanes rather than simply length, the proportion of total paved road capacity in the high-income countries would be even greater (World Bank, 2008). Africa, south of the Sahara, has the lowest paved road length among the world's regions (Figures 1, 2 and 3).

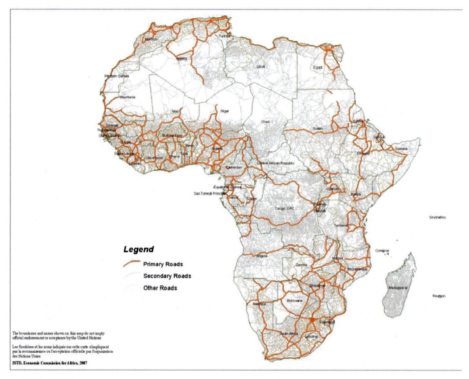

Source: AUC (2008).

Figure 3. Africa's Road Network

As reflected in Table 4, in general, Africa's (especially Sub-Saharan Africa) transport infrastructure lags well behind the rest of the world.

Africa's road density per 1,000 square kilometers is less than one-third of that even in the world's other poorest region, South Asia, and is less than 12 percent of that in the well-developed countries of the OECD. Only 25 percent of Sub-Saharan Africa's roads are paved, compared to 38 percent in South Asia, 82 percent in the OECD countries, and 50 percent worldwide. The thinness of Sub-Saharan Africa's road development in relation to landmass and the relatively low percentage of roads that are paved results in only about 34 percent of the rural population living within two kilometers of an all-season road, which is a good indicator of whether people have ready access to efficient transport for market access and purposes. By comparison, 65 percent of the rural population of South Asia enjoys such access. Quantity of road infrastructure is not the only issue. Quality is also important. The poor condition of Sub-Saharan Africa's roads makes overland transport so difficult and costly that Sub-Saharan Africa's diverse regions remain largely isolated from one another, severely curtailing internal trade. In addition, it has been asserted by the World Bank that improving the quality of transportation infrastructure plays a key role in reducing road traffic injuries, which are estimated to cost approximately 1 percent of GDP in low-income countries. Thus, an initial investment of $20 billion coupled with $1 billion annually for maintenance would expand overland trade by about $250 billion over 15 years, with major direct and indirect benefits for the rural poor (see also, Taylor, 2007).

Table 4. Sub-Saharan Africa's Transport Infrastructure with Regional and Income Comparisons

	Sub-Saharan Africa	South Asia	All Developing Countries	Middle Income	High Income OECD	World
Road Density (km/1,000 people)	3.3	2.4	5.0	7.0	17.3	6.7
Road Density (km/1,000 sq km of land	156	545	442	702	1340	841
Paved Roads (% of total)	25	38	41	52	82	50
Rail Density (km/1,000 sq km of land	3.7	18.8	16.3	23.3	46.2	23.1

Average from 1997-2002

Source: Taylor (2007).

Table 5. Proportion of Rural Population Living within Two Kilometers of an All-weather Road

Region	Proportion of Rural People
Sub-Saharan Africa	30
Middle East & North Africa	34
Latin America & Caribbean	38
South Asia	58
Europe & Central Asia	75
East Asia	94

Source: Roberts et al (2006).

The situation in rural Sub-Sahara Africa is even more worrisome (see also Table 5). The average road density in rural areas for SSA is 34 m/km2. This is only 23% of the density in China (Fan and Chan-Kang, 2004) and 4 percent of the density in India (World Bank, 2002). Poor road access leads to higher transaction costs for many farmers when selling their produce. For example, high transaction costs are equivalent to a value added tax of 15% for Kenyan farmers (Renkow et al., 2004). Transportation charges in rural Ghana and Zimbabwe are 2-2.5 times higher than in Thailand, Pakistan, and Sri Lanka (Torero, 2004).

Similarly, road safety remains a real concern in Africa, where there are 28 deaths per 100,000 inhabitants annually largely affecting the young population with a substantial number being young pedestrians and cyclists. In the age group 5 and 44 years, road accidents are the second cause of mortality. The cost of these road accidents in some middle-income countries represents 1 percent to 1.5 percent of GNP, that is, in some cases, more than the countries receive as development assistance. In Africa, this amount is estimated at US$10 billion, i.e. nearly 2 percent of GNP.

Transit traffic for landlocked countries is largely by land and in particular by road. Africa has fifteen (15) landlocked countries whose direct access distance to the sea is between 220 km in Swaziland and 1735 km in Chad.

Despite the existence of road transport regulation in the various African regions, conditions for its application represent another challenge. The multiple checks to which road transporters are subjected constitute real obstacles to the flow and performance of this mode of transport. In the final analysis, landlocked countries are at a serious disadvantage, as the inter-State transit costs are passed on to consumers.

In a study, which covered 24 countries comprising 85 percent of sub-Saharan Africa's GDP and assuming an average annual economic growth in Africa (through 2015) of 7 percent and an annual expenditure on infrastructure of 9 percent of GDP (including both original capital investment and operation and maintenance costs), it has been estimated that the annual infrastructure investment needs through 2015 of $22–24 billion (5.1 percent of GDP) and operating and maintenance expenses of $17–18 billion (3.9 percent of GDP), for a total of about $40 billion per year or 9 percent of GDP would be needed (see Taylor, 2007). These results are further broken out by sector, as reflected in Table 6. The analysis confirms the development importance of roads, which would need 43 percent of total infrastructure expenditures, including nearly $10 billion annually in construction costs, compared to $5.5 billion for electricity-related infrastructure and $4.5 billion for water and sanitation combined. The necessary expenses for operation and maintenance bring the totals in these sectors to about $17 billion annually for roads, almost $9 billion for electricity, and about $8 billion for water and sanitation.

Table 6. Sub-Saharan Africa's Estimated Annual Infrastructure Expenditure Needs to Meet the MDGs (By sector in billions ($) assuming $40 billion annual total)

	Electricity	Telecoms	Roads	Rail	Water	Sanitation	Total
Investment	5.5	3.2	9.8	0	1.8	2.7	22.8
Operation and Maintenance	3.3	2.0	7.4	0.8	1.4	2.1	17.2
Total	8.8 (22%)	5.2 (13%)	17.2 (43%)	0.8 (2%)	3.2 (8%)	4.8 (12%)	40 (100%)

Source: Taylor (2007).

In the absence of accessible, affordable infrastructure, poor people pay heavily in time, money and health. Recent estimates put annual investment needs for infrastructure (including rehabilitation and maintenance) at 5.5 percent of growth domestic product (GDP) in developing countries and 9 percent in the least developed countries (IMF and World Bank, 2005). Current spending falls far short, averaging 3.5 percent of GDP in developing countries. In sub-Saharan Africa, for example, annual infrastructure needs are USD 17-22 billion, while the annual spending (domestic and foreign, public and private) is about USD 10 billion. The sub-region's infrastructure financing gap is thus USD 7-12 billion per year, or 4.7 percent of GDP.

The current emphasis on infrastructure draws its inspiration from East Asia's economic history, including the experience of countries such as Japan, South Korea, Malaysia and Taiwan, China, which also made large investments in infrastructure. East Asia's accumulation of infrastructure stocks has outpaced infrastructure investment in other regions (Table 7). And East Asia's economic growth has outpaced the growth of other world regions. Between 1975 and 2005, East Asia's GDP increased ten-fold; South Asia's GDP increased five-fold; and all other regions' economies grew by factors of between two and three (Difference in GDP (PPP) in constant 2000 dollars between 1975 and 2005). For most policy-makers this is no coincidence.

Table 7. Growth of GDP and Infrastructure Stocks

1995 levels as multiples of 1975 levels				
	GDP	Electricity	Roads	Telecoms
East Asia	4.8	5.9	2.9	15.5
South Asia	2.6	4.4	2.5	8.2
Middle East & North Africa	1.8	6.1	2.1	7.2
Latin America & Caribbean	1.8	3.0	1.9	5.1
OECD	1.8	1.6	1.4	2.2
Pacific	1.7	2.0		4.3
Sub-Saharan Africa	1.4	2.6	1.7	3.9
Eastern Europe	1.0	1.6	1.2	6.9

GDP – PPP constant 2000 international $; Electricity – MW of generating capacity; Roads – km of paved road; Telecoms – number of main lines.
Source: Straub, Vellutini and Warlters (2008).

However, spending on infrastructure (both capital and recurrent costs, including maintenance) in low- and lower-middle income countries has declined from 15 percent of GDP in the 1970s and 1980s to about 7 percent since the early 2000s (World Bank, 2003). Since the mid-1990s all sources of infrastructure funding have fallen dramatically: government funding (which accounts for about two-thirds of spending), official development assistance (with a 50 percent drop in multilateral and bilateral aid to infrastructure; see World Bank, 2003) and private funding (which dropped from USD 128 million in 1997 to USD 58 million in 2002; World Bank, 2003). All sub-sectors and regions have been affected by the decline, with aid shifting to the social sector (see Figure 4). As a result many countries, especially in sub-Saharan Africa, suffer from a huge backlog of needed infrastructure investments.

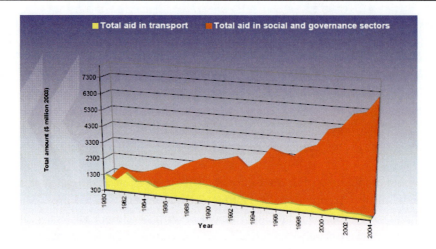

Source: AfDB/OECD Development Centre (2006)

Figure 4. Shift in ODA to Social Sectors

Despite its clear benefits for growth and poverty reduction, infrastructure spending is far below what is needed. Moreover, that gap widens as country incomes fall. Globally, more than 1 billion people have no access to roads, 1.2 billion do not have safe drinking water, 2.3 billion lack reliable sources of energy, 2.4 billion have no sanitation facilities and 4 billion no modern communication services. In the absence of accessible transport, energy and water, the poor pay heavily in time, money and health.

Africa's transport systems are poorly integrated and inefficient - transport and insurance represent more than 30 percent of the total value of exports compared with 14.6 percent for all landlocked countries and 8.6 percent for developing countries as a whole (see Figure 5). These place high cost premium on trade, travel and business, with crippling effect on Africa's trade competitiveness and its ability to participate in the world economy.

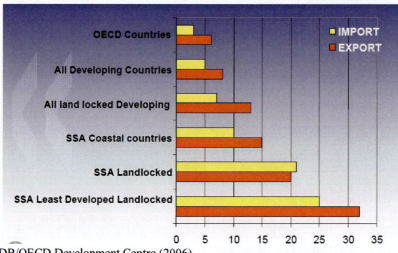

Source: AfDB/OECD Development Centre (2006).

Figure 5. Transport / Insurance Costs as Percent of Trade Value

To reduce poverty, the decline in infrastructure investment must be reversed. A significant increase in national, cross-border and regional infrastructure investment is needed to advance growth and reduce poverty in African countries. The UN Millennium Project estimates that between 2005 and 2015, sub-Saharan Africa's annual needs for infrastructure investment and maintenance equal 13 percent of GDP. Maintenance is especially important: according to World Bank estimates, more than two-thirds of partner countries' infrastructure spending needs in 2005 – 10 were for maintenance.

III. REVIEW OF RECENT LITERATURE

This section which is based on extensive literature survey primarily describes the implications of road infrastructure on poverty reduction both on a theoretical and empirical framework.

3.1 Linking Road Infrastructure to Poverty Reduction: A Framework

In past decades donors supported infrastructure investment because they believed that it contributed to growth, trickledown economic development and redistribution to poor people. Today the links between infrastructure development and pro-poor growth are better understood. Public investment affects rural poverty through many channels. It increases farmers' income directly by increasing agricultural productivity, which in turn reduces rural poverty. Indirect impacts come from higher agricultural wages and improved non-farm employment opportunities induced by growth in agricultural productivity. Increased agricultural output due to public investment often yields lower food prices, again helping the poor indirectly because they are often net buyers of food grains. In addition to its productivity impact, public investment directly promotes rural wages, non-farm employment and migration, thereby reducing rural poverty. For example, improved road access helps farmers set up small rural non-farm businesses such as food processing and marketing enterprises, electronic repair shops, transportation and trade, and restaurant services (Fan, 2004).

Infrastructure also affects non-income aspects of poverty, contributing to improvements in health, nutrition, education and social cohesion. Indeed, infrastructure makes valuable contributions to all the MDGs (bottom arrow in Figure 6) (see Willoughby, 2004a). The many benefits of infrastructure have also been confirmed by the UN Millennium Project (2005), which advocates a major increase in basic infrastructure investments to help countries (especially in Africa) escape the poverty trap, and by the Commission for Africa (2005). But to be effective in reducing poverty, infrastructure development must be coordinated with other important concerns, such as agricultural, environmental and trade policies.

Infrastructure investments can lead to higher farm and non-farm productivity, employment and income opportunities, and increased availability of wage goods, thereby reducing poverty by raising mean income and consumption. If higher agricultural and nonagricultural productivity and increased employment directly benefit the poor more than the non-poor, these investments can reduce poverty even faster by improving income distribution as well.

Infrastructure Supports Pro-Poor Growth by:

i) Enhancing economic activity and thus overall growth – for example, by reducing production and transaction costs, increasing private investment, and raising agricultural and industrial productivity (top arrow in Figure 6).
ii) Removing bottlenecks in the economy which hurt poor people by impeding asset accumulation, lowering asset values, imposing high transaction costs and creating market failures. Eliminating these bottlenecks allows the poor to contribute to growth directly through the employment and income opportunities created by the construction, maintenance and delivery of infrastructure services, and indirectly through better services (middle arrow in Figure 6).
iii) Generating distributional effects on growth and poverty reduction through poor people's increased participation in the growth process – for example, by increasing their access to factor and product markets, reducing risk and vulnerability, enhancing asset mobilization and use, and promoting their empowerment (bottom arrow in Figure 6) (OECD, 2007).

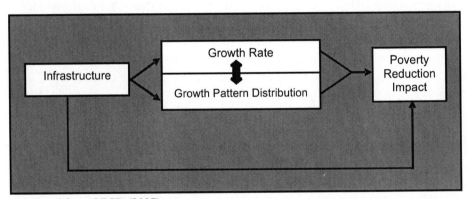

Source: Adapted from OECD (2007).

Figure 6. Infrastructure-Growth-Poverty Nexus

Transport difficulties inhibit poor people's access to health and education facilities. Accordingly, the social MDGs (2-6) indicate the need to improve transport services and facilities, and to link investments in transport with those in health and education. For example, reliable transport and communication services are a key reason maternal mortality rates have fallen in many countries, and health investments provide only additional benefits. Similarly, poor children's (mainly girls) school attendance – particularly in secondary education – is highly dependent on affordable transport services, with manageable distances and times from their homes. To strengthen the links between transport and poverty reduction, increasing use is being made of cross-sector accessibility planning at the district and community levels. Such planning takes into account all modes of passenger and freight transport, motorized and non-motorized. Community-driven development activities can help identify and ease bottlenecks.

Infrastructure investment affects poverty through multiple channels. For example, improved rural infrastructure will not only reduce rural poverty through improved agricultural productivity, but also affect rural poverty through improved wages and non-farm employment. To take account of the multiple pathways by which investments can impact on growth and poverty, the underlying conceptual framework is summarized in Figure 7.

Figure 7 summarizes the links from infrastructure investments (areas of intervention) through these determinants (areas of influence) to the poor's wages and employment (direct channel), on the one hand, and rural economic growth (indirect channel) that influences the supply and prices of basic goods, on the other. The final links are to real income/consumption of the poor and, consequently, poverty reduction (area of concern). The various links can be illustrated with an example. For example, a road investment could result in an increase in agricultural productivity, non-farm employment and productivity, directly raising the wages and employment of the poor and, hence, their economic welfare. This is the (direct) income distribution effect. In addition, higher productivity and expanded employment lead to higher economic growth, affecting the supply and prices of goods and, thus, the poor's well-being. This is the (indirect) growth effect (Ali and Pernia, 2003).

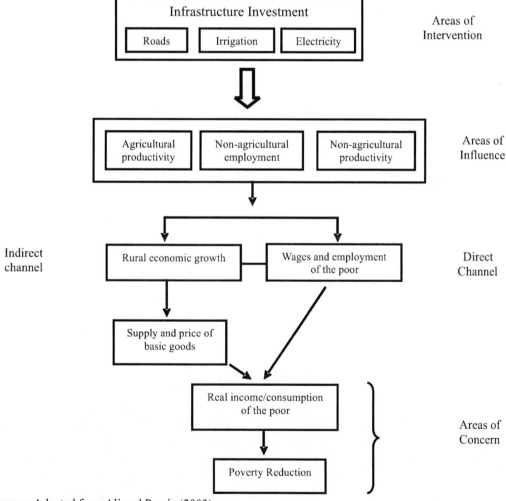

Source: Adapted from Ali and Pernia (2003).

Figure 7. Simple Analytical Framework Depicting the Links between Infrastructure and Poverty Reduction

The links between infrastructure services, growth and social outcomes like the Millennium Development Goals operate through multiple channels as depicted in figure 8. The delivery of services like water, sanitation, transportation and energy directly benefit households and can dramatically improve their welfare. But many of the benefits of infrastructure services accrue to firms – in France, for example, that input-output tables reveal that firms consume two-thirds of all infrastructure services (Prud'homme, 2004). Thus it is through this channel that costs are lowered and, most importantly, market opportunities are expanded (especially through telecommunications and transport). The resulting gains in competitiveness and production are what drive the gains in economic growth and ultimately welfare.

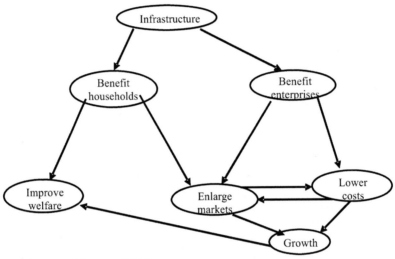

Source: Adapted from Prud'homme (2004).

Figure 8. Linkage between Infrastructure and Economic Development.

The extent to which transport infrastructure can directly contribute to poverty reduction seems to depend on its impact on income and non-income dimensions of poverty at the micro-level. In terms of income poverty, transport infrastructure opens up opportunities for the poor to raise the productivity of their limited resources. In rural areas, where most of the poor reside and where agriculture remains the main source of income, transport infrastructure lowers the costs of inputs and facilitates access to credit, extension services, and most importantly, output markets with better prices. It also facilitates the commercialization of farm and non-farm activities and often leads to agricultural diversification from low-value food grains to more perishable, high-value agricultural products.

Efficient operation of transport infrastructure and services is critical to attainment of the Millennium Development Goals (MDGs), and nowhere more so than in Africa. The large size of the continent and the wide spread of population inherently raise the significance of transport in almost all development decisions. Backlogs in maintenance and inefficiencies in operations have serious effects on many other sectors. Expensive and poor-quality trunk services reduce the competitiveness of African products. Inadequate and ill-maintained local infrastructures prevent large parts of the population from participating in the modern economy. The significance of transport services to each of the MDGs means that effective pursuit of the latter requires priority attention to those transport services, which are relevant to each. It is the essential contribution of transport to achieving these ends that links transport to the outcomes targeted by the Millennium Development Goals (see Figure 9).

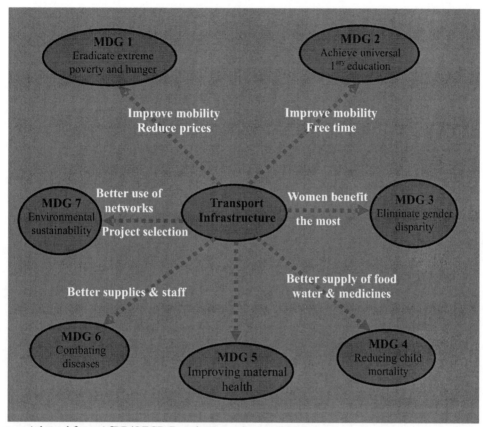

Source: Adapted from AfDB/OECD Development Centre (2006).

Figure 9. Transport Infrastructure and the MDGs

The experiences of China and India underscore the point that infrastructure does not have its positive effect on development in a vacuum, but rather in the context of a particular country and its economic starting point, its human and natural resources, and its policies and institutions. In much of Africa, the macroeconomic and market liberalization reforms of the 1980s and 1990s increased the emphasis on local, regional and international trade as drivers of development and poverty reduction and this increased the importance and potential value of roads and other basic transport infrastructure. One study looking at household-level poverty reduction in Uganda and Ethiopia following liberalization confirmed this by finding that whether the household had access to infrastructure and urban markets were an immensely important factor governing the growth in household income. It explains about half of the household consumption growth and poverty reduction in Ethiopia during 1989–95, and it was also quantitatively important for growth in Ugandan household income (Christiaensen et al., 2004).

3.2. Empirical Literature on the Impact of Road Infrastructure on Poverty

The empirical evidence points toward a negative relationship between poverty and road infrastructure. The importance of roads is borne out in many other studies and experiences in Africa and elsewhere:

- An econometric study found that Uganda's spending on rural roads had a "substantial" effect on agricultural growth and rural poverty reduction, as well as a large effect on per capita income, with an average benefit-cost ratio of 9.13 (Fan et al., 2005);
- According to a study based on 1994 and 1997 household surveys, a lack of rural "connectedness" due to a lack of widespread access to transport inhibited poverty reduction in Ethiopia because participation in export markets and access to education were "key characteristics" that help households move out of poverty, but these opportunities were limited largely to people living in towns (17 percent of the population) or in an area with modern road transport (30 percent). A 2000 household survey in Ethiopia showed that the average distance between rural households and an all-weather road is 11 kilometers (Willoughby, 2004b);
- Vietnam's market-oriented economic reforms beginning in the late 1980s produced rapid annual growth of about 8 percent in GDP and 4.8 percent in agriculture, and data from household surveys have shown "the considerable significance of infrastructure, and especially roads, in determining how widespread were the benefits of the growth-oriented reforms and the extent to which they reached the poor." One study found that the higher rural incomes in Vietnam correlate with closer proximity to a "motorable road" and that improvements in local roads have their greatest effect in areas with the lowest average incomes: "the presence of a village road in the poorest communities increased the probability of a resident's escaping poverty by 68 percent" (Deolalikar, 2001);
- Transport costs due to poor roads and other transport infrastructure are a particularly limiting factor for the trade prospects of landlocked countries, such as are prevalent in Africa. In one study, the median landlocked country was found to have transport costs 50 percent greater than the median coastal country and a 60 percent smaller trade volume (Lemao and Venables, 2001); and
- A country study in Uganda found that transport costs reduce the exporter's value added by about 30 percent, far more than the estimated 12.5 percent caused by foreign import tariffs, creating a strong internal disincentive to produce and export Ugandan goods (Weiss, 2003). Another study put the travel cost burden on exporters even higher, up to two-thirds of value added, with half of that being for the overland portion of the journey within Africa (Willoughby, 2002). Such costs make it virtually impossible to fulfill the vision of export trade making a significant contribution to Africa's growth and poverty reduction.

Reliable, efficient infrastructure is crucial to economic and social development that promotes pro-poor growth. By raising labor productivity and lowering production and transaction costs, economic infrastructure – transport, energy, information and communication technology, and drinking water, sanitation and irrigation – enhances economic activity and so contributes to growth, which is essential for poverty reduction. A number of studies point to a significant impact of roads on poverty reduction through economic growth. Access to roads has been shown in numerous studies to have a significant effect on rural poverty (Jacoby, 2000; Gibson and Rozelle, 2003). Kwon (2000), analyzing Indonesian data, estimates a growth elasticity with respect to poverty incidence of 0.33 for good-road provinces and 0.09 for bad-road provinces. This implies that poverty incidence falls by 0.33 percent and 0.09 percent, respectively, for every 1 percent growth in provincial GDP. Provincial roads also appear to directly improve the wages and employment of the poor, such that a 1 percent increase in road investment is associated with a 0.3 percent drop in poverty incidence over five years. Another study on Indonesia, using more disaggregative district level data, also reveals a significant effect of roads on the average incomes of the poor via growth, an estimated elasticity of 0.05 (Balisacan, Pernia, and Asra, 2002).

A parallel research on the Philippines, using provincial data, reveals that roads, particularly when complemented by schooling investment, exert significant indirect and direct impacts on the welfare of the poor (Balisacan and Pernia, 2002). The elasticities suggest that a 1 percent increase in road access coupled with schooling results in a 0.32 percent rise, via growth, in the mean incomes of the poor. Similarly, a 1 percent improvement in roads with schooling is directly associated with a 0.11 percent increase in the poor's incomes. A study by Fan et al. (2002), using provincial data, examines the effects of different types of government expenditures on growth and rural poverty in China. They find that roads significantly reduce poverty incidence through agricultural productivity and non-farm employment. The estimated elasticities with respect to road density are 0.08 for agricultural GDP per worker, 0.10 for nonagricultural employment, and 0.15 for wages of nonagricultural workers in rural areas. Among government infrastructure projects, rural roads are found to have the largest impact on poverty incidence: for every 10,000 yuan invested on rural roads, 3.2 poor persons are estimated to be lifted out of poverty.

A related research shows that road density has a significant positive effect on the consumption expenditure of rural farm households in poor regions of the PRC (Jalan and Ravallion, 2002). For every 1 percent increase in kilometers of roads per capita, household consumption rises by 0.08 percent. Research on Viet Nam reveals that poor households living in rural communes with paved roads have a 67 percent higher probability of escaping poverty than those in communes without paved roads (Glewwe et al., 2000). Likewise, an evaluation of a World Bank-funded rural road rehabilitation project in Viet Nam finds that the strongest positive impact was for the poorest households (Van de Walle and Cratty, 2002). In particular, the time savings to reach habitual places of destination were highly significant for the poorest 40% of households. A study on Nepal finds that providing extensive rural road networks results in substantial benefits, with the poor capturing an appreciable share (Jacoby, 1998). However, the poor's share is often not large enough to significantly reduce income inequality as the benefits from road extension could be greater for landholdings of the rich. Thus, the distribution of benefits from road extension may be ambiguous. The relevant question to ask is whether the benefits of a hypothetical road project are sufficiently large and distributed progressively enough to reduce overall income inequality, with benefits accruing more to the poor than the non-poor.

Qualitative research employing interviews and focus group discussions lends additional insights. One such study in two provinces of the Central Highlands of Viet Nam notes that the benefits of rural roads are generally perceived as largely social rather than economic in nature (Songco, 2002). While the rural poor appreciate road improvements, they clamor for other types of interventions, such as credit and health services. Nonetheless, rural roads are generally regarded as instrumental in creating opportunity, facilitating empowerment, and enhancing security (Asian Development Bank, 2002; World Bank, 2002).

The rural poor's lack of access to product and factor markets leaves them largely bypassed by the growth process. Infrastructure investments complemented by policy and institutional reforms enable markets to develop and function efficiently, thereby mainstreaming the poor. Making markets work for the poor is therefore a key element of a country's poverty reduction strategy. The main factors underlying rural poverty include farm productivity, as well as non-farm employment and productivity (Ali and Pernia, 2003). Infrastructure investments influence all the three sets of poverty determinants. Road investments, for example, could increase agricultural productivity, non-farm employment, and productivity, directly raising the wages and employment of the poor, and hence, their economic welfare. In addition, higher productivity and expanded employment lead to faster economic growth, affecting the supply and prices of goods that benefit the poor.

The magnitudes of effects of infrastructure investment on rural poverty transmitted through different channels, in the case of rural roads, are illustrated in the following table. The estimates presented are derived from two recent country studies on the China and India (Fan et al., 1999 and 2002). The total direct and indirect effects of road investments on poverty in the rural China are more than twice those in rural India. Given the importance of possible country-specific factors in the overall poverty-reducing impact, the decomposition results indicate the significance of all channels, viz., agricultural productivity, non-farm employment and rural wages, and the follow-on economic growth. The direct effect through the increase in agricultural productivity accounts for close to 20 percent and 30 percent of the total poverty-reducing effects in India and the China, respectively. The direct effects of increasing non-farm employment and rural wages contribute to over three quarters in India and one half of the total effect in the China, underscoring the particular significance of the rural labor market channel. The effect through labor markets is especially large in India, primarily because rural India has a significant proportion of landless or sub-marginal farmers, for whom rural road investment would open up gainful non-farm employment opportunities. On the other hand, the relative indirect follow-on effect of higher economic growth on rural poverty reduction is larger in the China than in India. Taken together, the results show that the infrastructure investments have significantly large direct effects on rural poverty reduction (Yao, 2003).

According to results from Kwon's (2005a) study of China, additional kilometer of high-class roads lift 9 rural poor above the poverty line and low-class roads lift 22 rural poor above the poverty line; while additional kilometers of high-class roads lift 6 urban poor above the poverty line, and low-class roads lift 4 urban poor above the poverty line

In addition, for Indonesia, Kwon (2005b) find that roads, of themselves, significantly affected poverty incidence, as did other variables. Roads influenced the performance of other variables in poverty alleviation as well. In other words, road capital alleviated poverty two ways: by itself (its own effect) and through its effect on the performances of other variables (the through-effect). To investigate the role of roads thoroughly, the sample was divided into the good- and bad- access provinces. Roads were found to be very important by themselves, regardless of the level of road capital available in a province. Remarkably, the through-effect had a much bigger magnitude in good-access provinces. When road investment increased 1 percent, poverty declined 0.3 percent - over five years, with everything else equal. The study finds that road investments improved the performance of provincial economic growth in poverty reduction, such that every one percent growth in provincial GDP led to a decline in poverty incidence by 0.33 percent in good-road provinces and 0.09 percent in bad-road provinces. This implies that the accumulation of road capital has a nonlinear contribution to poverty alleviation. As road capital is accumulated, the link between economic growth and poverty reduction becomes stronger.

Apart from its indirect contributions to poverty reduction, there is also increasing evidence to show that transport infrastructure can have a direct contribution to poverty reduction, independent of the growth channel. For instance, the same study by Kwon (2005a) reveals that road capital had its own explanatory power for poverty incidence, which was *not channeled through economic growth*. Provincial roads directly improved the wages and employment of the poor in Indonesia, such that a one percent increase in road investment led to a 0.3 percent drop in poverty incidence over five years. Meanwhile, Warr's (2005) study on road and rural poverty in Lao PDR shows that all-weather roads had a positive and highly significant impact on poverty: all-weather road access lowered poverty incidence by around six percent, and about 13 percent of the decline in rural poverty incidence between 1997–98 and 2002–03 can be attributed to improved road access alone.

For China, Fan and Chan-Kang (2005) find that in terms of poverty reduction, low-quality roads raise far more rural and urban poor above the poverty line per yuan invested than do high-quality roads. Road investments yield their highest economic returns in the eastern and central regions of China while their contributions to poverty reduction are greatest in western China (especially the southwest region). This implies different regional priorities depending on whether economic growth or poverty reduction is the most important goal for the country.

Using panel data of 1994-2002, as well as time series data of 1978-2002 in China, Zou et al. (2008) examine the effect of transport infrastructure on economic growth and poverty alleviation, and find out that the higher growth level in East and Central China comes, to a great extent, from better transport infrastructure. They compare the different effect of railways and roads in different regions, and find out that public investment on road construction in poor areas is of drastic importance to growth and poverty alleviation, and therefore should be a priority of policy choice.

Fan et al. (2002) take a more comprehensive approach to the problem. Using a model consisting of a system of equations to account for endogeneities, Fan et al. quantify the effects of rural infrastructure on growth and poverty reduction in rural China between 1970 and 1997. The authors find that public investments in roads, together with investments in education and agricultural research, helped to reduce rural poverty and regional inequality.

On micro-linkages, based on field research in India, Thailand, and the China, a 2005 Asian Development Bank study finds that rural transport improvements decreased costs to the poor for personal travel and goods transport. Rural transport improvements are also revealed to have generated farm income, promoted non-farm activities, and increased the range of opportunities for wage employment as well as the wage rates of labor in rural areas. In terms of non-income poverty, transport infrastructure can likewise generate direct impacts by lowering the cost of services needed by the poor, and by serving as a good complement to interventions that seek to improve access to health, education, and other social services.

Transport investments may also play an important role in mitigating risks faced by poor households. The same study finds that rural transport investments increased the availability and accessibility of education and health care services in rural areas, resulting in greater participation in these programs by the poor. Rural roads also facilitated the delivery of emergency relief to the poor in case of natural disasters (Setboonsarng, 2006).

Jalilian and Weiss (2004) find evidence of a direct relation between infrastructure and poverty reduction that is in addition to a growth effect. The average direct infrastructure poverty elasticity is relatively high at - 0.35 for the $1 a day headcount measure and –0.53 for the $2 headcount. For India, for example, a 35 percent increase in the infrastructure measure is required to bring the headcount down by 19 percent.

Jalan and Ravallion (2002) find that road density has a significant positive effect on the consumption expenditure of rural farm households in poor regions of China. For every 1 percent increase in kilometers of roads per capita, household consumption increases by 0.08 percent. Research on Vietnam reveals that poor households living in rural communes with paved roads have a 67 percent higher probability of escaping poverty than those in communes without paved roads (Glewwe et al., 2000). Similarly, an evaluation of a World Bank-funded rural road rehabilitation project in Vietnam finds that the strongest positive impact was for poorest households (van de Walle and Cratty, 2002). Escobal (2001) analyzed factors that determine market access for poor rural Peruvian farmers, showing the importance of key public assets such as rural roads in lowering transaction costs and in improving incomes of rural farmers.

Seetanah and Khadaroo (2008) investigated transport infrastructure as an element in poverty reduction at the macroeconomic level for the case of Mauritius. An aggregate poverty function, extended for the sake of the study with transport capital of the country for the period 1960-2005 was employed in a VAR framework to account for dynamism and endogeneity. Results from the analysis show that transport capital has been a sizable element in reducing poverty in the country with a reported coefficient of -0.14. Poverty is also found to be essentially a dynamic phenomenon and constitutes a vicious cycle. Indirect effects of transport capital is also confirmed as such type of capital is observed to have positive effects on output, employment, human capital and negative effect on inequality, all of which in turn reducing poverty level.

Other empirical studies identify poor transport infrastructure and border restrictions as significant deterrents to trade expansion. Drawing on new econometric results, Buys, Deichmann and Wheeler (2006) quantify the trade-expansion potential and costs of such a network. They use spatial network analysis techniques to identify a network of primary roads connecting all Sub-Saharan capitals and other cities with populations over 500,000. The authors estimate current overland trade flows in the network using econometrically-estimated gravity model parameters, road transport quality indicators, actual road distances, and estimates of economic scale for cities in the network. Then they simulate the effect of feasible continental upgrading by setting network transport quality at a level that is functional, but less highly developed than existing roads in countries like South Africa and Botswana. The authors assess the costs of upgrading with econometric evidence from a large World Bank database of road project costs in Africa. Using a standard approach to forecast error estimation, they derive a range of potential benefits and costs. Their baseline results indicate that continental network upgrading would expand overland trade by about $250 billion over 15 years, with major direct and indirect benefits for the rural poor.

Brenneman and Kerf (2002) finds strong evidence of positive impacts of infrastructure on education (particularly for transport and energy services), and on health outcomes (especially for water/sanitation, energy and transportation, although less so for telecommunications). Datt and Ravaillon (1998) find that between 1960 and 1990 rural poverty levels changed considerably in Indian states—and that states starting with better infrastructure and human resources saw significantly higher long-term rates of poverty reduction. Deninger and Okidi (2003) obtain similar results in exploring factors underlying growth and poverty reduction in Uganda during the 1990s. Their work indicates the importance of improving access to basic education and health care, but progress also depends on complementary investments in electricity and other infrastructure.

Fan et al. (2002) document the critical role of infrastructure development, particularly roads and telecommunications, in reducing rural poverty in China between 1978 and 1997. The authors show that poverty fell because of the growth in rural non-farm employment that followed expansion of infrastructure (see Briceño-Garmendia, C., Estache, A. and Shafik, N. (2004). The analysis of the relationship between poverty incidence and road development carried out by Warr (2005) suggests that about 13 percent of this decline in rural poverty in Lao can be attributed to improved road access alone. Other factors included a massive public investment in irrigation facilities. There is now a high return to providing dry weather access to the most isolated households of Lao PDR—those who have no road access at all. They constitute 31.6 percent of all rural households in Lao PDR and are being left behind by the development of the market economy. By providing them with dry season road access, rural poverty incidence could be reduced permanently from present 33 percent to 29.7 percent. A further reduction to 26 percent could be obtained by providing all rural households with all-weather road access.

Recent studies such as Jacoby (2000), Gibson and Rozelle (2003), and Jacoby and Minten (2008) focused on the effectiveness of road and transportation infrastructure. According to Jacoby and Minten (2008), a road that essentially eliminated transport costs in a small region of Madagascar would boost the incomes of the remotest households— those facing transport costs of about $75/ton—by nearly half, mostly by raising non-farm earnings.

In the rest of the paper, we investigate the direct poverty-reducing impact of road infrastructure using a panel data of African countries.

IV. THE MODEL AND DATA: IMPACT OF ROAD INFRASTRUCTURE ON POVERTY IN AFRICA

4.1. The Empirical Model

We use the cross-country data to analyze how international remittances affect poverty in Africa. Using the basic growth–poverty model suggested by Ravallion (1997) and Ravallion and Chen (1997) as well as the frameworks posited by Dollar and Kraay (2002), Ghura, Leite and Tsangarides (2002), Berg and Krueger (2003) and empirical works of Anyanwu and Erhijakpor (2008), Capistrano and Sta Maria (2007), and Jongwanich (2007), the relationship that we want to estimate can be written as:

$$\log P_{it} = \alpha_i + \beta_1 \log(g_{it}) + \beta_2 \log(y_{it}) + \beta_3 \log(Road\inf rast_{it}) + \beta_4 \log(X_{it}) + \varepsilon_{it} \quad (1)$$
$$(i = 1,...., N; t = 1,....., T)$$

where P is the measure of poverty in country i at time t; α_i is a fixed effect reflecting time differences between countries; β_1 is the elasticity of poverty with respect to income inequality given by the Gini coefficient, g; β_2 is the "growth elasticity of poverty" with respect to real per capita GDP given by y; β_3 is the elasticity of poverty with respect to road infrastructure (paved roads as percentage of total roads), Roadinfrast; X is the control variables, including international remittances (as percentage of GDP), primary education enrolment, inflation and openness; and ε is an error term that includes errors in the poverty measure.

The dependent variable in Equation (1), which is poverty, is measured using the Foster-Greer-Thorbecke (FGT) poverty indices- the poverty incidence, the depth of poverty and the severity of poverty (Foster, Greer and Thorbecke, 1984). The measures used for the dependent variables are the headcount ratio, poverty gap ratio and the squared poverty gap ratio, respectively. The poverty incidence is a measure of poverty which refers to the proportion of families with per capita income less than the per capita poverty threshold to the total number of families (see also, Anyanwu, 2005). The headcount measure is considerably the most commonly calculated poverty measure. The poverty depth indicates how far below the poverty line the average poor household's income falls, and is measured by the poverty gap ratio which is defined as the total income shortfall, expressed in proportion to the poverty line, of families with income below the poverty threshold, divided by the total number of families. The severity of poverty is the poverty measurement that is more sensitive to the income distribution among the poor. The measure used for the severity of poverty is the squared poverty gap ratio which is the total of the squared income shortfall, expressed in proportion to the poverty line, of families with income below the poverty threshold, divided by the total number of families. The severity of poverty defines how many families are located far below the poverty line. These people are labeled as the "poorest of the poor."

The measure of income inequality is the Gini coefficient. The Gini coefficient is the ratio of the area between the Lorenz curve and the diagonal (the line of perfect equality) to the area below the diagonal. As a measure of income inequality, the Gini coefficient ranges from 0 to 1. The larger the coefficient is, the greater the degree of inequality. Thus, the Gini coefficient limits 0 for perfect equality and 1 for perfect inequality. For the per capita income variable, the equation uses the per capita GDP as a measure.

The coefficient on our variable of interest, β_3 could be both positive and negative and we are interested in testing whether the impact of road infrastructure on poverty reduction is statistically significant. That is, controlling for income and its distribution, we test the hypothesis that countries receiving more road infrastructure will have less poverty. Theory predicts that international remittances would reduce poverty (see Anyanwu and Erhijakpor, 2008). The model also assumes that the level of income inequality affects poverty reduction. Since past work has shown that a given rate of economic growth reduces poverty more in low-inequality countries, as opposed to high-inequality countries, the income inequality variable is expected to be positive and significant. Therefore, the worse the income distribution and an increase in inflation tend to have a negative impact on poverty reduction so that their coefficients are expected to be positive.

The model assumes that economic growth—as measured by increases in mean per capita income— will reduce poverty. The relationship between poverty and the income variable is therefore expected to be negative and significant. Thus, the negative coefficient of β_2 is expected while income of the poor tends to grow proportionally with per capita growth. The literature shows that education increases the stock of human capital, which in turn increases labor productivity and wages (Anyanwu, 1998, 2005). Thus, while an increase in school enrolment increases opportunity of the poor to generate income, the coefficient associated with primary education is expected to be positive.

The coefficient associated with trade openness to poverty reduction is ambiguous (Berg and Krueger, 2003). On the one hand, trade liberalization could benefit the poor at least as much as the average person (Jongwanich, 2007). Trade liberalization could increase the relative wage of low-skilled workers and reduce monopoly rents and the value of connections to bureaucratic and political power. On the other hand, trade liberalization might also worsen the income distribution, particularly by encouraging the adoption of skill-biased technical change in response to increased foreign competition. Thus, if trade liberalization worsens the income distribution enough, particularly by making the poor poorer, then it is possible that it is not after all good for poverty reduction, despite its positive overall growth effects. A number of empirical studies using panel and cross-section data (e.g. Edwards, 1997; Ghura *et al.*, 2002; Dollar and Kraay, 2004) found no link between openness and the well-being of the poor beyond those associated with higher average per capita income growth.

4.2 The Data

Making use of poverty surveys beginning in 1990, the dataset consists of 33 African countries and 75 observations. Appendix Table 1 lists the countries and survey years of the dataset. The poverty and inequality measures used here are from the World Bank's PovcalNet database, which incorporates three measures of income poverty. The first is the poverty incidence (headcount poverty), which measures the percentage of the population living on less than one PPP dollar a day. The second is the poverty depth (poverty gap), which is the mean distance below the poverty line as a proportion of the poverty line, tells us how poor the poor are—how far below the poverty line the average poor person's income is. The third is the poverty severity (squared poverty gap), which is the mean of the squared distance below the poverty line as a proportion of the poverty line, is more sensitive to the distribution of the poor below the poverty line. The income distribution measure, the Gini coefficient, is available from the same survey data. The rest of the data series are from the World Bank World Development Indicators Online (see Appendix Table 2). In analyses of the impact of infrastructure at a macro level there is always a problem of how infrastructure is measured. Most possible infrastructure variables are relatively closely correlated so that the inclusion of several in the above equation will give biased results. A common approach (see also Jalilian and Weiss (2004)), which we adopt here, is to use one variable, in our case length of paved roads as a percentage of total roads, as a proxy for road infrastructure. International remittances are expressed as a ratio of the GDP of recipient countries. The income variable is per capita GDP in constant 1995 U.S. dollars while inflation rate is the percent change in the consumer price index. Other variables used are primary education enrolment rate and openness, measured by the ratio of imports plus exports to GDP. Tables 8 and 9 provide detailed descriptions of the dataset.

Table 8. Descriptive Statistics of Regression Variables

Variable	Observations	Mean	Median	Standard Deviation	Range
Paved Roads	50	28.64	18.3	23.03	72.1
Poverty Headcount	75	38.95	36.4	24.85	90.12
Poverty Gap/Depth	75	16.54	13.31	13.98	52.05
Poverty Severity	75	9.31	6.27	9.23	34.14
Gini Index	75	45.43	44.49	8.52	44.33
Per Capita GDP	75	711.24	412.2	772.77	3761.28
Remittances to GDP	64	3.79	1.42	1.42	49.33
Primary Education Enrolment	70	88.97	90.45	34.64	137.4
Inflation Rate	73	16.18	9.37	25.35	187.79
Trade Openness	70	6758.75	6037.346	3194.75	14857.23

Note: These are raw data before the log transformation.
Source: Authors' Calculations.

Before proceeding to the regression analyses, it is instructive to present bivariate relationships between key variables using simple scatter plots. Figure 10 show clear and unambiguously negative relationship between road infrastructure and poverty headcount in Africa. The same is true of the relationship between road infrastructure and both depth and severity of poverty in the continent.

V. EMPIRICAL RESULTS

5.1 OLS Results

Table 9 shows the results when Equation (1) is estimated using Ordinary Least Squares (OLS). The log transformation of all the variables allows us to interpret the coefficients as elasticities. Sub-regional dummies (North Africa and Sub-Saharan Africa) were introduced to control for fixed effects. The OLS estimates from our sample conform to the predictions of the model (Table 10).

The road infrastructure variable has a negative and statistically significant impact on each of the three poverty measures: headcount, poverty gap/depth, and poverty severity. Estimates for the poverty headcount measure suggest that, on average, a 10 percent increase in paved roads as a percentage of total roads will lead to a 5.4 percent decline in the share of people living in poverty.

Table 9. Bivariate Correlations of Regression Variables

Variable	Paved Roads	Poverty Headcount	Poverty Gap/Depth	Poverty Severity	Gini Index	Per Capita GDP	Remittances to GDP	Primary Education Enrolment	Inflation Rate	Trade Openness
Paved Roads	1.00									
Poverty Headcount	-0.67***	1.00								
Poverty Gap/Depth	-0.66***	0.99***	1.00							
Poverty Severity	-.65***	0.96***	0.99***	1.00						
Gini Index	-0.25*	0.28**	0.31***	0.32***	1.00					
Per Capita GDP	0.51***	-0.60***	-0.61***	-0.61***	0.31***	1.00				
Remittances to GDP	0.38**	-0.27**	-0.22*	-0.17	0.02	0.09	1.00			
Primary Education Enrolment	-0.14	0.04	0.05	0.05	0.13	0.08	-0.31**	1.00		
Inflation Rate	-0,07	0.32***	0.37***	0.40***	0.29**	-0.15	0.04	0.002	1.00	
Trade Openness	0.17	-0.13	-0.08	-.06	0.34***	0.36***	0.39***	-0.07	0.03	1.00

Note: *** Significant at 1 % level; ** Significant at 5% level; * Significant at 10% level.
Source: Authors' Calculations.

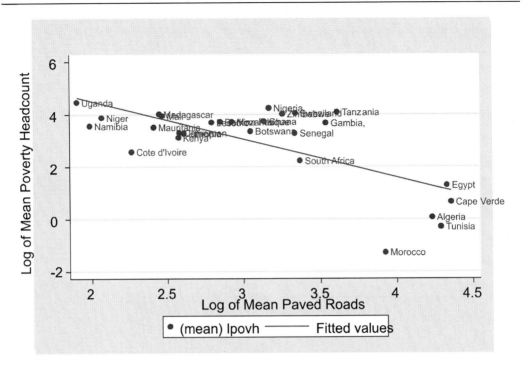

Figure 10. Scatter Plot of Log of Mean Poverty Headcount and Log of Mean Paved Roads

Table 10 shows that road infrastructure will have a slightly larger impact on poverty reduction when poverty is measured by the more sensitive poverty measures: poverty gap/depth and severity of poverty. It shows that on average, a 10 percent increase in paved roads as a percentage of total roads will lead to a 7.2 percent decline in poverty depth. Since the depth of poverty measures the distance of the poor people from the poverty line, it can be interpreted that as the length of paved roads increases, the distance of the poor people from the poverty line decreases. The results prove to be in accordance with expectations. For the severity of poverty (squared poverty gap), estimates imply that on average, a 10 percent increase in the length of paved roads brings about a 8.6 percent decline in the welfare of the people located far below the poverty line. These results are consistent with the magnitude found by Glewwe et al. (2000) for Vietnam and more recently by Jalilian and Weiss (2004) for developing Asian countries.

Regardless of the measure of poverty used as the dependent variable, per capita income has a negative and significant coefficient. International remittances have negative and significant effect on poverty headcount and severity. A positive and significant coefficient for the Gini index for poverty severity and depth indicates that greater inequality is associated with higher poverty. Other important dimensions of our results relate to the positive and significant effects of both trade openness on poverty severity and depth as well as the consistent, positive and significant impact of inflation rate on the three measures of poverty in Africa.

The coefficient on the dummy variable for Sub-Saharan Africa (SSA) represents the impact on poverty of unobservable SSA-specific factors with respect to the reference group (North Africa). In both the poverty headcount and severity estimations, the dummy variable for the SSA is positive – and negative for North Africa. In other words, if all the explanatory variables of the model had exactly the same levels in all the countries, poverty headcount, for example, would be some 127 percent higher in SSA countries. There would be equal corresponding fall in North African countries.

Table 10. Ordinary Least Squares Estimates of the Effects of Road Infrastructure on Poverty Measures in Africa

Variable	Poverty Headcount	Poverty Depth/Gap	Poverty Severity
Paved Roads(% of total)	-.54**	-.72**	-.86**
	(-2.20)	(-2.46)	(-2.52)
Inflow of International Remittances (ratio of GDP)	-.22**	-.21**	-.18
	(-2.34)	(-1.87)	(-1.41)
Gini Index	1.32	2.26*	2.82**
	(1.32)	(1.90)	(2.04)
Per Capita GDP (constant 2000 US$)	-.58**	-.88***	-1.14***
	(-2.74)	(-3.54)	(-3.91)
Sub-Saharan Africa	1.27**	1.03*	.79
	(2.74)	(1.87)	(1.23)
Primary Education Enrolment Rate	-.57**	-.44	-.33
	(-1.99)	(-1.30)	(-.83)
Trade Openness	.54	.89**	1.18**
	(1.45)	(2.01)	(2.29)
Inflation Rate	.27*	.40**	.50**
	(1.85)	(2.26)	(2.43)
Constant	-.73	-6.83	-10.96**
	(-.20)	(-1.59)	(-2.19)
R-Squared	0.82	0.83	0.82
Adjusted R-Squared	0.77	0.79	0.78
F-Statistic	18.54***	20.00***	19.21***
Prob>F	0.0000	0.000	0.000
N	42	42	42

5.2. IV-GMM Results

However, one possible problem with Equation (1) is that it assumes that all of the right-hand side variables in the model—including international remittances— are exogenous to poverty. However, it is possible that international remittances may be endogenous to poverty. Reverse causality may be taking place: international remittances may be reducing poverty, but poverty may also be affecting the level of international remittances being received. Without accounting for this reverse causality, all of the estimated coefficients in Table 10 may be biased. One way of accounting for possible endogenous regressors is to pursue an instrumental variables approach. Therefore, to deal with this problem, we follow Catrinescu et al (2006) and Aggarwal et al (2006) in estimating the equations instrumentalizing the remittances variable with its first and second lagged levels, using a the two-step (IV) efficient generalized method of moments (GMM) estimation method.

Table 11 shows the first-stage results from the IV-GMM estimations. We conduct and report two tests to show the validity of our instruments. First, we present the F-statistic for weak instruments. This is a test of the significance of our instruments in predicting remittances. The F-statistics is above the critical value, at 1 percent significance, indicating that our estimates do not suffer from a weak instruments problem. Second, we report the Hansen J test of overidenditfying restrictions. The joint null hypothesis in this case is that the instruments are uncorrelated with the error term and that excluded instruments are correctly excluded from the estimated equation. Again, these tests confirm the validity of our instruments.

Table 11. First-Stage IV-GMM Estimates for International Remittances to Africa

Variable	Coefficient	t-Statistics
Instruments		
First Lag of Inflow of International Remittances (ratio of GDP)	1.05***	9.18
Second Lag of Inflow of International Remittances (ratio of GDP)	.02	.20
Included exogenous variables		
Paved Roads (% of total)	.19	1.16
Gini Index	-1.08*	-1.66
Per Capita GDP (constant 2000 US$)	.10	.70
Sub-Saharan Africa	.51**	2.69
Primary Education Enrolment Rate	.29	1.58
Trade Openness	-.05	-.20
Inflation Rate	-.09	-.96
Constant	-3.22	-.87
N	40	
Shea Partial R-Squared	0.89	
F-Statistics of excluded instruments	115.17***	
P-value	0.0000	

Table 12 present the second-stage IV-GMM results. As for the impact of road infrastructure on of poverty, we continue to find that it has a negative and significant impact on all three measures of poverty in Africa.

Comparing the OLS and IV-GMM estimates for road infrastructure (Tables 10 and 12) yields similar results. For example, while the IV-GMM estimates for the poverty headcount measure suggest that, on average, a 10 percent increase in road infrastructure will lead to a 5.2 percent decline in the share of people living in poverty (Table 12), the OLS estimates suggest that a similar increase in road infrastructure will lead to a 5.4 percent decline in the share of poor people (Table 10). Indeed, comparing the OLS and IV-GMM estimates for road infrastructure (Tables 10 and 12), we find that the coefficients for the road infrastructure variable in Table 13 are slightly more negative for poverty incidence (-.52), and slightly lower for both poverty gap/depth (-.62) and severity of poverty (-.69) – but all highly significant. Considered as a whole, the IV-GMM results suggest that after instrumenting for the possible endogeneity of international remittances, road infrastructure still has a negative and statistically significant impact upon all three measures of poverty. Evaluated at the sample mean, an increase in $1 in road infrastructure (from 28.64 to 38.64 kilometers) will lead to a 0.18 percent [(38.64/28.64 - 1)*(-0.52)] reduction in the poverty headcount.

Table 12. IV-GMM Estimates of The Effect of Road Infrastructure onPoverty Measures In Africa

Variable	Poverty Headcount	Poverty Depth/Gap	Poverty Severity
Instrumented Endogenous Variable			
Inflow of International Remittances	-.21***	-.22***	-.22**
(ratio of GDP)	(-3.57)	(-2.99)	(-2.31)
Exogenous Regressors			
Paved Roads (% of total)	-.52***	-.61**	-.69**
	(-3.29)	(-2.82)	(-2.49)
Gini Index	1.69***	2.63***	3.20***
	(2.69)	(3.48)	(3.47)
Per Capita GDP (constant 2000 US$)	-.62***	-.93***	-1.18***
	(-4.55)	(-5.32)	(-5.38)
Sub-Saharan Africa	1.30***	1.08**	.86*
	(3.24)	(2.35)	(1.63)
Primary Education Enrolment Rate	-.53**	-.45*	-.36
	(-2.22)	(-1.70)	(-1.22)
Trade Openness	.67**	1.09**	1.43***
	(2.09)	(2.87)	(3.19)
Inflation Rate	.22**	.34**	.44***
	(2.19)	(2.83)	(3.13)
Constant	-3.22	-10.02**	-14.73***
	(-.87)	(-2.37)	(-3.01)
Centered R-Squared	0.83	0.84	0.83
Hansen J Statistic	1.569	1.792	1.771
p-Value	.210	.181	.183
Pagan-Hall Statistic	28.273	30.648	33.222
p-Value	0.898	0.828	.7301
N	40	40	40

As in the OLS results, income inequality, per capita GDP, trade openness and inflation rates continue to be significant determinants of all three measures of poverty in Africa. Income inequality continues to exact the largest positive impact on all three measures of poverty, increasingly progressively from the poverty headcount (coefficient of 1.69) to poverty gap (coefficient of 2.632) and to the severity of poverty (coefficient of 3.20). This is in conformity to Ravallion (2008). Again, regardless of the measure of poverty used as the dependent variable, per capita income has a negative and significant coefficient. Again, there was consistent, positive and significant effects of both trade openness and inflation rate on the three measures of poverty in Africa. These indicate the adverse poverty effects of the recent trade liberalization efforts in Africa and that of uncertainty represented by inflation. As expected, increase in human capital (proxied by primary education) has negative and significant effect on poverty in Africa. This conforms with the positions held by Berg and Kruger (2003) and Jongwanich (2007).

Also, the dummy variable for the SSA is more strongly positive than in the OLS results – and strongly negative for North Africa – on all three measures of poverty. For example, if all the explanatory variables of the model had exactly the same levels in all the countries, poverty headcount would be some 130 percent higher in SSA countries while there would be equal corresponding fall in North African countries.

VI. CONCLUSIONS AND POLICY IMPLICATIONS

This paper has used a new data set to examine the impact of road infrastructure on poverty in Africa. Some key findings and policy implications emerge. First, road infrastructure has a strong, statistically significant impact on reducing poverty in Africa. For example, a 10 percent increase in paved roads as a percentage of total roads will lead, on average, to a 5.2 percent decline in the share of people living in poverty. Indeed, the results provide strong, robust evidence of the poverty-reducing impact of road infrastructure in Africa. Two, per capita GDP strongly reduces all measures of poverty in Africa. Third, income inequality appears to be the strongest factor fueling all three measures of poverty in the continent. Fourth, both trade openness and inflation tend to reinforce poverty in Africa. Fifth, human capital strongly reduces the incidence and depth of poverty in Africa.

Our findings point to some key policy recommendations. In particular, our findings clearly indicate that there is considerable room for making road infrastructure more pro-poor. This has implications concerning policy, regulatory, and institutional measures that could help strengthen the impact of transport infrastructure on poverty reduction. In Africa, as in other developing countries, private sector investments have only been more extensive and successful in large urban cities or peri-urban populated areas. The track record of success has been in projects such as mass transit systems and toll roads. Thus, experience points to the fact that government is likely to continue to play a key role in transport infrastructure while new and innovative modes of financing will have to be tested. For their part, donors need to reverse the decline in assistance. Donor support for investment in infrastructure will continue to be important, especially where it can be used to generate pro-poor change. Current investment in infrastructure falls far short of even conservative estimates of what is needed.

Indeed, improved donor support for infrastructure offers some of the best opportunities for systemic pro-poor change. Road infrastructure is a sub-sector in which there is much scope for working with governments to strengthen accountability, encourage environmentally sound policies and increase social mobilization. Africa's development partners should therefore embraces this new approach to road infrastructure services as key to poverty eradication. Jointly working between governments and other providers of infrastructure services can contribute to efficiency and effectiveness and to achieving pro-poor growth. They need to seek opportunities to engage with national governments and multilateral agencies, building consensus for dealing with difficult agendas, so as to make road infrastructure services work better to eliminate poverty. Many bilateral agencies will increasingly want to provide financial support through government budgets, even if this support is subsequently passed on to commercial parastatal organizations or utilities. Such grant funding agencies are likely to be able to deliver significant support for policy development, for institutional strengthening, for human resource development and for piloting new approaches in the provision of road infrastructure services.

Project design including location of infrastructure investments is critical. Poverty reduction can be hastened if road interventions are made in locations that are pivotal in terms of distributive and multiplier effects favoring the poor.

In African countries, extending transport infrastructure to provide universal access should be a priority, but at the same time, there is clearly a pressing need to make poverty reduction an integral part of road transport infrastructure policy. To be effective in addressing poverty, there is a need to put asserted effort to explicitly identifying the poor or disadvantaged groups that will be affected by transport infrastructure projects; carrying out poverty analysis; and incorporating the results of such an analysis into project design. Components spelling out explicit activities should be incorporated to ensure that poverty issues are addressed throughout the project cycle.

Given our results with respect to the effects of inequality, equity considerations will require some form of targeting and prioritization of transport investments that have the greatest impact on poverty. For instance, among the different types of transport infrastructure, targeting investments to road infrastructure could make the most sense since it has been highlighted in the past as an important determinant of poverty reduction. Besides addressing the question of what to invest in, there is also the equally important question of where to invest. Given that poverty incidence tends to be higher in rural areas, targeting rural areas that lack access to basic transport infrastructure and services can be expected to have the biggest impact on poverty reduction.

Improving transport infrastructure's impact on poverty does not only entail physical access but affordability as well. This requires ensuring that the poor benefit from savings in operating costs, and that the resulting change in transport services is affordable to the poor. Here the primary policy instrument is to ensure effective competition in transport services, allowing operators to set their own fares and new operators to enter the market so that efficiency is encouraged. This is because, the lower the level of fare and entry regulation, the higher the chance of road infrastructure investment contributing to poverty reduction (see Setboonsarng, 2006).

Given increasing globalization, liberalization, and changing patterns in trade, providing regional public goods such as cross-border road infrastructure has become more critical in bringing benefits that may not materialize through domestic provision alone. Indeed, as had been recognized by the African Union/NEPAD as well as regional institutions like the African Development Bank, transport projects constitute one logical area for regional cooperation, considering the impact that infrastructure improvements could have on reducing trade costs and facilitating trade between participating countries. The goals of the NEPAD Transport Program include: reducing transport costs and improving the quality of services; improving the maintenance of transport infrastructure assets; attracting public and private investment inflows for transport infrastructure development; removing formal and informal barriers to the movement of goods and people; supporting regional cooperation and the integration of markets for transport services; and ensuring that transport makes the expected contribution to poverty eradication in Africa. The vision for Africa's transport is therefore geared towards completion of policy and institutional reforms; promoting knowledge sharing and innovation; achieving sector governance that is rule-based, predictable, transparent and participatory; creating conditions that favor participation of the private sector in operations as well as in financing; development of multi-sectoral economic development corridors; and prevention of the spread of HIV/AIDS by mainstreaming actions in transport program. Attaining this vision is therefore critical to poverty reduction in the continent. Indeed, the case for investing in cross-border transport infrastructure is most compelling for the fifteen land-locked African countries.

Remittances-receiving countries of Africa need to develop a strategy to maximize the benefits of remittances while minimizing their negative repercussions, including reducing the cost of sending remittances; improving data on remittances; the regulation of money transfer companies, broaden access of population to financial services by developing new products for households receiving remittances on a regular basis; establishing national and regional policies and strategies on remittances; and motivating senders and recipients of remittances to conduct their money transfer operations through formal financial institutions.

A major development concern from our findings relates to the poverty-reinforcing impact of trade openness, especially with the global trend towards trade liberalization, in spite of the problem of making significant headway in the Doha development round. We propose that African governments design complementary policies to mitigate the adverse income distribution and poverty consequences of trade reforms rather than abandoning such reforms all together. Such mitigation policies may range from setting up or improving safety nets, to better labor-market policies and institutions, and to investing in access roads to improve access by the poor to markets. In addition, well-designed additional policy interventions, especially those that improve education and infrastructure and address other "behind the border" investment climate reforms, can mitigate the adverse poverty changes that may result from trade liberalization.

Following our finding that inequality fuels poverty in African countries, policy makers need to tackle this challenge head-on. The literature has identified a number of possible policy instruments to deal with inequality, including, conditional cash transfers, guaranteed employment schemes, labor market training, greater access to health, nutrition and education through increased social investments, affirmative action, and land and property rights reforms, especially to benefit rural dwellers (particularly women). Evidence has shown that conditional cash transfers and expenditures (for education, for example) are effective levers of redistribution (see Levy, 2006; Kanbur, 2008). Improving access to education, for example, can reduce inequality (and hence poverty) both by increasing individual productivity and by facilitating the movement of poor people from low-paying jobs in agriculture to higher-paying jobs in industry and services. More importantly, public spending on education (as well as on health and other human capacity), when targeted toward the poor, can produce a double dividend, reducing inequality and poverty in the short run and increasing the chances for poor children to access formal jobs and thus break free from the intergenerational poverty trap. Increasing educational levels (and its quality) should be accompanied by a strong investment climate to ensure that productive jobs are created for the newly educated.

Given our finding that increases in human capital have negative and significant effect on poverty in Africa, effective education policies should be an essential component of any poverty-reduction strategy in the continent. Accordingly, a focus of economic policies on education in order to reduce poverty and to speed up development appears to be justified. Thus, since our findings provide an encouraging impetus for the use of education policies as part of anti-poverty programs, African governments, international development partners and the private sector can promote investment in education to increase enrolment rates, school attendance and length of time spent in education for children in African countries.

APPENDIX

Table 1. Countries in the Sample & Poverty Dataset Details Between 1990 and 2005

Country	Survey Year	Country	Survey Year
Algeria	1995	Namibia	1993
Benin	2003	Niger	1992
Botswana	1993	Niger	1994
Burkina Faso	1994	Nigeria	1992
Burkina Faso	1998	Nigeria	1996
Burkina Faso	2003	Nigeria	2003
Burundi	1992	Rwanda	2000
Burundi	1998	Senegal	1991
Cameroon	1996	Senegal	1994
Cameroon	2001	Senegal	2001
Cape Verde	2001	South Africa	1993
Central African Rep.	1993	South Africa	1995
Cote d'Ivoire	1993	South Africa	2000
Cote d'Ivoire	1995	Swaziland	1994
Cote d'Ivoire	1998	Swaziland	2000
Cote d'Ivoire	2002	Tanzania	1991
Egypt	1990	Tanzania	2000
Egypt	1995	Tunisia	1990
Egypt	1999	Tunisia	1995
Ethiopia	1995	Tunisia	2000
Ethiopia	2000	Uganda	2002
Gambia,	1992	Uganda	1992
Gambia,	1998	Uganda	1996
Ghana	1991	Uganda	1999
Ghana	1998	Zambia	1991
Kenya	1992	Zambia	1993
Kenya	1994	Zambia	1996
Kenya	1997	Zambia	1998
Lesotho	1993	Zambia	2004
Lesotho	1995	Zimbabwe	1990
Madagascar	1993	Zimbabwe	1995
Madagascar	1997		

Table 1. Continued

Country	Survey Year	Country	Survey Year
Madagascar	1999		
Madagascar	2001		
Malawi	2004		
Mali	1994		
Mali	2001		
Mauritania	1993		
Mauritania	1995		
Mauritania	2000		
Morocco	1990		
Morocco	1998		
Mozambique	1996		
Mozambique	2002		

Source: World Bank, PovcalNet Database.

Table 2. Description of Variables and Data Sources

Variable	Source
Paved Roads (as % of total roads)	World Development Indicators
Remittances (sum of receipts of worker remittances, employee compensation, migrant transfers) (as % of GDP)	World Development Indicators
Poverty indicators	PovcalNet database (available at http://iresearch.worldbank.org/PovcalNet/jsp/index.jsp.)
Gini index	PovcalNet database (available at http://iresearch.worldbank.org/PovcalNet/jsp/index.jsp.)
Per Capita GDP (constant 1995 US dollar)	World Development Indicators
Primary School Enrolment Rate	World Development Indicators
Trade openness ((imports + exports)/GDP)	World Development Indicators
Inflation (annual percentage change in CPI)	World Development Indicators

REFERENCES

ADB (Asian Development Bank) (2005). *Assessing the Impact of Transport and Energy Infrastructure on Poverty Reduction* http://www.adb.org/Documents/Reports/Assessing-Transport-Energy/

AfDB/OECD Development Centre (2006). *African Economic Outlook 2005/06: Promoting* Transport Infrastructure, OECD, Paris.

Aggarwal, Reena, Asli, Demirguc-Kunt, & Maria, Peria (2006). "*Do Workers' Remittances Promote Financial Development?*", World Bank Policy Research Working Paper No. 3957 (Washington: World Bank).

Ali, I & Pernia, E. M. (2003). *Infrastructure and Poverty Reduction: What is the Connection?*, ERD Policy Brief Series Number 13, Asian Development Bank, January.

Anyanwu, J. C. (1998). 'Poverty of Nigerian Rural Women: Incidence, Determinants and Policy Implications", *Journal of Rural Development*, Vol. 17, No.4, pp.651-667.

Anyanwu, J. C. (2005). "Rural Poverty in Nigeria: Profile, Determinants and Exit Paths", African Development *Review, Vol. 17, No.3, December*, pp. 435-460.

Anyanwu, John C. & Erhijakpor, A. E. O. (2008). Do International Remittances Affect Poverty in Africa?, Paper presented at the *African Economic Conference* 2008 on *"Globalization, Institutions, and Economic Development of Africa"*, Jointly Organized by the AfDB and UN-ECA at Ramada Hotel, Tunis, Tunisia, 12th–14th November.

Asian Development Bank. (2002). *Impact of Rural Roads on Poverty Reduction: A Case Study-Based* Analysis, IE-68, Operations Evaluation Department, Asian Development Bank, Manila.

AUC. (2008). First Session of the Conference of African Ministers of *Transport, 21 – 25* April 2008, Algiers, Algeria.

Balisacan, A. M., & Pernia, E. M. (2002). Probing Beneath Cross- National Averages: Poverty, Inequality, and Growth in the *Philippines. ERD Working Paper Series* No. 7, Economics and Research Department, Asian Development Bank, Manila.

Balisacan, A. M., Pernia, E. M. & A. Asra. (2002). Revisiting Growth and Poverty Reduction in Indonesia: What Do Subnational Data Show?, *ERD Working Paper Series* No. 25, Economics and Research Department, Asian Development Bank, Manila.

Berg, A. & A. Krueger. (2003). 'Trade, Growth, and Poverty: A Selective Survey', *IMF Working Paper* 03/30, International Monetary Fund, Washington DC.

Brenneman, Adam & Michel, Kerf. (2003). *Infrastructure and Poverty Linkages: A Literature Review,* mimeograph, Washington, D.C, The World Bank, December.

Briceño-Garmendia, C., Estache, A. & Shafik, N. (2004). Infrastructure Services in Developing Countries: Access, Quality, Costs and Policy Reform, World Bank Policy *Research Working Paper* 3468, December 2004.

Buys, P., Deichmann, U., & Wheeler, D. (2006). Road Network Upgrading and Overland Trade Expansion in Sub-Saharan Africa, World Bank Policy *Research Working Paper* 4097, December 2006.

Capistrano, L. O. & Sta. Maria, M. L. (2007). The Impact of International Labor Migration and OFW Remittances on Poverty in the Philippines.

Catrinescu, N., Leon-Ledesma, M., & Quillin, B. (2006). Remittances, Institutions, and Economic Growth, Institute for the Study of labor (IZA) *Discussion Paper* No. 2139, May.

Chen, S. & Ravallion, M. (2008). The Developing World Is Poorer Than We Thought, But No Less Successful in the Fight against Poverty, World Bank Policy Research *Working Paper* 4703, Washington, D. C., August.

Christiaensen, Luc, et al. (2004). "Macro and Micro Perspectives of Growth and Poverty Reduction in Africa", *World Bank Economic Review,* 2004.

Commission for Africa. (2005). *Our Common Interest: Report of the Commission of Africa.* London, 2005.

Datt, G. & Ravallion, M. (1998). "Why Have Some Indian States Done Better than Others at Reducing Rural Poverty?", *Economica* 65:17-38.

Deninger, K. & Okidi, J. (2003). *Growth and Poverty Reduction in Uganda, 1999-2000: Panel Data Evidence*, Washington DC., Development Policy Review, Volume 21 Issue 4 Page 481 - July.

Deolalikar, A. (2001). "The Spatial Distribution of Public Spending on Roads in Vietnam and Its Implications," A Report for the Asian Development Bank.

Dollar, D. & Kraay, A. (2002). 'Growth is Good for the Poor', *Journal of Economic Growth*, Vol. 7 (3): 195-225.

Dollar, D. & Kraay, A. (2004). 'Trade, Growth, and Poverty', *Economic Journal*, Vol. 114 (493): F22-F49.

Edwards, S. (1997). 'Trade Policy, Growth, and Income Distribution', *American Economic Review*, Vol. 87 (2): 205-10.

Escobal, J. (2001). *The Determinants of NonFarm Income Diversification in Rural Peru.* World Development, Vol 29, No 3, pp 497-508.

Fan, S. (2004). Infrastructure and Pro-poor Growth, Paper presented at the OECD DACT POVNET Agriculture and Pro-Poor Growth, Helsinki Workshop, 17-18 June 2004.

Fan, S. & Chan-Kang, C. (2005). Road Development, Economic Growth, and Poverty Reduction in China, Research Report 138, IFRI, Washington, DC.

Fan, S. et al. (2005). "Public Expenditure, Growth, and Poverty Reduction in Rural Uganda," DSGD Discussion Paper No. 4, IFPRI, Washington, DC.

Fan, S., Zhang, L. & Zhang, X. (2002). 'Growth, inequality, and poverty in Rural China: the role of infrastructure', *Research Report 125, International Food Research* Institute (IFRI), Washington D.C.

Fan, S., Hazell, P. & Thorat, S. (1999). Linkages between Government Spending, Growth, and Poverty in Rural India, *IFPRI Research Report* 110, International Food Policy Research Institute, Washington, D.C.

Foster, J., Greer, J., & Thorbecke, E. (1984). "A Class of Decomposable Poverty Measures", *Econometrica*, Vol. 52, No.3, pp.761-776.

Ghura, D., Leite, C. A. & Tsangarides, C. (2002). 'Is Growth Enough? Macroeconomic Policy and Poverty Reduction', *IMF Working Paper* 02/118, International Monetary Fund, Washington DC.

Gibson, J. & Rozelle, S. (2003). "Poverty and Access to Roads in Papua New Guinea", *Economic Development and Cultural Change.*

Glewwe, P., M. Gragnolati, and H. Zaman (2000), Who Gained from Vietnam.s Boom in the 1990s? An Analysis of Poverty and Inequality Trends, World Bank *Working Paper* 2275, Washington, D.C.

Jacoby, H. G. & Minten, B. (2008), On Measuring the Benefits of Lower Transport Costs, World Bank Policy Research Working Paper 4484, January 2008.

Jacoby, H.G. (2000). "Access to markets and the benefits of rural roads", *Economic Journal*, 100, July, 717-737.

Jalan, J., & Ravallion, M. (2002). Geographic Poverty Traps? A Micro Model of Consumption Growth in Rural China, *Journal of Applied Econometrics*, 17(4):329-46.

Jalilian, H. & Weiss, J. (2004). Infrastructure, growth and poverty: some cross country evidence, *Paper presented at the ADB Institute Annual conference on 'Infrastructure and development: poverty, regulation and private sector investment'*, 6 December 2004.

Jongwanich, J. (2007). Workers' Remittances, Economic Growth and Poverty in Developing Asia and the Pacific Countries, UNESCAP Working Paper, WP/07/01, January.

Kanbur, R. (2008). Poverty and Distribution: twenty Years ago and Now, paper presented at the 3rd African Economic Conference, African Development Bank, Tunis, November 2008.

Kwon, E. (2005a). 'Infrastructure, Growth and Poverty Reduction in Indonesia: A Cross-Sectional Analysis', Paper presented at the ADBI Workshop on Transport Infrastructure and Poverty Reduction, ADB Manila, 18–22 July 2005.

Kwon, E. (2005b). 'Road Development and Poverty in the People's Republic of China.' Presented at the ADBI Workshop on Transport Infrastructure and Poverty Reduction, ADB Manila, 18–22 July 2005.

Kwon, E. K. (2000). Infrastructure, Growth, and Poverty Reduction in Indonesia: A Cross-sectional Analysis, *Asian Development Bank*, Manila, Processed.

Lemao, N. & Venables, A. (2001). "Infrastructure, Geographical Disadvantage, Transport Costs, and Trade," *World Bank Economic Review* 15(3) 451–479.

Levy, S. (2006). Progress Against Poverty: Sustaining Mexico's Progresa-Opportunidades Program, Brookings Institution Press, *Washington*, D. C.

OECD. (2007). Promoting Pro-poor Growth: Policy Guidance for Donors OECD, *Paris, March*.

Prudhomme, R. (2004). *Infrastructure and Development*, Washington DC, Paper prepared for the ABCDE (*Annual Bank Conference on Development Economics*), May 3-5, 2004.

Ravallion, M. (1997). "Can High-Inequality Developing Countries Escape Absolute Poverty?", *Economics Letters, Vol.* 56, pp. 51–57.

Ravallion, M. & Chen, S. (1997). "What Can new Survey Data Tell us About Recent Changes in Distribution and Poverty?", *World Bank Economic Review*, Vol. 11.

Renkow, M., Hallstrom, D.G. & Karanja, D. D. (2004). Rural infrastructure, transaction costs and market participation", *Journal of Development Economics*, 73, pp349-367

Roberts, P., Shyam, K. C., & Rastogi, C. (2006), Rural Access Index: A Key Development Indicator, *World Bank Transport* Paper 10.

Seetanah, B. & Khadaroo, A. J. (2008). Transport Infrastructure and Poverty Reduction in Mauritius: Macroeconomic *Evidences*, http://s09.cgpublisher.com/proposals/422/index_html

Setboonsarng, S. (2006). Transport Infrastructure and Poverty Reduction, *ADBI Research Policy* Brief No.21.

Songco, J. (2002). Do Rural Infrastructure Investments Benefit the Poor? *World Bank Working* Paper 2796, Washington, D.C.

Straub, S., Vellutini, C. & Warlters, M. (2008). Infrastructure and Economic Growth in East Asia, *World Bank Policy Research Working Paper* 4589, April 2008.

Taylor, M. R. (2007). Beating Africa's Poverty by Investing in Africa's Infrastructure, Partnership to Cut Hunger and Poverty in Africa, October.

Torero, Maximo & Chowdhury, Shyamal. (2004). Infrastructure for Africa: Overcoming Barriers to Development", *Brief prepared for the 2020 African Conference, Kampala*, Uganda, April 1-3, 2004.

Van de Walle, D. & Cratty, D. (2002). *.Impact Evaluation of a Rural Road Rehabilitation Project*, World Bank, Washington D.C.

Warr, P. (2005). "Road Development and Poverty Reduction: The Case of Lao PDR", ADB Institute, *Research Paper Series*, No 64.

Weiler, F. (2004). Transport and Poverty The Direct *Contribution of Transport Infrastructure to Poverty* Reduction, KFW, Frankfurt.

Weiss, J. (2003). 'Infrastructure Investment for Poverty *Reduction: A Survey of Key Issues'*, ADB Institute Research Policy Brief No. 5.

Willoughby, C. (2002). "Infrastructure and Pro-Poor Growth: Implications of Recent Research," A paper prepared under contract to Oxford Policy Management for the United Kingdom Department for International Development.

Willoughby, C. (2004a). "How Important is Infrastructure for Achieving Pro-Poor Growth?", sponsored by DFID.

Willoughby, C. (2004b). "Infrastructure and the MDGs", sponsored by DFID.

World Bank. (2002). Socioeconomic Impact Assessment of Rural Roads: Methodology and Questionnaires, Roads and Rural Transport TG and Transport Economics and Poverty TG, World Bank, Washington D. C. Draft.

World Bank. (2008). Safe, Clean, and Affordable Transport for Development: The World Bank Group's Transport Business Strategy 2008-2012, The World Bank Group, Washington, DC.

World Bank, World Development *Indicators* (WDI) Online.

Yao, X. (2003). Infrastructure and Poverty Reduction —Making Markets Work for the Poor, ERD Policy Brief Series Number 14, Asian Development Bank, May.

Zou, W., Zhang, F., Zhuang, Z. & Song, H. (2008). Transport Infrastructure, Growth, and Poverty Alleviation: Empirical Analysis of China, Annals of Economics and Finance, Vol. 9, No.2, 345–371.

In: Poverty in Africa
Editor: Thomas W. Beasley

ISBN: 978-1-60741-737-8
© 2009 Nova Science Publishers, Inc.

Chapter 2

WE ARE THE FIRST DOCTORS HERE AT HOME: WOMEN'S PERSPECTIVES ON SANITARY CONDITIONS IN MOZAMBIQUE

Maja Söderbäck and Malin Udén
School of Health, Care and Social Welfare,
Mälardalen University, Sweden

ABSTRACT

Lack of sanitation is an important public health issue in low-income countries. Globally, the lack of sanitation affects some 2.8 billion people, mainly the poor, women and children. The people affected are deprived of their dignity and at risk for several severe diarrheal diseases. However, improvements are often hindered by the fact that human excrement is a sensitive issue, and feasible solutions fail to consider cultural and gender issues.

With this background, this chapter focuses on women's sanitary conditions in a rural African village (Mozambique). An ethnographic approach was used to investigate the everyday sanitary conditions, understood through a theoretical framework of equity in health, and gender was used for understanding. During a two-month stay in the village, women in three households were followed and observed in their everyday work to explore the sanitary prerequisites. Furthermore, official and traditional leaders in the village were interviewed about their perceptions of the women's sanitary situation.

The findings show that every woman and her family members are obligated to deal with their human waste on an individual basis, creating solutions mostly from what could be obtained free within the confinements of their yard. This unhygienic situation rendered the women fearful of disease and accidents, especially for their children, resulting in both psychological and physiological discomfort. Maintaining sanitation was female work. However, only men were allowed to build new latrines, causing difficulties for the many women without husbands. Several positive forces also existed: openness, interest, knowledge and an already existing net of community development. Improvements are instead held back by poverty and gender disparities, depriving women of control over their own home and health.

Keywords: determinants of health, ethnography, Mozambique, poverty, rural, sanitation, women

INTRODUCTION

Today some 2.8 billion people globally lack adequate sanitation. It is mainly a problem of the poor, women and children in low-income countries, causing deadly diseases in the form of diarrhoea and intestinal worms. Too many die from this preventable cause. In Africa, two out of three individuals lack an acceptable sanitary situation (Vlugman, 2006). As this chapter is written, a new cholera epidemic raging in Zimbabwe has gained the world's attention. The neighbouring country, Mozambique, where this chapter is set, is also at risk of the spreading epidemic (World Health Organization [WHO], 2008).

Sanitation is a governmental public health issue, but it often tends to fall behind when governments and organisations work for improved living conditions for the poorest. This has been suggested to partly depend on a lack of recognition for how culture and gender affects this often awkward subject. Sanitation is not merely a public health problem due to lifestyle or personal habits; it is a complex subject, affected by emotions, taboos and obvious equality problems. Few people are comfortable in a discussion of human faeces and urine.

Lack of sanitation affects women in a special way: they carry the main responsibility for maintaining hygienic standards. They often adhere to stricter privacy demands, while at the same time having less power to improve their situation. This chapter will focus on women's sanitary conditions in a rural African village (Mozambique), their perceptions of and preferences for what creates a sanitary home. That knowledge can be of general interest to public health workers and others who want to understand rural low-income families' sanitary prerequisites.

BACKGROUND

The Setting

Mozambique

Mozambique, officially the Republic of Mozambique, is a country in southeast Africa bordering the Indian Ocean to the east, Tanzania to the north, Malawi and Zambia to the northwest, Zimbabwe to the west and Swaziland and South Africa to the southwest. Within an area of 801,590 km² the population is estimated at 21,284,701 (2008). The official language is Portuguese. There are about 13 other national languages (Embassy of the Republic of Mozambique, 2008). After World War II, while many European nations were granting independence to their colonies, Portugal's dictator António de Oliveira Salazar clung to the concept that Mozambique and other Portuguese possessions were overseas provinces of the mother country, and emigration to the colonies soared (Mozambique's Portuguese population was about 250,000 in 1975). The drive for Mozambican independence developed apace, and in 1962 several anti-colonial political groups formed the Front for the Liberation of Mozambique (FRELIMO), which initiated an armed campaign against Portuguese colonial rule in September 1964. After 10 years of sporadic warfare and Portugal's return to democracy, Mozambique became independent on June 25, 1975. Portugal's policy of underdeveloping its colonies, combined with the rapid exodus of Portuguese people, left Mozambique with few internal human resources. FRELIMO established a one-party Socialist state, and quickly received substantial international aid from Cuba and the Soviet bloc nations (Embassy of the Republic of Mozambique, 2008).

In 1982, Renamo, an anti-Communist group sponsored by the Rhodesian Intelligence Service in the mid-1970s, and sponsored by the apartheid government in South Africa as well as the United States after Zimbabwe's independence, launched a series of attacks on transport routes, schools and health clinics. The country descended into civil war. In 1990, with apartheid crumbling in South Africa, and support for Renamo drying up in South Africa as well as the United States, the first direct talks between the Frelimo government and Renamo were held. In November 1990 a new constitution was adopted. Mozambique was now a multiparty state, with periodic elections and guaranteed democratic rights. The General Peace Accords were signed in Rome in October, 1992. A UN Peacekeeping Force (ONUMOZ) oversaw a two-year transition to democracy (Embassy of the Republic of Mozambique, 2008).

When the civil war ended, the country's infrastructure was devastated. People had lost social security from their extended families. Schools and hospitals were destroyed and the state was virtually bankrupt (Alberts & Hirvonen, 1993; Ferrell, 2002). During the last decades the economic situation and the infrastructure has improved (Van den Bergh-Collier, 2000), but the national incidence of poverty was in 2006 still 54 percent, according to Mozambique's PARPA[1]. The poverty incidence in the Gaza region—where Maciene, the village in which this chapter is set—is just above the average, while the neighbouring Inhabame region reaches up to 81 percent (Republic of Mozambique, 2005).

After the liberation from the colonial power, women's emancipation was important on the political agenda and equal rights were included in the constitution (Ferrell, 2002). However, the political and legislative power is still favours men, who occupy most of the parliament seats, senior government and civil servant positions. In everyday reality, men are often seen as the main breadwinners, further complicating women's entrance in the labour market, who are given lower salaries and uncertain employment forms. The absence of income makes it difficult for women to invest when they are denied bank loans, despite being more likely to meet their payments. Poverty is especially common among female-headed households and families in which women are discriminated against (Van den Bergh-Collier, 2000).

The Mozambican women carry the responsibility of caring for most of the nation's food production, child care and household maintenance. They make up just over half of the labour force, and 90 percent of the economically active women work in farming. Peasant farming is, however, not visible in national economical statistics, as it is simply seen as an extension of women's natural responsibilities. Sanitation, water and waste are often women's responsibilities in Mozambique (Van den Bergh-Collier, 2000).

---

[1] Plan for the Reduction of Absolute Poverty) are documents written by the of world's poorest countries on The PARPAs (Action how they will tackle poverty, to be eligible for cooperation with the World Bank (Republic Mozambique, 2005).

Lack of potable water and sanitation has been a serious problem in Mozambique for a long time. The majority of the population still uses onsite solutions such as latrines or septic tanks. Children below five who suffered from malnutrition totaled 41% 2005, with diarrhoea as the main risk factor (United Nations Development Program [UNDP], 2005). Latrine and sanitation programs have been promoted several times since independence, but many advances were lost during the civil war. Both expanded sanitation and improved gender equality are PARPA goals aiming to improve the nation's human capital (Republic of Mozambique, 2005).

Life Conditions in Maciene

Maciene, the rural village focused on in this chapter, has about 1,000 inhabitants in the centre, while 6,500 inhabitants in the surrounding settlements are connected to the school, health centre and the Anglican Church ("Mälardalen Encounters Mozambique", n.d.). The health centre aids about 3,500 persons per month. The village hosts a school for grades one through eight. However many children, especially girls, drop out early. Most inhabitants live of peasant farming, cattle breeding and small-scale fishing. Many men work outside the village in the capital Maputo, or in South Africa, leaving the village with a high percentage of women, children and elderly. The houses in the village are made of bricks or sand and branches. Running water and electricity is unusual outside the main road. The setting is Christian, and the majority of the villagers belong to the Anglican Church (Anglican Church, 1999; 2001).

Earlier studies shows that the households consist of extended families, not limited to the closest blood relatives. There is a clear hierarchy in the households, with seniority and men in favour as the as the main decision makers. Women carry the main responsibilities of the households, while boys can help out as an additional chore. The boys describe themselves as being in a fortunate position (Gidlund, 2006; Wiltfalk, 2008).

To fetch water, some households use the community well, others use wells or open waterholes or the nearby lake. However, Holtmar and Wreetling (2004) describe that the nearby lake is contaminated, as it is used to wash clothes that release detergents, and when cattle are led there to drink. Lindén (2005) found that for the villagers the contaminated water was a problem. The hospital has many patients with sanitation-related diseases like diarrhoea, malnutrition and urinary tract infections.

Sanitation and Public Health

Sanitation is a public health issue that mainly affects low-income settings, especially rural communities and women and children. The meaning of sanitation is the separation of people from human and animal faeces; urine does not pose the same risks. For people to uphold the criteria of separation, they need hygienic ways of disposing of human excrement, together with good waste disposal of solid and liquid waste. Sanitation and pure water are closely connected, because it can become a bearer of pathogens in many ways. Animals drinking from the same sources as humans and flies flying from exposed faeces to a family's water container are such examples. When faeces enters the body it brings bacteria, virus or parasites, causing a number of diseases. Typhoid fever, cholera and intestinal worms are common examples with diarrhoea as the most prominent problem, causing dehydration, malnourishment and anaemia (Avvannavar & Mani, 2008; Cairncross, 2003; Landon, 2006; Vlugman, 2006).

A user-friendly and a medically-correct sanitary system are dependent upon a range of factors, including technical, cultural, political, social, environmental and economic factors.

Open defecation in canals, roads or fields is an inadequate solution. Pit latrines, where faeces is dropped and stored on site, have less effect on the environment, but instead pose a bigger risk of leaking pathogens into the groundwater. In practical terms, good sanitation and the avoidance of diseases is obtained through a septic tank or by connecting to a public sewage net (Cairncross, 2003; Vlugman, 2006).

Avvannavar and Mani (2008) mean that the social function of toilets is often forgotten in sanitation promotion. One such example is how organisations often favour ecologically sound latrines in rural development programs, but what people really want is water closets like in the cities resulting in failure of the projects. A study of rural Benin families showed that for the families a toilet represent safety, health, wealth and prestige. It could become something to leave behind as a proof of achievement during one's lifetime (Jenkins & Curtis, 2005).

However, Cairncross (2003) states that hygiene practices in fact might play an even more important role for people's health, than having a sanitary latrine. Equally important is washing of hands after performing ones needs, and not performing them in the field that can contaminate crops. To keep good hygiene people need good water for cleaning In areas without sewage the only water available is often the drinking water, that often ends up as the place where people have to throw their solid and liquid waste. The connections between families who have toilets and their lower diseases risk is more confounded by the fact that they often are more educated, and thus more likely to keep good hygiene. (Avvannavar & Mani, 2008; Landon, 2006).

The need to defecate and urinate is a primal need that ideally should be performed in a safe, private and comfortable place. What this means can differ among ages, sexes and whether one has any disabilities. If people lack a latrine, or have a deteriorated version, they can be at risk for accidents, insect bites or sexual assaults. A good latrine or toilet can thus be physiologically important if it can generate a feeling of safety. People can then perform their needs regardless of weather, if others are present and after dark. On the other hand, some individuals prefer to relieve themselves in the open; men especially can choose to perform their needs in the open even if there is a latrine or toilet nearby (Avvannavar & Mani, 2008; Jenkins & Curtis, 2005; Water Supply and Sanitation Collaborative Council [WSSCC], 2006).

Culture and religion are presets for how people view their excrement and how it should be cared for. Human excreta are tied in to sexual morality and personal hygiene. Faeces and discussions about it are taboo to some extent, while people generally have a more relaxed attitude towards urine. Fear of faeces is somewhat rational, but can become an obstacle if it causes avoidance behaviour. Children's faeces are considered more harmless. The taboo nature of the excreta can diminish the efforts put towards improving sanitation from private actors, organisations and governments (Avvannavar & Mani, 2008; Vlugman, 2006).

Gender Issues

All over the world women can be observed as responsible for producing household goods and services and caring for children (Kulick, 1987), while at the same time having minimal access to power over politics, civil society and labour markets (Van den Bergh-Collier, 2000). This division is often defended from a biological point of view, saying that men and women have different destinies depending on their reproductive roles. In this chapter that view is discarded, claiming that what appears to be biology is in fact constructed in individual minds and culture (Kulick, 1987; West & Zimmerman, 1987). The theory of social construction is based on the assumption that gender differences are created and sustained over time simply by applying them. A key factor is that children learn as they are very young what it means to be male or female (West & Zimmerman, 1987).

However, most gender theories are based on the experiences of white western women (West & Fenstermaker, 1995). From the African woman's point of view gender theory can be seen as not applicable; saying gender oppression is primarily a European invention. But it can also be valid, seeing for example old costumes testifying of disparities, like lack of inherence rights and arranged marriages (Aina, 1998; Ata Aidoo, 1998).

Views on women's bodies and their waste products are a culturally loaded factor. Security, dignity, comfort and privacy are all issues that have been shown to be especially important in order for women to be pleased with their sanitation (Jenkins & Curtis, 2005; WSSCC, 2006). Women are expected to be more private about their primal needs than men, and that becomes difficult if sanitary facilities are missing or inadequately equipped for women's needs (WSSCC, 2006).

If a latrine is missing women are sometimes forced to wait to relieve themselves until they can seek shelter in the darkness (Avvannavar & Mani, 2008). Waiting can become a health problem when it sets constraints on liquid intake and thus causes dehydration as well as urinary tract infections and constipation (Vlugman, 2006). Washing haphazardly after menstruation is a risk factor that can arise when women are ashamed of their bodies and their waste products (WSSCC, 2006).

Women's empowerment is thus inextricably linked to sanitation (WSSCC, 2006). Women's work in the households is very time consuming, limiting their opportunities to do other productive activities or resting, and exposes them to pathogens. However, the producing of household goods and services also give women a vast amount of knowledge and vested their own interests of the families' sanitary conditions (Vlugman, 2006). Development and maintenance of technical solutions related to water and sanitation have been shown to be more sustainable if handled by women, but women are often seen as biologically unfit for technical work (WSSCC, 2006). In reality women's involvement in development work are often hindered by gender structures. Loosening social constraint on women's say and decision making is thus an important factor for sanitation development (Mello Souza, 2006).

Equity and the Determinants of Health

The majority of the sanitation related literature claims that poverty is the main underlying cause of bad sanitation, rather than individual hygiene behaviours. Since the Alma Ata declaration in 1978 the World Health Organisation (WHO) and the United Nation have equity in health as a prime objective of the public health policy (Scott, Stern, Sanders, Reagon, & Mathews, 2008; WHO, 1978). 'Determinants of health' are used to describe personal, social, economic and environmental factors that determine the health statues of individuals or populations (WHO, 1998). Dahlgren and Whitehead (2007) state that equity oriented health policies is aiming to reduce the health hazards for less privileged, and make the healthy choice as easy for them as for the most affluent groups.

Dahlgren and Whitehead (2007) ecological model contains four different 'policy levels' with determinants that can threaten, protect, or promote health and can be affected by different types of political actions (see Figure 1). Such a holistic perspective takes in to account that one determinant can be affected by all levels in society; different determinants can interact with each other and they can have different effects on different people. The core of the model represents individual factors like age, sex and the genes. These factors must be included for understanding, but can hardly be seen as open for change. The first adjustable layer is instead lifestyle behaviours, like diet, smoking and exercise. For people to be able to change their lifestyle public health efforts should focus on giving the individual information and tools for change. Layer two represents the people that surround and give support to the individual, such as family, friends and the local community. For change to happen on this level, efforts should focus on helping the local community, and to give social support to individuals and families. The aim should be to help people find their intrinsic strength to reduce their health hazards (Dahlgren & Whitehead, 2007).

Layer three consists of the material and social conditions people live in. Sanitation is represented there, together with other similar services like water, education and health care. Improvements on that level should focus on policies and strategies. In the uttermost level are the major structures of the nation, the region and the world. At the highest level interventions require changes cutting across all sectors, and aim at long-term structural efforts.

The fact that the model is layered does not mean that different issues are only attributed to one level. Smoking for example is not only an individual lifestyle question; it is also a question of laws and taxes belonging to level four (Dahlgren & Whitehead, 2007).

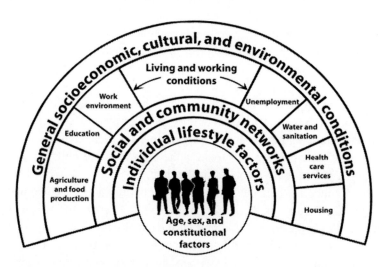

Figure 1. The main influences on health according to Dahlgren and Whitehead

Source: Dahlgren and Whitehead (2007, p. 11)

METHODOLOGY

Ethnographic Approach

The aim of this chapter is to describe women's sanitary household conditions in a Mozambican rural village (Maciene) with focus on the impact of inequity and gender relations. The overall design for the research is built on an ethnographic approach for international public health research (Crang and Cook, 2007; Dahlgren, Emmelin and Winkvist, 2004; Pilhammar Andersson, 2008). The ethnographic way of working and the Mozambican conditions is well known by the first author (Söderbäck, 1999; Söderbäck & Christensson, 2007). For this chapter the fieldwork was made by the second author.

An ethnographic approach suits to understand the local conditions as it strives to *"understand parts of the world more or less as they are experienced and understood in the everyday lives of people who 'live them out'"* (Crang & Cook, 2007, p. 1). No setting can be expected to be a homogenous society. It is important to search for diverging views, to expose different manners and experiences. To understand others one must get to know them and their surroundings. The ethnographer participates in social relations going on in the setting. The knowledge from the field-research is therefore neither objective nor subjective, but inter-subjectively created within the relationships. It is therefore important to get as close as possible to everyday sanitary dealings in the setting from the women's perspective, while at the same time trying to stand aside and see actions that they might not always even acknowledge themselves. To gain a holistic view the fieldwork in the setting was done for a prolonged period of time.

The Informants

The key-informants in the village are women. Six women were contacted via a gatekeeper, the rest through snowball sampling. The final sample contained women between 16 to 78 years of age, who all cared for their households. The daily life in three households were observed. One household consisted of a married couple, living in a large household with several separate houses, running water and electricity. That made it possible for them to own things like a refrigerator and a TV. They could enjoy these relative comforts because they had employments before retiring.

The two other households were run by women whose husbands had left them and their children to find work elsewhere. One woman lived in a family with two other grown women, of whom one had an employment that made it possible for them to afford a stable house of bricks and concrete. The other woman lived alone with her five children in a small house made of sticks and zinc. Her only income was the field.

The household's incomes reflected their sanitary conditions: the couple had a septic tank with a flush toilet (see Picture 3), the larger family had a concrete latrine (See Picture 2) and the third woman had a plastic cover for her pit latrine (see Picture 1).

To fully understand sanitation and hygiene on a community level, the local systems of political, community and religious leaders are also important. Four such leaders were included, representing the church, the hospital, the political and the traditional leadership. The traditional leader is a part of Mozambique's heritage from before the national state (Cipire,

1992). The political leader has the official political power, but the two work together for a balanced community.

Picture 1.

Picture 2.

Picture 3.

Data Collection

The interviews always focused on women and sanitation, but the questions were somewhat different with the women and with the leaders. The main themes for the women were caring for sanitation and what they thought of their situation. The village leaders were interviewed about cooperation above household level, their view on the villages' situation, development needs and possibilities. The interviews were kept semi-structured to facilitate the translation process. The informants spoke either Portuguese or the local language Shangana. Two translators were helpful in the process.

Participant observations were made in the three households. During the observations activities at the field and at home were followed by the fieldworker. No special schedule was constructed before the observations. Instead the observations included all personal hygiene practices that could be observed, and housework like washing, cleaning and showering with regards to how it was done and by who (and who did nothing). During the observations field notes and pictures were taken. Burgess (1984) might call that "observer-as-participant" rather than the ideal participant observer that fits seamlessly in to the lives of the informants.

The ethical considerations were performed to fulfil the Swedish Scientific Academy's ethical requirements for social science and humanistic research (The Governing Board of the Swedish Research Council, 2002). The informants were notified of everything that might affect their will to participate in the interviews and observations, such as the aim of the study, its purpose, promise of confidentiality and the freedom to abort at any moment. When cameras and audio records were used, consent was sought. For the village officials a letter of approval was written by the gatekeeper, to inform them about the field researcher's status as an official guest of the church.

Analysis of Data

The interviews and observations were continuously transcribed. The women have been given confidential names, and the leaders have been given codes. The quotes used in the findings section are also modified by removing repeated words and cleared up grammatically (Kvale, 1996), the latter probably a shortcoming of the translation rather than the informants. The observation records are written according to an analysis schedule containing six headings: descriptions of the setting, the people's interaction with the setting, the observers own participation in the setting, reflexions on the setting, methodological reflexions and personal reflexions.

The diary and the transcripts are analysed by using qualitative content analysis, following Lundman and Hällgren Granheim (2008). Meaning-units, sentences or words, in the transcriptions were concentrated to construct categories and themes for the findings. This method is suiting for ethnographical work because the form of the text for the 'units of analysis' does not matter. The method is also holistic, because all fragments like sentences or words can be traced back to the full text from which they were derived.

Writing Ethnography

The findings in this chapter are written in a narrative style to tell the story of the informants and their surroundings and capture the everyday life of the women's mastering of their sanitary conditions. The findings section is descriptive, that is staying close to the informants own words. Interview and observation records are mixed. The focus has been to highlight diverging views of the informants, to show that not even a small community like Maciene is a single unity (Sandelowski, 1998).

FINDINGS

Caring for Sanitation

Personal Hygiene

The households in Maciene cared for their excrements in different ways depending on their economic situation. Most households needed to create solutions to take care of their needs within the confinements of their own land. A few families had an income that allowed them to install a septic tank, running water and a flush toilet. These toilets were appreciated, but often flushed poorly why faeces stayed in the bottom of the bowl.

The basic construction of a latrine was based on a 'drop-and-store' method starting with a deep hole that was stabilized at the top with thick branches. To give the users privacy and avoid smells and flies spreading to the yard, the latrines placed to be hidden by other structures or at the outskirts of the yards. On top of the holes the families' constructed different seating or squatting arrangements made from wood or pots. For example one woman had taken a clay pot, pierced a big hole in the bottom and then fastened it in the sand upside-down (see Picture 1).

If the family could afford it they had improved their latrines by buying a plastic or concrete plate to place above the hole to stabilize the structure. Most latrines had bought or makeshift lids, like pieces of palm trees, to reduce the number of flies. The lids were however rarely used, and some families lacked covers all together. Old magazines were sometimes used as toilet paper.

Because the latrines were moved once the holes filled up, maintenance and construction were of secondary importance. The construction of the latrine walls was often unstably made of palm leaves or bamboo sticks, the latter sturdier but had to be bought. The latrines almost always lacked roofs, and because of this one woman said she could not perform her needs during rain. It was not uncommon for a family to have at least two latrines, in varying conditions to make it easier for visitors to find a free latrine. If a family employed contractors or maids they were confined to the household's oldest latrine.

The families cleaned their latrines and toilets with water, coal and detergents to remove germs and bad smells. They did not keep any water basins for washing their hands at the latrine, but the women mentioned washing with water as an important practice. When the latrines filled up they were covered in sand and a new hole was dug. The time to fill a latrine differed. For one family it took two years; another woman said that heavy rains could fill up or cause their latrines to collapse within three months.

There were occasions when people performed their needs outside of the latrine, and a few households still lacked latrines altogether according to a leader. One option observed was to urinate in the shower. This was explained by not having to feel the smell of the latrine unless it was absolutely necessary. Sometimes the women had seen villagers defecating at the field, which was seen as unhygienic and dangerous.

The shower construction reminded of the latrines, but because they were rarely moved the households could invest in sturdier constructions (see picture 4). The showers were considered less private than the latrines, and were often placed closer to the yard, with an open door. The women disliked having to stand on the sand and put stones or old bags to stand on, or bought a concrete floor if they could afford. An alternative to the outside shower, used by some households, was a shower or bathtub with running water. Children showered and changed clothes before school, while the women cleaned after finishing the day's fieldwork and cooking. Showering used about 20 litres of water and they used rags from old food sacks and stones to scrub body and feet. The young often took care of their own showering, which could be less than thoroughly performed.

Picture 4.

To care for their menstruation the women used either cotton, disposable or reusable pads and cleaned themselves in the latrine or in the shower. The menstruation articles were kept private; one woman who cleaned her menstruation pads hung them to dry in her room where no one else could see them.

Food Hygiene

Preparing food took the largest parts of the women's days. First at the fields, then preparing meals and lastly doing dishes. Food and water was mostly stored in large quantities in sacks or buckets inside to shield it from flies, thieves and birds. However sometimes food was just left on the ground with the animals, for example when the maize was dried in the sun. Water was gathered at different places depending on where the families lived and their economic situation. One family that had installed tap water kept backups in the form of rain water in a cistern for when the tap water lost pressure, which often happened. The other two observed families had five minutes' walk to a hand pump and a shallow well in a swamp area.

The buckets for storing water could be used for other things like washing dishes. The families were more careful with the cups for scooping up water that were always kept clean, and used solely for that reason. The water was either boiled or drunk as it was; none of the families used any special purifiers in their water. The water accompanying meals was often in the form of tea, but when drunk between meals it was not cooked. To cook the food and water, firewood had to be gathered at the fields. The women walked between two to twenty-five minutes to gather the amount of wood required for about one family meal.

Most families lacked an indoor kitchen and prepared their food sitting close to the dusty ground and the animals, in the shadow of a tree in the yard. The kitchens and their utensils could sometimes be shared with friends and family. When preparing food it was mostly cleaned in some way, either mechanically by peeling it or picking out dirt, or by soaking it with water. It did happen that people ate food that was not cleaned. One woman was for example observed crushing maize full of dirt and bird feathers and especially children picked fruits directly from the ground to eat.

The observed women often washed their hands after they got visibly dirty but they did not to any great extent wash their hands before preparing or eating food. One of the families did however wash their hands before meals, but only if the boy working for them was around. He then brought water, a basin and a towel to allow everyone to rinse.

The women in this study worked hard to live in a household that looked and felt clean. Everything that was used in the daily work was often cleaned both before and after using it, like dishes, water basins and the dish rack. Getting rid of visible dirt was especially important and therefore they scrubbed long and hard to make things look like new. This could for example be seen with the pans where food was cooked. Every day the metal got blackened by the soot, and after every meal they were scrubbed hard to shine again. Soap, coal to kill germs, something to scrub with and cold water were the basic items for washing most items in the household. If they could afford it special detergents and washing up liquids were used. The water was always conserved, for example lightly dirty water from showering could be re-used to wash the shower floor.

In all the observed families the dishes were done outside in the shadow on a construction of branches and tin roof (see picture 5). The dishes were done in big plastic or tin basins, which could be the same ones as for showering and carrying water. Dishes were done to be hygienic and to make things look nice. When having tea for example, the outside of the thermos was always washed as well as the inside. Some items were never washed and rarely even rinsed; this was often the larger awkward items like the big wooden mortars.

Picture 5.

House Hygiene and Waste—Activities in the Yard

From a sanitation perspective, the yards became littered when people threw dirty water or old food into the yards, and when animals were allowed to run free. The observed households took their sweeping of the yard with different levels of seriousness. In one household the yard was swept spotless first thing every morning, for several hours, by the father and their employees. The two other observed families could go several days without sweeping. Food and water could sometimes become dirty of coal and sand dust from the cleaning of the outdoor kitchens.

Much like the human excrements, waste created at the yards during cleaning and cooking had to be removed under the condition that it had to be deposited on their own land. The solid waste was gathered in big piles or holes and burned and covered to lessen in size. This practice also avoided rodents, insects, mosquitoes and snakes. Dirty water from washing the latrine, showering or washing clothes could be poured out at all places in the yard, so that the sand could absorb it. Water from cleaning and showering could be canalized away a few meters by digging a ditch or installing a pipe. One family reused this water, and it from the shower to a tree for watering.

Exceptions from those solutions were the dirty water from washing babies' nappies, or from the menstruation cleaning process. This was either poured in the latrine or far away in the bush. Disposable pads from menstruation were left in the latrine. The water from menstruation was considered very dirty; one woman said that in her youth they believed that women could spread the menstruation-pain to each other, and therefore kept private basins for washing.

All the visited households kept animals, including chickens, pigs and ducks. The chickens could be allowed to stay in the house or the kitchen if they were sitting on eggs, otherwise the animals ran free in the village during the days, trying to stay as close to food as possible. The chickens were especially prone to walk on the dishes and ran over the plates when people sat down to have a meal, leaving their droppings where they walked. Most of the timethe chickens went unnoticed when walking on dishes or food, but if they approached while cooking or eating the families tried to chase them away with sticks.

When the young children played they used whatever had been left at the yard, like a water basin and kitchen utensils, subsequently attracting their parents' anger and worry. The smaller children liked to roll around in the sand and go scavenging on the waste heaps where they could find things to put in their mouths.

The Informants Perceptions and Preferences of the Sanitary Conditions

The Everyday Sanitary Conditions

Most of the women were afraid of falling ill in their households because they judged their sanitary conditions to be inadequate. Their fears included diseases like cholera, malaria, worsened HIV and tuberculosis, and accidents, insects, snakes and rats. Sometimes people's health was described as governed by forces outside of the individual, why there was hardly any point in being afraid. Most of the time they however tried to control it by cleaning their house, themselves and their food as thoroughly as they could:

"Because we need to care about our homes before we go and see the doctor in the hospital. Because we are the first doctors here at home, we have to care about our environment. And after that we can go and see the doctor if we get ill."

—Translation of Sofia

Even though most women were afraid of falling ill, only one woman thought that her family had actually suffered from lack of sanitation when everyone got diarrhoea. Within the households some saw equal risks for all in the family, while others perceived women and children as the most exposed. Those that saw women being at risk connected it to their household work:

"[2]although in this community women are the ones who spend most time at home, when men are working outside. And that is why we have more women exposed to the waste and sanitary bacteria."

—Translation of village leader 3

A third way of looking at risk was given by a woman who felt that everyone in the household would fall ill if a woman was reckless when cooking or cleaning, regardless of age and sex. For children it was their reckless play that was seen as causing increased risks. When one girl was asked why she disliked field defecation she explained that children ran around everywhere and could get in contact with that "mess".

The informants' views on their present sanitary conditions differed, partly depending on what they had to begin with. The women with toilets and running water were generally satisfied with their sanitary conditions. They viewed their homes as sanitary, even though they felt their interiors could be improved.

The women who had latrines felt that they wanted to improve them in some way regarding its stability, comfort, hygiene or the way they constantly had to move them. The latrines were hard to clean, could collapse during heavy rains and the walls often deteriorated before the latrine was filled. One woman expressed a worry about the hygiene of having a yard full of filled holes. The concrete latrine was a good option from a stability and hygienic point of view, but what the women really dreamt of was a bathroom with a tub, flush toilet and a septic tank like in the city:

"although it is *latrina melhorada* [concrete latrine] she does not feel comfortable... So as to give us one example of the toilets we have in the flat and in some houses in Maputo... She says that after finishing this house they would like to build something like those kinds of toilets. Although those toilets are beautiful she would like to have one like that because of the hygiene."

—Translation of Sofia

---

[2] Quotations key: ... = a few words has been left out.
--- = an entire sentence or more has been left out.
[ ] = word inserted by author for understanding.

Sofia knew that she did not have the best there was to offer. When she was asked further questions whether she ever felt ashamed, because the answer was 'no', it was because she shared this reality with everyone else in the village. A leader said that the latrines could in all their simplicity still be said to be a kind of improvement. In the older days and in other villages open defecation was still practiced, and the village had come far in that sense and thereby avoided many diseases. One woman did express some gratitude, and said that the latrine construction was comfortable.

Regarding showers, the women wished for construction improvements for the purpose of cleaning and stability. The younger girls in particular dreamed of bath tubs and tap water. One girl said that sometimes snakes entered through the stick walls and she would be protected from that if she could afford brick walls. Improved canalization of the water was another issue for the women who were afraid that it would provide breeding grounds for germs and mosquitoes. By having a better shower a girl said that it would improve her menstruation procedures and that she would feel cleaner when washing. Otherwise the women were mostly pleased or had no comments about how they could improve their ways of maintaining hygiene during menstruation.

Some things were simply not questioned; upon asking why the women always washed their underwear in the shower no one knew the reason for this tradition. It was what they had been taught and was just a custom. Sometimes the women did not explicitly wish for improvements but at the same time did not say that they were satisfied. This feeling was expressed typically by a woman when she was asked about what she felt about her latrine:

> "this is the way that God has given her. The only way."
>
> —Translation of Rosana

Sanitation Related Responsibilities

Responsibility for the household sanitation was in about half of the cases described as a shared workload among all of the household members. This could either be expressed as work division with men caring for the outside while women cleaned the inside, or simply as a freedom of choice:

> "She is saying that the work division varies. Sometimes it is her that cleans the toilet while the boys are wiping the floors and caring about the waste, and it happens the other way around."
>
> —Translation of Maria

Other informants said that according to cultural values women were the main household carers, meaning they were the ones who had daily dealings with sanitation, cared for their family's health and taught their children to care for the house. One woman perceived gender equality as an important matter and had taught all of her children and her husband to cook and clean. But a man performing a woman's work could also become embarrassing, breaking the traditional rules of behaviour:

"if a man wakes up and takes a basin and puts clothes with detergents... people around will think that this man is crazy. Yeah because the work he is doing is women's work."
—Translation of village leader 1

With women's responsibilities over the household followed problems and opportunities. One problem was the time it consumed and simply locked them to their households:

"If women could they would [change]. --- Since the beginning women are the ones who care about their kids, who care about their homes, this is an obstacle... since women are the ones who stay at home."
—Translation of Vitória

This view was nuanced by a woman who said that women in the rural areas could not stay home *enough*. In the cities the women could afford to be real housewives because they did not have to work in the fields and therefore had time to really clean their homes. Women's family responsibilities made it difficult to hold official positions, as was pointed out by a female leader. Women in such positions were overall unusual and their decision making power within the household was limited, why it became difficult to improve sanitation even if they wanted to:

"She is saying that women depend on men, and if they want to change something in the sanitary situation they have to ask men for permission. --- She is saying that it should change, it should change."
—Translation of Theresa

Even if all other chores were described as divided, construction work were always to be done by men. This could put women without grown men in their households in difficult positions because they had to pay an outsider whenever they wanted to move the latrine. The overall reason for the work division was explained either through women's weaker bodies, culture or personal interests. A few informants mentioned that they could very well perform the duties of the other sex; they simply followed the common rules of behaviour.

Regardless whether it was culture or interest that made it so, developing one's household could be said to be a part of being a woman. One woman, for example, had made significant changes by building a latrine instead of continuing to practice open defecation as her household had in the past. One informant expressed the subject this way: Even if women lack the knowledge of how to build a latrine they were still the ones who were going to get it done, because men lacked initiative on the matter.

Responsibilities for sanitation were also related to the role of being a good Christian. The church had a responsibility to be involved in the village's public health because of the bible's description of Jesus as a man that cared for others. Helping your neighbour is seen as a part of being Christian, and based on the thought that what happens to another might happen to me. A common perception by the women was that there was a connection to Christianity simply because the priest talked about sanitation during service.

A fuller explanation was that God had put the humans on Earth to live a long and healthy life; therefore, things that could threaten it, like dirty homes, should be avoided:

> "She is saying that the Cord, theLord of the creation says that we have to clean the house. So this is part of these laws, of the commandments."
> —Translation of Maria

Support and change of the sanitary conditions

Poverty was the main obstacle against all improvements of sanitary-related constructions mentioned by women and by village leaders. Therefore, many of the wishes expressed earlier were not seen as realistic, because they knew they lacked the necessary funding and infrastructure:

> "She is saying that she would like to change her sanitary situation but since she does not work or her husband does not work also they do not have this possibility to improve their sanitary situation if they had they would."
> —Translation of Alice

The leaders could be a bit more optimistic and had already been part of improvements like the communal water pump, but questions about possible projects or interventions were often followed by statements like 'If there were a donor…'. The younger girls were among the more optimistic, because they thought they might be able to find work when they got older. Another aspect of lacking money was lacking control over it. One girl said that her family had money, but she could not access it because the decisions were made by the most senior man. Other priorities were another issue. An old woman who lived alone without income was very unhappy about her situation, but did not think that her problems were of high priority:

> "If the church had money she believes that they would do that [help her]… Yeah and she is saying that the church does not help them because they have children to help. I think that they have identified a group of children, HIV parents' orphans, to help…"
> —Translation of Amélia

But lack of money was sometimes expressed as a possibility by forcing people to be creative and help each other. A leader took an example from the hospital. They could not afford to clean their buildings but once in a while they called up the village to help them free of charge instead.

Support could be received in the form of teaching and knowledge. The practical help and coordination that the women could receive was limited. Developed infrastructure with safe tap water was available but limited due to the monthly fee. By coming together, many informants felt that improvements could be made to the sanitary situation, but none had any visions about what could be done. Some informants said that the households used to gather to clean and care for the common grounds in the village, like clearing a road or remove breeding grounds for mosquitoes. Others thought it would be impossible to cooperate over sanitation because of the sensitivity of the matter and lack of spirit:

"They don't support each other… Each household cares about each house. … She is saying that since the beginning there was no spirit of cooperation and each person cares about his life or his household."
—Translation of Rosana

When the women were asked if they ever affected anyone else's sanitary situation the answer was always that they had made a friend aware of a problem in her household. This could be said directly, but if the women felt that it would embarrass their friends; the traditional leader could act as a medium and call up a general meeting. One woman was concerned about young mothers and tried to teach them what she knew:

"She influenced someone, a friend of hers… She said that once she arrived in her friend's house and she found everything spread, and the babies' nappies were dirty. Then she said please wash your babies' nappies and clean the house, otherwise you are going to get ill."
—Translation of Camila

People were not always susceptible to advice; one woman said that jealousy could be in the way. No one wanted to listen to her because she already had a nice house with running water and flush toilet.

Support for change could be received from the village institutions, mainly in the form of information and practical teaching. At the hospital the women received individual advice, while the church and the leaders held community meetings. Their advice could be very specific and sometimes contained an element of shame for those who had a dirty household. Different volunteer groups were also engaged in sanitation, especially aimed at HIV-affected families, and one informant suggested that those groups could be seen as a way that the households were actually helping each other more than they thought.

The village institutions could be perceived as easily accessible and as closed by different women, in regards to their possibilities to affect their sanitary situation through them. Some felt that it was easy to contact the leaders about suggestions:

"She is saying that it is not difficult to talk to the community leader. And the only thing she can say is to give the information about what is wrong. The leader has got power, with her power she can influence the rest of the population."
—Translation of Vera

The women who on the other hand felt that the institutions were inaccessible said that the leaders would be offended or afraid to be overthrown if ordinary people came with suggestions. In fact very few villagers approached the leaders to talk about sanitation:

"People do not approach; it is the church that approaches people… If the church says that today we are going to rake the ground at the cemetery, everyone has to go there and clean. So it is part of the church that convinces people, not the people who convinces the church."
—Translation of village leader 1

The information from the village institutions and volunteer groups often targeted women, who were overrepresented at the village meetings. The explanation was different factors related to their household responsibilities which made them the most common visitors at the hospital and most likely to care for their children while men worked elsewhere. The leaders of the village felt that there were gender disparities, but did not take any active measures against it. One leader said that there was a general world development promoting gender equality; another meant that they do address the entire village when talking about sanitation, but then the households makes the division.

Regarding knowledge one informant meant that the village as a whole needed more education on construction and prevention, for example learn how to build a proper concrete latrine and how to then spread that information in an effective way. Otherwise many of the women and the leaders were satisfied with the overall knowledge on sanitation related diseases and hygiene practice. There were however exceptions, young women were a few times said to be lacking in effort and knowledge. Some families were said to still not understand the concepts of bacteria and therefore rely solely on witch doctors.

According to the hospital those families were diminishing and that the knowledge level had increased significantly in recent years, partly due to the schools good education of young women. Before when they provided mosquito nets and water purifiers few were interested, but today they never had enough to meet the demand. This was by a few described as a result of the villages relatively good infrastructure, with a school, a care centre and an active church that gathered almost everyone in the village. The church had provided a link between the people and modern medicine, explaining diseases from the bible and making people trust the nurses' advices:

> "…they have been aware for a long time. … Because you see the church … is the school, everything the infrastructure that we have they date from a long time. And from this moment people opened this awareness."
> —Translation of village leader 4

To conclude the description of the sanitary conditions different views on the future are shown, to express how differently the situation can be perceived by an old woman, a young girl and a leader (bold style implies question):

> "This is the only way. And they might bring disease but nothing can be done."
> —Translation of Paula

> "… *is it possible now, a year from now or when you grow up?* … She does not know."
> —Translation of Vitória

> "*Do you see any obstacles against improving the waste and sanitary situation?* There is no obstacle."
> —Translation of Village leader 2

Conclusion According to the Ecological Model of the Determinants of Health

In this section the findings are concluded by summarizing them according to Dahlgren and Whitehead's (2007) ecological model of the layers of 'determinants of health'.

Layer one—lifestyle factors:

- The women placed great value on, and were described as very interested in, keeping their households clean to keep hygiene and feel comfortable in a beautiful home. Even though they were afraid, very few thought that *they* had actually been affected by their sanitary situation.
- Many households tried to improve their sanitary conditions if they could, like buying a concrete latrine or facilitate water drainage. Some informants expressed an indifference to the situation, or had simply chosen to accept their inability to change.
- Upholding a sanitary life for the family were in some families described as women's responsibility, while in others it was everyone's business.
- Attitude and habit-problems that the informants mentioned were people that still did not belie in modern medicine young women being less careful with cleaning and men not bothering to maintain what they created.

Layer two—social and community networks:

- In the village there were many possibilities to be educated about sanitation through the community networks. Some informants felt shut out from this system, and perceived the village institutions as closed for suggestions.
- The community networks yielded less of practical help and cooperation. Many women wished for more support, but had trouble seeing how, or if, that could happen.
- The most important network was the social net of the family. Here most women had learnt how to care for sanitation, and their children could sometimes help them with construction work.
-

Layer three—living and working conditions:

- There was no infrastructure that could support sanitation, why all waste entering the household had to stay there. The women with latrines saw their sanitary situation as unhygienic, while those with toilets were more pleased with their situation.
- Because most informants worked at their own yards and in the fields they were constantly exposed to their lack of sanitation. This exposure was in some cases higher for women, because they were responsible for cleaning.
- A leader proposed that the situation could still be seen as a kind of achievement, as open defecation was becoming less common.

Layer four—general socioeconomic, cultural and environmental conditions:

- Most informants' perceived poverty as the main obstacle against improvements of the sanitary situation.
- Gender disparities were the reality some informants lived within, which affected who did what and who was in charge. Women were often responsible for producing food,

caring for the children and maintaining their households, while men were the main decision makers and responsible for construction-work.

DISCUSSION

Discussion of Findings

Lifestyle and Community Networks

Analysing this setting's sanitary conditions from a lifestyle perspective includes attitudes, knowledge and habits relating to what people are in control over (Dahlgren & Whitehead, 2007). When comparing the findings this chapter with previous research it seems that even though some attitudes and habits can be questioned, several problems in Maciene are less tangible than have been reported from elsewhere. The women took their duties to uphold sanitation seriously. The demand for improved sanitation was closely related to a wish for a healthier household, as they saw a connection between their personal behaviour, their responsibilities and their family's health. Hence the title 'we are the first doctors here at home' as delightfully expressed by one woman, is relevant. There is a common foundation of knowledge and interest where health professionals and the villagers can meet, as opposed to Cairncross' (2003) observations in the Pacific,

Sanitation was among the women to some extent an embarrassing subject, but not so that it caused avoidance behaviour, otherwise common in sub Saharan Africa (Avvannavar & Mani, 2008). The women were surprisingly open, and often used words that the gatekeeper had advised the translators to avoid, so not to insult the informants. Another indicator of relative openness was how the showers mostly lacked doors; nudity did not seem as shameful as latrine visits might be. Menstruation was to some extent an embarrassing and private matter, especially menstruation pads, but was not identified by the women as a health problem as Jenkins and Curtis (2005), Vlugman (2006) and WSSCC (2006) have described.

Embarrassments can also cause positive behaviours when it encourages people to uphold hygiene in the process of keeping appearances. A clean household could show that the families were good Christians. Religion can be positive key factor defining people's sanitary behaviour (Avvannavar & Mani, 2008).

There were also habits and attitudes among the women that can be improved. The sanitary situation could improve if the families would wash their hands before cooking and eating, use the lids on their latrine, always cover their water and keep animals away from food, water and kitchen items. Children's reckless behaviour might be the most troubling. Their carelessness can easily spread diseases as they forget to wash, or play at the waste heaps.

Some attitudes among the women were difficult to interpret. Considering how Lindén (2005) has shown that cholera is a common disease in Maciene it was surprising how few of the women thought that lack of sanitation had actually affected *them*. This discrepancy might have been created by chance, or the women denied or failed to see the connection. In the same way one might ask if the groups who seemed to have accepted their situation were in need of being motivated, or if acceptance is a good thing when ones possibilities for change are small.

It is through the social and community networks that the village can take control over their health (Level two in Dahlgren & Whitehead, 2007). Social networks related to sanitation took different shapes at various degrees between institutions, friends and volunteer groups; always with a focus on information and teaching. The different paths of information-sharing fill different needs. The hospital give targeted adjusted advice to special groups like young mothers. The church and the leaders give general information to the entire population, and advices between friends are made on site in accordance with what was observed as wrong. Still family-connections played the most important part in learning.

The women and the leaders had different views on how well cooperation worked. One possible explanation as to why some women saw no cooperation is that the top-down governing style does not really meet the definition of cooperation. Gidlund (2006) has suggested that people in Maciene often are full of ideas, but sometimes does not believe in themselves and their own voices. Applying a more grassroots-oriented perspective could perhaps loosen these constraints. This is also what is meant by the vision for Maciene written by the Anglican Church (1999; 2001)

Living Conditions, Poverty and Sanitation

The living and working conditions set the prerequisites from which the women could create their health (Level three in Dahlgren & Whitehead, 2007). Sanitation is a part of that foundation and should be adjusted to what people want regarding safety, privacy and comfort. For the majority of women that was not the case in this setting, either for the latrines or for the showers. The constant moving of latrines, risk of bites and diseases, deteriorating walls and lack of running water were all factors risking the women's physiological health, and the subsequently by worry lowering their psychologically well-being (Avvannavar & Mani, 2008; Jenkins & Curtis, 2005).

The simple latrines were a health risk in some households as they could contaminate water and soil, but still an improvement in comparisons with open defecation. From a female perspective they were positive as they offered relative privacy, and could be visited during the day. Much space is the sanitary advantage of living in rural areas as Avvannavar & Mani (2008) state, but causes problems when it makes expanding infrastructure more expensive (Mwanza, 2003; WSSCC, 2006).

Cairncross (2003) and Jenkins and Curtis (2005) have described the importance of cultural understanding. Many of the hygiene customs practiced in Maciene setting seemed logical, expected and recognisable, but there were surprises that confirmed the relevance of local adjustments. Such an example was how important it was for the women to keep their feet clean while showering. Seeing how they got dirty as soon as they stepped outside again it was complicated to understand why. Nevertheless that was the way they most definitely wanted their showers to be constructed.

If level three set the conditions for health, the living conditions must in turn be based on the general terms of life (Level four in Dahlgren & Whitehead, 2007). On a larger scale the nation's poverty set the tone for what can be achieved infrastructure-wise in a rural village. With lack of roads, sewage systems and few work opportunities the households' options are limited, and left to care for their own needs. For an individual household lack of cash meant an inability to have a hygienic toilet or good water drainage. This situation was observed and identified in Maciene by the women. The lack of money means that if the village institutions want to improve the sanitary situation they need donors. In light of Vlugman's (2006) claim that organisations and governments often fail to acknowledge the importance of sanitation that might become an obstacle. But by installing piped water in Maciene the church has also come to show that they can improve the infrastructure despite low resources (The Anglican Church, 1999, 2001).

Gender and Sanitation

The gender situation focused on in this chapter can be related to the general level four of Dahlgren and Whitehead (2007). Crang and Cook (2007) argue that simply because a single setting is studied, the researcher should not expect a coherent culture with a single set of beliefs. This statement was highly relevant when trying to understand what gender meant in the village. Some informants felt that household work was equally divided between men and women, while others perceived women as the main family careers who were tied down by their responsibilities. The latter was also confirmed in other fieldwork done in the village by Gidlund (2006), Schwarts and Widefjäll (2006) and Wiltfalk (2008), and on a national Mozambican level by Ferrell (2002) and Van den Bergh-Collier (2003).

The informants' different experiences can be examined from different angles, the first being to take their different experiences at face value. Mozambique has a legacy of an active women's rights movement that played an important part during the independence war, and this could have affected some households in the setting (Ferrell, 2002). Another option is that the women were never even oppressed to begin with, for example Ata Aidoo (1998) suggests that gender inequality is primarily a western way of organising society. However because the Maciene setting is influenced by Christianity, that explanation seems less plausible.

The women claiming that gender equality existed in the setting can be questioned. One building block of the gender theory applied in this chapter is that disparities are hidden behind the veil of social construction (West & Zimmerman, 1987). The women were more inclined to answer that they had the main responsibility if asked indirectly, like through questions about diseases risks. A counter argument against that notion is the researchers with a western background, do not understand the African woman's view on equality. West and Zimmerman (1987) might on the other hand claim that this is exactly the accomplishment of gender, making unfair arrangements seem equal. In the Maciene setting there were statements such as 'if a man goes outside and starts washing up he will be the laughing stock of the surroundings'. No man is an island, and even if some families have made their way out of an unequal living situation, they still live in a society whose overall picture is different.

West and Zimmerman (1987) offer an explanation to why gender inequalities appear through the construction of power structures hidden beneath biology. Some statements from the interviews strengthen this view, like when men were explained to be the main constructors of latrines because of their superior physique. To the fieldworkers as visitors from another culture that statement seems strange, as the physique of the women in the setting would more than suffice for heavy and straining employment in Europe. As Kulick (1987) has shown what is clearly impossible for men or women in some cultures might very well be their best feature in others. But not all women and leaders explained their different work tasks as attributable to biology. Male and female informants said that they knew that they could do what the other sex did, but that it would be wrong in accordance with their culture. In that case their system of gender inequality, or the doing of difference, is upheld by some unknown force that could not be identified in this chapter. Further, the women are of greater risk of infection because of their household work and concerned with keeping a high level of sanitation. Development work should thus include their knowledge. However, female leaders are rare and their voices are worth less than those of men, also in the Maciene setting (Van den Bergh-Collier, 2000; Wiltfalk, 2008).

Ferrell (2002), Mayanja (2006) provide examples of case studies showing the benefits of combining gender equality work with sanitation and water development. However, for women to have time to improve their situation they must be freed of some of their responsibilities (Vlugman, 2006). For example the traditional leader in this chapter witnessed of troubles when trying to combine her official position with caring for her family, a problem facing women all over the world (West & Zimmerman, 1987). Levelling out responsibilities is for some families however impossible, when the national poverty forces men to leave their families as migrant workers. This comes to show what Dahlgren and Whitehead (2007) have already stated: there is a limit to what the individual and their community can do to tackle issues belonging to the highest level.

Equity in Health

This chapter demonstrates that equity in health is not a reality in a rural setting as Maciene. Money, rather than needs, guides the distribution of opportunities for well being, as achievement of good sanitation. The skewness this creates can be illustrated in the connection between Dahlgren and Whitehead's (2007) levels one and three: that different living conditions create different demands on lifestyle.

A family with a pit latrine that gathers their water in a well and stores it in buckets are more often at risk of diseases, because the system is 'open'. They must always remember to put the lid on their latrine and cover the water, otherwise for example flies can spread diseases between the two (Landon, 2006). For a family with a flush toilet and tap water that risk is smaller, because water and faeces is sealed off in a tube or septic tank until needed. Thus for a family who cannot afford the better option the demands on them to uphold a perfect lifestyle are higher. It might be difficult but doable for adults, however impossible for children.

Accordingly the family with a septic tank have a higher probability of being able to uphold that perfect lifestyle. With higher income the probability of them being both husband and wife increases and probably has the possibility of hiring maids (Republic of Mozambique, 2005). This injustice is further enhanced by the fact that women without husbands also are those that has to pay for a new latrine pit.

Discussion of the Ethnographic Approach

Ethics and Objectivity

Performing an ethically accepted study in an unfamiliar setting is complicated. For this chapter the traditional ethics policy (The Governing Board of the Swedish Research Council, 2002) was challenged and personal dilemmas often appeared for the fieldworker. It was difficult to uphold confidentiality of the informants. When the fieldworker needed to rely on help to identify them their identities were revealed to powerful villagers and other informants. It is not by default something compromising, but could result in conflicts of interest. It can also be questioned if the 'informed consent requirement' was upheld, considering that many informants were illiterate. They might not have understood that their actions could come in to question. The illiteracy of the informants and the language barriers means that in its current form this chapter is inaccessible to those who made it possible.

Perhaps the most complicated ethical problems are not covered by ethical principles. The principles protect the individual's rights, but give fewer guidelines for a white researcher from a rich country in an African low-income setting, and all of the power issues that follow (Crang & Cook, 2007). For the fieldworker, this conflict became clearest when looking at the balance of exchange. A few informants wanted something back after the interview, but were met with a 'no'. The answer was given, but it was more difficult to shake the uneasy feeling that arose when asking people who have so little to open up about personal issues to someone who has so much, without being able to give anything back.

> *"Indeed, in the end of a process... you are likely feel that, despite your best efforts, your ethics have been compromised; that they are, in fact, quite grubby, and that, if you had been a better person (or at least got more sleep), you would have been able to do a better job. We have all certainly felt all of this. And this is surely normal"*
> (Crang & Cook, 2007, p. 32).

Close to the issue of ethics is objectivity in research. According to Kapborg and Berterö (2002), it becomes more difficult to be fair and objective in studies of unfamiliar cultures. When the researcher cannot see the entire picture, things can appear simpler and more polarised than they actually are. That risk was in this chapter most obvious for the gender analysis. Many writers have pointed out Western researchers' inability to correctly portray African gender relations at the risk of describing African men as the only 'villain' in development work and forgetting the importance of global politics. That is partly a shortcoming of this chapter as well. To minimize this risk, the researchers constantly tried to account for alternate takes, and clearly display all of the arguments about the gender situation in the findings discussion.

Implementation of the Ethnographic Design

Solidity is the criterion used to measure the consistency of qualitative research, or whether it was performed in a logic way (Crang & Cook, 2007). Good solidity means to be able to step outside of the theory and into reality (Dahlgren et al., 2004). The thread, or solidity, of this chapter was the poverty focus with a holistic, or cultural, approach. That theme can be traced through the description of sanitation and the theoretical framework via the ethnographic approach to the results in the findings and discussions.

In an unfamiliar setting like Maciene, the research design always has to be discarded at some point, because one is forced to accept some loss of control to others. According to Crang and Cook (2007), this might be the very essence of ethnographic research. Some of the deviations from the original plan were successful. The interviews were altered to include some observations, which became a good tool for both informant and fieldworker. Other adjustments were more difficult, like trying to get the women to open up more during interviews. The fieldworker changed the order of the questions, the place for the interviews and what kind of questions to ask, but ultimately could not overcome whatever bridge needed to be crossed.

The observations and the interviews complemented each other in a way that strengthens the credibility of this chapter. Together they triangulated the issue of practice and perceptions of sanitation (Dahlgren et al., 2004). But how well did the methods manage to measure the *conditions*? The informants' answers probably came to depend as much on their personalities as the factual situation (if such a measure exists). Some saw no possibilities at all, while others did not even see lack of money as an obstacle. Seen separately, the interviews might thus not have answered the aim, but when combined a more diverse picture appeared that came closer to the truth.

For the performance of the observations, one notable problem was how the household members adjusted their behaviours in the presence of the field researcher. Cleaning up for guests is probably a common courtesy all over the world, and maybe (probably) especially when that guest has already interviewed the host about her hygiene practices. The solution to this problem is normally to stay in the field for several months until people start to relax (Burgess, 1984; Pilhammar Andersson, 2008), but that was not an option in this case. As the women's dedication to caring for their households was confirmed in the interviews with the village leaders, it seems that the observation records are still valid.

The performance of interviews rendered more questions than the observations, because they involved spoken communication. This caused, or showed, cultural clashes and translation problems that made the plan of deep interviews into a mixture of surveys, observations and conversation. The presence of the translation process made the conversations stilted and interrupted. It was probably one of the reasons that the interviews remained too shallow (Kapborg & Berterö, 2002). The translation disturbed the non-spoken communication (Crang & Cook, 2007). Laughter was, for example, difficult to interpret—did the informant perceive it as a fun or funny question?

Regarding the sampling of informants, diversity was the strength of this chapter (Burgess, 1984; Dahlgren et al., 2004). Interviewing both women and leaders triangulated the aim from their different positions. This raised the credibility of the study, as it showed both issues of unity (Dahlgren et al., 2004), and exposed contradictions, untruths and confusions (Crang & Cook, 2007). One such example is the large number of women who seemed to be keen to talk about sanitation with the leaders, while the subsequent leader interviews showed that in fact very few did so.

Good sampling should be replicable (Burgess, 1984), but because the sampling in this chapter was based on local knowledge and snowball method that criteria could not be met. There were also limitations to the spread within the group of women. Career women and disabled or sick women were unconsciously excluded, probably because the field researcher had asked for informants who were responsible for handling the household. Jama (2008), who conducted fieldwork in the same village, has shown, for example, how difficult it becomes for HIV-affected families in the setting to manage everyday life, of which sanitation plays one part.

The translation process was problematic in the findings analysis because the method's credibility is built on being able to show that themes are derived from the informants' own words (i.e., the transcripts). One problem was that the translators summarised the informants' answers; another that they sometimes changed the questions by adding their own examples. These problems were foreseen, and measures were taken to lessen their effect, like agreeing on the translation of important words. Random mistranslations were more difficult to control, which comes down to everyone's language skills. Using the same translators throughout the study, one would hope, decreased these problems over time (Kapborg & Berterö, 2002).

In this case, the transcripts became a hybrid of the feelings, assumptions and values of not only the informants, but also of the translators and the field researchers (Crang & Cook, 2007). To highlight this ambiguity, the quotes in the findings section were kept as they are, expressed by a third person. Despite this, the researchers maintain that the main findings are credible. Words like 'poverty', 'cleaning' and 'not satisfied' are not abstract descriptions of complicated relationships; the message came through even if it was wrapped in grammatical mistakes. The credibility of the analysis was strengthened by having the material coded by both authors (Lundman & Hällgren Granheim, 2008).

Because ethnographic research is descriptive, demographic comparisons of transferability are not entirely puritanical (Dahlgren et al., 2004). As the data was available it can still be highlighted that many of the female informants were rather typical, in the sense that most of them were unemployed farmers, lived in an average poverty region (Republic of Mozambique, 2005) and lacked acceptable sanitation, defined as a septic tank (UNDP, 2005). Thus, many women in Mozambique probably face at least similar prerequisites as described in this chapter.

Conclusion

The findings in this chapter demonstrate that the basis of all sanitation work means caring for one's own waste, in one's own yard, constructing latrines and showers out of free items. The simplest latrines put the villagers at risk for infections and accidents, as well as causing physiological discomfort. Those who could afford it instead bought materials to build sturdier constructions and, if possible, also installed a septic tank.

Some women in the Maciene setting chose to accept their sanitary conditions, but many wanted improvements to decrease the health risks and increase comfort. The main obstacles against improvements were poverty, lack of motivation for practical cooperation, low self-confidence and the perceived discrimination against women. The women perceived themselves as the maintainers of their household's sanitation and hygiene, while men cared for construction work and were the main decision makers.

Several positive forces also exist that could help women take control over their own and their families' health. The women are open about this often awkward subject, and motivated to improve whenever a chance arises. Community development work is already in place in the Maciene setting. Together the school, the hospital, the church, volunteers, friends and family work to spread information (Anglican Church, 1999). This also helps the women gain knowledge about the importance of sanitation from a health perspective.

ACKNOWLEDGMENTS

This fieldwork was made possible by the cooperation between Mälardalen University and the Lebombo diocese in the Mozambique Anglican Church. The field period was funded by the Swedish Mission Council. Dean Carlos Matshine coordinated the stay in Maciene, and provided necessary insight on how to locally adjust the fieldwork. The conversations with the informants were made possible by Lurdes Macie and Celeste Mabuluco, who assisted as laymen translators. Lastly, this fieldwork could never have been possible without the women and households who invited the fieldworker into their homes and shared both their public and private moments.

REFERENCES

Aina, O. (1998). African women at the grassroots. In Nnaemeka, O. (Ed.) *Sisterhood, feminism & power. From Africa to the Diaspora* (pp. 65-88). Asmara, Eritrea: Africa World Press.
Alberts, R., & Hirvonen, S. (1993). *Kvinnoliv i Moçambique* [Women's life in Mozambique]. Stockholm: Afrikagrupperna.
Anglican Church. (1999). *Maciene Vision.* Unpublished manuscript, Maciene, Mozambique.
Anglican Church. (2001). *Maciene Vision.* Unpublished manuscript, Maciene, Mozambique.
Ata Aidoo, A. (1998). The African woman today. In Nnaemeka, O. (Ed.) *Sisterhood, feminism & power. From Africa to the Diaspora* (pp. 39-50). Asmara, Eritrea: Africa World Press.
Avvannavar, S. M., & Mani, M. (2008). A conceptual model of people's approach to sanitation. *Science of the Total Environment, 390*, 1-12.
Burgess, G. R. (1984). *In the field. An introduction to field research.* London: Routledge.
Cairncross, S. (2003). Sanitation in the developing world: current status and future solutions. *International Journal of Environmental Health Research, 13*, 123-131.
Cipire, F. (1992). *A Educação Tradicional em Mozambique.* [The traditional education in Mozambique] Registo no Ministério da Cultura No 988/92. Maputo, Mozambique: Litografia Globo, Lda.
Crang, M., & Cook, I. (2007). *Doing ethnographies.* London: SAGE Publications.
Dahlgren, G., & Whitehead, M. (2007). *Policies and strategies to promote social equity in health* (2nd ed.). Stockholm: Institute for Futures Studies.
Dahlgren, L., Emmelin, M., & Winkvist, A. (2004). *Qualitative methodology for international public health.* Umeå, Sweden: Print & Media Umeå University.
Embassy of the republic of Mozambique. (2008). *History of Mozambique.* Retrieved 12 December 2008 from www.embassymozambique.se/us/.

Ferrell, B. J. A. G. (2002). Community development and health project: a 5-year (1995–1999) experience in Mozambique, Africa. *International Nursing Review, 49*, 27–37.

Gidlund, A. (2006). *Everyday life conditions and beliefs regarding health & wellbeing. An ethnographical study among households in Maciene community Mozambique*. Unpublished master's thesis, Mälardalen University, Västerås, Sweden.

Governing Board of the Swedish Research Council (Vetenskapsrådet). (2002). *Riktlinjer för humanistisk-samhällsvetenskaplig forskning* [Guidelines for humanistic and social science research]. Stockholm: Author.

Holtmar, M., & Wreitling, N. (2004). *The water issue in the village of Maciene – An actor perspective approach to rural Mozambique*. Unpublished bachelor's thesis, Mälardalen University, Västerås, Sweden.

Jama, A. (2008). *"Some are infected but we all are affected" – experiences among household member's [sic] affected by HIV/AIDS in Maciene, Mozambique*. Unpublished master's thesis, Mälardalen University, Västerås, Sweden.

Jenkins, M. W., & Curtis, V. (2005). Achieving the 'good life': Why some people want latrines in rural Benin. *Social Science & Medicine, 61*, 2446-2459.

Kapborg, I., & Berterö, C. (2002). Using an interpreter in qualitative interviews: does it threaten validity? *Nursing Inquiry, 9*, 52-56.

Kulick, D. (Ed.) (1987). *Från kön till genus. Kvinnligt och manligt i ett kulturellt perspektiv* [From sex to gender. Female and male in a cultural perspective]. Stockholm: Carlsson Bokförlag.

Kvale, S. (1996). *InterViews: An introduction to qualitative research interviewing*. Thousand Oaks, CA: SAGE Publications.

Landon, M. (2006). *Environment, health and sustainable development*. Berkshire, United Kingdom: Open University Press.

Lindén, A. (2005). *Waste in Maciene – what kind of issue? A case study of rural Mozambique*. Unpublished bachelor's thesis, Mälardalen University, Västerås, Sweden.

Lundman, B., & Hällgren Graneheim, U. (2008). Kvalitativ innehållsanalys [Qualitative content analysis]. In Granskär, M., & Höglund-Nielsen, B. (Ed.) *Tillämpad kvalitativ forskning inom hälso-och sjukvård* (pp. 159-173). Lund, Sweden: Studentlitteratur.

Mayanja, R. (Ed.) (2006). *Gender, water and sanitation. Case studies on best practice*. New York: United Nations.

Mello Souza, S. (2006). Brazil: A story of women leaders in water preservation. In Mayanja, R. (Ed.) *Gender, water and sanitation. Case studies on best practice* (pp. 1-9). New York: United Nations.

Mwanza, D. D. (2003). Water for sustainable development in Africa. *Environment, Development and Sustainability, 5*, 95-115.

Oyewumi, O. (2004). Conceptualizing gender: Eurocentric foundations of feminist concepts and the challenge of African epistemologies. In *African gender scholarship: Concepts, methodologies and paradigms* (pp. 1-9). Dakar, Senegal: Council for the Development of Social Science Research in Africa.

Pilhammar Andersson, E. (2008). Etnografi [Ethnography]. In Granskär, M., & Höglund-Nielsen, B. (Eds.) *Tillämpad kvalitativ forskning inom hälso- och sjukvård* (pp. 41-57). Lund, Sweden: Studentlitteratur.

Republic of Mozambique (2005). *Action plan for the reduction of absolute poverty 2006-2009 (PARPA II)*. Maputo, Mozambique: Author.

Sandelowski, M. (1998). Writing a good read: Strategies for re-presenting qualitative data. *Research in Nursing & Health, 21*, 375-382.

Schwarts, M., & Widefjäll, L. (2006). *Women and agriculture – A case study of a rural village in Mozambique*. Unpublished bachelor's thesis, Mälardalen University, Västerås, Sweden.

Scott, V., Stern, R., Sanders, D., Reagon, G., & Mathews, V. (2008). Research to action to address inequities: the experience of the Cape Town Equity Gauge [Electronic version]. *International Journal for Equity in Health, 7(6)*.

Söderbäck, M. (1999). *Encountering parents: professional action styles among nurses in pediatric care*. Göteborg, Sweden: Acta Universitatis Gothoburgensis.

Söderbäck, M., & Cristensson, K. (2007). Care of hospitalized children in Mozambique: nurses' beliefs and practice regarding family involvement. *Journal of Child Health Care, 11(1)*, 53-69.

United Nations Development Program. (2005). *Mozambique national human development report 2005*. Maputo, Mozambique: Author.

Van den Bergh-Collier, E. (2000). *Towards gender equality in Mozambique*. Stockholm: Swedish International Development Cooperation Agency.

Vlugman, A. (2006). Progress of the MDG water supply and sanitation target. *Global Watch, 1(1)*, 77-100.

Water Supply and Sanitation Collaborative Council. (2006). *For her it's the big issue. Putting Women at the centre of water supple, sanitation and hygiene. Evidence report*. Geneva, Switzerland: Author.

West, C., & Fenstermaker, S. (1995). Doing difference. *Gender and Society, 9(1)*, 8-37.

West, C., & Zimmerman, Don H. (1987). Doing gender. *Gender and Society, 1(2)*, 125-151.

Wiltfalk, J. (2008). *Perceived health and human rights issues in everyday life – with a group of adolescents in Maciene, Mozambique*. Unpublished master's thesis, Mälardalen University, Västerås, Sweden.

World Health Organization. (1978). *Declaration of Alma Ata*. Geneva, Switzerland: Author.

World Health Organization. (1998). *Health promotion glossary*. Geneva, Switzerland: Author.

World Health Organization (2008). *Cholera in Zimbabwe*. Retrived Januari 5, 2009 from http://www.who.int/csr/don/2008_12_02/en/index.html

APPENDIX 1

Definitions

Low-income country: According to the World Bank[1] a country with a gross national income per capita of $935 or less. In 2007 the world had 49 such countries, including Mozambique (World Bank, n.d.).

Household: A group of people living together who are usually economically interdependent. The household often includes multiple generations and extends over a wide geographical area and is based upon reciprocal rights and duties (Foster, 2002). The physical structure of the home is referred to as *housing*. Sanitation is a part of housing but it also includes, amongst others, ventilation, drainage, crowding and insulation (McMichael, Kjellström, & Smith, 2006).

Hygiene: "*...cleanliness, removing of dirt and pathogenic substances* [own translation]" (Janlert, 2000, p. 135). In the findings hygiene is used in this generic sense including all chores associated with sanitation, such as cooking, waste handling and cleaning. In this thesis hygiene is mentioned in reference to human actions, while *sanitation* are the physical structures that enables the separation of faeces from humans (Avvannavar & Mani, 2008).

Socio-economic group: "*Individuals that because of their social (i.e. employment) and economical (i.e., income) situations are viewed as one group* [own translation]" (Janlert, 2000, p. 306). The term is used to express a group's position within the social structure (Janlert, 2000).

REFERENCES

Foster, G. (2002). Understanding community responses to the situation of children affected by AIDS: Lessons for external agencies. In Sida (Series Ed.) & Sisak, A. (Vol. Ed.) *One step further – Responses to HIV/AIDS: Sida studies no - 7* (pp. 91-116). Stockholm: Swedish International Development Cooperation Agency.

Janlert, U. (2000). *Folkhälsovetenskapligt lexikon* [Public health dictionary]. Stockholm: Natur & Kultur.

McMichael, A. J., Kjellström, T., & Smith, K. R. (2006). Environmental health. In Merson, M. H., Black, R. E., & Mills, A. J. (Eds.) *International public health. Diseases, programs, systems, and policies* (pp. 393-445) (2nd ed.). Boston: Jones and Bartlett Publishers.

World Bank (n.d.). *Country Classification*. Retrieved September 23, 2008, from http://go.worldbank.org/K2CKM78CC0 and http://go.worldbank.org/D7SN0B8YU0

ABOUT THE AUTHORS

Maja Söderbäck, PhD, BcS, RNped is an assistant professor at the School of Health, Care and Social Welfare at Mälardalen University, Sweden. She has taught as a senior lecturer in public health, nursing and care sciences, appeared as a guest senior lecturer for three years in Mozambique, conducted ethnographic research in Sweden and in Mozambique, and managed a master field study program in a low-income setting in Mozambique (Maciene). Her research has focused on families and children's involvement in health and hospital care.

Malin Udén, MPH, has conducted field work research in a rural low-income setting in Mozambique.

In: Poverty in Africa
Editor: Thomas W. Beasley

ISBN: 978-1-60741-737-8
© 2009 Nova Science Publishers, Inc.

Chapter 3

LIVELIHOOD DIVERSIFICATION, DE-AGRARIANISATION AND SOCIAL DIFFERENTIATION: COMPARATIVE ANALYSIS OF RURAL LIVELIHOODS FROM SOUTH AFRICA AND KENYA[1]

Miyuki Iiyama [*,1]
World Agroforestry Centre (ICRAF), Nairobi, Kenya

ABSTRACT

Livelihood diversification, de-agrarianisation and social differentiation along differential access to off-farm incomes and non-agrarian assets turn out to be dominant features of rural poverty in contemporary Africa. They pose methodological challenges for researchers to conceptualise sociological typologies of rural African populations in the processes of de-agrarianisation and increasing social differentiation, while the existent development theories apparently underestimate their considerable implications on rural development. In response to the increased recognition of these features, the livelihood study has emerged to lead the focus of rural poverty analysis from an agriculture-centred, sector-level viewpoint to a household or individual-level viewpoint. The livelihood study, through synthesising empirical evidence across, should contribute to facilitating the analysis of social changes from the perspective of households/ individuals and to refining existent development theories and policies.

This study attempts to search for effective criteria to identify typologies of rural Africans that reflect heterogeneities in livelihood diversification portfolios of farm and

---

[1] This chapter is a revised version of the Ph.D dissertation of the author submitted to and accepted by the faculty of economics, University of Tokyo. Iiyama (2008), *Livelihood Diversification, De-agrarianisation and Social Differentiation: Case Studies on Rural Livelihoods from South Africa and Kenya*. The author greatly acknowledges the guidance provided by Prof. Lungisile Ntsebeza of University of Cape Town to complete this chapter manuscript

[*] Contact address: M.Iiyama@cgiar.org

off-farm activities within and between communities, and to apply them to case studies from South Africa and Kenya. The South African case describes heterogeneous reactions by rural sub-populations to cope with social transitions (unemployment) and secure rural livelihoods. The Kenyan case examines heterogeneous reactions by rural sub-populations to de-agrarianisation over agricultural intensification.

The case studies reveal that de-agrarianisation processes, i.e., their causes, directions, extents and impacts on rural development and agricultural intensification, have shown considerable variations between South Africa and Kenya, depending on the local experiences of colonial histories, state policies, demographic and agro-ecological conditions, i.e., under-farming in South Africa and governance issues in Kenya. Nevertheless, it has also been found that de-agrarianisation and livelihood diversification in South Africa and Kenya have been similarly accompanied by the increasing social differentiation with differential accesses to non-agrarian assets. Synthesising the analytical results can contribute to deriving theoretical and policy implications on agrarian change in the era of globalisation.

1. INTRODUCTION

While globally the number of people who live in absolute poverty has been declining for 25 years, in Africa it is still increasing (Collier 2007). Kates and Dasgupta (2007) edited the special feature on poverty and sustainability science in an academic journal to seek scientific perspectives on poverty worldwide. The seven articles were contributed by leading scholars, ranging from an orthodox economist (Collier 2007), to an unorthodox political economist (Hyden 2007). Six of the seven articles focused on sub-Saharan Africa (SSA). An African exceptionalism dominates the development needs of today and will require different strategies from those used elsewhere.

The overall assessment by Kates and Dasgupta (2007) is that geopolitics, poverty, governance and geography all contribute to African exceptionalism, although their respective importance varies by region, country and place. Yet, some authors argue that the causes of rural poverty lie not in African peculiarities but rather in geographic features that globally cause problems but are disproportionately pronounced in Africa (Collier 2007). Others stress African socio-economic and political peculiarities in which the majority of poor are only marginally captured by market institutions and instead rely on solving their problems 'outside the system' (Hyden 2007).

In this study I attempt to present a new insight into the uniqueness of African rural poverty and developmental challenges by examining the interactions between Africa's inherent geographic/ socio-economic conditions and the impacts of greater exposure to wider social dynamics. This chapter synthesises a range of recent research and case studies to examine two major research agendas.

The first is to reveal two dimensions of the dominant features of rural poverty in contemporary Africa. One dimension includes low levels of the division of labour and underdevelopment of factor markets, which are attributed to Africa's inherent biophysical, demographic and historical conditions that have made investment in agricultural intensification and market development risky. The other dimension includes off-farm income diversification, de-agrarianisation and social differentiation, which are among the emerging features of African rural poverty in the era of globalisation. Interactions between these two dimensions have complicated the developmental challenges.

The second research agenda is to analyse how greater exposure to wider social dynamics affects rural development and poverty in Africa. To assess this, one must not only understand the driving factors of the livelihood diversification, but also examine the impacts of de-agrarianisation and increasing social differentiation on rural social relations which were initially defined by Africa's inherent conditions. I assume that the trend of de-agrarianisation and increasing social differentiation is a universal phenomenon across Africa as a result of heterogeneous reactions by rural sub-populations to opportunities and risks through the adoption of distinctive livelihood diversification portfolios. In turn, the impacts of de-agrarianisation and increasing social differentiation on rural social relations are diverse across regions due to local-specific historical backgrounds, policies and market/infrastructure.

The identification of driving factors of social changes in response to greater exposure to wider social dynamics, and the examination of factors causing the extent of diversity between and within rural economies, would contribute to understanding and alleviating rural poverty in Africa. Yet, there have been too few intensive field studies. More concrete evidence on rural livelihoods is still much needed.

This chapter presents case studies from agropastoral communities in remote rural areas of South Africa and Kenya. The study areas, a Transkeian community in South Africa and a Rift Valley community in Kenya, were respectively selected to represent typical rural communities in both regions: i.e., southern Africa, where most rural households have heavily depended on off-farm income sources for survival while farming has stagnated for years; and eastern Africa, where diversification into stable off-farm income sources has often been associated with investment of cash/capital in agricultural intensification. The Transkeian and Rift Valley communities have experienced divergent development paths in terms of the colonial histories, state interventions in indigenous institutions, institutionalisation of rural-urban migration, and extents of market penetration. In turn, they share some similarities. In both areas, rural households depend on various combinations of farm and off-farm activities for their livelihoods. Both study areas are located in remote peripheries with poor access to large urban markets. The environment in both is semi-arid, and the populations are traditionally agropastoralists.

As a result, these case studies reveal contrasting experiences between the southern and eastern African rural societies in the extent of the impacts of de-agrarianisation on agricultural development and rural poverty. At the same time, they reveal similar experiences of typical rural agro-pastoral societies in both southern and eastern Africa in terms of increasing social differentiation as a result of heterogeneous livelihood diversification strategies by rural sub-populations in reactions to risks and opportunities provided by greater exposure to wider social dynamics.

This chapter is organised in the following way: Section 2 discusses the contemporary features of rural poverty in Africa, consequent emerging research agendas and theoretical as well as methodological challenges; Section 3 presents comparative analyses of rural livelihoods from South Africa and Kenya; and Section 4 concludes the chapter by summarizing findings and discussing policy implications.

2. CONTEMPORARY FEATURES OF RURAL POVERTY IN AFRICA

2.1. Changing Nature of Rural Poverty

Rural areas in SSA are among the most under-developed regions in the world (Kates and Dasgupta 2007). Seventy per cent of the total population there depends on mixed crop-livestock systems (Thornton et al. 2002) for their livelihoods. Yet, combinations of arid/semi-arid climate, severe agro-ecological (soil, vegetation) conditions, low levels of infrastructural development and poor government services have created a risky environment for agricultural development. The response of rural populations to such risks has been to diversify their livelihoods into various farm (crop/livestock) and off-farm activities (de Haan 2000).

Livelihood Diversification

Initially, African livelihoods were purely for subsistence. Severe climatic and agro-ecological conditions are thought to have limited agricultural potential and carrying capacity of the land (Boserup 1965; Platteau 2000). With low levels of population pressure, each household practised extensive farming, by allocating family labour, i.e. men took care of livestock while women tended arable plots. Customary land tenure systems guaranteed community members usufruct rights to arable plots and grazing rights on commonage, and consequently social differentiation was not so marked. The absence of completely landless sub-populations was in turn closely associated with low levels of specialisation, as division of labour was within households rather than between households (Hyden 1980; Low 1986).

Throughout the twentieth century, colonialism brought about tremendous changes to rural livelihoods. Where colonial farmers came to settle in substantial numbers, such as in the eastern and southern Africa, the colonial governments often exercised coercive means to expropriate land in agriculturally high potential zones from indigenous populations and pushed them into designated reserves in marginal zones (Welch Jr. 1977). With the increased population pressure, agro-pastoralists found it challenging to cope with the decreasing resource bases. For most poor rural families, farming on its own could no longer provide sufficient means of survival (Ellis 2000; Francis 2000; Bryceson 2002).

Colonialism also brought rural Africans into cash economies through paying taxes, buying food, and selling their crops and their labour. Even after independence, education as well as greater exposure to wider social dynamics has further promoted lifestyle changes from subsistence to Westernised consumption patterns (Francis 2000; Bryceson et al. 2000; Bryceson 2002), while expanding urban economies and public sectors (i.e. offices, schools) provided opportunities to earn cash. While returns from farming may fluctuate highly due to risks of crop failure and animal diseases, off-farm activities provide more reliable sources of income (Reardon 1997; Bryceson 2002; Tiffen 2003).

De-agrarianisation

For the past few decades, there has been accelerated shift in the nature of livelihood diversifications from a more or less subsistence mode to one more involved in off-farm cash income activities (Bryceson 2002) under rapidly changing macro-environment. Before the

1980s, the majority of SSA countries followed largely an inward-oriented development strategy, and they largely experienced slow growth. After the 1980s however, many SSA countries increasingly searched for ways to accelerate their participation in the global economy. Some of them significantly liberalised their trade and investment policy regimes as part of Structural Adjustment Programme (SAP).

While the positive impacts of globalisation have not been adequately transmitted to growth and poverty reduction in SSA countries, the openness has exposed rural Africans to more in cash economies than ever. "While returns from commercial agriculture were becoming less certain, daily cash requirements increased under the economic stringency of SAP. In addition to the removal of agricultural subsidies, bankrupt African governments removed subsidies on educational and health services. School fees and user fees at health centres became a high priority in rural household budges, Price inflation reached rural consumers through rising import costs of agricultural inputs, and enticing consumer goods that private traders brought to village markets" (Bryceson 2002, 729).

One of the reactions is to pursue more diversified livelihood patterns into off-farm income activities to earn ready cash for daily requirements. Several reviews confirm some discernable patterns that non-farm/off-farm incomes predominate over farm incomes in many African settings. Reviewing 23 case studies conducted from the 1970s to the early 1990s in regions distributed over Eastern, Western and Southern Africa, Reardon (1997) shows that on overage between 30% and 50% of rural household income was derived from non-farm sources. Bryceson (2002) provides higher figures for the contribution of off-farm activities to total income, ranging between 60% and 80%, based on data from systematic surveys conducted in six African countries during the late 1990s, attributing the increase to the impacts of trade liberalisation in many of the SSA countries.

Bryceson has called these phenomena 'de-agrarianisation', defined as 'economic sectoral change arising from contraction of rural populations that derive their livelihood from agriculture' (Bryceson et al.2000) or 'a long-term process of occupational adjustment, income earning reorientation, social identification and spatial relocation of rural dwellers away from strictly agricultural-based modes of livelihood' (Bryceson 1999; 2002).

Regional Diversity

While de-agrarianisation seems to be a universal phenomenon, its processes and extents have been diverse across regions within SSA, as 'there are local histories of impoverishment and accumulation just as there are many different local presents, different predicaments, different ways of being locked into markets and different responses' (Francis 2000). Especially, the effects of de-agrarianisation on agricultural intensification are spatially and temporally specific.

For example, case studies from South Africa and Kenya provide contrasting findings on the degrees and directions of de-agrarianisation. A comparison of recent economic indicators for South Africa and Kenya is given in Table 1. In both Southern and Eastern Africa, during the earlier colonial periods, European settlers took over much of the high potential agricultural land and pushed Africans into increasingly crowded reserves. Colonial governments devised policies to suppress commercial farming by Africans in reserves to induce migrant labour to mines or farms. By the 1930s, the collapse of reserve agriculture was reported in both regions due to serious soil erosion and environmental degradation (Bundy 1988; Tiffen et al.1994).

After the 1940s, however, state policies in the southern and eastern Africa diverged. During the industrialisation initiated by the mining sector, the South African government further suppressed African farming under the segregated regime (Ntsebeza and Hall 2007). As Bundy (1988) documents in *Rise and Fall of the South African Peasantry*, by the mid-twentieth century, most adult males were absent from home to work in thriving mines, factories or white farms, and the relative contribution of farming to livelihoods became increasingly marginal against remittances and other transfer incomes. The process was not reversed after the 1980s, when falling gold prices and the restructuring of the industry led to large-scale job losses. Today most rural households with unemployed adults survive on the state welfare system, with which food and necessities are purchased, while arable fields except home gardens are not even cultivated (McAllister 2001; Bank 2005).

Table 1. Economic and Social Indicators of South Africa and Kenya

	South Africa 2000	South Africa 2005	Kenya 2000	Kenya 2005
statistics*				
surface area(sq.km)	1,2 million	1,2 million	580.4 thousand	580.4 thousand
population, total	44.0 million	46.9 million	30.7 million	34.3 million
population growth (annual%)	2.5	1.1	2.2	2.3
GDP (current US$)	132.9 billion	242.1 billion	12.7 billion	19.2 billion
GDP per capita (US$)	3,020	5,162	414	560
GDP growth (annual %)	4.2	5.1	0.6	5.8
inflation (annual %)	8.8	4.8	6.1	7.2
agriculture, value added (% of GDP)	3.3	2.5	32.4	27.0
industry, value added (% of GDP)	31.8	30.3	16.9	18.5
services, etc., value added (% of GDP)	64.9	67.1	50.7	54.4
rural population share (%)	38.3		66.0	
dominant rural income sources	pension, wage, remittances casual work, small business		crop / livestock incomes charcoal making	
openness indicators**				
exports of goods & services (% of GDP)	27.9	26.8	21.6	26.7
imports of goods & services (% of GDP)	24.9	28.3	29.6	34.1
openess = exports+imports as % of GDP	52.8	55.1	51.2	60.8
main export	gold, diamonds, platinum other metals and minerals machinery and equipment		tea, horticultural products coffee, petroleum products fish, cement	

(Sources) *:World Development Indicators database, April 2007 (http://devdata.worldbank.org)
**: Global Integrity Report 2006 (http://www.globalintegrity.org/report)

In contrast, in the 1950s the Kenyan colonial government reversed its policies and promoted African smallholder farming by allowing them to grow high-value cash crops. The post-colonial state continued this practice and implemented land redistribution in some parts of the country (Francis 2000). In zones either adjacent to large markets, such as central and parts of eastern Kenya, or with high agricultural potential, such as the white highlands (land formerly settled by Europeans), rural households reinvested their urban earnings in improving farming technologies (Collier and Lal 1984; Evans and Ngau 1991). As Tiffen et al. (1994) document in their book *More People, Less Erosion*, these households invested off-farm incomes in various soil conservation measures (e.g. terraces) to reverse environmental degradation which had been aggravated by severe population pressure. This pattern, however, does not necessarily apply to remote areas, where investment in education is regarded more promising to secure livelihoods than in agriculture (Francis and Hoddinott 1993).

By the late twentieth century, de-agrarianisation resulted in 'the stagnation of farming in the southern African periphery' (Low 1986), and 'greening' of Machakos District (eastern Kenya) (Tiffen et al. 1994). Different consequences of the diversification into off-farm activities on agricultural intensification are due to local-specific historical backgrounds, colonial/state policies and market/infrastructure which will require further empirical investigation through comparative studies.

Social Differentiation

The processes of de-agrarianisation, though diverse across regions, have coincided with increasing exposures of African national economies to the global economy and structural unemployment (Bryceson 1999; Francis 2000; Bryceson et al. 2000).

For example, both South Africa and Kenya are among the top ten developing countries in terms of the largest proportionate tariff reductions since the early 1980s, and especially during the 1990s while the openness indicator, majored as the value of exports plus imports as a percentage of GDP, improved as shown in Table 1. In South Africa, there has been its insertion into the global economy as a result of the ending of apartheid regime. Kenya has also become more open during this period, although not in such dramatic circumstances (Jenkins 2004). Yet, the openness to the global economy has failed to bring about sufficient employment growth. The rate of unemployment has steadily increased since the late 1970s to around 40% in the early twenty-first century, and it often exceeds 50% in rural areas, especially among the unskilled and the youth (Kington and Knight 2004).

As few opportunities for remunerative employment are available only for a small number of highly educated/skilled workers, off-farm income diversification has accentuated rural social differentiation between regular and casual income earners. Educational attainment is one of the most important determinants of salaried and skilled employment, while the uneducated, women, and youth rarely enjoy the same access to remunerative opportunities as do educated males (Francis 2000; Barrett et al. 2001). According to Bryceson (1999), it is recognised in rural Africa that income diversification switches from being a coping to an accumulation strategy when pursued by wealthy and medium-income households. The superior skills and asset endowments of wealthier households yield far greater returns than poorer households with fewer off-farm agrarian skills, means of transport and essential contacts. Poor households in turn harvest less in bad weather years and have little choice but to pursue off-agrarian income-earning activities in easy-entry markets that are already saturated. Thus, over time income diversification may serve to exacerbate rather than alleviate inter-household economic differentiation.

2.2. Emerging Research Agenda

De-agrarianisation processes in Africa correspond to the period when all other developing country regions have shown marked improvement in key indicators of economic development, except SSA. Understanding the nature of African poverty and contributing to its reduction is therefore one of the grand challenges of researchers (Kates and Dasgupta 2007). Then it is essential to acknowledge that there are two dimensions in the features of rural poverty in the contemporary Africa.

One dimension is attributed to Africa's inherent biophysical, demographic and historical conditions which have kept investment in agricultural intensification and market development risky. One of the dominant features of rural Africa is the relatively low population density which is attributed to severe biophysical conditions (Collier 2007). In 2000, the population density in mixed rainfed farming zones in Africa was estimated at 68/km^2 against 139/km^2 in Southeast Asia and 289/km^2 in South Asia (Thornton et al. 2002). The low population pressure has constrained the intensification of agriculture and the development of the factor markets (Boserup 1990). The division of labour is often rather along gender lines within a household that pursues highly diversified livelihood strategies than between households (Low 1986). As a result, in rural Africa, labour markets remain thin and tenancy is almost entirely absent (Ellis 2000), while there are powerful interactions with the urban labour market through migration and remittances (Collier and Lal 1984).

The other dimension includes off-farm income diversification, de-agrarianisation, and social differentiation, which are among the emerging features. As reviewed in the previous sub-section, the 1980s and the 1990s witnessed in rural Africa the increasing divergence of rural livelihoods away from purely agrarian modes and the increasing income inequality. The main factors contributing to rural poverty in Africa in general still do not reflect much lack of access to land (Ellis 1998; Bryceson 2002; Eastwood et al. 2006), except in extremely overpopulated regions (Jayne et al. 2003). Rather accesses to regular off-farm incomes, livestock and educational attainment most contribute to social differentiation. Off-farm income diversification reinforces social stratification as high-income earners redirect portions of their income to more lucrative activities (Bryceson et al. 2000).

In summary, low levels of the division of labour, underdevelopment of factor markets, and high household-level livelihood diversification, are among the dominant features of rural poverty in Africa and apparently attributed to Africa's inherent biophysical, demographic and historical conditions. On the other hand, livelihood diversification into off-farm activities, de-agrarianisation, and increasing social differentiation due to differential access to off-farm incomes and non-agrarian assets are emerging features of the contemporary rural Africa. The uniqueness and complexity of African rural poverty and development challenges may lie in the interactions of these two features - inherent geographic/socio-economic conditions and the impacts of greater exposure to wider social dynamics.

Still, until recently, rural development debates rarely paid attention to the emerging features, i.e., livelihood diversification into off-farm activities, or de-agrarianisation (Ellis 2000). Rural Africans were assumed to operate purely as smallholders, and focus was on how to stimulate growth through agriculture (Ellis and Biggs 2001). Sectoral policy instruments were recommended to give rural farmers the right incentives to increase farm production. Liberalisation reforms however generally failed to bring about the desired growth in the agricultural sector, while recessions and downsizing of the states aggravated unemployment. The fact that rural families operate as farmers as well as wage earners and business people has made effects of sectoral-policy instruments unpredictable, for changing relative prices are internalised within households rather than acting as an external stimulus to the free movement of resources (Ellis 2000; Bryceson et al.2000).

Only after the late 1990s, research started to reveal that in SSA farming often provides a surprisingly small proportion of the incomes of rural households relative to off-farm activities (Reardon 1997; Ellis 1998; Francis 2000; Barrett et al. 2001; Bryceson 2002). The emerging research agenda is to develop a methodology to investigate the interactions of these features in relation to existent models.

2.3. Search for Alternative Theory/Methodology

Theoretical/Methodological Challenges

In development studies, there are often the formalist/substantivist debates between economists and anthropologists/rural sociologists, which is termed as "the conceptual pivot for the bifurcation of sociologically oriented peasant studies and the smallholder economic development approach" (Bryceson et al. 2000, 13-14).

In pure forms, both schools attempt to seek for the causes of rural underdevelopment in Africa's inherent conditions, either biophysical/demographic conditions (formalist) or peculiar social structures (substantivist). Both formalist/substantivist theories have not adequately treated in their analyses emerging features of rural poverty – off-farm livelihood diversification, de-agrarianisation and social differentiation. The analysis of African rural poverty in the era of increasing openness to the global economy requires a new framework that allows the identification of driving factors of off-farm diversification, de-agrarianisation and social differentiation, as well as the examination of their effects on social relations which were initially constrained by inherent conditions. To do so, the methodological formalist/substantivist dichotomy needs to be overcome, as argued below.

The identification of driving factors of off-farm livelihood diversification may be better served by methodological individualism (formalism) than methodological collectivism (substantivism). Many African specialists have acknowledged that livelihood diversification is a response not only to risks but also to an economic opportunity for private accumulation (Ellis 2000; Francis 2000; Bryceson et al. 2000; Barrett et al. 2001). An African community consists of heterogeneous individuals with often conflicting interests (de Haan 2000) that make them respond differently to risks and opportunities provided by greater exposure to wider social dynamics. It is thus rather natural to interpret social changes in response to wider social dynamics, as formalists do, from perspectives of individuals who are risk averse but at the same time keen to improve private wealth.

In contrast, formalist or deductive approach has its limit to acknowledge peculiar aspects of rural social relations in Africa in order to understand why market cannot be a driving force for agricultural transformation. Substantivists, for example, Hyden, highlight "the lack of functional interdependence between rural households in productive activities" on one hand and the social mobility of the poor on the other hand, relative to those in Asia and Latin

America, as distinguishing features of rural social relations in Africa. It is argued that the lack of functional interdependence between rural households in productive activities has made forward and backward linkages difficult to develop in rural settings.

> There is no functional interdependence bringing them (individual households) into reciprocal relations with each other and leading to the development of the means of production. ... To the extent that there is co-operation among producers in these economies it is not structurally enforced but purely a super-structural articulation rooted in the belief that everybody has a right to subsistence. Consequently, co-operation among peasants is temporary, for example, at the time of an emergency, rather than regular and formalized (Hyden 1980,13). Much of the productive efforts are still carried out by individual households quite independently of the work in other such production units. It is as if everybody is paddling his own canoe rather than accepting the implications of working on a larger sailing vessel, where roles are assigned according to functional needs (Hyden 1980, 205).

What effects of greater exposure to wider social dynamics have had on the functional interdependence between rural households in productive activities and the status of the poor in Africa? De-agrarianisation and increasing social differentiation may lead to individualising social relations and dismantling the economy of affection, but, due to high household-level livelihood diversification, may not necessarily lead to deepening the divisions of labour in productive activities. If so, greater exposure to wider social dynamics promotes the involvement of rural villages into cash economies but simply increases their vulnerability to exogenous shocks, while failing to integrate driving forces of rural development and agricultural transformation through forward/backward linkages. These effects require inductive analysis.

Search for Sociological Typologies

In empirical application, the analysis of the reaction to wider social dynamics needs the examination of socio-economic characteristics of households, i.e. education, skills, labour, and other livelihood assets, which determine their ability to adopt distinctive livelihood strategies to deal with risks and opportunities. In turn, the analysis of these impacts on rural social relations requires the examination of the functional interdependence between households in productive activities.

To facilitate these analyses, it is necessary to identify sociological typologies of rural African populations that reflect these heterogeneous livelihood strategies. There are yet methodological challenges to conceptualise sociological typologies of rural African populations.

In the field of rural sociology, smallholder producers in Africa have often synonymously been treated as 'peasants' (Bryceson et al. 2000). African peasantries were being formed through the imposition of colonial rule and the expanding world market. The peasant is understood to stand somewhere between the 'primitive agriculturalist' and the 'capitalist farmer' (Welch Jr.1977; Hyden 1980). In a more formal definition, the peasant is characterised by a range of attributes, including (a) the pursuit of an agricultural livelihood which combines subsistence production with commodity production; (b) internal social organisation based on family labour whereby the family serves as the unit of production, consumption, reproduction, socialisation, welfare and risk-spreading; (c)external subordination to state authorities and to regional or international markets; and (d) village settlement and traditional conformist attitudes and outlook (Bryceson et al. 2000, 2-3).

However, with a global tendency towards de-agrarianisation, there have been dynamic fluctuations in the ratio of rural producers involved specifically in the peasant labour process, which Bryceson defines as peasantisation/de-peasantisation (Bryceson et al. 2000). It becomes difficult to draw a boundary between peasants and non-peasants in rural Africa. Attempts are made to divide rural households into 'rich', 'middle' and 'poor' peasant categories in terms of access to land and other agrarian assets, but the dividing line between them is necessarily arbitrary (Raikes 2000). As peasants become definitionally problematic, it is therefore necessary to search for alternative criteria to effectively reflect heterogeneous reactions of rural sub-populations to risks and opportunities in the era of increasing openness to the global economy, especially diversification into either remunerative or low-return off-farm activities.

As researchers and policy makers have recognised that rural production and social relations are diverging away from agrarian livelihoods, the livelihood approach has gained popularity as an analytical framework for rural poverty in Africa (Ellis and Biggs 2001). The 'livelihood approach' has been developed to effectively describe heterogeneous livelihood diversification strategies among rural sub-populations within a particular local context. This approach can be effectively employed to empirically assess the effects of de-agrarianisation on local processes of social differentiation on rural social relations from a household or individual perspective.

2.4. Livelihood Approach

The livelihood approach has led the focus of rural poverty analysis from 'an agriculture-centred, sector-level, viewpoint, to a household or individual-level viewpoint' (Ellis 2000). The livelihood approach is an analytical framework to facilitate precise understanding of what people are actually doing and striving to make a living in low-income countries. In its framework, the livelihood is defined as the assets (natural, physical, human, financial and social capital), the activities, and the access to these (mediated by institutions and social relations) that together determine the living gained by the individual or household. Five main categories of capital assets in the livelihood definition are presented in Box 1.

Box 1. Categories of Capital Assets in Livelihood Approach

iv) Natural capital: the natural resource base
v) Physical capital: assets brought into existence by economic production processes, e.g. infrastructure, tools, and machines
vi) Human capital: education level and health status of individuals and populations
vii) Financial capital: stocks of cash (savings) that can be accessed to purchase either production or consumption goods, and access to credit
viii) Social capital: social networks and associations in which people participate and from which they can derive support that contributes to their livelihoods.

The livelihoods approach requires timely and cost-effective means of capturing the livelihood strategies of the poor. In empirical analysis, income is often used as a proxy to measure livelihood at initial stages of analyses. While livelihood and income are not synonymous, the composition and level of individual or household income are nevertheless the most direct and measurable outcome of the livelihood process (assets/activities) (Ellis 2000). In implementing the survey, major livelihood (income earning) activities in a particular research site are first identified. Major income earning activities are generally classified into (on-)farm/off-farm income sources. Farm and off-farm categories are further disaggregated into different sub-categories of activities, as reflecting different features of the resources required to generate them, accessibility to them depending on assets and skills, and their location nearby or remote.

The livelihood approach usually takes a household, consisting of co-residents plus migrant members, as a basic analytical unit. To guide research, I assume associations between particular livelihood strategies and assets, as following; at village or community level, different households will adopt different livelihood strategies according to their particular asset and access status. Furthermore, within the household, the strategies of individuals are likely to be constrained by, and to overlap with, the livelihood strategy of the household or homestead group. For example, households with more assets (especially educated members) are likely to adopt strategies including regular off-farm income activities and are often engaged in farm activities as they can afford to purchase inputs. They can also afford to invest in higher education of family members as part of their diversification strategy. However, households without assets tend to be engaged in low-return off-farm activities while failing to invest in productive farm activities and in the education of family members.

One should note that there is a caution in regard to the relation between livelihood strategies and social capital among five types of the livelihood assets. Donor agencies such as the World Bank often assume that horizontal associational ties of trust within the community, i.e., 'civil society', provide the basic trust upon which the transaction costs of everyday economic exchange can be minimised and thus argue that investment in social capital within the rural community would pave the way for improving resource access by individuals and for enabling a sustainable environment for their community. On the other hand, Ellis (2000) and Bryceson et al. (2000) claim that social capital's horizontal associational ties cannot be assumed to exist or to be necessarily desirable, as the processes that create 'insiders' and 'outsiders' with respect to social capital sometimes result in the 'social exclusion' of particular individuals or groups within rural communities. Furthermore, livelihood diversification, de-agrarianisation, increasing social differentiation in the era of increasing openness to the global economy should affect the way rural social relations are organised.

Therefore, in empirically analysing the reaction to greater exposure to wider social dynamics and increasing openness to the global economy, I examine the relations between particular livelihood strategies and capital asset endowments of households, i.e. education, skills, labour, and other livelihood assets, except social capital assets, by assuming that these determine ability of households to deal with risks and opportunities provided externally vis-à-vis rural institutions, while the effects of social capital is undetermined. In turn, the effects of greater exposure to social dynamics on social capital are examined in regard to the impacts of de-agrarianisation and social differentiation as a result of livelihood diversification on social relations between rural households and their functional interdependence in productive activities.

2.5. Application to South African Case

In the former homelands of South Africa, it has been long recognised that rural livelihoods have diverged away from purely agrarian activities well over a century. Each household was given restricted access to land whose area was too small for vital commercial farming. With few economic opportunities in the homelands, the residents were destined to be migrant workers (Bundy 1988). After the 1980s, due to the recession in the mining and commercial farming sectors which had traditionally employed the majority of unskilled rural African workers, many retrenched workers returned home in economic distress. In the meantime, there emerged a few elites who accumulated wealth within the homelands. The South African government funnelled money into the homelands to expand bureaucracies and educational institutions which boosted the number of homeland citizens earning reasonable salaries. Thus, by the 1980s, rural African societies became differentiated in terms of access to regular employment and wages, intensifying local-level social tensions (Beinart 1994).

After the abolishment of the homeland systems in 1994, the pace of economic growth was lagging behind the increase in the number of new entrants into the labour market. The unemployment rate rose to 41% which was especially high among the youth (Burger and Woolard 2005). The proportion of households with unemployed members has more than doubled from 13.4% in 1995 to 27% in 2002 (Pirouz 2004). On the other hand, after 1994, the old-age pension system became suddenly equalised and increased for Africans. Women aged over 60 and men aged over 65 are eligible to receive a pension, and thus the state welfare system provides a kind of vital social security for the majority of the poor in the former homelands (Bank 2005).

Thus, while off-farm income diversification and de-agrarianisation were already the dominant features of rural livelihoods in South Africa under the colonialism/apartheid, social differentiation along with access to a regular income, such as wages, remittances or pensions, became more pronounced along with the transition to democracy.

Recently the livelihood approach was used in rural South African studies in an attempt to reveal heterogeneous logics of and reactions by rural sub-populations to the social transition. For example, Francis (2000) indicates that the households could be grouped into the following three typologies in terms of their ability to cope with social changes: (1) households which have experienced income growth since the 1970s or which have accumulated land, access to land or capital equipment; (2) households whose income is relatively stable and/or which are managing from month to month with more than half of them containing one or more members receiving a pension; and (3) households which are falling into greater poverty, which are obviously not coping (Francis 2000).

On the other hand, revenues from sales of maize, vegetables and livestock products consist of a small portion (less than 10%) of total household income in the former homelands (Leibbrandt et al. 2000; Eastwood et al. 2006). Still, some authors attempt to re-evaluate the 'hidden' role of subsistence farming in or in-kind contributions from land-based activities to rural livelihoods (McAllister 2001; Ainsile 2005), while the post-apartheid agrarian reform needs to improve the welfare of the historically marginalised (Ntsebeza and Hall 2007). If I only pay attention to off-farm cash income activities, I could fail to understand long-term livelihood strategies of accumulation and investment. For example, assume that there are two households that derive income from old-age pension, and one owns some livestock and grows maize for home consumption while the other does not. The household with more animals and that grows maize is more food secure than the other household.

Thus it is important to deliberately take the values of land-based activities into consideration when applying the livelihood approach to rural South Africa in order to capture heterogeneous reactions to social changes by rural sub-populations. The criteria to classify household typologies need to reflect livelihood portfolios, i.e., proportional contributions of sub-categories of off-farm income activities (pension, wage/business, remittance, casual income) as well as in-kind contributions of land-based activities (maize production, livestock) to livelihoods.

2.6. Application to Kenyan Case

The Kenyan economy has been principally based on agriculture without a strong industrial sector, and the extent/process of de-agrarianisation has been more modest and gradual than that of South Africa. Nevertheless, off-farm income diversification has become a significant feature of livelihoods in rural Kenya. The rapid population growth since independence has threatened the shrinking agricultural resource basis on which Kenyan economy primarily depends. The primary concern is therefore whether diversification into off-farm activities could contribute to sustainable agricultural intensification by providing rural households with capital and by allowing them to mitigate risks that would otherwise arise from specialisation in farming.

Reportedly, diversification into off-farm activities has been accompanied by sustainable agricultural intensification in already highly populated areas with high agricultural potential and with better market access, such as in central and parts of eastern Kenya as well as the former white highlands (Hyden 1980; Collier and Lal 1984; Evans and Ngau 1991; Tiffen et al. 1994).

In contrast, the development did not reach the rural peripheries in the semi-arid/arid zones until the mid-twentieth century or later (Hyden 1980). With low population density, people in these zones survived on slash-and-burn agriculture combined with extensive grazing of indigenous animals. In the recent few decades the arrival of infrastructural development and education has gradually transformed rural livelihoods away from an autarchy. Concurrently, more people have migrated from high potential zones (that are already over-populated) into marginal zones in search of unoccupied land. Initially, people resorted to opening up indigenous forests to expand arable and grazing activities, as few alternative cash earning opportunities were locally available (Francis and Hoddinott 1993; Freeman and Ellis 2005). These exploitative practices led to the depletion of vegetation and the degradation of inherently fragile soils. Rising population pressure coupled with increasing demand for cash to cater for westernised consumption patterns have made it necessary for rural dwellers to intensify and commercialise their farming practices to achieve both welfare and environmental goals.

Along with the infrastructural development, development agencies (either government or non-governmental) have arrived in such peripheries to alleviate poverty and reverse environmental degradation by providing residents with new farming technologies. Reports indicate that, even within a small area, rural households respond heterogeneously to adopting new technologies (Tittonell et al. 2005; Iiyama et al. 2008). Households that diversify into regular off-farm income activities are more likely to adopt intensive farming and resource management, while a substantial number of the poor without access to regular off-farm incomes survive either on conventional extensive farming methods or on exploitation of forests to make charcoal for sale. The differential dependence on natural resources among sub-populations should raise serious governance concerns (Iiyama et al. 2008).

The application of the livelihood approach to rural Kenya therefore should reveal the effects of local processes of social differentiation on governance and sustainable agricultural intensification by examining the association between the particular livelihood diversification strategies and the adoption of resource management. In typical agro-pastoral communities in remote semi-arid regions of Kenya, while there is little variety in off-farm income activities (regular, casual or remittances), most households adopt diverse crop (staple, fruits, drought-resistant, commercial) and livestock (cattle or small ruminants, indigenous or exotic) varieties, each with different economic returns and resource management incentives. Proportional contributions of diverse crop and livestock activities along with off-farm income sub-categories are effective criteria to categorise heterogeneous households into relatively homogenous groups with similar livelihood diversification strategies and resource management levels.

3. ANALYSIS AND DISCUSSION

3.1. Study Areas

To gain empirical information on inter-household heterogeneities in livelihood strategies, I decided to focus on the households residing within a boundary of the smallest administrative units both in rural South Africa and Kenya.

In South Africa case, the households residing in two sub-villages in the former Xhalanga District, located in the south-western part of the former Transkei, were chosen for interviews. The Transkei was the largest and poorest of the former homelands. In the study area, major livelihood activities are off-farm income activities, with some subsistence maize and livestock production. In the past, communal labour practices, such as exchanging labour, draught oxen, and farming implements among neighbouring households, helped households without capital to plough for subsistence. Such practices however became gradually obsolete due to increasing inter-household inequalities especially after the 1980s of structural unemployment. These days cultivation is replaced by tractor services, which costs the cash equivalent of or more than a month's off-farm income for a poor household in the study area. As a result, cash-/stock-less poorer farmers cannot afford to cultivate arable fields but parts of garden plots. Several visits were made with the 69 households between May 2000 to January 2006 to implement interviews and participant observations on their livelihoods.

The Kenyan study area is located along the Kerio Valley in Keiyo District in the Rift Valley Province of western Kenya. The region can be roughly subdivided into three agro-ecological zones – the highlands (altitude 2,500–3,000 m) to the west, the escarpment (1,300–2,500 m) in the central region, and the lowland or valley floor to the east (1,000–1,300 m). This study focused on households representing the valley floor community in one sub-location. Until the early 1970s, it was considered unviable to do farming in the valley floor because of no permanent sources of water. Still, infrastructural development after the 1980s accelerated immigration and population growth. Today, farm activities include grain production (maize, beans, and sorghum), horticulture, and livestock (indigenous, exotic). Fruits and exotic animals such as dairy cattle and goats were introduced by NGOs and initially adopted by a few individuals. Off-farm activities include a few regular income opportunities (formal employment and small business) and casual (charcoal making) activities. Remittance is less a dominant source of income in this community remote from industrial towns. Recently serious governance problems have arisen, as poorer households who can not afford to undertake productive farming exploit indigenous trees for firewood and charcoal, threatening natural resource bases for the whole community. The household survey was conducted in 2006 with all 177 households in the sub-location.

Table 2. Livelihood Clusters

	cluster[A]	cluster[B]	cluster[C]	cluster[D]	cluster[E]
South Africa Activities	remittance/casual	pension	remittance/casual & livestock	pension & livestock	wage/business & livestock
% of the surveyed hh	19%	25%	16%	26%	14%
mean disaggregated sources' contribution to total wealth					
wage & business income(%)	0	1	0	4	56
remittance (%)	55	6	13	2	1
pension income(%)	0	86	0	20	0
casual income(%)	35	1	8	0	0
estimated maize value(%)	3	3	1	1	3
estimated livestock value(%)	7	2	77	72	40
mean estimated values of household wealth					
total wealth(US$)	583	968	2,140	4,750	4,283
total wealth(R)	4,783	7,936	17,552	38,958	35,122
total off-farm income(R)	4,292	7,549	3,727	10,353	20,204
estimated aize value(R)	152	222	252	505	1,098
estimated livestock value(R)	338	165	13,573	28,100	13,910
	Cluster[1]	cluster[2]	cluster[3]	cluster[4]	cluster[5]
Kenya Activities	specialisation in casual off-farm	specialisation in traditional livestock	staple crop & traditional livestock	integration of fruits & exotic animals	specialisation in regular off-farm
% of the surveyed hh	34%	12%	11%	19%	23%
each component's					
drought-resistant crop(%)	1	1	3	2	0
staple food crop(%)	6	8	59	5	6
fruits(%)	5	0	2	32	6
commercial crop(%)	0	0	0	4	2
traditional livestock(%)	8	73	16	9	8
exotic livestock(%)	1	0	0	14	7
regular off-farm income(%)	0	2	1	8	72
casual off-farm income(%)	78	9	11	10	0
remittance(%)	0	6	7	12	0
land rental(%)	1	1	1	4	0
mean annual gross income					
total gross income (US$)	527	680	1,164	1,374	2,338
total gross income (ksh)	36,957	47,625	81,510	96,213	163,666
crop-income[ksh]	6,579	5,481	49,237	44,424	27,337
livestock income[ksh]	3,668	31,687	13,703	28,037	21,456
off-farm income[ksh]	26,589	10,400	17,690	22,361	115,295
land rental income[ksh]	121	57	870	1,391	244

The following sub-sections present comparative analyses of the livelihood diversification patterns between the former Transkei and the Rift Valley households, in regard to the examinations of the identified livelihood strategies (3.2), the regional diversity in de-agrarianisation (3.3), the factors driving social differentiation (3.4), and the impacts of off-farm livelihood diversification, de-agrarianisation and increasing social differentiation on rural social relations (3.5), on which theoretical/methodological implications (3.6) are derived.

3.2. Livelihood Clusters in South Africa and Kenya

I attempted to identify dominant livelihood strategies in the particular local context and classify each household according to the typologies of the livelihood strategies. The criteria were chosen to capture local processes of social differentiation. In the former Transkei, the contributions of diverse off-farm income activities and subsistence land-based activities, i.e., estimated values of maize yields and livestock, to a household's wealth were chosen as criteria to reflect the heterogeneous reactions to South African social transitions by rural sub-populations. In Kenya, the sub-categories of farm and off-farm activities with different economic returns and resource management incentives were chosen as criteria to reflect diverse responses among rural sub-populations to the challenges of agricultural intensification. Then, the cluster analysis (Everitt and Dunn 2001) was employed to group households with similar sets of livelihood activities.

The results are shown in Table 2. For both Transkei and Rift Valley communities, the five distinctive livelihood strategies or five clusters of households were identified. Below I interpret each of the clusters for South African community and for Kenyan community.

In rural South Africa, overall, the particular off-farm income activities the households depend on and whether they own livestock seem to define a livelihood strategy, while a proportion of estimated maize value, 1-3% across the clusters, hardly contributes to differentiating the households.

The five clusters identified were; [A] remittance/casual only (19% of the total households), [B] pension only (25%), [C] remittance/casual with livestock (16%), [D] pension with livestock (26%) and [E] wage/business with livestock (14%). Cluster [A] on average derived most (90%) of their wealth (estimated at 4,783 rand [R] or US$583 at R8.2/US$) from off-farm income activities, either remittance from absent family members or casual activities, such as washing, cleaning and collecting firewood for neighbours. Cluster [B] earned 86% of their wealth (estimated at R7,936 or US$968) from old-age pension. Cluster [C] derived 77% of their wealth (estimated at R17,552 or US$2,140) from livestock, while also receiving remittance or casual off-farm incomes. Cluster [D] earned 72% of their wealth (estimated at R38,958 or US$4,750) from livestock, while pension accounted for 20%. Cluster [E] derived 56% of their wealth (estimated at R35,122 or US$4,283) from regular off-farm incomes, either wage or business incomes, while holding 40% of their assets in the form of livestock.

In rural Kenya, some households were classified according to various types of crop and livestock activities with different levels of intensification and economic returns, while households fallen into the lowest/highest income clusters were found to derive over 70% of incomes from off-farm activities, either casual or regular. The five clusters identified were; [1] specialisation in casual off-farm income (34% of the total households), [2] specialisation in traditional livestock (12%), [3] staple crop & traditional livestock (11%), [4] integration of fruits and exotic animals (19%) and [5] specialisation in regular off-farm income (23%). Cluster [1] on average derived 78% of their total annual gross income (valued at 36,957ksh or US$527 at 70ksh/$US) from casual off-farm activities, mainly consisting of charcoal burning and casual labour. Cluster [2] earned 73% of their income (47,625ksh or US$680) from subsistence pastoral activities with traditional livestock, 9% from casual off-farm sources and 8% from staple crops. Cluster [3] (11% of the households) derived 59% of their total gross income (81,510ksh or US$1,164) from staple crops, 16% from traditional livestock and 11% from casual off-farm income. Cluster [4] earned on average 96,213ksh or US$1,374 of the annual gross income from diversified sources; 32% from fruits, 14% from exotic animals and 12% from remittances. Cluster [5] (23% of the households) earned 163,666ksh or US$2,338 on average, far higher than the other clusters. They derived 72% of their gross income from regular off-farm earnings, 7–8 % from traditional and exotic animals and 6% from staple crops and fruits.

3.3. Factors Affecting the Extent of De-Agrarianisation

While de-agrarianisation seems to be a widely observed phenomenon across rural Africa today, its causes, directions, extents and impacts on rural development have been spatially and temporally specific, reflecting diverse local histories, colonial/state policies, and agro-ecological, demographic and political conditions.

In rural South Africa, most households depend critically on off-farm income activities. At the time of survey, all of the households were receiving some forms of off-farm income with different levels. Two-thirds of the households owned at least an animal (cattle, sheep, goat), but livestock holding was also fairly skewed among the households in the community as shown in Table 3. Clusters [A] and [B] derived most of their income from a single low-return off-farm activity (casual, remittance or pension) and rarely owned livestock, in comparison to clusters [C] and [D] which also depended on those off-farm activities, but held more wealth in the form of livestock. Cluster [E] earned more off-farm income than the others (twice to five times as much), and also kept livestock. On the other hand, though most households (91%) were at least engaged in growing maize (often intercropping with beans) for subsistence purpose, contribution of crop farming to income/wealth seems minimal. Poorer clusters [A] and [B] had access to smaller sizes of plots but cultivated less than the well-off clusters. In relation to cluster [C], [D] and [E] households (56% combined), cluster [A] and [B] households (44% combined) may be comparatively more vulnerable to possibilities of losing off-farm income sources, as they rarely had livestock assets and cultivate maize for subsistence.

The causes of de-agrarianisation in the former homelands of South Africa can be traced to the colonial administration to establish migrant labour systems under the segregationist regime. Migrant remittances were rarely invested in either upgraded intensive agricultural technologies or soil conservation measures in the homelands. Nevertheless, migrant remittances had been somewhat invested in the form of livestock for rural households and subsistence farming had been maintained through communal labour among neighbours. When urban economies start contracting after the 1980s, economic differentiation between those with or without regular incomes widened. Cash-strapped households with retrenched workers could no longer afford to cultivate their arable fields, when the communal labour practice became obsolete and replaced by expensive tractor ploughing service. Today, many rural households survive on old-age pensions, with which food and necessities are purchased. Otherwise, households headed by unemployed youth struggle to survive on casual off-farm income.

In contrast to South Africa, the Kenyan economy has been principally based on agriculture without strong industrial and state sectors, and the extent/impact of de-agrarianisation on rural livelihoods has been more modest and gradual. Nevertheless, off-farm income diversification has become a significant feature of livelihoods over the past few decades, even in semi-arid zones which used to be considered marginal areas. Increasing demand for cash incomes for education and consumption has necessitated agropastoralists either to expand their farming activities or to diversify into more profitable off-farm activities. Considering the fragile ecological conditions on which rural peoples depend in semi-arid zones, diversification into off-farm activities could contribute to sustainable agricultural intensification.

Table 3. Land Access, Use and Livestock Holdings

South Africa	cluster[A] remittance/ casual	cluster[B] pension	cluster[C] remittance/ casual &	cluster[D] pension & livestock	cluster[E] wage/business & livestock
land access/use					
land access(ha)	1.2	2.4	1.7	2.3	4.1
land use(ha)	0.3	0.6	1.1	1.5	3
% of area cropped/owned	25	25	62	65	73
mean livestock holding					
no. of cattle	0.1	0	5.2	9.2	3.9
no. of sheep	0	0	0.8	23.4	17.6
no. of goats	1.5	1.6	4.5	5.1	6.4

Kenya	Cluster[1] specialisation in casual off-farm	cluster[2] specialisation in traditional	cluster[3] staple crop & traditional	cluster[4] integration of fruits & exotic	cluster[5] specialisation in regular off-farm
land access/use					
land access(ha)	1.5	2.6	3.8	3.5	4.7
land use(ha)	0.4	0.5	1.9	1.3	1
% of area cropped/owned	27	19	50	37	21
mean livestock holding					
total no. of livestock(TLU*)	1.63	13.11	6.82	5.44	5.25
no. of exotic animals(TLU)	0.02	0	0.10	2.41	1.44
no. of traditional	1.59	13.11	6.72	3.05	3.79

*Total Livestock Unit (TLU) is calculated as follows: a bull is equivalent to 1.29TLU, cow 1 TLU, calf 0.7TLU, sheep and goat 0.11TLU.

In the Rift Valley community, some households which had educated family members and access to training could diversify into regular off-farm income activities, adopt more intensive and commercial farming methods, such as clusters [5] and [4]. However, due to limited availability of remunerative off-farm income activities, most poor households lacking the assets necessary to undertake productive farming were observed to open up indigenous forests either to make charcoal for selling (cluster [1]) or to expand arable and grazing activities (clusters [2] and [3]) without undertaking sustainable management. The differential dependence on natural resources among sub-populations, which are in turn closely associated with the differential access to remunerative off-farm activities, has caused serious governance concerns.

Different consequences of the diversification into off-farm activities on agricultural intensification, i.e. under-farming in the former Transkei and governance problems in Rift Valley community, have been attributed to local-specific historical backgrounds, state policies, market/ infrastructure, and increasing social differentiation along with differential access to non-agrarian assets. The Kenyan situation may somewhat apply to rural peripheries in the eastern Africa (Evans and Ngau 1991; Freeman and Ellis 2005; Tittonell et al. 2005), while the former Transkei case may look too extreme but be observed commonly across rural areas in the southern Africa (Francis 2000; McAllister 2001; Bank 2005; Eastwood et al. 2006).

3.4. Driving Forces of off-Farm Income Livelihood Diversification, De-Agrarianisation and Social Differentiation

Examinations of the association between particular livelihood strategies and capital assets may reveal which asset endowments would enable households better to respond to risks and opportunities externally brought about by wider social changes. Socio-economic characteristics of households may serve as proxies for household's human and financial capital asset endowments. The basic socio-economic variables of the five dominant livelihood strategy clusters identified respectively in the former Transkei community and in the Rift Valley community are compared in Table 4.

Table 4. Socio-Economic Characteristics of Households in Livelihood Clusters

South Africa	cluster[A] remittance/casual	cluster[B] pension	cluster[C] remittance/casual & livestock	cluster[D] pension & livestock	cluster[E] wage/business & livestock
age of the head	41	74	51	69	54
education years of the head	5.2	3.2	6.3	4.6	6.5
family labour	5.7	7.4	7.2	9.2	8.1
Kenya	Cluster[1] specialisation in casual off-farm	cluster[2] specialisation in traditional livestock	cluster[3] staple crop & traditional livestock	cluster[4] integration of fruits & exotic animals	cluster[5] specialisation in regular off-farm
age of the head	45	61	50	53	35
education years of the head	5.5	2.7	4.6	5.2	10.9
family labour	3	3.3	2.8	3.8	3.6

In the former Transkei community in South Africa, on average, cluster [A] (remittance/casual only) household heads were the youngest (41 years old) followed by their [C] counterparts with livestock (51 years old), while cluster [B] and [D] (pension with or without livestock) heads were the oldest (74 and 69 years old respectively). Older heads of clusters [B] and [D] were the least educated (3.2 and 4.6 schooling years), while cluster [E] (wage/business and livestock) heads (6.5 years) were the most educated. While the cluster [A] (remittance/casual only) heads were younger than those of cluster [C] (remittance/causal with livestock), cluster [A] heads had fewer years of education than cluster [C] heads (5.2 years vs. 6.3 years).

In Rift Valley community in Kenya, household heads of cluster [5] (regular off-farm income) were the youngest (35 years old), followed by those of [1] (casual off-farm income), while those of [2] (traditional animals) were the oldest (61 years old). With respect to education, household heads belonging to cluster [5] had attended school for more years on average (11 years), followed by those of clusters [1] (6 years), [4], [3] and [2], in decreasing order. Clusters [4] and [5] are also characterised by larger households than clusters [1] and [3].

Overall, both in South Africa and Kenya, within a small area, there existed substantial inter-household heterogeneity in the adoption of livelihood strategies and the levels of assets. In turn, despite the differences in criteria to categorise households, there were some similarities in identified social groups in terms of their associations with household asset levels. Education is often interpreted as one of the most important human capital assets in the livelihood literature (Ellis 2000; Francis 2000). Higher education has been necessary to get local employment or start business. For example, the well-off households belonging to cluster [E] in South Africa and cluster [5] in Kenya earned substantial portions of their wealth/income from regular off-farm income activities while also gaining some from crop-livestock activities. In contrast, the poor households that belonged to clusters [A] in South Africa and [1] in Kenya depended on low-return casual off-farm activities. Their heads were relatively young but less educated than their counterparts in clusters [E] and [5]. Among households headed by relatively old heads, clusters [D] and [4] households derived relatively more wealth/incomes from livestock/crop-livestock activities, their heads were more educated, and families were larger than those of households in clusters [B] and [2] with the oldest heads. Clusters [C], [D], [E] in South Africa and [3], [4], [5] in Kenya cultivated proportionally more land areas, while clusters [A], [B] and [1], [2] cultivated less areas.

These findings correspond to the general empirical observation reported by livelihood specialists that access to regular off-farm incomes, livestock and educational attainment most contribute to reinforcing social differentiation in rural Africa (Ellis 2000; Francis 2000; Bryceson 2002; Eastwood et al. 2006). While high-income earners with more capital assets redirect portions of their income to more lucrative activities and to investments in farming, the poor lacking capital assets have little choice but to specialise in unskilled off-farm labour (Evans and Ngau 1991; Barrett et al. 2001; Freeman and Ellis 2005; Tittonell et al. 2005). While comparisons reveal substantial regional diversity, de-agrarianisation and social differentiation along differential access to non-agrarian incomes and assets seem to be a universal feature of contemporary rural Africa.

3.5. Impacts of Livelihood Diversification, De-Agrarianisation and Social Differentiation on Social Relations

Elsewhere in Africa, rural households have become more and more involved in off-farm activities and cash economies at various degrees. At the same time, it is reported that substantial mobility barriers to high return niches exist within the rural off-farm economy (Reardon 1997; Ellis 2000; Barrett et al. 2001; Bryceson 2002; Ellis and Freeman 2005). In both rural South Africa and Kenya, though many households depend on off-farm activities, organised off-farm labour markets do not exist. Relatively high-paying formal employment opportunities are limited to a few civil servant, teaching, or development agency positions, while a few local elites are engaged in petty trades. In contrast, many rely on more temporal and far less remunerative self-employment options. This divide in rural off-farm economy is in turn reflected in that in farming; those with regular off-farm incomes are more likely to invest in farming while those without cannot afford to do so.

These substantial barriers to high return niches within the rural economy both in off-farm and farm sectors, which are somehow related to 'the lack of functional interdependence between rural households', are another distinguishing feature of the contemporary rural poverty and underdevelopment in Africa.

Hyden (1980) regards the lack of functional interdependence between rural households in productive farming activities, relative to that in Asia and Latin America, as one of distinguishing features of rural social relations in African underdevelopment and argues that it has made forward and backward linkages difficult to develop in rural African settings. The reality is far more complicated than Hyden anticipates due to the effects of greater exposure to wider social dynamics and increasing openness to the global economy on rural social relations. To assess the substantive effects of off-farm income diversification, de-agrarianisation and social differentiation on the functional interdependence between rural households in both farm and off-farm activities, the social relations between the rural sub-populations pursuing the distinctive livelihood diversification strategies are examined below.

In South African case, the most important criteria to cluster households into groups pursuing similar livelihood diversification strategies were the contributions of diverse off-farm income activities on one hand and estimated livestock values among the subsistence land-based activities to a household's wealth on the other hand. The former homeland households were heavily dependent on off-farm sources for their cash incomes, reflecting the extreme extent of de-agrarianisation in the southern African peripheries. Most sources of the dominant off-farm incomes were of non-rural, non-local nature, such as migrant remittances, pension (state welfare system), salaries (NGOs/schools/offices), while business (self-employment, petty trades) and casual incomes (helping neighbours' domestic tasks, collecting firewood and grass) were of local nature but without much forward/backward linkages. In turn, subsistence livestock and crop farming has also lacked the functional interdependence between households. In rural South Africa communal labour used to be practiced among neighbouring households by mutually exchanging labour, tools and draught cattle at the planting season, but these exchanges were organised at temporary bases and not formalised (McAllister 2001). Even such a communal labour practice became obsolete and has been replaced by the tractor ploughing service by wealthy villagers. Today, while livestock are owned by individual households, subsistence maize production is operated by family members of individual households who hire tractor service.

In Kenyan case, rural households were found pursuing livelihood strategies with different economic returns and resource management incentives, either low-return portfolios of casual off-farm (charcoal making) with subsistence farming (drought-resistant/staple crops, traditional livestock) or high-return portfolios of regular off-farm (salaried employment/petty trades/urban migration) with commercial farming (fruits/ commercial). Unlike rural South Africa under the influence of the strong capitalist and state sectors, the limited variety of off-farm income sources was available in the remote Rift Valley village. While regular/remittance income sources were accessed by the minority of households, substantial numbers of households were earning casual off-farm income by felling trees on the communal land and processing them into charcoal that can be sold at remote markets. On the other hand, in the study area crop farming has long been operated by individual households independently on plots while indigenous livestock owned individually have been grazed on unfenced areas. Recently, some households started undertaking intensive horticulture, but they managed most tasks for horticulture by family labour, while poorer households tend to exploit natural resources through extensive farming. Today, well-off households adapt themselves to changing environment by diversifying into high-return farm/off-farm activities, but they are doing so quite independently, while poor households tend to 'exit' or remain 'uncaptured', to use Hyden's (1980) terms, for survival.

Thus it appears that both in South African and Kenyan rural communities the functional interdependence between households in productive farm and off-farm activities was, and has remained, weak, while individual households independently pursue livelihood portfolios extensively diversified into off-farm income sources. In the former Transkei community, both in off-farm and farm activities, there have been no formalised divisions of labour in either subsistent farming or off-farm activities, for example, between the poorer cluster households ([A] remittance/casual, [B] pension, [C] remittance/casual & livestock) and the relatively well-off cluster households ([D] pension & livestock, [E] wage/business & livestock), while each household has been heavily dependent on off-farm income sources of non-local (urban sectors), non-farm (state, private sectors) nature. In Kenyan Rift Valley community, too, there have been no formalised labour exchanges, for example, between the poorer cluster households ([1] casual off-farm, [2] traditional livestock, [3] staple crop & traditional livestock) and the relatively well-off cluster households ([4] fruits & exotic animals, [5] regular off-farm) while the poorer resort to exploitation of natural resources or retreat into subsistence.

On the other hand, negative impacts of de-agrarianisation on rural development are more pronounced in rural South Africa than in rural Kenya especially in regard to the vulnerability of the poor to external shocks. With the penetration of capitalism since the early twentieth century, rural South Africans have long been regarded as proletariats while the distorted communal system, which guaranteed access to homestead plots, has worked as a 'smoke screen for the real extent of proletarianisation (Hendricks 1990). Migrants may have kept faith in building family farms in the villages under the migrant labour system. However, with the structural unemployment that started in the 1970s–1980s, there has been a shift from remittances to welfare grants as the main source of rural income and a subsequent shift of functional families to pension-dependent households that neither farmed effectively nor received regular remittances from absent industrial workers (Bank 2005). Increasing social differentiation has led to the collapse of communal labour and of the economy of affection if they had ever been, and the young unemployed have found themselves extremely vulnerable to economic shocks and while not afford even to practice subsistence farming without inputs and implements.

Unlike South African counterparts, the Kenyan poor seem to have some options for survival "outside the systems" (Hyden 2007), by retreating into subsistence or exploiting the nature surrounding them. However, because not only the poor but also the relatively wealthy have claims on common natural resources, survival strategies "outside the systems" by the poor raise serious governance concerns, while increased population pressure is expected to intensify competitions for such resources and to necessitate agricultural intensification.

3.6. Theoretical/Methodological Implications

While rural African individuals have become more involved in off-farm activities and cash economies, market forces have failed automatically to transform African rural agriculture. Rural villages have failed to consolidate driving forces of social transformation to stimulate rural labour markets and to create local on-farm/off-farm employment opportunities.

Existent development models have perceived low levels of market development and consequent agricultural underdevelopment in rural Africa as geographically (Platteau 2000; Collier 2007) or historically (Hyden 1980; 2007) unique phenomena. Both formalists and substantivists try to rationally explain the causal relations between low levels of market development and agricultural underdevelopment, by either the population pressure or the social relation as a key determinant factor. For example, formalists claim that the functioning of markets or division of labour requires well-enforced property rights and trust in economic dealings, which are critically conditioned by the thickness of economic space that is indeed determined by population density. They argue that market development will remain very incomplete if populations are thinly spread over large areas of land as in many parts of rural Africa (Platteau 2000). In contrast, substantivis search for the structural determinants of African underdevelopment in African peasants' behaviour embedded in personalised relationships with the affective ties based on common descent or residence, in which investment in maintaining their position in community may pay off in the long run by expanding their potential claims on their risk bearing capacity. As a result, the pre-capitalistic production relations are being defended against the intrusions of the market economy while retarding the growth of productive forces (i.e., capital goods) (Hyden 1980).

Both existent formalist and substantivist models try to search for key determinants of rural market and agricultural underdevelopment in Africa in either physical/demographic conditions or peculiar social structures. Yet, causes of African poverty are much more complicated today due to the impacts of greater exposure to wider social dynamics. Off-farm livelihood diversification, de-agrarianisation and increasing social differentiation along with differential access to non-agrarian assets, which were attributed to colonialism, rural-urban migration and increasing openness of national economies to the global economy, have had considerable implications on rural market and agricultural development in the contemporary Africa, i.e., under-farming in South Africa and governance issues in Kenya.

Peculiarities of African poverty in the contemporary era need to be examined not only by examining the inherent physical/demographic or socio-economic conditions, but also by assessing the considerable implications of greater exposure to wider social dynamics upon the inherent conditions. To do so, the existent develop models need to be modified and integrated beyond the methodological formalist/substantivist dichotomy so that they can deal with both social dynamics triggered in the response to risks and opportunities provided by greater exposure to wider social dynamics and their impacts on rural social relations.

On the analysis of social dynamics, it is natural to assume that rational individuals are not only risk averse but also responsive to externally brought about economic opportunities provided externally, as formalists do. Social dynamics are regarded as the result of the aggregation of the decisions of rational economic agents who manage risks while invest in private accumulation. Social dynamics are then accompanied by increasing social differentiation and conflicting norms among rural sub-populations due to their heterogeneous reactions to risks/economic opportunities. The penetration of the cash economy may further alter social norms that individuals should follow within African communities.

On the other hand, this assumption does not answer why the divisions of labour and factor markets remain underdeveloped in Africa while the extents of de-agrarianisation are highly diverse across regions within Africa. With rural markets under-developed, African rural social relations will remain key focus on the inductive research. De-agrarianisation and increasing social differentiation may lead to individualising social relations and dismantling the economy of affection but not to deepening the divisions of labour between rural households in productive activities. Individual households have rather extensively been dependent on off-farm income sources of non-local nature (South Africa) or have retreated into subsistence or resorted to exploiting common natural resources (Kenya). Greater exposure to wider social dynamics and increasing openness of the national economies to the global economy promotes the involvement of rural villages into cash economies but simply increases their vulnerability to exogenous shocks, while failing to integrate driving forces of rural development and agricultural transformation through forward/backward linkages.

In summary, the empirical analysis of the peculiarities of African rural poverty requires a framework that incorporates the perspective of individual households who strive to cope with changes brought about externally through off-farm income diversification which in turn drives de-agrarianisation and social differentiation on one hand, and the assessment of their effects on the functional interdependence between rural households in productive activities on the other hand, by overcoming the methodological formalist/substantivist dichotomy.

4. CONCLUSION

Deepening rural poverty, sluggish performance of the agricultural sector, accelerated resource depletion and environmental degradation in Africa have always concerned policy makers and researchers and urged them to search for effective research and policy tools. This chapter has attempted to reveal peculiarities of contemporary African rural poverty and to examine how greater exposure to wider social dynamics has affected developmental challenges, through extensive survey of the livelihood literature and empirical comparisons of rural livelihoods of agro-pastoral communities in the South African and Kenyan peripheries to examine the extent of diversity between and within rural economies. This section concludes this chapter by briefly summarising the findings and discussing policy implications.

The major objective of this chapter has been to present a new insight into the peculiarities of African rural poverty and developmental challenges by examining the interactions between Africa's inherent geographic/socio-economic conditions and the impacts of greater exposure to wider social dynamics and increasing openness to the global economy.

The comparative analyses of the rural livelihoods revealed that de-agrarianisation processes, i.e. their causes, directions, extents and impacts on rural development and agricultural intensification, have shown considerable variations between South Africa and Kenya, depending on initial local conditions. Nevertheless, it has also been found that de-agrarianisation and livelihood diversification in South Africa and Kenya have been similarly accompanied by the increasing social differentiation due to the heterogeneity in adopting distinctive portfolios of livelihood diversification strategies among rural sub-populations with differential accesses to non-agrarian assets, while the availability of remunerative livelihood opportunities has been limited in rural peripheries.

In general, across rural Africa, the poor have been identified as lacking capital assets, especially human capital, to adopt high-return livelihood strategies in response to risks and economic opportunities provided by greater exposure to wider social dynamics. Yet, the fact that rural households pursue diversified livelihood diversification portfolios may make the effectiveness of policy tools aimed at only the agriculture sector unpredictable. Instead, the following policy implications are derived from the micro-level findings.

First, rural poverty alleviation and promotion of sustainable agricultural development require meso-/macro-level policies encompassing the promotion of multi-sectoral development rather than focusing on agriculture. From a household/individual perspective, motivations to diversify income sources include risk management and economies of scope. The findings in South Africa and Kenya have shown that households diversifying into regular off-farm income activities are more endowed with human capital assets, especially education and skills, and also are more likely to invest in agriculture and resource management. In contrast, households engaged in low-return casual off-farm income activities lack the assets necessary to undertake productive farming activities and thus have little incentive to manage resources properly. Diversification into remunerative off-farm activities appear to provide the necessary capital for farming and to reduce the risks arising from specialisation in farming. Therefore, meso-/macro-level development policies need to be multi-sectoral, encompassing education and farm and off-farm activities.

Second, community-level projects require effective targeting. Within a small community, households are sharing physical, natural capital. In turn, our findings have revealed that the increasing social differentiation due to heterogeneous endowments in human and financial capital have led to skewed access to and dependence on common natural resources among community members, while making customary practices, which formerly ensured coordination among community members either in communal work or in the management of common resources, less binding and alienating the poor from the benefits arising from social capital. Projects aimed at enhancing the diversity and profitability of livelihood portfolios of the poor and at augmenting their capital asset bases may be more effective than efforts solely focused upon restricting access to common resources, as is often the case. Classifying households according to the dominant livelihood strategies in a particular local context can serve for efficient targeting.

In concluding this chapter, I stress the importance of more inductive research on rural African livelihoods. As rural livelihoods in Africa have been continuously changing, rather than searching for deductive models, inductive studies can not only facilitate the analysis of social changes from the perspective of households/individuals but will fill the empty spots in the knowledge of development and enrich models.

REFERENCES

Ainsile, A. (2005). Farming Cattle, Cultivating Relationships: Cattle Ownership and Cultural Politics in Peddie District, Eastern Cape. *Social Dynamics,* 31(1), 129-156.

Bank, L. (2005). On Family Farms and Commodity Groups: Rural Livelihoods, Households and Development Policy in the Eastern Cape. *Social Dynamics,* 31(1), 157-181.

Barrett, C.B., Reardon, T., & Webb, P. (2001). Nonfarm Income Diversification and Household Livelihood Strategies in Rural Africa: Concepts, Dynamics and Policy Implications. *Food Policy,* 26, 315-331.

Beinart, W. (1994). *Twentieth-Century South Africa. Cape Town and Oxford.* Oxford University Press.

Boserup, E. (1965). *The Conditions of Agricultural Growth: The Economics of Agrarian Change under Population Pressure.* Aldine: Chicago.

Boserup, E. (1990). *Economic and Demographic Relationships in Development.* Essays Selected and Introduced by T. Paul Schultz. Baltimore and London: The Johns Hopkins University Press.

Bryceson, D.F. (1999). African Rural Labour, Income Diversification and Livelihood Approaches: A Long-Term Development Perspective. *Review of African Political Economy,* 26(80), 171-89.

Bryceson, D., Kay, C., & Mooij, J. (2000). *Disappearing Peasantries? Rural Labour in Africa, Asia and Latin America.* Warwickshire: ITDG Publishing.

Bryceson, D.F. (2002). The Scramble in Africa: Reorienting Rural Livelihoods. *World Development,* 30(5), 725-739.

Bundy, C. (1988). *The Rise and Fall of the South African Peasantry.* Second Edition, London and Cape Town: James Currey Ltd. and David Phillip.

Burger, R., & Woolard, I. (2005). *The State of the Labour Market in South Africa After the First Decade of Democracy.* CSSR (Centre for Social Science Research) Working Paper No.133. Cape Town: University of Cape Town.

Collier, P., & Lal, D. (1984). Why Poor People Get Rich: Kenya 1960-79. *World Development,* 12(10), 1007-1018.

Collier, P. (2007). *Poverty Reduction in Africa.* PNAS (Proceedings of the National Academy of Sciences of the United States of America), 104(43), 16763–16768.

De Haan, L. (2000). Globalization, Localization and Sustainable *Livelihood. Sociologia Ruralis,* 40(3), 339-365.

Eastwood, R., Kirsten, J., & Lipton, M. (2006). Premature Deagriculturalisation? Land Inequality and Rural Dependency in Limpopo Province, South Africa. *Journal of Development Studies,* 42(8), 1325-1349.

Ellis, F. (1998). Household Strategies and Rural Livelihood Diversification. *The Journal of Development Studies,* 35(1), 1-38.

Ellis, F. (2000). *Rural Livelihoods and Diversity in Developing Countries.* Oxford: Oxford University Press.

Ellis, F., & Biggs, S. (2001). Evolving Themes in Rural Development 1950s-2000s. *Development Policy Review,* 19(4), 437-438.

Evans, H.E., & Ngau, P. (1991). Rural-Urban Relations, Household Income Diversification and Agricultural Productivity. *Development and Change*, 22, 519-545.

Everitt, B.S., & Dunn, G. (2001). *Applied Multivariate Data Analysis*: Second Edition. London: Arnold.

Francis, E., & Hoddinott, J. (1993). Migration and Differentiation in Western Kenya: A Tale of Two Sub-Locations. *The Journal of Development Studies*, 30(1), 115-145.

Francis, E. (2000). *Making a Living: Changing Livelihoods in Rural Africa*. London and New York: Routledge.

Freeman, A.H., & Ellis, F. (2005). *Implications of Livelihood Strategies for Agricultural Research: A Kenya Case Study*. In F. Ellis, & AH. Freeman (Eds.) Rural Livelihoods and Poverty Reduction Policies (pp.198-212). London and New York: Routledge.

Hendricks, F.T. (1990). *The Pillars of Apartheid: Land Tenure, Rural Planning and the Chieftaincy*. Stockholm: UPPSALA, Almqivist & Wiksell International.

Hyden, G. (1980). *Beyond Ujamaa in Tanzania: Underdevelopment and Uncaptured Peasantry*. Berkeley and Los Angeles: University of California Press.

Hyden, G. (2007). Governance and Poverty Reduction in Africa. PNAS (Proceedings of the National Academy of Sciences of the United States of America), 104(43), 16751–16756.

Iiyama, M., Kariuki, P., Kristjanson, P., Kaitibie, S., & Maitima, J. (2008). Livelihood Diversification Strategies, Incomes and Soil Management Strategies: A Case Study from Kerio Valley, Kenya. *Journal of International Development*, 20, 380-397.

Jayne, T.S., Yamano, T., Weber, M.T., Tshirley, D., Benfica, R., Chapoto, A., & Zulu, B. (2003). Smallholder Income and Land Distribution in Africa: Implications for Poverty Reduction Strategies. *Food Policy*, 28, 253-275.

Jenkins, R. (2004). Globalization, Production, Employment and Poverty: Debates and Evidence. *Journal of International Development*, 16, 1-12.

Kates, R.W., & Dasgupta, P. (2007). African Poverty: A Grand Challenge for Sustainability Science. PNAS *(Proceedings of the National Academy of Sciences of the United States of America)*, 104(43), 16747–16750.

Kington, G.G., & Knight, J. (2004). Unemployment in South Africa: The Nature of the Beast. *World Development*, 32(3), 391-408.

Leibbrandt, M.V., Woolard, C., & Woolard, I. (2000). The Contribution of Income Components to Income Inequality in the Rural Former Homelands of South Africa: a Decomposable Gini Analysis. *Journal of African Economics,* 9(1), 79-99.

Low, A. (1986). *Agricultural Development in Southern Africa: Farm-Household Economics & Food Crisis*. London: James Curry, Portsmouth: Heinemann, Cape Town: David Philip.

McAllister, P. (2001). *Building the Homestead: Agriculture, Labour and Beer in South Africa's Transkei*. Hampshire: Ashgate Publishing Limited.

Ntsebeza, L., & Hall, R. (2007). *The Land Question in South Africa*. Cape Town: HSRC Press.

Pirouz. F. (2004). Have Labour Market Outcomes Affected Household Structure in South Africa? A Preliminary Descriptive Analysis of Households, Paper Submitted to the Conference "African Development and Poverty Reduction: The Micro-Macro Linkage" hosted by the DPRU and TIPS in association with Cornell University, Cape Town 13-15 October 2004.

Platteau, J-P. (2000). *Institutions, Social Norms, and Economic Development*. Amsterdam: Harwood Academic Publishers.

Raikes, P. (2000). *Modernization and Adjustment in African Peasant Agriculture*. In D. Bryceson, C. Kay, & J. Mooij. (Eds.) Disappearing Peasantries? Rural Labour in Africa, Asia and Latin America (pp.64-80). Warwickshire: ITDG Publishing.

Reardon, T. (1997). Using Evidence of Household Income Diversification to Inform Study of the Rural Nonfarm Labour Market in Africa. *World Development*, 25(5), 735-747.

Thornton, P.K., Kruska, R.L., Henninger, N., Krisjanson, P.M., Reid, R.S., Atieno, F., Odero, A.N., & Ndegwa, T. (2002). *Mapping Poverty and Livestock in the Developing World*. *Nairobi*: ILRI (International Livestock Research Institute).

Tiffen, M., Mortimore, M., & Gichuki, F. (1994). *More People, Less Erosion: Environmental Recovery in Kenya*. Chichester: John Wiley & Sons.

Tiffen, M. (2003). Transition in Sub-Saharan Africa: Agriculture, Urbanization and Income Growth. *World Development*, 31(8), 1343-1366.

Tittonell, P., Vanlauwe, B., Leffelaar, P.A., Rowe, E.C., & Giller, K.E. (2005). Exploring Diversity in Soil Fertility Management of Smallholder Farms in Western Kenya I. Heterogeneity at Region and Farm Scale. *Agriculture, Ecosystems & Environment*, 110, 149-165.

Welch Jr., C.E. (1977). Peasants as a Focus in African Studies. *African Studies Review*, 20(3), 1-5.

In: Poverty in Africa
Editor: Thomas W. Beasley

ISBN: 978-1-60741-737-8
© 2009 Nova Science Publishers, Inc.

Chapter 4

POVERTY AND MATERNAL HEALTH IN MALAWI

C.P. Maliwichi-Nyirenda[*,1] *and L.L. Maliwichi*[2]

[1] National Herbarium and Botanic Gardens of Malawi, P.O. Box 528, Zomba, Malawi.
[2] Department of Family Ecology and Consumer Science, University of Venda, P/B. X5050, Thohoyandou, 0950, South Africa.

ABSTRACT

A large proportion of Malawi's population is poor and unable to meet their basic needs. The country has not experienced a significant economic growth over the years to help eradicate extreme poverty and hunger. Poverty is one of the main contributing factors towards maternal mortality because women cannot afford conventional medical care. Malawi is the 13th poorest country with high maternal mortality rate of 984 maternal deaths per 100,000 live births. Although the government has made investment in health sector, most health facilities, which provide free services, lack essential drugs and equipment. Better services are provided by district and central hospitals but these are few and not readily accessible. People from rural areas are only attended to by district and central hospitals if they have a referral letter from health centres. In addition, private hospitals, which are fully equipped and readily accessible, charge exorbitant fees.

This study investigated, through participatory rural appraisal and questionnaire interviews, how maternal problems are managed in rural areas of Mulanje District in Malawi. Thirty three diseases were documented. There were mixed responses towards the causes of maternal mortality. Uterine rupture however seemed to be the major cause of maternal deaths. According to Ministry of Health and Population, uterine ruptures are caused by use of medicinal plants hence bans use of medicinal plants by pregnant women. Despite the ban, the study found that people still use medicinal plants. Trained traditional birth attendants, who are prohibited by the Ministry of Health and Population from using medicinal plants, were also found using medicinal plants. Thirty-two ailments prevalent among pregnant women were documented. Ten medicinal plant species used for six commonly prevalent maternity cases were also documented. Continued use of medicinal plants was attributed to inaccessibility of conventional health facilities, cultural reasons and poor reception at conventional hospitals. Despite being resource-limited,

---

[*] Corresponding author email: nyirendacecilia@yahoo.co.uk

traditional medical practitioners especially traditional birth attendants, undertake substantial amount of child deliveries (at least 1,100 per month).

It is anticipated that for as long as the problems facing modern maternal healthcare delivery services prevail, people shall continue to use medicinal plants. There is there fore, a need to investigate if there is any link between medicinal plant use and maternal deaths so as to facilitate the safe consumption of these medicinal plants.

INTRODUCTION

Maternal death forms one of the main challenges facing developing countries. Poverty is one of the main causes because poor women cannot afford quality healthcare and proper antenatal care [Lanre-Abass, 2008]. Matthews [2002] confirms that the most common causes of maternal mortality are linked to poverty. These are: anaemia and haemorrhage (resulting from poor nutrition) and abortion-related difficulties (due to failure to afford quality healthcare provided by private hospitals). Due to non-affordability of modern healthcare facilities, about half of all child deliveries occur outside these facilities thus making childbirth risky [Save the Children, 2008]. Due to the grave extent of maternal mortality, one of the United Nation's millennium development goals is to reduce maternal mortality ratio by three quarters by 2015 [The Health Foundation Consortium, 2007]. Techniques that have been proposed to be used in the reduction efforts include training of traditional birth attendants, antenatal risk screening and increasing skilled medical attendance during delivery [Bergsjo 2001, Bergstrom and Goodburn 2001, and Starrs 2000 as cited by Matthews, 2002].

Socio-Economic Status of Malawi

Malawi is one of the highly populated countries in Tropical Africa [Anon. 1995].

The country has 13 million people [National Statistical Office, 2004]. It is the thirteenth poorest country in the world with 64.3% of the population living below the poverty line of 41USD cents per person per day [Benson et al., 2002]. The entire population's health status is low [Ministry of Health and Population, 1999a]. Indicators include very high maternal, infant, under-five and child mortality rates and low life expectancy [Malawi Government, 1993]. Life expectancy has been reduced to 35 years from 48 years in 1990 [Ministry of Health and Population, 1999b].

To help people access medical facilities, the government has made substantial investment in the health sector such that about 80% of the population lives within 8km radius of free primary healthcare facility [Malawi Government, 1993]. Despite this investment, most of the facilities in rural areas lack essential drugs and laboratory equipment due to financial constraints. Better services are however provided by district and central hospitals but these are not readily accessible. Primarily, people are supposed to get medical attention from health centres. They are only attended to by district and central hospitals if they have referral letters from health centres. Sufficient services are nonetheless provided by private hospitals; but these charge exorbitant fees. This has resulted in most of the people relying on traditional remedies for solving primary health care problems.

Status of Maternal Health in Malawi

Malawi is one of the poorest countries in the world with a maternal mortality rate of about one per cent (984 deaths per 100,000 live births). In the local Chichewa language, the words used to describe pregnant women are 'pakati', meaning 'between life and death', and 'matenda', meaning 'sick' The leading maternal health problems identified among a population of 3171 women across 172 women's groups in Mchinji district were anaemia (present in 87 per cent of the groups), malaria (80 per cent), retained placenta (77 per cent) and obstructed labour (76 per cent). (Online) http://www.ucl.ac.uk/news/news-articles/0609/06092805 (accessed 20th Jan. 2009).

In general, older women from rural areas, women from the Central Region of Malawi, women with low education, women who are not working for cash, and women in the lowest wealth quintiles identified lack of money and distance as the major constraints to accessing health services.

(Online)www.measuredhs.com/pubs/pdf/FR175/09Chapter09.pdf (Date Accessed 16th Jan. 2009). Women and children living in rural areas are most likely to be deprived of basic information, health, education, water and sanitation. (Online) http://www.childinfo org/files/MICSLaunch_TheDailyTimes.pdf (accessed 20th Jan. 2009).

Women and children are a priority on Malawi government's developmental agenda. However, mortality rates still remain high during childbirth. Malawian women mainly die due to pregnancy and childbearing complications and high fertility rates. The fertility rates are one of the world's highest [Malawi Government, 1993; National Statistical Office, 2001]. Throughout a woman's reproductive period, she gives birth to an average of 7.6 children, thus putting her at an estimated lifetime risk of dying of 1 in 32 [Malawi Government, 1993]. With respect to maternity morbidity and mortality, the main causes are: anaemia, postpartum haemorrhage, common grand multiparity, lack of expertise in management of third stage of labour, large portion of high risk pregnancies, poor access to obstetric services and poor obstetric services [Ministry of Health and Population, 1999b]. Other contributing factors include low levels of maternal education, short intervals between births, type of assistance rendered to the woman during delivery, insufficient medical infrastructures and HIV/AIDS epidemic [Malawi Government, 1993; Maliwichi, 1994; National Statistical Office, 1994].

The Government of Malawi is tirelessly trying to find strategies of improving the health status of people through the "health for all" campaign. In terms of maternal health, there are efforts to improve the health status of mothers through the Safe Motherhood Programme. The programme is aimed at reducing maternal and child mortality through, among other things, creating awareness, at community level, of the risks of pregnancy and the need for utilizing conventional health services. The Government also recognizes that Traditional Birth Attendants (TBAs) are the major implementers of Safe Motherhood initiatives. The TBAs are part of traditional medical practitioners (TMPs). They are the only group of TMPs who have been fully integrated in orthodox/ western health care delivery services.

Poverty is one of the underlying factors towards maternal mortality because women cannot afford conventional medical care. Maternal mortality is estimated at 984 maternal deaths per 100,000 live births [National Statistical Office, 2004]. There are many cases where pregnant women experience complications like obstructed labour, prepartum and postpartum haemorrhage, uterus ruptures and even death. Contemporary doctors attribute some of these problems to use of medicinal plants for labour enhancement (Pitocin). Thus, the

Ministry of Health has been banning people from using medicinal plants in its efforts to bring down maternal mortality rate. Despite this, no research has been carried out to determine the extent to which medicinal plants are used in maternity-related cases. Besides, no study has been undertaken to investigate if people are following the ban. In addition, despite the majority of Malawi's population being poor, no study has been done to investigate how maternal health issues are managed from traditional perspective.

Objectives

The overall objective of the study was to investigate how poverty-stricken rural women manage maternal cases. Specific objectives of the study were to:

ix) investigate accessibility of modern healthcare delivery services
x) assess contribution of traditional medical practitioners to maternal health and challenges they face in delivery of their services
xi) investigate linkages between traditional and modern medical practitioners
xii) document prevailing maternal diseases
xiii) assess how the ailments are managed traditionally
xiv) explore possible causes of maternal mortality
xv) investigate accessibility of medicinal plants

METHODOLOGY

Study Area

The study took place in Mulanje District, south of Malawi (Figures 1, 2 and 3). It took place in villages that were readily accessible around Mulanje Mountain. Traditional Authorities (T.A.) Nkanda and Mabuka were selected because in the former, the district hospital is far away while the latter is closer. Two villages were selected in each T.A. i.e. Chipoka and Likhomo (T.A. Mabuka) and Kazembe and Nakhonyo (T.A. Nkanda).

Mulanje district borders Mozambique. The district is dominated by tea estates. Tea is one of the major foreign exchange earners for Malawi after tobacco. The district contains Mount Mulanje (also known as Mulanje Massif), the highest mountain in south- central Africa. It is 22 by 26 km in size and rises to about 3000km above sea level. The mountain is a protected area although its boundaries have been heavily encroached. The vegetation of the mountain is dominated by rolling grasslands and forested slopes. The mountain has numerous endemic animal and plant species. Endemic animal species include dwarf chameleon, skinks, geckos and birds [NASA Earth Observatory, 2009]. In terms of endemic plant species, Mulanje cedar (*Widdringtonia whytei*), Malawi's national tree, is one of the popular species. A timber species, Mulanje cedar is currently endangered due to illegal logging and fire [Bayliss *et al*, 2007].

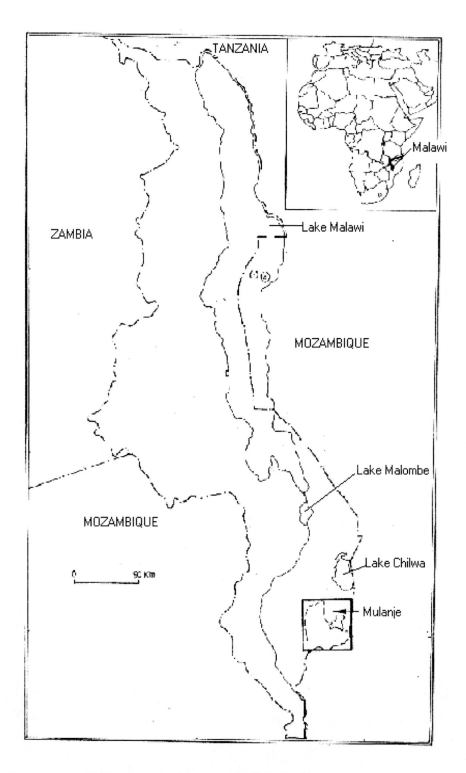

Figure 1. Map of Malawi showing location of Mulanje district

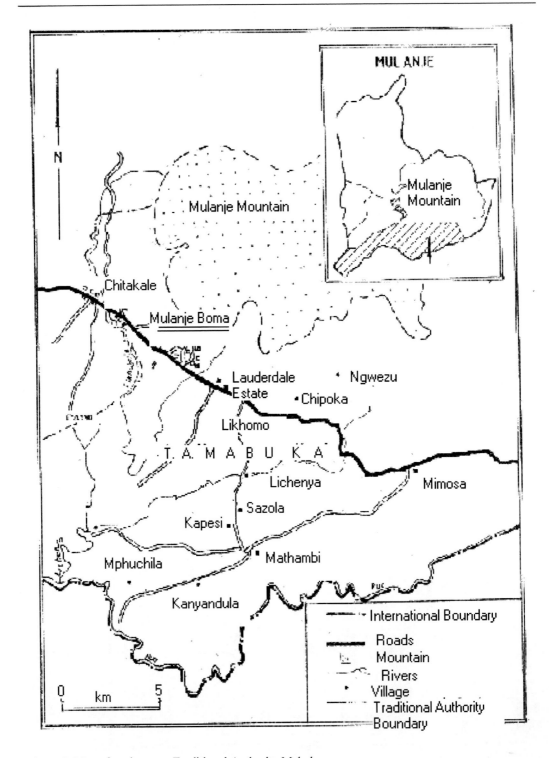

Figure 2. Map of study area - Traditional Authority Mabuka

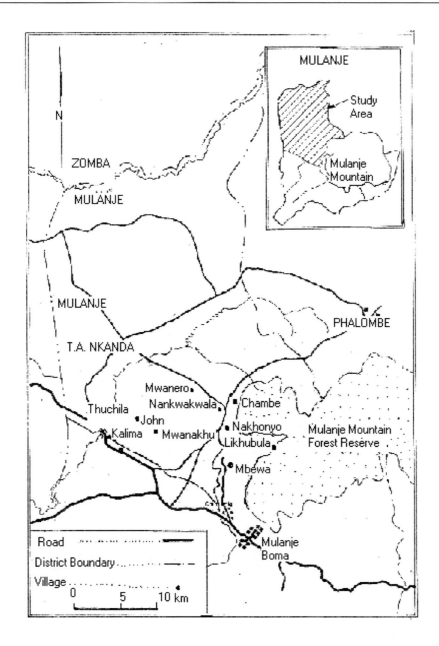

Figure 3: Map of study area - Traditional Authority Nkanda

Data Collection

The study was undertaken in 1999. Qualitative methods involving Participatory Rural Appraisal (PRA) were used. In particular, Focus Group Discussions (FGDs) were used. These involved sixty-one people from local communities, twenty-nine Traditional Medical Practitioners (TMPs) and twelve hospital staff. The issues that were discussed included: identifying main maternal problems; management of maternal problems; type of healthcare delivery service preferred; contributing factors to the choice of healthcare delivery service.

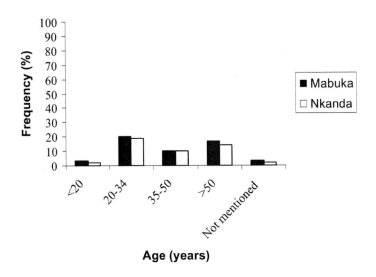

Figure 4. Age classification of questionnaire respondents

Quantitative research methods were also used employing semi-structured questionnaires. The questionnaires were administered to one hundred and thirteen respondents. Sixty-one of these were from T.A. Mabuka while the rest were from T.A. Nkanda. For questionnaire interviews, most of the respondents were aged between 20 and 34 years (~23%) and >50years (~20%) (Figure 4). With respect to focus group discussions, none of the respondents were aged below 20. However, in terms of marital status and religion, the scenario was similar to the one observed during questionnaire interviews i.e. the majority were married (Figures 5 and 6).

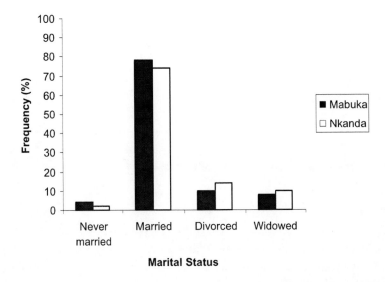

Figure 5. Classification of questionnaire respondents according to marital status

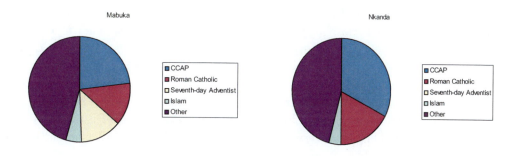

Figure 6. Classification of questionnaire respondents according to denomination

In terms of major denominations, most of the respondents belonged to Church of Central Africa Presbyterian (CCAP) and Roman Catholic (RC). However, a substantial number of people belonged to smaller denominations namely African Mother, Ambassador, Anglican, Assemblies of God, Bahai, Church of Christ, Jehova's Witness, Judea United, Providence Industrial Mission, Samaria, Topia and Zion.

Medical Inventories

List of diseases affecting pregnant women was documented in vernacular language. Corresponding symptoms were also documented in order to identify the ailments correctly. Conventional medical doctors were consulted to translate the vernacular terminologies into English / Scientific medical equivalents.

Plant Species Identification

Plant species used in treating maternal diseases were documented in vernacular names. Voucher specimens were collected and identified into scientific names at National Herbarium and Botanic Gardens of Malawi in Zomba.

Data Analysis

Data from focus group discussions was analysed manually by attaching it to similar information obtained from questionnaires. Questionnaire information was analysed using Statistical Package for Social Scientists (SPSS) Computer Programme. The data was coded, entered into SPSS and analysed using descriptive statistics to calculate frequencies and make cross tabulations.

MODERN HEALTHCARE DELIVERY SERVICES AVAILABLE IN THE STUDY AREA

There are three main healthcare service providers in Malawi. These are Ministry of Health and Population (MOHP), Christian Hospitals Association of Malawi (CHAM) and the private sector. In the entire Mulanje district, there were three main referral hospitals. These were: Mulanje District Hospital, Mulanje Mission Hospital (also known as Ulongwe Hospital) and Phalombe Mission Hospital. MOHP owns the district hospital while Church of Central Africa Presbyterian and Roman Catholic Church, respectively, run Mulanje and Phalombe Mission hospitals. The mission hospitals are under CHAM. Due to recent political demarcations, Phalombe Mission Hospital is now in Phalombe District. The District Health Officer (DHO), who manages the district hospital, is based at Mulanje District Hospital. The DHO has the responsibility of overseeing all health-related activities affecting the people of Mulanje and Phalombe districts and surrounding areas.

Apart from the main hospitals, there are twenty health centres and twenty-two dispensaries that play a big role in health delivery services. Of these, twenty belong to MOHP; sixteen to estates fraternity (under the private sector) and CHAM runs the rest (Table 1). In the healthcare delivery system, the lowest is a health centre followed by a dispensary and then hospital. The hospital is the main referral centre and it is the largest in terms of staff and equipment. The three main hospitals handle a wide range of health problems, maternal and child health inclusive, while almost all health centres and dispensaries have out patient departments which mainly provide first aid services like dispensing antimalarial drugs, oral rehydration salts and pain killers. Lujeri and Chambe are the only health centres that have maternity facilities and a midwifery nurse.

Apart from Lujeri and Chambe, all health centres and dispensaries do not have maternity health facilities and midwifery nurses. These health centres and dispensaries register the pregnant women that are within their catchment area. They later send them to the district hospital for antenatal check up. When due for delivery, they are given free transport to and from the main hospital. Postnatal clinics are however done at the health centres and dispensaries.

Table 1. List of health units available in entire Mulanje District according to funding agencies

Christian Hospitals Association of Malawi	
Dispensary	Chiringa, Thembe
Health Centre	Mwanga, Namasalima, Namulenga, Sukasanje
Hospital	Mulanje Mission, Phalombe Mission
Ministry of Health and Population	
Dispensary	Chitekesa, Kalinde, Kambenje, Mimosa, Mulomba, Phalombe
Health Centre	Bondo, Chambe, Chinyama, Chonde, Mbiza, Milonde, Mkhwayi, Mpala, Mpasa, Muloza, Nambazo, Namphungo, Nkhulambe, Thuchila
Hospital	Mulanje District
Private / Estate	
Dispensary	Chikuli, Eldorado, Esperanza, Glenorchy, Lauderdale, Likanga, Limbuli, Minimini, Phwazi, Makande (Agricultural Development and Marketing Canning Factory), Ruo, Sayama, Tea Research Foundation (Mimosa), Thornwood
Health Centre	Chisambo, Lujeri

Glenorchy, Phwazi and Esperanza dispensaries have dressers (these were initially ward attendants or cleaners in a main hospital but through experience have been upgraded to a post like that of a medical assistant). In the remaining delivery points, there are medical assistants (who have undergone general training). Excluding private and mission hospitals, all government medical services are free. However, child delivery is charged and it depends on the type of delivery. If it is normal, it costs less. The cost increases if an operation is made.

Mulanje District is the main referral hospital for all health centres, dispensaries and the mission hospitals. In T.A. Mabuka, people usually go to the District Hospital while in Nkanda they visit Chambe Health Centre. In terms of accessibility, T.A. Nkanda is far away from Mulanje District and Mulanje Mission hospitals. It is about 45 km and 60 km away from Mulanje District and Mulanje Mission hospitals respectively. T.A. Mabuka is nearer to the district hospital than the mission hospital (between 5km and 20km respectively).

Mulanje District and Mulanje Mission hospitals operate differently. In the case of Mulanje Mission Hospital, anyone can go to the hospital for medical attention provided she or he has money. Although the district hospital provides free services, people cannot get medical treatment anyhow if they have a health centre nearby. Instead, they first go to the health centre where they are attended to. If their case is complicated, they are given a referral letter which allows them to get medical attention from the district hospital. The referral letter certifies that their case cannot be managed at the health centre.

Mulanje District and Mulanje Mission hospitals have a variety of drugs, equipment and specialists. Therefore, they have the capacity of providing better services than any other type of healthcare facility in the area. For example, they are able to have long-term in-patients and they are able to undertake surgeries.

There are few government-owned health centres in the study area. These provide free services but they are smaller than the referral hospitals. Unlike referral hospitals, the health centres do not have specialists hence they provide basic healthcare services. They are primarily for outpatients. In T.A. Nkanda there is only one health centre, Chambe (one of the two health centres that provide maternity health care services). There was also one health centre in T.A. Mabuka, Bondo.

In terms of estate-owned health centres, there are two in T.A. Mabuka namely Lauderdale and Sayama. In T.A. Nkanda, there is one called Glenorchy. The health centres in T.A. Mabuka are within a distance of at least 5km and 10 km respectively. In T.A. Nkanda, it is within at least 5km distance. Due to the conditions laid out by estates, their health care facilities are only accessed by their employees and their immediate families (husband/wife and children). Nevertheless, the services provided are free.

There are also a couple of privately-owned clinics in the area. For example, near Mulanje District Hospital, there is a Marie Stopes-funded clinic locally called 'Banja La Mtsogolo'. It specializes in family planning services. It also provides primary healthcare services. Both family planning and primary healthcare services are on outpatients scale and the services are not for free. There are also individually-owned private clinics in the study area. Although these were not counted to determine how many they are, it was clear that there were more that government and estate-owned health centres.

By virtue of having government health centres, estate health centres and privately owned clinics in T.A. Mabuka and Nkanda, one would assume that the communities have sufficient health care delivery services. However, this is not the case because these have shortfalls. In the case of government health centres, although their services are free, they do not have enough facilities to treat most of the medical problems. Besides, they do not have experts to undertake major medical services like operations and there is bureaucracy of requiring a referral letter for one to be treated at a district hospital. Therefore, only critical patients have to be referred to the district hospital. In order for patients to reach the referral hospital, they use ambulances that are provided by the government through Ministry of Health and Population. Due to financial constraints facing the ministry, the ambulances are not sufficient. Coupled with the fact that Mulanje District is big and the road network is poor, the few ambulances travel long distances to collect patients. The arrangement is usually on first come first served basis (Maria[†], pers. comm. 2008). Therefore, once a patient is referred to the main hospital, she is not picked straight away. In some cases it can take more than 24 hours. Where the patient can manage to use public transport, some just use it to get to the referral hospital quickly. However, due to financial constraints, only few people can afford public transport. In addition, the public transport is not regular. The situation is complicated when it is a maternity case because the patient cannot use public transport if labour has started. Therefore, the woman has no choice but wait for the ambulance.

In view of these problems, the government of Malawi launched Safe Motherhood project to help pregnant women. The aim of the project was to encourage people to get prepared in advance (if one of the family members is pregnant) by keeping money for hiring a motorcycle or bicycle to ferry them to the hospital. Despite this intervention, people still cannot afford to keep money because of the high poverty levels that are prevalent in the villages.

In terms of Banja La Mtsogolo and individually-owned private health facilities, their services are very expensive such that the majority of the rural people cannot afford. Therefore, the affordable services are those provided by government-owned health facilities i.e. Chambe Health Centre and Mulanje District Hospital. However, due to the aforementioned constraints, people have no choice but rely on home-based therapies. In terms of pregnant women, they rely on Traditional Birth Attendants and Traditional Medical Practitioners who live within the communities.

In the case of estate-owned health centres, their services are not enjoyed by every person but only estate employees and their immediate families. This is difficult for people who live nearer to the estate-owned health centres than government-owned health facilities. For example, Chipoka and Likhomo villages in T.A. Mabuka. Since there is no government-owned health centre in the area, it means that pregnant women have to walk up to Mulanje District Hospital. Where they can afford, they can use public transport. Unlike women living in areas where there are government-owned health centres, like in T.A. Mabuka, people in T.A. Nkanda are at a disadvantage because they do not have a benefit of using an ambulance. Moreover, being maternity cases it is risky to use public transport in case labour starts while in transit. In such cases, it would have been ideal if the government was to negotiate with estates so that pregnant women and any critical cases could be handled at estate-owned health centres. By virtue of the estates being situated in places where people used to live (i.e. villagers were moved to remote areas in order to give land to estates), the estates have a social responsibility over the surrounding communities. As a way of compensating the villagers, the government could ask the estates to provide health delivery services to surrounding communities. The estates could also be urged to provide their ambulances to ferry critical cases which require attention at the district hospital.

[†] Trained TBA (not real name) based in T.A. Nkanda.

Despite the aforementioned constraints, some people still shun government hospitals. In the study area, many people prefer Mulanje Mission Hospital mainly due to the fact that they are better attended to by the members of staff than at the District Hospital or Ministry of Health and Population health centres where the staff is alleged to be rude. Even pregnant women in T.A Mabuka were found to pass Mulanje District Hospital and go to Mulanje Mission Hospital for antenatal clinics and delivery. The poor reception in government healthcare facilities is not unique to Mulanje. It is a country-wide scenario. For example, findings by Safe Motherhood Project [2001] stated that in Blantyre, Nsanje, Zomba, Phalombe, Chiradzulu, Mangochi, Thyolo and Chikwawa districts, pregnant women reported to be mocked by hospital staff during labour. The staff sings mocking songs, shouts at the women and even hit them.

By virtue of rural pregnant women not fully utilizing government healthcare facilities, it means they do not receive the needed medical attention during pregnancy. For instance, pregnant women (and babies) are supposed to get vaccines that are only available in main hospitals, dispensaries and health centres. A pregnant woman gets *Tetanus toxoid* to protect the unborn child from Tetanus infection while the newly born child is given BCG (used to protect the baby from *Tubercle bacillus* (TB) infection) and Polio 0 at birth; Diphtheria, Whooping cough and Tetanus (DPT1) and Polio 1 after at least six weeks of age; DPT2 and Polio 2 one month after first dose; DPT3 and Polio 3 at one month after second dose; and measles vaccination after at least nine months. DPT is for Diphtheria, Whooping cough and Tetanus prevention while Polio is for *Poliomyelitis* prevention.

All in all, the conventional health services are not enough because the majority of the people live near health centres or dispensaries that mostly render first aid kind of treatment. Coupled with the alleged rudeness of hospital staff and long traveling distance to main hospitals, most people are still disadvantaged from the investment made by various bodies into the healthcare delivery system. In view of these constraints, pregnant women have no choice but resort to home-based remedies.

CONTRIBUTION OF TRADITIONAL MEDICAL PRACTITIONERS TO MATERNAL HEALTH

Traditional Medical Practitioners, also known as traditional healers, comprise traditional birth attendants (TBAs) and general traditional medical practitioners (referred to as TMPs in this study). TBAs specialize in maternity-related issues while TMPs provide general medical treatment. The study found that TBAs and TMPs in the study area render services to people within Mulanje, neighbouring districts and as far as Mozambique. Most of the respondents mentioned that TBAs and TMPs play an important role in maternal health. All focus group discussion participants acknowledged that the role played by TBAs and TMPs was very important. Some of reasons mentioned were that these service providers are readily accessible. Moreover, where one does not have money, she or he can pay in kind e.g. chicken. Besides, the service providers are flexible in that they can provide treatment to a patient and they get the payment later when the patient gets the resources. For instance, at one TBA's place one mother failed to pay after delivering her child. Instead, she left her blouse and skirt as surety that she would pay the bill later when she finds money. Although services provided by traditional healers are generally lower than those provided by modern hospitals, some of the people still cannot afford [Maliwichi, 1997]. This reflects the situation at national level whereby most people in Malawi live under hard economic conditions. Settling of traditional medical costs in kind occurs in many poverty-stricken countries. For example, in Ecuador, most people fail to pay the bill in cash; hence they pay in kind [Baquero, *et al,* 1981].

According to the respondents' feedback, the general impression that they had was that the objective of the TBAs and TMPs is not to make financial gains like what the private hospitals portray. Instead, the TBAs and TMPs' priority is to serve the communities. The role played by TBAs and TMPs was also highlighted during questionnaire interviews. In both T.A. Mabuka and Nkanda, 92% of respondents mentioned that TBAs and TMPs were important because they cure mothers and children and they cure diseases that cannot be treated at a modern hospital. Examples of ailments that cannot be treated at a modern hospital include mental disorder and epilepsy. 7% of the respondents did not regard the services provided by TBAs and TMPs as important. They viewed the services provided by modern hospitals as better than those provided by the traditional healers. The remaining 1% could not determine the role of TBAs and TMPs since they had never consulted them because of their religion which bans them from using traditional medicine.

For the 92% of the respondents who regarded the TBAs and TMPs as important, they stated that their contribution to maternal health is the same because they play complementary roles. They mentioned that TBAs specialize in maternity-related cases which TMPs cannot treat. The respondents also said that the role played by TBAs and TMPs is similar because both parties have the same goal of saving people's lives.

The study found that the TMPs and TBAs' fields of practice are gender-specific. The TMPs are dominated by males. For instance, in T.A. Nkanda, 26 males were reported while in T.A. Mabuka there were 34 males. Of these, less than half were females. There were 108 traditional birth attendants in the study area (98 in T.A. Mabuka and the rest in T.A. Nkanda). Out of the 108 TBAs, only one was a male. The fact that the TBA profession is dominated by women is not unexpected. This is because culturally, women assist fellow women while men assist fellow men. The study found that the sole male TBA has been unable to deliver his services because women are not comfortable with him. He therefore trained his wife to carry out the services on his behalf.

The cultural resistance is not only restricted to traditional scenarios but also modern hospitals. For instance, at a workshop recently organized by White Ribbon Alliance for Safe Motherhood Malawi (WRASM) in Blantyre, Malawi, male nurses complained that rural women shun them by refusing to undress before them. The women also refuse to be attended to by a male nurse during child delivery [The Daily Times, December 2008].

All in all, the important role played by TBAs and TMPs reflects the real situation countrywide. TBAs and TMPs assist about 90% of Malawi's total population due to their ready accessibility and insufficient government health facilities [Msonthi and Seyani, 1986].

Child Deliveries Made by Traditional Birth Attendants Vis-À-Vis Availability of Resources

Mulanje district hospital records showed that Traditional Birth Attendants (TBAs) attend to about 1,100 child deliveries per month in the entire district. It was however difficult to determine how many of these deliveries were provided by TBAs in Traditional Authorities Mabuka and Nkanda. The study found that out of the 108 TBAs that were known by the Ministry of Health and Population (MOHP), about half of them had not received training. Therefore, these do not receive any assistance from the ministry to help them in their child delivery services. Besides, there are numerous TBAs who are still unreported. For example, during this study a middle aged and a 70 years old TBA were discovered in T.A. Nkanda. These were not yet known by the Ministry. The 70 year old TBA had trained her three daughters and three granddaughters who were helping her in the practice.

The MOHP identifies active and committed TBAs during under-five clinics by asking mothers the person who attended to their last child delivery. After being traced, the TBAs undergo training during which they are taught ways of handling prenatal and postnatal services and actual deliveries. TBA coordinators, who, by profession, are community health nurses, facilitate TBAs' training programme (Nkhata, Traditional Birth Attendant Coordinator, *pers. comm.*, 1999). During the training, the TBAs receive intellectual and technical support. Intellectually, the TBAs are trained to ensure that the tools they use are sterile and the place where delivery takes place is clean. They are also trained to have a placenta pit where they dispose of the placenta. They also get training in keeping records of their work. The records are periodically supervised by Mulanje District Hospital staff. The records comprise details of every delivery undertaken by the TBA such as name of mother, home village, number of children born at that time (e.g. one, twins or triplets), sex of the child/children and outcome of delivery (whether mother or newly born child/children are alive or dead). The trained TBAs further observe their clients through antenatal clinics and they also have a separate house where the deliveries take place. For instance, Maria (a trained TBA - not real name) has two separate houses that are solely used for maternity services. One is used for keeping pregnant women awaiting delivery and for actual delivery while the other is used for keeping newly born children awaiting discharge.

In terms of technical assistance, the TBAs get a delivery kit which comprises various items useful in child delivery (Table 1). The delivery kit is supplied by Ministry of Health and Population after a TBA completes training. The items are replenished whenever the Ministry gets new supplies. The period can be as long as once a year (personal observation). The TBAs also attend refresher courses periodically. Though scarce, sometimes there can be donations. In such cases, the TBAs get various type of technical assistance ranging from infrastructure, uniforms, pieces of cloths, ambulance bicycles and ordinary bicycles.

In the case of untrained TBAs, they do not have a delivery kit (or part of it), a delivery house or placenta pit. In addition, they do not keep records. To undertake child delivery, they follow their clients to their respective homes.

The differences between trained and untrained TBAs have made trained TBAs win people's confidence, hence gaining more clients than their counterparts. For instance, Janet (not real name), an untrained TBA in the study area lost most of her clients. They now deliver at Maria's place. However, such cases are only applicable where a trained TBA is readily accessible. Where trained TBAs are not easily accessible, women deliver with the assistance of an untrained TBA.

Table 1: List of items that Ministry of Health and Population supplies to every trained traditional birth attendant

Serial No.	Item	Quantity
1	2m Mackintosh	1
2	Basin	1
3	Bowl	1
4	Cord ligatures with spirit	Varies
5	Cotton wool 500 grams	1
6	Eye ointment	1 tube
7	Gloves	12 Pairs
8	Hand towel	2
9	Iron tablets	Varies
10	Lifebuoy soap	2 bars
11	Medium-size receiver	1
12	Nail brush	1
13	Oral Rehydration Salts (ORS)	10 Sachets
14	Plastic apron	1
15	Razor blades	2 packets
16	Record delivery forms	10
17	Referral forms	10
18	Shoulder bag	1
19	Soap container with cover	1

Practically, there is no difference between trained and untrained TBAs. Although trained TBAs receive assistance from MOHP, the assistance is not enough and it is not regular. As a result, the quality of the services rendered by trained and untrained TBAs is the same because they both lack necessary resources and infrastructure. For example, due to irregular replenishing of delivery kit material, trained TBAs resort to using locally available materials. For instance, during the study, Maria ran out of mackintosh and gloves. Instead she sew together several pieces of sugar bales to use as mackintosh for women to sleep on during delivery. Instead of proper gloves, she was wearing empty sugar packets. In terms of infrastructure, the MOHP does not afford to give trained TBAs delivery shelters. Thus the TBAs their own resources to have delivery houses. Due to poverty and the fact that they charge nominal fees[‡], the TBAs cannot to have delivery houses of good quality. For instance, even Maria who had many customers, she only managed to build two grass thatched houses, one for delivery and the other for newly born babies (Figure 7). The sleeping space is inadequate such that chances of infestations with lice are high since the place is most of the time busy and full. The sleeping mats are also dilapidated. The labour room is also very small such that it only accommodates two people at a time. Besides, all houses are poorly ventilated

---

[2] Initially, after a child was born at a Traditional Birth Attendant's place, whether dead or alive, the mother used to pay MK2.00 (1USD = MK68.62 as at the time of the study). This was gradually raised to MK70.00 per baby. If there was a miscarriage the payment was MK50.00. An additional MK2.50 was charged if the mother did not bring a razor blade for cutting the umbilical cord. The increases were made upon Ministry of Health and Population's recommendation.

because the windows are very small (30cm x 30cm size). This makes the rooms dark. In the room where newly born babies are kept, there is no window such that the door is the only source of ventilation.

Figure 7a. Front view of delivery suite for Maria, a trained traditional birth attendant of Mulanje.

Figure 7b. Back view of the Maria's delivery suite. Note the reed mat which pregnant women sleep on.

Figure 7c. A house where Maria's newly delivered babies stay awaiting discharge. The left hand door is entrance to a kitchen

A trained TBA is supposed to undertake antenatal clinics. For example, at Maria's place these take place every Friday. For one to start the clinics, the payment was MK20.00. The rest of the clinics are attended free of charge. If Maria has iron tablets, she gives every pregnant woman 7 tablets during the clinic. The woman takes one tablet everyday until the next Friday. If, however, the TBA runs out of the iron tablets, the women go without any. This is also the case with women who deliver at an untrained TBA. Although trained TBAs conduct the clinics, most women do not attend consistently. There are also some people who start the checkups as late as six or seven months. For instance, out of the fifty-nine respondents who attend to pregnant women, six (i.e. 3.0%) stated that their clients do not attend antenatal clinics until delivery time. Sixteen (8.0%) of the respondents reported that the women start the clinics when they are less than three months pregnant. Twenty-eight (i.e. 14%) reported that their clients start attending antenatal check ups when their gestation period is three to less than six months pregnant. Nine respondents (4.5%) start attending to their clients when they are six to nine months pregnant.

Similarly, the TBAs do not dispense any vaccines. For instance, at Maria's place since she started her work more than 20 years ago, vaccines have never been dispensed at her place. So far, a Health Surveillance Assistant of the area gave only two vaccines. To ensure that every woman and baby gets the vaccines, the Ministry of Health and Population urges them to go to the health centres. Even though this seems to be ideal, there are some associated problems. Health centre staff usually collects the vaccines from the District Hospital. With transport problems that exist in the district, the acquisition of vaccines by the health centres is not systematic because it depends on when hospital staff travels. This affects the time when either the mother or the baby becomes vaccinated. Since the vaccine is given at specified times, once the vaccine is not available at that time, it means the consumer will be disadvantaged. Considering the fact that most people live far away from a health unit, they can be discouraged to come again for the same vaccine. Hence it is likely that some do not receive all the required vaccines.

Despite the constraints faced by TBAs, most women prefer home deliveries with the assistance of a TBA. An indicator of this is long-term constant influx of patients at TBA's place. Independent interviews with the patients at Maria's place revealed that her clients like her because she is caring, kind, charming and committed. When some patients do not have food she provides them with some at no charge. She often spends her free time with the patients telling them stories and dancing with them. She is always ready to help even at odd times and often times she sleeps at the delivery suite rather than her own house. Despite T.A. Nkanda having Chambe health centre which has maternity facilities, many women prefer to deliver at Maria's place. Maria's records showed that she delivers 30-60 babies per month and she has never experienced any maternal death.

Challenges Faced by Traditional Birth Attendants in Providing Maternal Healthcare Delivery Services

The effect of poverty in provision of quality maternal healthcare by traditional medical practitioners, especially traditional birth attendants, is evident in the previous section. Coupled with poverty and the fact that the TMPs charge nominal fees for their duties, the traditional healers cannot successfully solve most of the problems they face since they are not on Government's payroll like the other health workers. Furthermore, due to poverty, they fail to provide ideal conditions for child delivery hence compromising on the safety and hygiene of the pregnant women and the newly born babies.

69% of T.A. Mabuka respondents and 82% of T.A. Nkanda respondents confirmed that all traditional healers face problems in their profession. The problems mentioned in T.A. Mabuka, included lack of appreciation by clients who do not pay after being cured (mentioned by 22% of the respondents), transport problems to get to places where medicinal plants are found and scarcity of the medicinal plants (19%), and lack of money to enable the patients afford transport to take them to referral hospitals after being referred (14%). The rest of the respondents (14%) mentioned the following problems:

i. traditional healers have multiple occupations such as subsistence farming hence difficult for them to concentrate on traditional healing
ii. lack of permits to enable the practitioners collect traditional medicine material from Mulanje Forest Reserve
iii. jealousy friends, relatives and other members of the public who make it difficult for the practitioners to succeed in their practice

In T.A. Nkanda, 36% stated non-willingness of the clients to pay after being treated as one of the problems facing traditional healers. 21% mentioned of lack of transport to enable the practitioners collect plants and follow up their clients. 15% mentioned that the traditional healers have multiple occupations hence do not have ample time to practice as traditional healers.

Collection of medicinal plant material is also a problem in Malawi particularly in rural areas. Coupled with environmental degradation, traditional medicine resources are now scarce. Due to financial problems, people do not afford transport costs. Consequently, people have to walk or ride bicycles for long distances to get medicinal plant resources although modern hospitals are within short distances. People are prepared to walk or cycle to as far as Mozambique due to poverty.

One of the frequently mentioned hitches faced by traditional healers was their involvement in multiple occupations. This is not only restricted to the traditional healers. Rather, it is a common situation countrywide. Malawi being an agro-based economy, many people rely on subsistence farming. Thus, they are involved in farming in addition to other jobs. The other reason for engaging in multiple occupations is to diversify income.

Collaboration between Traditional Healers and Modern Doctors

In view of the shortfalls facing traditional and modern medical healthcare delivery services, there have been some attempts to ensure collaboration between traditional healers and modern doctors. The efforts have been facilitated by Ministry of Health and Population. However, it is mainly traditional birth attendants (TBAs) who have been fully recognized since 1987 [Witte, 1995]. As mentioned earlier, the TBAs are given intellectual and technical support.

With respect to the Traditional Medical Practitioners (TMPs), the collaboration is in terms of public health programmes particularly HIV/AIDS and *Tubercle bacillus* (TB). In such programmes, TMPs attend training workshops organized by the ministry. During the workshops, the TMPs are advised to refer patients to modern hospitals for TB diagnosis when they cough for over three weeks.

31% and 58% of T.A. Mabuka and Nkanda respondents mentioned that there is collaboration between modern doctors and traditional healers. Although the aforementioned respondents affirmed existence of the collaboration, the rest felt that there was no collaboration. The 69% of T.A. Mabuka who indicated that there was no collaboration, mentioned that the following are the contributing factors:

i. the government has never created a conducive environment for the collaboration to take place
ii. the government is reluctant to have the collaboration for fears that the allowances its staff receive will have to be shared with the traditional healers
iii. there is no institution to unite the two schools of thought
iv. the two systems cannot collaborate because their practices are mutually exclusive

In Nkanda, the 42% of the respondents who said that there is no collaboration between traditional healers and modern doctors, mentioned of the following reasons:

i. modern doctors are pompous such that they do not want to collaborate with TMPs (mentioned by 34% of the respondents)
ii. TMPs are pompous hence they cannot agree to collaborate with modern doctors (mentioned by 10% of the respondents)
iii. each system believes its school of thought is superior than the other

The respondents however suggested various strategies that would make the collaboration effective and successful. These included:

i. the two systems should practice under one roof. This will enable patients access the two therapies at one place hence making healthcare delivery service readily accessible (mentioned by 33% of Mabuka respondents and 29% of Nkanda respondents)
ii. TMPs should be allowed to work full-time in hospitals because the aim of their job is similar to that of modern doctors i.e. saving people's lives (mentioned by 21% of Mabuka respondents and 20% of Nkanda respondents)
iii. TMPs should only work part-time to enable them go into the wild to collect traditional medicine resources (mentioned by 18% and 8% of Mabuka and Nkanda respondents respectively)

However, some respondents were of the opinion that there should not be full collaboration (38% in Mabuka and 33% in Nkanda). They mentioned that an agreement should be made between the two systems so that they only complement each other rather than practicing under one roof. They were against the idea of the TMPs practicing in the modern hospitals. They further stated that TMPs' prescriptions are supposed to be home-based hence relocating them to modern hospitals would create chaos. An example of such prescriptions was treatment for migraine headaches which involves beating of drums.

The respondents further mentioned pieces of advice which they thought would be useful to be considered by TMPs and modern doctors. According to the respondents, they felt that if these were heeded to, services rendered by both parties would be efficient (Table 2).

Although there is no full collaboration at the moment, most respondents were hopeful that collaboration would be an ideal way forward. This would enable the health-for-all strategy that was adopted in 1979 to be achieved. For the strategy to be realized, joint diagnosis is the most appropriate therapy as confirmed in Kandy, Sri Lanka [Aluwihare, 1982 and Chirambo, 1987]. In the context of Malawi, probably if the pieces of advice that were suggested by the respondents (Table 2) were to be considered, collaboration between the two parties would be effective. Nonetheless, some people do not desire full collaboration; there is a feeling that the approach used by the ministry is not attractive. The approach is seen as top-down in that the modern doctors dictate on how the traditional healers should conduct themselves. For example, the banning of TBAs from using medicinal plants. The top-down approach has resulted in lack of cooperation from traditional healers [Chikuni et al, 2002].

Diseases Prevalent among Pregnant Women

Thirty-three diseases were documented to prevail among pregnant women (Table 3). Of these, ten were mentioned in both Traditional Authorities Mabuka and Nkanda. The ten were: backache, diarrhea, drowsiness, gonorrhea, headache, high blood pressure, malaria, pneumonia, post-delivery stomachache and release of water from the vagina.

Table 2. Pieces of advice suggested by respondents of Traditional Authorities Mabuka and Nkanda aimed at making the services rendered by traditional medical practitioners (TMPs) and modern doctors effective

ADVICE	FREQUENCY OF MENTION (%)	
	Mabuka	Nkanda
TMPs and modern doctors should cooperate and be trustworthy	31	31
Both parties should render assistance to their patients quickly and lovingly	5	19
They* should be polite	5	14
They should work with commitment	11	6
They should give appropriate medicine to their patients	7	6
They should refer cases to each other	8	4
Modern doctors should not ill-treat patients	5	4
They should have enough supply of medicine	0	6
They should endure in their practices	5	0
Modern doctors should not ill-treat patients	3	2
They should be honest	3	2
Modern doctors should be dedicated; they should start work at the right time	2	2
They should hold meetings regularly to share information	2	2
TMPs should continue assisting their patients quickly	3	0
TMPs should continue being cheerful to patients	3	0
Government should intervene to ensure that the services rendered by the two parties are good	2	0
Modern doctors should not despise medicinal plants; they should appreciate that most of the medicines they use originate from plants	2	0
Modern hospitals should be brought closer to the people	2	0
Modern doctors should not look down upon TMPs	2	0
They should accept that collaboration cannot work because they belong to different schools of thought	2	0
TMPs should be clean to ensure that the services they render are hygienic	0	2
TMPs should refrain from telling lies	0	2

*They = TMPs and modern doctors

Causes of Maternal Mortality

There were differences in attitude between hospital staff and community members in terms of causes of maternal mortality. According to the former, uterus rupture is the main contributing factor. The hospital professionals stated that the uterus ruptures emanate from use of medicinal plants for speeding up the labour process (pitocin). This results into short-spaced but strong contractions which are beyond the normal body capacity. Although the hospital staff was not able to determine the medicinal plant species involved, they suspected *Ampelocissus* sp. or *Cissus* sp. (locally known as Mwanamphepo).

Table 3. Some diseases prevalent among pregnant women in Traditional Authorities Mabuka and Nkanda.

COMMON NAME		SYMPTOMS
Medical terminology	Vernacular	
Abnormal menstruation	Kusambamo movutikira	- Problems in menstruation
Backache	Nsana	- Weakness
Barrenness or infertility	Nansula	- Failure to conceive
Celebral malaria	Malungo aakulu	- Unconsciousness
Diarrhoea	Kutsekula m'mimba	- Passing out watery stool - Vomiting
Dizziness or drowsiness	Chizumbazumba or chizungulire	- Feeling dizzy - Falling down whenever standing
High blood pressure	Kuthamanga magazi	- Fast heart beat - Headache - Weakness
HIV / AIDS	Edzi	- immunity breakdown
Malaria	Malungo	- Fever - Nausea - Weakness
Nausea	Nselu	- having a nauseatic feeling

On the other hand, community members boldly refused that there were any harmful plant species. They reported that witchcraft, failure of the people to reach the referral hospitals in time (after being referred to by TBAs), and early pregnancies were the factors contributing to maternal mortality. They also mentioned that most often when people go to hospitals, they are insulted by hospital staff. Therefore, people prefer home-based child delivery. According to them, witchcraft causes post-maturity while failure to go to the hospital in time results in people attempting to deliver complicated cases at home. Furthermore, early pregnancies mean immature bodies becoming pregnant and failing to cope up with labour contractions.

Utilisation of Medicinal Plants

Due to the concern that most maternal deaths are a result of consumption of medicinal plants, Ministry of Health and Population (MOHP) discourages use of medicinal plant concoctions by pregnant women. Despite the ban, this study found that people still use medicinal plants for maternity-related cases. People mentioned the following reasons as contributing factors to the continued use of medicinal plants:

i. use of medicinal plants is a tradition that has been there since time immemorial hence it cannot be stopped now
ii. medicinal plants are cheap and readily accessible as opposed to conventional drugs which are expensive (where they are available) and inaccessible (where they are provided freely)
iii. pregnant women are insulted by conventional hospital staff hence they prefer to be attended to by traditional healers and traditional birth attendants (TBAs) who are kind though poor

Conventional hospital staff also confirmed that pregnant women use medicinal plant concoctions. They mentioned that they have had several cases where pregnant women had confessed, during antenatal clinics, to have used medicinal plants for various reasons. The most popular reasons for use of medicinal plants were to induce labour and hasten it. To curb this problem, conventional hospital staff mentioned that MOHP teaches trained TBAs to stop giving medicinal plant preparations to pregnant women. Thus the ministry believes that it is only untrained TBAs who give medicinal plant concoctions to pregnant women.

Contrary to this belief, this study found that even trained TBAs use medicinal plant preparations. Some of the reasons why trained TBAs use medicinal plant concoctions are due to the nature of their job and their culture whereby traditional medicines are part and parcel. In addition, the trained TBAs alleged that they had been using the concoctions for several years but they had never experienced any maternal death. Moreover, despite the ministry banning them from using the concoctions, the TBAs are not given enough medication to use when providing their services. Therefore, they do not have any choice but resort to traditional remedies.

The study documented ten plant species which are used in treating five commonly prevalent maternity-related cases (Table 4).

Table 4. Medicinal plant species reported to be used in treating selected maternity-related ailments in Traditional Authorities Mabuka and Nkanda

Disease		Plant species used		Part(s) used
Medical terminology	Vernacular name	Botanical name	Local name	
Anaemia	Kuchepa magazi	*Lagenaria sphaerica*	Sopa	Bark
Avoiding miscarriage	Kupewa mimba isatayike	*Ormocarpum kirkii*	Muimiko	Bark
Damage in the stomach for a woman who has just delivered a child	M'mimba moonongeka mayi atangobereka	i. *Pennisetum purpureum* ii. *Annona senegalensis*	i. Nsenjere ii. Mpoza	i. Leaves ii. Leaves
Miscarriage-related stomach pains	M'mimba mopita pachabe	*Vitex doniana*	Ntonongoli	Leaves
Post maturity	Kumangidwa	*Tragia benthamii*	Mzaza	Leaves and roots

Conclusion

The study has shown that it is difficult to access quality health care delivery services in rural areas. The contributing factors include lack of basic medical facilities in government health centres; poor reception in government health facilities; poverty of the rural masses which prevents them from affording expensive services rendered by private hospitals; bureaucracy which makes it difficult for the villagers to access referral hospitals if they live near government health centres; and banning of the villagers from accessing estate-owned clinics. These factors, plus cultural reasons, compel the people to use traditional remedies for primary healthcare. In terms of child delivery, they rely on traditional birth attendants who live within the communities. Reliance on traditional birth attendants is widespread in Africa [Musila, 2000].

This study has also shown that despite various diseases prevailing among pregnant women, most women resort to traditional remedies and home-based child delivery. The study has further shown that the role played by traditional medical practitioners (TMPs) in maternal health is vital. Despite the TMPs having insufficient resources, they still attend to many people. Their services are more of life-saving than making money. Although the role of TMPs is vital, there is no full collaboration between them and modern doctors. Lack of collaboration is one of the reasons why healthcare delivery services continue to be inaccessible to most people in Malawi. Tied with poverty, people do not have a choice but resort to cheaper services. Despite Ministry of Health and Population's policy which bans use of traditional remedies especially medicinal plants, this study has demonstrated that rural people still use them. It is apparent that for as long as these factors prevail, people shall continue to use medicinal plants. This is evident in the fact that despite some medicinal plant species being found in far away places, people still walk long distances in order to collect them. In addition, where modern hospital facilities are available e.g. Chambe (in Nkanda) and Mulanje District Hospital (in Mabuka), some people prefer to deliver their children with the assistance of Traditional Birth Attendants. There is therefore, a need to recognize the role of traditional methods in maternal health.

Although there were differences between communities and hospital staff in their attitude towards causes of maternal mortality, maternal mortality is a national concern. At national level, it is believed that the main cause is uterine ruptures. As this study has established, there are several factors that people believe cause maternal mortality. It is important that all possible causes should be investigated to establish the extent to which they cause mortality. Unless this is known, the prevailing high maternal mortality rates will not decrease. Alternatively, maternal mortality cases should be followed up to verify if any medicinal plant species were used. In order to make people cooperative, it would be ideal to create a friendly environment rather than demonizing traditional remedies. As the situation is at the moment, it is difficult for the causes to be established because the hospital staff put the blame on the communities while the latter blame the former.

REFERENCES

Aluwihare, APR. (1982). Traditional and western medicine working in tandem. World *Health Forum*, 3, 450-451.

Anon. Southern Africa Awareness Project. Lusaka: The Royal Netherlands Embassy; 1995.

Baquero, H., Sosa, R., Baquero R. & Pinto, E. Traditional Birth Attendants Training Programme Supervision, Evaluation and Follow-up Services. In: Mangay-Maglacus A; Pizurki H editors. *The TBA in Seven Countries: Case Studies in Utilisation and Training*. Geneva: World Health Organisation; 1981; 9 - 21.

Bayliss, J., Makungwa, S., Hecht, J., Nangoma D. & Bruessow, C. Saving the Island in the Sky: the plight of the Mount Mulanje cedar Widdringtonia whytei in Malawi. *Oryx*, 2007, 41, 64-69.

Benson, T., Kaphuka, J., Kanyanda, S. & Chinula, R. (2002). Malawi: An atlas of social statistics. Zomba and Washington DC: National Statistical Office and International Food Policy Research Institute.

Chikuni, A. C., Saka, J. K. & Maliwichi-Nyirenda, C. P. Traditional medicine and medicinal plants: research, practice and policy: Workshop report presented to International Development Research Centre. Mangochi, Malawi; 4-5 Apr. 2002.

Chirambo, M. C. Primary eye care in Malawi. *World Health Forum*, 1987, 8, 204-207.

http://www.ucl.ac.uk/news/news-articles/0609/06092805 (accessed 20th Jan. 2009).

http://www.measuredhs.com/pubs/pdf/FR175/09Chapter09.pdf (Date Accessed 16th Jan. 2009).

http://www.childinfo.org/files/MICSLaunch_TheDailyTimes.pdf (accessed 20th Jan. 2009)

Lanre-Abass, B. A. (2008). Poverty and maternal mortality in Nigeria: towards a more viable ethics of modern medical practice. *International Journal of Equity in Health, 7*, 11-19.

Malawi Government. Situation Analysis of Poverty in Malawi. Lilongwe: Government of Malawi; 1993.

Maliwichi, C. P. (1994). *Socio-economic Status of Malawian Women and its Implications on Maternal and Child Health*. Unpublished Undergraduate Thesis Submitted to Demographic Unit, University of Malawi, Zomba.

Maliwichi, C. P. The importance of traditional medicine in the health care delivery systems in Malawi: A paper presented at Medicinal Plants and Biodiversity workshop, Chancellor College, Zomba; 2-3 April 1997.

Matthews, Z. Maternal mortality and poverty. London: DFID Centre for Sexual and Reproductive Health; 2002.

Ministry of Health and Population. To The Year 2020: A Vision for the Health Sector in Malawi. Lilongwe: Ministry of Health and Population; 1999a.

Ministry of Health and Population. Malawi Fourth National Health Plan: 1999 - 2004. Lilongwe: Ministry of Health and Population; 1999b.

Msonthi, J. D. & Seyani, J. H. The status of research on medicinal plants of Malawi- an overview. Paper presented at the IFS workshop / Training course on Pharmacological screening on medicinal plant products, Harare; 1986.

Musila, W. A. Preliminary Survey of Medicinal Plants Used by Kamba Traditional Midwives in Mwingi District, Kenya. Unpublished Report Submitted to UNESCO, Nairobi; 2000.

NASA Earth Observatory. Mulanje Massif [online]. 2009 [cited 2009 January 04]. Available from: www.earthobservatory.nasa.gov/images/imagerecords/ 0/412/ aral_amo_2008229_250m_geo.tif.
National Statistical Office. Malawi Demographic and Health Survey Report. Zomba: National Statistical Office; 1994.
National Statistical Office. Demographic and Health Survey 2000 - Preliminary Report. Zomba & Calverton: National Statistical Office and ORC / Macro International Inc.; 2001.
National Statistical Office. Demographic and Health Survey. Zomba: Government Printer; 2004.
Save the Children. Statistics on the effects of poverty on maternal health and saving newborn lives [online]. 2008 [cited 2008 December 15]. Available from: http://www.savethechildren.org/programs/health/saving-newborn-lives/rates.html.
The Daily Times. Expectant women reject us, male nurses say. Blantyre: Blantyre Newspapers Limited; 2008.
The Health Foundation Consortium. Reducing maternal death rates in Malawi. Lilongwe: Unpublished progress report; 2007.
Witte, D. Mulanje district annual report. Lilongwe: Ministry of Health and Population; 1995.

ACKNOWLEDGMENTS

The authors would like to thank United Nations Educational, Scientific and Cultural organisation (UNESCO), for sponsoring the study. The authors also thank all who contributed to the successful execution of this study. Specifically, we would like to thank the following: Mulanje District Commissioner for allowing the study to take place in the district; the District Health Officer and matrons of Mulanje District and Mission Hospitals for offering a venue for focus group discussions (FGDs); members of staff for Maternal and Child Health and Public Outreach departments for participating in the FGDs; Mrs. Chingwalo for technical support; Group Village Headmen Chipoka and Nkanda and Village Headmen Kazembe and Nakhonyo for allowing the study to occur in their villages; Traditional healers and traditional birth attendants for providing invaluable information;

Dorothy Chilingulo (posthumous) and staff of Likhubula Forestry Office for providing a venue for interviews for research assistants; Hankey Pangani, Chrissie Mwachande, Mike Liuma and Ernest Lumbe for helping with data collection; Augustine Chikuni for assisting with questionnaire drafting and proof reading of the script; Shaibu Kananji for helping with questionnaire drafting, administration and plant identification; Mrs. Mwachande for offering to cook for the research crew; Dean Nyirenda for helping with financial reports; Messrs Chinunga, Kazembe and Kazeze for driving the research team.

In: Poverty in Africa
Editor: Thomas W. Beasley

ISBN: 978-1-60741- 737-8
© 2009 Nova Science Publishers, Inc.

Chapter 5

OYSTER MUSHROOM CULTIVATION FOR RESOURCE-POOR FARMERS IN SOUTHERN AFRICA

E.C. Kunjeku[*1] *and L.L. Maliwichi*[2]

[1]Department of Plant Production, University of Venda, P B X5050, THOHOYANDOU 0950. South Africa.
[2]University of Venda, Department of Family Ecology and Consumer Science, P/B. X5050, Thohoyandou, 0950, South Africa.

ABSTRACT

Oyster mushrooms of the genus *Pleurotus* are cultivated widely in the world, and are being cultivated on a large scale in most developing countries. However this mushroom cultivation technology has not been widely adopted and developed in most of tropical Africa. It has been neglected in spite of the advantages it has for the resource-poor farmers. Subsistence farmers often do not have enough land to produce crops on an economic scale, and often lack capital to initiate projects that require expensive infrastructure and investment. Oyster mushroom cultivation has the potential to provide food and also alleviate poverty from the sale of excess production. There is no requirement for land, and investment in mushroom house construction is minimal. Oyster mushrooms are primarily wood decomposing fungi, growing mostly in forest situations on tree trunks and wood detritus. However, they can be grown artificially in all kinds of environments and on various cellulosic waste products. The cultivation is done in built-up structures, and therefore the mushroom cultivation does not compete with field crops for space. The investment on infrastructure is minimal. Resource-poor families in Zimbabwe trained in this technology are cultivating oyster mushrooms as a source of food and also as an income-generating venture. Markets for the mushrooms range from boarding schools and hospitals to hotels. The other attraction for growing oyster mushrooms is that they utilize agricultural waste as a substrate.

Oyster mushrooms have a lot of similarities with wild mushroom which are a delicacy for most rural populations in Africa. They are a rich source of protein and vitamins, and are often used as a substitute for meat. In most of tropical Africa, wild

---

[*] Corresponding author Tel: +27 15 962 8078; Fax +27 15 962 8598. email: Ednah.kunjeku@univen.ac.za

mushrooms are picked during the summer season. They therefore tend to be a food source for only a limited time in the year, unlike the commercially grown mushrooms which are available throughout the year. Cultivation of *Agaricus* mushrooms requires large capital investment and specialized skills, and is not suitable for poor farmers. Wild mushrooms differ from the *Agaricus* species in their texture and taste. Like the tropical wild mushrooms, oyster mushrooms tend to be chewy, closely approximating meat texture. Oyster mushrooms are a rich source of protein, comparing favourably with meat and eggs. They are also a source of carbohydrates, minerals (such as calcium, phosphorus and iron), and vitamins such as thiamin, riboflavin and niacin. Various studies have put the protein content of oyster mushrooms from 15% up to 30% of their dry weight, depending on the substrate on which they are grown. They contain amino acids and enzymes that have been said to boost the immune system. They have also been shown to contain anti-oxidants that boost the immune system by acting as free radical scavengers. They are easily digestible, an essential component especially for sick people with sensitive digestive systems. They are therefore an ideal food for immunocompromised individuals such as people living with HIV/AIDS, as they improve the nutritional status as well as boosting the immune system.

INTRODUCTION

The Millennium Development Goals (MDG) set for the period 1995-2015 by the UN aim to reduce the number of people suffering from hunger and also to reduce by 50% the number of people living on less than US$1 per day. As at 2004, in Africa, 50% of the population was living below the international poverty line. In Sub-Saharan Africa, 33% of the population is under-nourished compared to 14% for the world and 17% for developing regions. 25% of the children in Africa are underweight and more than a third of the children are stunted. To meet the MDG targets, the annual GDP for African countries needs to grow by 7%, but by 2003, only 10 countries had GDP growth of 5% or more. The implication is that 42% of the population will still be poor in 2015 compared to the target of 24%. (IFPRI, 2004)

Poverty is the greatest cause of hunger in Africa, where over 350 million people in Sub-Saharan Africa survive on less than US$1/day. Over 184 million people suffer from malnutrition; 50% of the population has no access to health care. One in every six children dies before reaching the age of 5 years. Only 57% of the children are enrolled in primary education; and only 33% will complete school (IFPRI, 2004). As if the effects of poverty were not enough, 50% of all the war casualties in Africa are children (Smith, 2002).

Hunger, which is the recurrent and involuntary lack of access to food, mostly begins and ends with poverty. The FAO has defined poverty as "lack of, or the inability to achieve a socially acceptable standard of living, i.e., lack of command over economic resources; the inability associated with capability failure to participate in society" (Bellu & Liberati, 2005). Poverty is principally the inability to earn income to purchase food or the inability to grow enough food to feed the family unit. The primary source of livelihood for 65% of the African population is agriculture. Agriculture also produces 30-40% of the GDP and earns 60% of the export income. Over 90% of agricultural production is from the small-scale farms, and on these farms are found 75% of all the undernourished children in Africa (Smith, 2002). Many reasons have been cited as causes of hunger, among them low land productivity, inadequate infrastructure especially in the rural areas, vulnerability to natural disasters, high levels of insecurity due to civil conflict, wars and political instability; as well as the high prevalence of HIV/AIDS which has led to decreased labour productivity, erosion of assets and a blocking in the transfer of knowledge from one generation to the next.

Hunger is a consequence of food insecurity, the limited or uncertain ability to secure nutritionally adequate and safe foods; or the inability to acquire these foods in socially acceptable ways (Holben, undated). The main indicators of poverty are lack of income, lack of healthy living conditions and lack of status in the society. Poverty has been defined in terms of absolute poverty (referring to the barest minimum subsistence and minimum diet), or relative poverty, which places the position of people in a distribution. However it is defined, poverty varies with time and space, and is always linked to food security. Food security depends on:

- Availability of food, in terms of production, storage and ability to import;
- Stability, in terms of market functioning and integration; and
- Accessibility, in terms of purchasing power.

People are hungry in Africa because they do not have purchasing power. It is not because food is not available, as is often argued. The world produces excess food, but Africans do not have the ability and capacity to buy the food; they are poor and hence they go hungry.

Apart from food insecurity, the effects of poverty extend to alienation from the community and inability to participate in the community. Poverty also leads to fragmentation of families as members move away in search of ways to alleviate the situation. Homes for the poor, where they exist, are often overcrowded. The poor do not have access to health care, and disease is a problem that is closely linked to poverty. Stillwaggon (2001) states that pre-existing health conditions have a key role to play in susceptibility to disease, citing Louis Pasteur's quote: "the microbe is nothing, the terrain is everything". Malnutrition compounds the infection by parasites, and this is further compounded by lack of access to medical care. The HIV/AIDS pandemic has severe consequences for the poor. Between 1970 and 1997, Sub-Saharan Africa is the only region in the world to have experienced a decrease in food production. In countries like Zimbabwe, Kenya, Uganda, Zambia and Malawi, the protein supply fell by 15%, and these countries have some of the highest rates of HIV/AIDS cases (Stillwaggon, 2001). In many cases, HIV prevalence is strongly correlated with falling protein intake, falling calorie consumption arising from unequal income distribution, as well as labour migration (Stillwaggon, 2001). Parasitic infection and malnutrition undermine the body's specific and nonspecific immune response. Deficiencies in micronutrients weaken the immune response, while parasites deprive the body of these essential nutrients even further.

The Initiative to End Hunger in Africa (IEHA) was launched by USAID in 2002 and its aim is to help increase agricultural production and fulfill the MDG set by the UN. Some of the suggestions are that economic growth led by agriculture can be achieved through innovations coming from universities through science and technology programmes and also by linking farmers to markets and reducing the vulnerability of the poor to drought or floods, conflicts and market crashes. Increasing economic opportunities by raising incomes, improving health and increasing educational attainments are some of the ways suggested as ways to reduce poverty. Freedom from conflict and strife is also essential, as is empowering the poor through greater political participation so their voices can be heard. Seasonal variation in income has to be reduced. For example in Zambia, vegetable production has been seen as a way of alleviating poverty (Chileshe, 2007). Women produce about 30 bags of maize for sale per season (i.e. after 6 months) giving an income of about US$450 per year at US$15/bag. Producing vegetables year round produces extra income of about US$3 per week, earning an extra US$150 /year, which not only increases income, but reduces seasonal variation in access to ready money throughout the year.

While vegetable production offers a viable option to increase income, in most African countries, availability of extra land is a limiting factor to diversifying agricultural production. Innovations that require limited access to land as well as those that require low investment are essential to alleviate poverty. Mushroom cultivation is one of these options. Mushrooms are high-value products that can diversify farming systems, and at the same time mitigate climate change by utilizing agricultural wastes that would otherwise be destroyed by burning. Mushroom cultivation can be carried out throughout the year, thereby enabling access to income. Even though the artificial cultivation is labour intensive, this labour requirement can be met without difficulty by most families.

MUSHROOMS IN ECOSYSTEMS

Mushrooms, as with the other fungi, occupy an important place in the biosphere by virtue of being primary recyclers. They can convert dead wood matter and return nutrients to the environment. Apart from this, mushrooms are also a food source for many communities. Edible mushrooms are found in all the three ecological groups that are recognized for mushrooms: mycorrhizae, parasitic and saprophytic. In the mycorrhizae group, there is a mutually dependent and beneficial relationship between mushrooms and roots of the host plants. The mushroom mycelia increase the plant's ability to take up nutrients, nitrogen and essential elements, while the mushroom gets carbon from the plant's falling leaves. Very few edible mushrooms are found in this group. Parasitic mushrooms damage trees but they also create new habitats. This group of mushrooms lives off the host, endangering the health of the host. Few edible mushrooms are parasitic; most parasitic mushrooms have medicinal uses. The third ecological group is the saprophytic mushrooms and most edible mushrooms are found in this group. Most are recyclers and wood decomposers. Mushroom mycelia grow between cell walls and produce enzymes and acids which degrade large molecules into simple compounds and in this way are able to return carbon, hydrogen, nitrogen and minerals into the ecosystem. Primary decomposers have fast growing mycelia, which attach to and decompose plant tissue, especially wood, e.g. oyster mushrooms. Secondary decomposers depend on the previous activity of other fungi. These mushrooms grow from composted material e.g. button mushrooms of the *Agaricus* spp. Tertiary decomposers are typically soil dwellers that grow in reduced substrates.

Increasingly, mushrooms are also being used for bioremediation in the environment where they absorb poly-chlorinated biphenyls, pentachlorophenols, oils, pesticide residues and radioactive wastes.

Medicinal Mushrooms

About 1 800 species of mushrooms are known to have medicinal value, acting to reduce blood cholesterol, inhibit tumors, as well as stimulate the body's immune system. Mushrooms have been used as herbal medicines for a long time, especially in the Orient, particularly mushrooms such as *Ganoderma* spp, *Trametes* spp, *Lentinus* spp and *Tremella* spp (Jong & Donovick, 1989; Jong & Birmingham, 1992). They have been used for a variety of ailments, including as anti-cancer agents, antioxidants, anti-hypertensive agents, cholesterol lowering agents, for liver protection, anti-inflammatory agents, anti-fibrotic, anti-diabetic, anti-viral and antimicrobial agents (Jong & Birmingham, 1992). *Pleurotus tuber-regium* has been used as a cure for headaches, stomach ailments, colds and fever (Oso, 1997) and for asthma, smallpox, and high blood pressure (Fasidi & Olorunmaiye, 1994). *Auricularia* spp have been used to cure haemorrhoids and stomach ailments (Chang & Buswell, 1996). Studying wild mushrooms in Portugal, Barros *et al* (2007) found that the mushrooms had antioxidant activities due the presence of phenolic compounds and organic acids, as well as anti-microbial activities due to the presence of phenols and flavonoids. *Ganoderma lucidum* has been shown to suppress cell adhesion and cell migration of invasive breast and prostate cancer cells *in vitro* (Silva, 2003).

Mushrooms as Nutriceuticals

More recently, a billion dollar industry has arisen from mushroom cultivation. This is the nutraceutical or nutriceutical industry. Nutriceuticals are compounds extracted from fungal mycelia or fruiting bodies, and are regarded as functional foods with potential to prevent disease or have the potential to contribute to disease prevention. The definition of nutraceutical varies and includes nutritional supplements, health foods, or food supplements (Chang & Buswell, 1996), functional foods, supplements, natural and organic foods (Aryantha, 2005), or to encompass potentially healthful products as dietary supplements (Smith, Rowan & Sullivan, 2002). Basically the definition puts these products beyond traditional nutrients. Aryantha (2005) puts the value of the nutriceutical industry at US$180 billion worldwide, with US$860 million in Africa. If more of these mushrooms can be grown in Africa, this would be an additional source of income with potential to alleviate poverty.

Mushroom Production as a Source of Income

Mushroom cultivation is an activity that is carried out by both the young and old, in groups or individually. People from many tribes in Africa traditionally collect, eat and sell wild mushrooms. The high rise in inflation and the HIV/AIDS pandemic has caused economic hardships as the number of orphans, families headed by children, and teenage pregnancy are on the increase. Many developing countries are now encouraging small holder farmers (especially, women and youth) to start mushroom production projects to reduce poverty and to improve economic conditions through generation of income.

Mushrooms as a Food Source

Mushrooms are not strange or alien to African culture. Wild mushrooms are a delicacy for most rural populations in Africa, often being used as a meat substitute because of the protein content. However the wild mushrooms are seasonal, often being available in the rainy season only. Technologies exist now for some of these wild mushrooms to be cultured artificially in mushroom houses, which do not require extra land and therefore do not compete for land requirements with the traditional farming practices. These tropical mushrooms are a good source of nutrition, and additionally have medicinal value.

Mushrooms have been used as a source of food since time immemorial, especially in the Orient where they have also been used as medicines (Buswell &Chang, 1993). About 2 000 - 5 000 species of mushrooms are used as food. Mushrooms have high protein content, ranging between 1.75% and 5.9% of fresh weight. Even though there is no documented evidence of mushrooms being used as a food source and having medicinal value in Africa, oral history and folklore are full of anecdotal evidence on the use of mushrooms (personal; information collected during community engagement projects in Zimbabwe and South Africa). The prevalence and availability of wild mushrooms is being reduced because of changes in land use patterns. As more land is assigned for settlement and for agriculture, natural habitats of mushrooms are being reduced. The fact that some of these mushrooms can now be cultivated under artificial conditions makes the practice more attractive, not only as an activity that can be carried out throughout the year to generate food and income, but also as a way of preserving biodiversity. Not only will the mushrooms provide food, they can also earn income that can be used to purchase other foods. Additionally because of their digestibility, they can be used as a food source for people with sensitive digestive systems such as HIV/AIDS patients.

Mushrooms contain digestible protein, with protein content above that of vegetables, but less than meat and milk. Protein content in mushrooms varies between 10 to 40% dry weight depending on species as well as how the mushrooms are grown. Mushrooms contain essential amino acids, being especially high in lysine and leucine (Chang, 1991). Mushrooms also contain between 3 -21% carbohydrates, and 3-35% dietary fibre. They also contain vitamins, especially thiamine (B1), riboflavin (B2), niacin, biotin, ascorbic acid (vitamin C), and vitamin D (by conversion from beta-carotene and ergosterol through exposure to ultraviolet) (Buswell & Chang, 1993). Mushrooms have a low fat content, with a high proportion of the fat being polyunsaturated. *Pleurotus ostreatus* has been found to have anti-cancer and immunomodulating effects due to the beta-glucans which have biological response modification properties, as well as having lavastatin, a compound with cholesterol lowering properties, as well as anti-viral, anti-diabetic and anti-inflammatory properties (Gunde-Cinnerman, 1999).

PLEUROTUS SPP AS FOOD SOURCE, MEDICINE AND A UUTRICEUTICAL

Along with other mushrooms, *Pleurotus* spp have been shown to have medicinal properties. They have been shown to have antitumor properties, mainly due to stimulating the immune response. *P. florida* and *P. pulmonarius* extracts with methane, have been shown to reduce significantly solid tumors in mice (Jose & Janardhanan, 2000); *P. ostreatus* extracts inhibited tumors growth *in vivo*, and induced apoptosis of human carcinoma cells, and were the most effective when compared to other mushroom extracts (Gu & Sivam, 2006). The active components in these extracts are water-soluble polysaccharides. *P. ostreatus* extracts induced apoptosis *in vitro* in colon cancer cells. *P citrinopileatus* polysaccharide extracts decreased the number of metastatic tumor nodules in mice (Wasser, 2002). These polysaccharides are also present in *P. tuber-regium* and have been shown to have anti-tumor effects *in vitro* due to cytotoxicity and anti-proliferative effects, leading to apoptosis (Wasser, 2002).

Gregori, Svagel & Pohleven (2007) cite various other compounds apart from the water-soluble polysaccharides in *Pleurotus* spp that have antitumor properties. Proteins, proteoglycans and nucleic acid extracts have been shown to have antitumor effects *in vitro* and *in vivo* for several cancers such as sarcoma, hepatoma, and leukemia. They also cite immunomodulatory and antimitogenic activities in *P. citrinopileatus, P. florida, P. sajor-caju,* and *P. eryngii*. Extracts from these species have been shown to have immunostimulatory activities on cell-mediated immunity in mice, where administration resulted in increased number of macrophages, CD4+ and CD8+ cells. Filipic, Umek & Mlinaric (2002, cited in Gregori *et al.* 2007) found antigenotoxic and anti-mutagenic effects in *P. cornucopiae* extracts against some bacteria species. Antioxidant, radical scavenging and iron chelating properties were reported to be higher in *P. ostreatus* and *P. cystidiosus* than other commercially cultivated mushrooms. *Pleurotus* spp have been shown to have hypocholesterolaemic and blood pressure lowering effects, as well as having antimicrobial and antiviral activities. Hot water extracts of *P. pulmonarius* and *P. sajor-caju* have been shown to have inhibitory effects against (HIV)-1 reverse transcriptase, and a protein extracted from *P. ostreatus* showed anti-HIV activity (Gregori *et al*, 2007).

Nutrient Content of Pleurotus spp

In common with all other wild mushrooms, oyster mushrooms are a good source of proteins, carbohydrates, vitamins, minerals, dietary fibre and fats. In a study of four wild mushroom species in Nigeria, Adejumo & Awosanya (2005), found that the wild mushrooms had crude protein content ranging from 29% to 37% of dry weight, carbohydrates content of around 70% and crude fibre in excess of 7%. Barros *et al.* (2008) also found the crude protein content of five wild mushrooms species in Portugal ranged from 2.1g to 3.4g per 100g fresh weight.

The nutrition content of mushroom depends on the substrate used for cultivation. For example, Bonatti *et al* (2004) compared nutrient content of *P. ostreatus* and *P. sajor-caju* grown on banana waste and rice straw. They found that the protein content in both species was higher on banana than on rice (*P. ostreatus* 16.9g/100g dry weight on banana compared to 13.1g/100g on rice; *P. sajor-caju* 18.4g/100g on banana and 13.0g/100g on rice). Total fat tended to be higher in *P. ostreatus* on rice than *P. sajor-caju*, but no differences were observed on banana. Carbohydrate content was not affected by substrates, while the ash content was higher on rice than on bananas for both species, even though the values for ash are much lower than those from other publications. Bonatti *et al* (2004) reported ash content of 9% on average for *P. ostreatus* on wheat, while Dundar, Acay & Yildiz (2008) reported values of 35% ash for the same species on the same substrate. Patrabansh & Madan (1997) reported ash content of 18% for *P. sajor-caju* on wheat, while Bonatti *et al* (2004) reported ash content of about 10% on the same substrate.

Mushrooms have a low fat content and a high proportion of polyunsaturated fatty acids. Dundar *et al* (2008) reported a 72-85% proportion of polyunsaturated relative to the total fat content. Mushrooms also have a high content of linoleic acid, a polyunsaturated omega-6-fatty acid responsible for wound healing (Dundar *et al.* 2008).

Pleurotus Cultivation

Mushroom development is favoured by hot and humid conditions and under natural conditions, wild mushroom development is limited to the rainy season in most tropical and sub-tropical regions which have seasonal rainfall. The remainder of the year is characterized by a long dry season where humidity is low and temperatures are high. These conditions are not conducive for natural mushroom growth. Humidity is therefore limiting for mushroom growth in these tropical regions. In the equatorial region, mushrooms grow throughout the year. Successful cultivation of mushrooms depends on identifying a mushroom species from the natural world and growing it in an environment that gives the mushroom advantage over other competing organisms, such as other fungi and bacteria. Artificial mushroom culture draws heavily on what happens in nature at the different growth stages. A mushroom house, therefore, has to closely approximate the ideal climatic requirements: temperature, relative humidity, light and air exchange. The basic procedures for mushroom cultivation are the same across most species and are basically as listed below:

- Isolation of pure mycelium to use as starter culture
- Preparation of inoculum (spawn) by expansion of mycelia on agar media and then onto grain
- Inoculation of sterilized or pasteurized substrate with quality spawn
- Initiation of fruitbody (the mushroom) and its development

Each of these Stages has Specific Environmental Requirements.

The choice of which mushroom to grow depends on the resources available to the farmer. Primary decomposers, such as the oyster mushroom, are able to colonize and decompose dead plant tissue and are the choice for resource-poor farmers. They are not as capital intensive as the button mushrooms, for example. Because they are secondary decomposers, button mushrooms are grown on composted substrates. Secondary decomposers have strict temperature and air exchange requirements that necessitate construction of controlled environment in the growing rooms. Oyster mushrooms can also benefit from controlled-environment houses, but their cultivation is possible with less sophisticated requirements.

Understanding the life cycle of mushrooms helps in appreciating why certain procedures are carried out or why they are carried out at a particular time. However it is important to remember the following:

- Mushrooms are the fruit of the mushroom plant (the mycelia) and occur only briefly in the life cycle of the plant.
- Fruiting only occurs under optimum conditions of temperature, humidity and nutrition.
- The mushroom serves to perpetuate the species by the production of spores.
- Mycelia can lie dormant for long periods of time and only produce primordia following periods of intense growth when nutrients, temperature and humidity are ideal.
- Primordia formation is central to the yield of mushroom.

Important considerations in mushroom cultivation that we encountered in Zimbabwe are:

- Source and quality of spawn, and access to it
- Availability of substrate that is easy to process
- Investment in mushroom house
- Production level
- Disposal of the mushrooms. This is an important factor because mushrooms are perishable and cannot be stored for long periods in the absence of cold storage facilities.

Moisture is important in facilitating enzymatic reactions. Enzymes work in an aqueous environment to digest the available nutrients for advancement of the mycelium. In the absence of water, the mycelium will desiccate and die. Favorable pH and temperature are required for the growth of fungi. The optimum pH for most fungi is in the range of pH 6-7 and under natural conditions, the fungus can regulate its own pH. However, for a mushroom grower, the pH has to be regulated before inoculation. Temperature is very crucial especially on the stability of the enzymes being produced by the fungus. The ambient temperatures for most enzymes produced by fungi is between 25 -35^{0}C. High temperatures will denature enzymes; it also leads to high water evaporation hence desiccation of the mycelium. It should however be noted that the temperatures for mycelia growth are higher than the temperatures needed for fruiting. The low temperatures reduce mycelia advancement and stimulate fruiting. Aeration and light are important because oxygen is needed on all metabolic processes. In oyster mushroom, high carbon dioxide content promotes vigorous mycelia growth. Low carbon dioxide is very important for fruiting to occur in most cultivated fungi. Light intensity, duration and wavelength are important for fruitbody production. Fruitbody development is phototrophic.

For poor farmers cultivating mushrooms, all these conditions have to be regulated by the way the mushroom house is constructed. Mushroom growing structures depend on building costs, the type of technology/technique to be used for production (tray, bag, rack, column, mound/bed, log) as well as the physical requirements of the mushroom i.e. temperature, moisture, light, aeration and humidity. To minimize insect pest and disease problems, mushroom houses should be built away from potential contamination sources such as compost heaps. Since environmental conditions are regulated by the mushroom house, the design and construction of the mushroom house is critical. It can make or break the cultivation success. The general shape of the room should preferably be rectangular and should allow for good air circulation. A curved roof structure serves to reduce dead air pockets, but a roof can also be heaped or flat. For flat roof structure, care must be taken to avoid condensation. In Zimbabwe, we initially recommended that the basic structure be made of wood, bricks, concrete block or metal frame with plastic cover and with cement floor. Provision for water drainage should be made to allow excess water to drain, and this could be achieved through slightly inclined cemented floors. Wooden structures should have interior walls, ceilings and exposed wood surfaces lined with plastic or treated with enamel or plastic based paint to protect wood from water damage and to make the room airtight. Brick structure should have inside walls plastered and all cracks, seams, joints or crevices should be sealed. Most important feature of a mushroom house is the ability to maintain a constant temperature; therefore, a mushroom house should be well insulated to save energy and to be able to better control the environmental conditions. Insulation materials that can be used include Styrofoam (where farmers can afford it), plastic lining, as well as thatch roofs. The house should be made insect-proof to prevent insects from entering. To give farmer full control over the fresh air supply, provision for control of fresh air supply made through windows and door that have wire mesh. The inside surfaces should be easily cleaned.

Cultivation of *Pleurotus* spp makes up 14.2% of the total world edible mushroom production (Gregori *et al*, 2007). The main species cultivated worldwide are *P. ostreatus*, *P. pulmonarius*, *P. sajor-caju*, *P. cornucopiae*, *P. eryngii*, *P. tuber-regium* and *P. florida*. Other less known *Pleurotus* spp that are cultivated include *P. citrinopileatus*, *P.djimur*, *P cystidiosus*. *Pleurotus* spp are primary wood decomposers that are able to degrade lignocellulosic residues. They occur naturally in tropical and subtropical regions, but now they are extensively cultivated under artificial conditions using agricultural and industrial wastes that would otherwise be destroyed by burning. In the spirit of Zero Emission Research Initiatives (ZERI), a concept put forward by the United Nations University in 1994, this is sustainable utilization of lignocellulosic wastes. The concept as propounded states that "the earth cannot produce more: man has to do more with what the earth produces". Cultivation of these mushrooms therefore has the added advantage of being environment friendly, in addition to the lignocellulosic waste being used for producing protein rich foods, and at the same time reducing environmental pollution (Anon, 2005; Chang, 2007). The spent substrate can be used for feeding ruminant livestock (Albores *et al*, 2006) or to increase digestibility and nutrition value of wheat straw for animal feeds (Streeter *et al*, 1982; Adamovic *et al.*, 1998; Villas-Boas, Esposito & Mitchell, 2002). The spent substrate has also been used for biogas production. Bisaria, Madan & Mukhopadhyay (1983) found that spent straw from cultivation of *P. sajor-caju* used in an aerobic digester produced more biogas (100 l/kg) than untreated straw (65 l/kg), with more methane being produced (60% from spent straw compared to 55% in untreated straw).

When grown artificially, oyster mushrooms have the advantage of having a shorter growth time compared to other mushrooms. They also require few environmental controls. They are also much more tolerant of pests and diseases. They grow very easily and are much cheaper to grow than other mushrooms. At the cheapest, oyster mushrooms can be grown on logs, but the incubation periods are long and yields are very low. Production outdoors is also very environment-dependent. The type of tree also affects the biological efficiency, for example production on alder has a biological efficiency of 3% while on beech wood the biological efficiency is 21% (Gregori *et al.,* 2007). Artificial production can use any organic waste but some wastes such as sawdust require pre-treatment to get rid of inhibitory components. Supplements might also need to be added.

Artificial production can be on the shelf, in a bag, in a bottle, on a tray, or in a jar, but the most common methods are shelf, bag and bottle. Bottles tend to be expensive and out of reach of most poor farmers.

The basic requirements for cultivation are substrates that contain lignin, cellulose and little amounts of hemi-cellulose (pectin and starch). The substrate should have a high water-holding capacity, and also be able to provide air. The carbon: nitrogen ratio in the substrate is important, as is the cellulose: lignin ratio (Gregori *et al* 2007). The basic production steps are:

- Chopping or shredding or grinding of the substrate
- Wetting and pasteurizing, this can be done by hot water or steam
- Spawning at temperatures around 25oC under sanitary conditions. The spawning rate varies widely from 1% to 5% of dry weight of the substrate
- The spawn run, where the mycelia grow to cover the substrate, requires carbon dioxide and oxygen, and temperatures lower than the spawning (i.e. 15-20°C) and light.

SUBSTRATES AND SUBSTRATE PREPARATION

Substrate types as well as additives to the substrate affect the biological efficiency, spawn run and spawning periods and yields. The nutrient content of the mushrooms is also affected by substrate. While adding micronutrients and macronutrients can increase yield, this might be an added expense for resource-poor farmers. For example, adding manganese at 50ug/g increased the biological efficiency of straw (Rodriguez Estrada & Royse, 2007). A wide range of substrates has been used in oyster mushroom cultivation, ranging from agricultural wastes, through industrial wastes to weed species. Substrates can be used alone or as mixtures to improve either water holding capacity or aeration. The preparation of the substrates also varies widely. In general, composting substrates for oyster mushroom cultivation reduces the biological efficiency. Usually composting is carried out to reduce the number of competitive microorganisms. The indigenous microorganisms in the substrate metabolize compounds to generate heat and this leads to temperature increases in the substrates. The temperatures range from 50-70°C and these temperatures are maintained for several days, after which the substrate is cooled and spawned. This works well for mushrooms that are secondary decomposers like the *Agaricus* spp, but not for primary producers such as *Pleurotus* spp. Hernandez, Sanchez & Yamasaki (2003) found that the biological efficiencies for substrates ranged between 60% and 94%, depending on the type of composting as well as the composting period. In that study, the composting removed the need for pasteurizing the substrate that was made up of 70% grass and 30% coffee pulps. Calcium hydroxide at 2% was added for pH adjustment, which also impacted on removal of competing species.

Various weeds have been used to culture mushrooms. Das & Murkerjee (2007) used weed species to grow *P. ostreatus*. The weeds used were *Leonotis* spp, *Sida acuta*, *Parthenium argentums*, *Ageratum conyziodes*, *Cassia sophera*, *Tephrosia purpurea* and *Lantana camara*. Biological efficiencies were better on *Leonotis* spp than on rice straw when these substrates were used individually. However 1:1 mixtures of the two had better biological efficiencies. Not all weeds however were suitable substrates. In this study, *T. purpurea* was the least effective as a substrate alone, with a biological efficiency of 23%, which improved slightly when used in a mixture with rice straw.

Yildiz *et al* (2002) used agriculture and plant–based industrial wastes that are usually burnt or left to rot. Tilia leaves, aspen leaves, spruce needles, rice stalks and sawdust were used as the main substrates, with wheat straw, bran, sawdust, grass and gypsum as additives, and evaluated for biological efficiency and yield. The best yield and highest biological efficiency (121%) was when wheat straw was mixed with waste paper in a 50:50 mix. The second best was sawdust and hazelnut (50:50, biological efficiency 102%). The best biological efficiency for a main substrate used alone came from wheat (80%). Some additives had adverse effects, e.g. bran attracted bacteria diseases in that study.

Wang, Sakoda & Suzuki (2001) cultivated *P. ostreatus* on spent beer grains with success.

Shashirekha, Rajaratham & Bano (2002) used spent rice straw enriched with oilseed cake and found that mushroom yields were increased and the spawn run periods reduced. Vetayasuporn, Chutichudek & Cho-Ruk (2006) used bagasse, the residual cane fibre after sugar processing, in varying mixtures with sawdust. A 50:50 mixture produced up to nine flushes of *P. ostreatus*, with biological efficiency of 107%. A 75:25 (bagasse: sawdust) mixture gave the same biological efficiency but less flushes. Vetayasuporn (2007) also assessed cattails, an invasive weed in Thailand for production of *P. ostreatus*. Even though the weed is used as a food source, with the roots having medicinal value, the aggressive development of the perennial weed makes it undesirable, especially in the wetlands. The weed by itself is not a suitable substrate for *P. ostreatus*, with a biological efficiency of 45% and producing only three flushes compared to sawdust alone with average yield of 112g/kg substrate weight (biological efficiency 95%; 6 flushes, 537g/kg). A 75:25 mix of cattails and sawdust improves the figures somewhat (biological efficiency 56%; 5 flushes; 289g/kg). Shah, Ashraf & Ishtiaq (2004) also found that even though leaves were not a good substrate by themselves for production of *P. ostreatus*, yields increased when added as a 25% mixture with sawdust, almost equaling the biological efficiency and yield of sawdust alone. Sawdust tends to be expensive in some areas so a mixture reduces the cost.

Various other mixtures have been used. Zhang, Li & Fadel (2002) used a rice and straw mixture for *P. sajor-caju*, and found that rice straw produced higher yields than wheat straw alone, but that a 2:1 mixture of rice: wheat straw was just as good.

Supplementation of substrates with micronutrients has been tried. Rodriguez Estrada & Royse (2007) found that yields of *P. eryngii* increased significantly when manganese was added at 50ug/g in the presence of soyabean than in mixtures of cottonseed/sawdust without supplementation.

Preparation of substrates also varies. The substrate can be chopped or ground to produce various substrate sizes. The size of pieces varies between 2 cm and 5 cm. Zhang *et al.* (2002) found that ground straw gave better yields and had higher biological efficiency than chopping, and they attributed this to the fact that grinding ruptures cell walls more than chopping so that nutrients are more accessible. Growth of the mushrooms was also faster by 5 days on ground substrate than chopped substrate (Zhang *et al.* 2002).

The way the substrate is sterilized also varies. Composting has been tested to kill competing organisms, but is not suitable for oyster mushrooms. The most widely used technique for pasteurizing is heating the soaked substrate to temperatures higher than 55°C or alternatively soaking the substrate in hot water at 80 °C for 2-4h to ward off other saprophytic fungi which would otherwise compete with mushrooms during spawn run. Balasubramanya & Kathe (1996) placed punctured polythene tubes containing substrate in anaerobic digesters for a week to kill off competing fungi. They found this to be equally effective as the hot water treatment, but then growers would have to invest in digesters. Other alternatives to hot water treatment include steam sterilization (Yildiz et al, 2002).

PLEUROTUS CULTIVATION IN ZIMBABWE

A pilot study for cultivation of *Pleurotus* spp was carried out in Zimbabwe starting in 2000. The Dutch Government through the Biotechnology Trust of Zimbabwe funded the project. The targeted recipients were resource-poor farmers, particularly households headed by women. Traditionally in Zimbabwe, households are headed by men, but women become heads either because the women are widowed or their husbands have left homes to seek jobs in towns. Where these jobs are available, they are lowly paid and the husbands are not able to send money home; their earnings were not enough to support their stay in towns and their families back home. The pilot studies were carried out in the two poorest districts in Zimbabwe. A total of 12 sites were chosen. The village communities selected about six to seven deserving recipients who were also known to be hard working. The project financed most of the materials used in the construction of mushroom houses, but the participants had to mould bricks and contribute their labour in the construction process. This ensured that the farmers would take ownership of the project. The mushroom houses were constructed cheaply so that when the technology was adopted, the cost to the people would be low. The ultimate aim of the project was to improve the nutrition status of the villagers, particularly the children, as well as earn some income for the families.

The pilot mushroom houses measured 8m X 6m and were constructed of brick and mortar, with a thatch gable roof to maximize air circulation. However the gable roof had to be replaced by a flat one due to the expense of roofing timber. The walls were plastered with cement inside, but the outside was left as bare bricks. A ceiling made of Hessian sacking material was recommended to increase and retain high relative humidity. There were two windows on each of the longer walls and one each on the shorter walls to provide adequate ventilation. The windows had a wire mesh cover to preclude pests. A double door was recommended, the outer consisting of a wire mesh screen. Outside the entrance was placed a footbath to minimize contamination of the mushrooms. The floor was concrete and covered with about 2cm of river sand for moisture retention. Figure 1 shows the prototype mushroom house. Inside the house were timber poles running the length of the house spaced about 1m to 1.5m apart on which the mushroom bags were hung.

Various materials were used as substrates depending on availability at the sites. Substrates used were banana leaves, maize stover and maize cobs, soyabean stalks, groundnut stalks and shells, thatch grass and sedges. These were materials that were readily available in large quantities in the immediate vicinity of the project sites. Mixtures of these substrates were also used. The best combination of substrates giving the highest biological efficiency and yield was a 50:50 combination of thatch grass and banana leaves, which was better than either substrate alone. Supplementing substrates with groundnut shells or soyabean stalks and hulls to increase the nitrogen content did not improve mycelial growth; neither did addition of inorganic fertilizers. Addition of ammonium nitrate and ammonium phosphate delayed mycelial development. In any case, these additions would have proved too expensive for the farmers.

Before use, the substrate was chopped into 5cm pieces, or pounded into small pieces in the case of maize cobs. The substrate was then soaked in water overnight or for two hours, after which it was boiled for an hour. It was allowed to cool and then packed tightly into bags and a layer of spawn spread every 6cm. This was the equivalent of about 1% spawning rate. Both clear plastic and opaque plastic bags were used so that the farmers could observe the spawn run.

Figure 2 shows women chopping the substrate, and Figure 3 shows the substrate being pasteurized by boiling on a wood fire. Figure 4 shows packaging and spawning. Both *P. ostreatus* and *P. sajor-caju* were cultivated. *P. ostreatus* gave higher yields in summer months and *P. sajor-caju* did better in the cooler months.

Figure 1. Prototype mushroom house at one of the project sites.

Figure 2. Chopping substrate.

Oyster Mushroom Cultivation for Resource-Poor Farmers in Southern Africa

Figure 3. Pasteurizing substrate

Figure 4a. Preparing to spawn and package.

Figure 4b. Spawning and packaging

Figure 5. Inside a mushroom house

The floor of the mushroom house was kept moist by watering frequently to retain high relative humidity. The bags were suspended on the poles and the house was kept dark throughout the spawn run. Figures 5 shows suspended bags inside a mushroom house. Depending on the season, the spawn run lasted about 3 – 4 weeks. During this period, the house was kept in complete darkness. After the substrate was completely colonized by mushroom mycelia, holes were punched in the bags to allow pinhead formation. This was 5 – 6 weeks post spawning. Opening the house early in the morning for a few hours and again late evening reduced the temperature of the mushroom house. Pinheads formed within a week, and after a further 5-7 days mushrooms were ready for harvesting.

Keeping the river sand on the floor of the house moist and opening and closing the door and windows controlled relative humidity. Once the pinheads started forming, the bags were sprayed with a fine drizzle of water to keep them moist. Figure 6 shows mushrooms ready for harvesting. The first and second flushes always produced the largest yield, with usually four flushes being economic for harvesting. Under certain circumstances, up to six flushes were possible. At the end of harvesting, the spent substrate was used as manure for vegetables or as feed for ruminants.

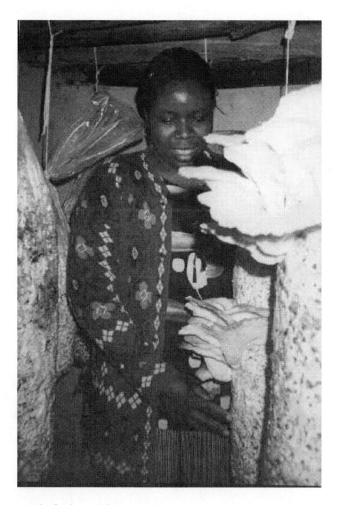

Figure 6. Mushrooms ready for harvesting

Adoption of the Oyster Mushroom Growing Technology

Once the mushrooms were ready, open days were held so that the communities could see. The mushrooms were used primarily as a food source and the surplus was sold. The mushrooms had a ready market from other members in the community, local boarding schools and hospitals. Even people from towns were driving to these rural areas to buy the mushrooms so much that the demand always exceeded supply. Once other people in the communities had seen the benefits of mushroom cultivation, demand for training also increased. The people who had adopted the technology were trained to train others. Even though the technology had been meant for people to use agricultural waste, the urban poor also started to cultivate mushrooms in their back yards using weeds or mown lawn grass as substrates.

In the rural areas, variations of the mushroom houses were constructed according to farmers' means. The photographs show some of these adaptations. Farmers reported that production from the mushroom houses was similar to production from the prototype houses. The rate at which the mushroom cultivation was adopted showed that the farmers were benefiting. After the substrate was spent, farmers used it for chicken feed, animal feed as well as manure for vegetable growing.

Rough calculations indicated that the cultivation of mushrooms was making a 30 to 40% returns on investment when all the costs were factored in. The farmers who adopted the technology reported being able to send their children to school and also being able to buy other foods from the proceeds of mushroom sales.

Figure 7. Alternative mushroom houses

Figure 8. Alternative mushroom houses

Challenges to Adoption of Technology in Zimbabwe

By 2002, the technology had been widely adopted so much that spawn production began to be a limiting factor. The University of Zimbabwe and the Biotechnology Research Institute which were responsible for producing spawn for sale to growers could not cope with demand for spawn.

Another limiting factor was the expense involved in pasteurizing the substrate. Using firewood for boiling the water was not environment-friendly. Other options for pasteurizing the substrate were being investigated, such as using sodium hypochlorite to kill off the competing species while the substrate was soaking overnight. The challenge here would be to identify a dose that does not kill the spawn as well.

Access to water became another limiting factor in Zimbabwe. Because of the requirement for high relative humidity throughout the cultivation, farmers had to ferry water frequently from the sources, and at some sites, the water source was a long distance away from the mushroom house. This is a serious consideration in most subtropical countries where there are often very severe droughts.

The preservation of mushrooms could potentially become a problem when supply exceeds demand. Mushrooms are 90% water and are also very fragile. The way mushrooms are harvested and the timing of the harvesting are both critical. Damaged pinheads are quickly parasitized by other microorganisms and fly maggots. Mushrooms are short-lived and decay quickly after harvesting, if they are not kept in a cool place. Mushrooms can be preserved by drying, freezing or canning. Freezing and canning are not options for resource-poor farmers. Drying is probably the most practicable under that situation. Mushrooms are essentially all water, and removal of water by drying stops all the life processes in the mushroom. The key to successful drying is removing as much water as possible, without introducing undesirable changes in the mushroom, such as darkening the colour. Drying should be completed in 24-48 hours, whether in open air (or using a dryer where available). Under most situations, the mushrooms must be cut into thin slices to quicken the loss of water. Simple drying racks can be constructed, the essential element being to allow air circulation. Once dried, the mushroom can be kept in tightly closed containers and under these conditions, they will keep for a long time if there is no repeated opening. Introduction of moisture in the containers leads to spoilage by moulds or bacteria, or infestation by insects. Dried mushrooms may be rehydrated by pouring boiling water over them and allowing them to soak for 15-30 minutes before use.

The way the technology is introduced for poverty alleviation in any country has a bearing on the adoption of the technology. Mushroom projects have been introduced in several countries in Africa; most through the ZERI projects with headquarters in Namibia. Other countries have projects that were initiated by farmers who requested training in the technology. One of the countries which had projects initiated by government is Swaziland, where farmers were supplied spawn-impregnated bags in the pilot phase. Farmers took the bags to their mushroom houses and tended them. Initially the project seemed to be working well as the distribution centres bore most of the production costs. The distribution centres themselves were using sugarcane bagasse as substrate, and initially this was free as the milling companies were throwing the bagasse away. However, as soon as the companies realized that their waste was being used for economic production, they started using it for other purposes. The distribution centres had to find other substrates or pay for the bagasse. By 2002, the technology in that format had to end, and a farmer driven initiative is being investigated (Choi, 2004).

Conclusion

Based on the Zimbabwe experience, oyster mushroom cultivation has the potential to reduce poverty in many parts of Africa. The technology is easy to grasp. The investment is low, although the labour requirements are quite high. A range of substrates can be used in the cultivation depending on availability. They could be industrial wastes or agricultural residues. Weeds can also be used, especially invasive weed species such as the water hyacinth. Mushrooms have the potential to alleviate poverty in addition to providing food. Additionally, growing other mushroom species that have nutriceutical values can be considered, especially in view of the emerging market for nutriceuticals. Even though the cultivation is labour-intensive, most households have enough labour within the family unit to make cultivation possible. For cultivation for the nutraceutical industry, families can pool their production to satisfy a larger market requirement.

Acknowledgments

Information on mushroom cultivation in Zimbabwe draws heavily on experiences on the mushroom project funded by the Biotechnology Trust of Zimbabwe while one of the authors (ECK) was principal investigator of the project. The work was carried out by staff and students from the Department of Biological Sciences (University of Zimbabwe) in conjunction with research staff from the Biotechnology Research Institute (Scientific & Industrial Research and Development Centre).

REFERENCES

Adamovic, M., Grubic, G., Milenkovic, I., Jovanovic, R., Protic, R., Stretenovic, L & Stoicevic, L. (1998). The biodegradation of wheat straw by *Pleurotus ostreatus* mushrooms and its use in cattle feeding. *Animal Feed Science and Technology 71*:357-362.

Adejumo, T. O. & Awosanya, O. B. (2005). Proximate and mineral composition of four edible mushroom species from South Western Nigeria. *African Journal of Biotechnology 4* (10): 1084-1088.

Albores, S., Pianzzola, M.J., Soubes, M. & Cerdeiras, M.P. (2006). Biodegradation of agroindustrial wastes by *Pleurotus* spp for its use as ruminant feed. *Electronic Journal of Biotechnology 9 (3)*: 215-220.

Alicbusan, R V. Mushroom production technology for rural development. www.unu.edu/unupress/unupbooks/80434e/80434E0m.htm. Accessed 21 November 2008.

Anon. ZERI Regional Project for Africa. Annual Report 2005.

Aryantha, I. N. P. (2005). Development of nutriceutical based on Indonesian edible mushrooms. www.sith.itb.ac.id/mgbm. Accessed 20 November 2008.

Balasubramanya, R. H. & Kathe, A. A. (1996). An inexpensive pretreatment of cellulosic materials for growing edible oyster mushrooms. *Bioresource Technology 57*: 303-305.

Barros, L., Baptista, P, Correia, D. M., Casal, S., Oliveira B. & Ferreira, I. C. F. R. (2007). Fatty acid and sugar compositions, and nutritional value of five wild edible mushrooms from Northeast Portugal. *Food Chemistry 105*: 140-145.

Barros, L., Cruz, T., Baptista, P., Estevinho, L.M. & Ferreira, I.C.F.R. (2008). Wild and commercial mushrooms as sources of nutrients and nutraceuticals. *Food & Chemical Toxicology 46*: 2242-2747.

Bellu, L.G. & Liberati, P. (2005). Impacts of policies on poverty: The definition of poverty. FAO. From www.fao.org/tc/easypol. Accessed 15 November 2008.

Bisaria, R., Madan, M. & Mukhopadhyay, S. N. (1983). Production of biogas from residues from mushroom cultivation. *Biotechnology Letters 5(12)*: 811-812.

Bonatti, M., Karnopp, P., Soares, H. M. & Furlan, S.A. (2004). Evaluation of *Pleurotus ostreatus* and *Pleurotus sajor-caju* nutritional characteristics when cultivated in different lignocellulosic wastes. *Food Chemistry 88*: 425-428.

Chang, S.T. & Buswell, J.A.B. (1996). Mushroom nutriceuticals. *World Journal of Microbiology & Biotechnology 12*: 473-476.

Chang, S.T. (2007). Mushroom cultivation using the "ZERI" principle: Potential for application in Brazil. *Micologia Aplicada International 19 (2)*: 33-34.

Chang, S.T., Lau, O.W. & Cho. K.Y. (1981). The cultivation and nutritional value of *Pleurotus sajor caju*. *Applied Microbiology & Biotechnology 12*: 58-62.

Chang. 1991. Cultivated mushrooms. In *Handbook of Applied Mycology 3*: 221-240. Marcel Dekker, New York.

Chileshe, D. (2007). Vegetable Business- a way out of poverty. From: http://ipsnews.net/fao_magazine/vegetable.shtml. Accessed 15 November 2008.

Choi, K.W. (2004). Mushroom Project in Swaziland: a government initiated mushroom bag distribution center. Chapter 2 in Mushroom Growers Handbook 1: Oyster Mushroom Cultivation. MushWorld.

Das, N. & Mukherjee, M. (2007). Cultivation of *Pleurotus ostreatus* on weed plants. *Bioresource Technology 98*:2723-2726.

Dundar, A., Acay, H. & Yildiz, A. (2008). Yield performance and nutritional contents of three oyster mushroom species cultivated on wheat stalk. *African Journal of Biotechnology 7 (19)*: 3497-3501.

Fasidi, I A. & Olorunmaiye, K. S. (1994). Studies on the requirements for vegetative growth of *Pleurotus tuber-regium* (Fr.) Singer, a Nigerian mushroom. *Food Chemistry 50*: 397-401.

Gregori, A.,Svagel, M. & Pohleven, J. (2007). Cultivation techniques and medicinal properties of *Pleurotus* spp. *Food Technology and Biotechnology 45(3)*: 238-249.

Gu, Y.H. & Sivam, G. (2006). Cytotoxic effect of oyster mushroom *Pleurotus ostreatus* on human androgen-independent prostate cancer PC-3 cells. *Journal of Medicinal Foods 9*: 196-204.

Gunde-Cimerman, N. (1999). Medicinal value of the genus *Pleurotus* (Fr.) P.Karst (Agaricales S.I. Basidiomycetes). *International Journal of Medicinal Mushrooms 1*: 69-80.

Hernandez, D., Sanchez, J E. & Yamasaki, K. (2003). A simple procedure for preparing substrate for *Pleurotus ostreatus* cultivation. Bioresource Technology 90: 145-150.

Holben, D.H. (undated). The concept and definition of hunger and its relationship to food insecurity.

IFPRI. International Food Policy Research Institute (2004). Ending hunger in Africa: prospects for the small scale farmer. From www.ifpri.org. Accessed 01 November 2008.

Jong, S.C. & Birmingham, J. M. (1992). Medicinal benefits of the mushroom *Ganoderma*. *Advances in Applied Microbiology 37*: 101-134

Jong, S.C. & Donovick, R. (1989). Antitumor and antiviral substances from fungi. *Advances in Applied Microbiology 34*: 183-262.

Jose, N. & Janardhanan, K. K. (2000). Antioxidant and antitumor activity of *Pleurotus florida*. *Current Science 79*: 941-943.

Oso, B.A. (1977). *Pleurotus tuber-regium* from Nigeria. *Mycologia 69*: 271-279.

Patrabansh, S. & Madan, M. (1997). Studies on cultivation, biological efficiency and chemical analysis of *Pleurotus sajor-caju* (Fr.) Singer on different bio-wastes. *Acta Biotechnology 17*: 107-122.

Rodriguez Estrada, A. E. & Royse, D .J. (2007). Yield, size and bacterial blotch resistance of *Pleurotus eryngii* grown on cottonseed hulls/oak sawdust supplemented with manganese, copper and whole ground soyabean. *Bioresource Technology 98*: 1898-1906.

Shah, ZA, Ashraf, M. & Ishtiaq C.H. (2004). Comparative study on cultivation and yield performance of oyster mushroom (*Pleurotus ostreatus*) on different substrates (wheat straw, leaves, saw dust). *Pakistan Journal of Nutrition 3(3)*: 158-160.

Shashirekha, M N., Rajaratham, S. & Bano, Z. (2002). Enhancement of bioconversion efficiency and chemistry of the mushroom, *Pleurotus sajor-caju* (Berk and Br.) Sacc. produced on spent rice straw substrate, supplemented with oil seed cakes. *Food Chemistry 76*: 27-31.

Silva, D. (2003). *Ganoderma lucidum* (Reishi) in cancer treatment. *Interactive Cancer Therapies 2 (4)*: 358-364.

Smith, J. (2002). Facts on poverty in Africa. From www.helium.com/items/989607-facts-on-poverty-in-africa. Accessed 11 November 2008.

Smith, J. E., Rowan, N. J. & Sullivan, R. (2002). Medicinal mushrooms: a rapidly developing area of biotechnology for cancer therapy and other bioactivities. *Biotechnology Letters 24*: 1839-1845.

Stillwaggon, E. (2001). AIDS and poverty in Africa. From www.thenation.com/doc/20010521/stillwagon. Accessed 20 November 2008.

Streeter, C. L., Conway, K. E., Horn, G. W. & Mader, T. L. (1982). Nutritional evaluation of wheat straw incubated with the edible mushroom, *Pleurotus ostreatus*. *Journal of Animal Science 54*: 183-188.

Vetayasuporn, S. (2007). Using cattails (*Typha latifolia*) as a substrate for *Pleurotus ostreatus* (Fr.) Kummer Cultivation. *Journal of Biological Sciences 7* (1): 218-221.

Vetayasuporn, S., Chutichudet, P & Cho-Ruk, K. (2006). Bagasse as a possible substrate for *Pleurotus ostreatus* (Fr.) Kummer Cultivation for local mushroom farms in the Northeast of Thailand. *Pakistan Journal of Biological Sciences 9*: 2512-2515.

Villas-Boas, S G., Esposito, E. & Mitchell, D A. (2002). Microbial conversion of lignocellulosic residues for production of animal feeds. *Animal Feed Science and Technology 98*: 1-12.

Wang, D., Sakoda, A. & Suzuki. M. 2001. Biological efficiency and nutritional value of *Pleurotus ostreatus* cultivated on spent beer grain. *Bioresource Technology 78*: 293-300

Wasser, S. P. (2002). Medicinal mushroom as a source of antitumor and immunomodulation polysaccharides. *Applied Microbiology and Biotechnology 60*: 258-274.

Yildiz, S., Yildiz, U. C., Gezer, E. D. & Temiz, A. (2002). Some lignocellulosic wastes used as raw material in cultivation of the *Pleurotus ostreatus* mushroom. *Process Biochemistry 38*: 301-306.

Zhang, R., Li, X. & Fadel, J.G. (2002). Oyster mushroom cultivation with rice and wheat straw. *Bioresource Technology 82*:277-284.

In: Poverty in Africa
Editor: Thomas W. Beasley

ISBN: 978-1-60741-737-8
© 2009 Nova Science Publishers, Inc.

Chapter 6

CHINESE POLICIES TOWARDS AFRICA: POVERTY ALLEVIATING OR POVERTY PROMOTING?

Jacqueline M. Musiitwa
Esq., Adjunct Professor of International Law at Central Michigan University, USA

ABSTRACT

Rationale

Over the past few decades poverty has emerged as a global problem and a global agenda item in need of action. For that reason, the United Nations made its eradication the first Millennium Development Goal (MDG). The MDGs' plan is for extreme poverty to be eliminated by 2015. Poverty is more of a concern on the African continent than elsewhere. As China's involvement in Africa increases, China has been forced to deal with the issue of poverty. Although China's interest in Africa started with its interest in acquiring natural resources and extending its geopolical influence, due to poverty and other development issues that end up affecting trade, China has since developed a donor-recipient relationship with Africa. Despite China's involvement in development and poverty alleviation, there is a strong argument that China's assistance acts as a double-edged sword because on the one hand China participates in poverty alleviation and on the other hand it engages in practices that create and promote poverty, such as violating labor laws, trading in illegal timber and supporting governments that perpetuate human rights violations against their citizens.

OBJECTIVES

This paper seeks to evaluate the impact China's move into Africa has had on the alleviation of poverty in Africa. It is argued that because of China's disregard for human rights and disregard for the environment, factors closely related to poverty, China demonstrates that it is not interested in alleviating Africa's poverty. Additional factors that make China a negative influence on the alleviation of poverty is China's inability to enforce domestic laws that govern China's conduct while trading abroad, that would help regulate China's behavior while trading. The non enforcement of trade related laws is a problem because both Chinese and African businesses are sometimes labeled corrupt. This paper will focus on China's willingness to facilitate warfare at the expense of basic needs of people by trading in and providing arms to tyrant rulers. The examples of Zimbabwe and Sudan will be used. With respect to dehumanizing work conditions, particular focus will be paid to Chinese treatment of Zambia's mineworkers. The West African timber industry will be used as an example of China's failure to abide by positive environmental standards. On the other hand, China's dual role as trade partner and donor could as Ethiopia's Prime Minister pointed out, be developing a new development model, one that promotes equality between countries and has few to no punitive measures. The arguments that China unlike the West acts condescendingly towards Africans but instead treats Africans as equal or that the common historical affiliation with Communism/Socialism or similarities in social norms are slowly gaining ground in strengthening China's positive perception in Africa.

Conclusion / recommendations

Despite China's donor aid to Africa, on balance, China is doing more to encourage poverty than it is doing to alleviate it. What can China do to reverse that perception? China can do more to alleviate poverty by ensuring that the countries it trades with are democratically ruled and also take an interest in human rights. China can also conduct environmental assessments before engaging in activities that will have substantial impact on the environment. Further, China can use its diplomatic core to improve its image as a rogue business partner into an ethical business partner that cares for more than merely the bottom line. Lastly, China can incorporate and push to the forefront of its corporate expansion and marketing campaign, corporate social responsibility.

INTRODUCTION

Over the past twenty years, China has significantly increased its trade with and investment in African countries. Not only has China developed as a significant trade partner, it has also developed as a significant development aid partner. In this chapter, China and Chinese business refer to businesses owned by the government of China as well as privately owned Chinese businesses that are registered in China and governed by Chinese law. With respect to China as a trade partner, China has received a lot of scrutiny about its management of aid, the lack of transparency in the aid sector, what constitutes a responsible transfer of resources including the need to consider social, environmental, fair labor procedures and safe guarding human rights.[1] Despite these criticisms, China has taken an active role in assisting with development goals rather than simply increasing trade relations and its geopolitical influence.

---

[1] Penny Davies " Chinese Development Assistance to Africa: Implications and Challenges." The China Monitor, Issue 28. April 2008, 8-10.

There has been intense commentary in the West about China's involvement in Africa. The discourse on China in Africa can not take place without comparison with the other major foreign entity in Africa, the West. Some view the conversation between China and the West with respect to Africa as stemming from the alleged concern of who will have greater ability to reap the reward of investment in Africa. China's entrance into Africa is challenging the idea that Western neocolonialism is being replaced with Chinese neocolonialism. On the one hand, it is perceived that, "The West, architect of the African state system and its economic foundations, seeks to tie its prevailing commercial dominance to an ambitious agenda of structural change for the continent. By way of contrast China has entered Africa simply to feed the insatiable hunger of its own infant market economy, and has little interest in Africa's internal problems or politics."[2] "Part of the reason that there has been a shift in attitude towards China in Africa on the part of some Western governments has much to do with changes in the international system and the accompanying impact that these have had on China's perception of its role in world affairs."[3] Some of these factors include the effects of the fall of the Berlin wall and China's admission to the World Trade Organization (WTO) in 2001.

Theories on China's Role in Africa

In the discourse of Sino-African relations, there are three competing views with respect to China's future plans in Africa. One theory is that China is a development partner. In this capacity, "China's involvement in Africa is part of a long-term strategic commitment to the continent, one that is driven by its own economic needs, a commitment to transmit its development experience to the continent and a desire to build effective cooperative partnerships across the developing world."[4] . In fact, Arguably, this is demonstrated by the fact that bilateral trade between China and Africa was US$50 billion by the end of 2006, which is phenomenal compared to US$1 billion in 2000. Additionally, China has continued to provide development aid to many countries on the continent. Lastly, the increase in South-South cooperation is another indication that China plans to share its development lessons as well as remain a long term trading partner with not only Africa, but the rest of the global South.

The second view is that China is an economic competitor. According to this theory, China is competing with Africa by engaging in a short-term 'resource grab' much like the West did during colonialism and continues to do during this neocolonialist era. This theory also implies that China does not pay much attention to the local economic, social, political and environmental development because it does not plan to maintain a long term relationship. If this is the case, Africa is in a disadvantaged position because China is dictating the terms of the relationship implying that Africa is unable to equally compete and gain from its relationship with China.[5] This theory is flawed for several reasons. China's trade with Africa has significantly increased direct foreign investment in many African countries as China

---

[2] Chris Alden, China in Africa, Zed Books, New York, 2007, 93.
[3] Chris Alden, China in Africa, Zed Books, New York, 2007, 114.
[4] Chris Alden, China in Africa, Zed Books, New York, 2007, 5.
[5] Chris Alden, China in Africa, Zed Books, New York, 2007, 5-6.

continues to purchase mines, forests, farms and formulate incentives for its citizens to migrate to Africa. Additionally, if even the colonial powers are still actively involved in African affairs why would China leave Africa? China has been involved with several Africa countries since colonial times and its increased involvement over time demonstrates an intention to remain in Africa long-term. This theory also discounts the amount of development aid China has given and the amount of corporate social responsibility Chinese companies are engaged in. If China were in Africa for the short term, it makes little business sense to have made such significant contributions to development and the reduction of poverty.

One is that this school of thought reflects the 'absence of pro-active African diplomacy as well as the African voice on African perceptions of the relations with China.[6]

The last interpretation involves several sub-issues. The third view is that of China as a colonizer. The theory is that China has long term plans to stay in Africa and exert its geopolitical influence. With intentions to stay in Africa for the long term, the theory is that China plans to develop long term partnerships within various sectors of development as well as the potential gain of political control of African territories.[7] This theory seems less likely than the other theories. Despite the existence of neocolonialism, in the current international political climate, it is unlikely China would violate the sovereignty of another state. In fact, China's non interference policy is a strong indicator that China does not plan to assume the role of colonizer. Despite the number of theories on what Sino-African relations might evolve into, current Chinese policy towards Africa indicates China's interest in maintaining a long term mutually beneficial relationship with Africa.

CHINA'S POLICY IN AFRICA: POVERTY ALLEVIAION

Introduction

Of particular focus in this chapter is Target 1 of Goal 1 of the Millennium Development Goals (MDGs), which is to eliminate poverty and hunger. Poverty affects political stability, development, human resource productivity, likelihood of disease and mortality, human rights, and so on. The goal of the MDGs are that between 1990 and 2015, the proportion of people whose income is less than $1 a day would be reduced to half. According to the United Nations, nine of the ten countries with the largest percentage of people earning less than US$1 a day are in Africa. That means that Africa has from 49% to a staggering 73%, of its population living in extreme poverty conditions.[8] "Between 1981 and 2001 the percent of total people in Sub-Saharan Africa living on less than $1 a day increased to 93%, from 164 million to 316 million."[9] Needless to say, any non-African country investing in Africa will encounter poverty and the limitations it sets on the African society. Based on such statistics, it

---

[6] Francia A. Kornegay, "Africa's Strategic Diplomatic Engagement with China." New Imulses from the South: China's Engagement of Africa, edited by Hanna Edinger with Hayley Herman & Johanna Jansson. Stellenbosch, RSA, center for Chinese Studies, 2008, 3.

[7] Chris Alden, China in Africa, Zed Books, New York, 2007, 6.

[8] United Nations Development Programme, United Nations Environment Programme, The World Bank, World Resources Institute. 2005.

[9] *United Nations Development Programme, United Nations Environment Programme, The World Bank, World Resources Institute. 2005.*

becomes imperative that Africa's trade partners following Africa's lead create a viable plan to work towards poverty alleviation.

The Significance of Partnerships

There are many key players in the fight against poverty in Africa. Governments are working with civil society, the private sector and international agents (governments, multilateral organizations and aid organizations). Before partnerships can be effective, Africa needs to develop a plan of action for eliminating poverty. Only then can it call on outside parties to assist it achieve its goal. This chapter will focus on civil society, the African Union and China.

African civil society plays a vital role in social, political and economic development by creating sustainable programs with guiding goals such as the MDGs. "The rise of the third sector springs from a variety of pressures, from individual citizens, outside institutions and governments themselves. It reflects a distinct set of social and technological changes, as well as a long-simmering crisis of confidence in the capability of the state."[10] Even with this backdrop, civil society works in conjunction with the state, the commercial sector and foreign entities to promote the common goal of poverty alleviation. This cooperation highlights the importance of partnership between sectors.

Another integral player in tackling the issue of poverty has been by the New Partnership for Africa's Development (NEPAD). NEPAD was developed by the Organization for African Unity in 2001 to develop an integrated socio-economic development framework for Africa. "The NEPAD framework extols the virtues of African self-reliance, ownership and leadership as well as good economic, political and corporate governance as the bedrock of its development agenda."[11] The creation of this framework gave Africa a better idea of its goals and how to create the necessary cooperative framework with countries such as China. However, despite China's involvement in the development arena, it is speculated that, "The emergence of China as a key player in Africa could undermine the NEPAD vision since it could make African countries increasingly reliant on China rather than on their own domestic resources and the resourcefulness of their people."[12] To prevent this from happening, t the joint meeting of the AU Commission and the NEPAD Secretariat suggested that the NEPAD framework should be taken in the broad and dynamic sense, which includes synchronization, harmonization among African countries before allowing foreign entities to enter.[13]

---

[10] Lester M. Salamon, "The Rise of the Nonprofit Sector", *Foreign Affairs*, July/August 1994.

[11] John Rocha, "A New Frontier in the Exploitation of Africa's Natural Resources: The Emergence of China" African Perspectives on China in Africa ed, Firoze Manji and Stephen Marks, Mkuki na Nyota Publishers, Dar es Salaam, 2005, 25.

[12] John Rocha, "A New Frontier in the Exploitation of Africa's Natural Resources: The Emergence of China" African Perspectives on China in Africa ed, Firoze Manji and Stephen Marks, Mkuki na Nyota Publishers, Dar es Salaam, 2005, 25.

[13] Abraham, Kinfe, "Partnership and the Cooperative Framework of NEPAD", China Comes to Africa: The Political Economy and Diplomatic History of China's Relation with Africa, 351.

Africa's Aid Needs

The discourse on China's involvement in Africa is arguably one sided in that it tends to focus on what China needs to do for Africa, rather than what Africa needs China to do for Africa. That said Africa needs to redefine its negotiating strategy to make it a more competitive player in the global market. The following are good initial steps: better terms for trade and aid without conditionalities.

Western versus Chinese aid Assistance

China's involvement with Africa has highlighted the difference in the manner in which Western aid is administered versus the manner in which Chinese aid is administered. According to Alden, it has been an achievement for NGOs and like-minded African governments to convince "Western governments and corporations to support development and investment, respectively, built on principles of good governances and transparency." [14] The issues raised by China's administration of aid are as follows: whether civil society and African governments will have to apply the same tactics for the Chinese government and Chinese corporations to support the same goals of good governance and transparency, how China's policy of "non interference" has challenged the international consensus on governance and development and sanctions and what conditions, if any, Chinese aid will have as compared to Western aid.

Chinese aid

There are two main questions this paper seeks to answer. One is whether China's presence in Africa has contributed to poverty reduction or increased the incidence of poverty as the title of this paper questions. The other question that arises is how China's aid to Africa can offset the negative results of trade with China such as pollution, destruction of rainforests, negative labor relations and assistance of undemocratic regimes.. Despite the progress in education, health and the status of women, Africa is still said to be the only continent not on target to meet the MDGs by 2015. There are several arguments that China is not doing enough to alleviate poverty. These are because China does not have a clear policy with respect to poverty alleviation in Africa so its projects do not have a common thread, China's conditionalities on aid hinder development, China's use of Chinese labor for projects deprives Africans of jobs, and that unequal trading positions between Africa and China further leads to poverty. The negative perception of China is compounded by evidence of purchasing illegal timber, lack of a social and corporate responsibility agenda, engagement with regimes that do not respect human rights and good governance among others.[15] The result has been increasing anti-Chinese sentiments.

---

[14] Chris Alden, China in Africa, Zed Books, New York, 2007, 111.
[15] Ibid, 17-21; Ian Taylor, "Unpacking China's Resource Diplomacy in Africa", China in Africa, Current Issues No.33 compiled by Henning Melber, Nordiska Africanstitutet, Uppsala, 2007, 20.

Despite increasing anti-Chinese sentiment, China's aid to Africa continues to grow annually. In fact, China's entrance into Africa has seen an increase in funding for various development projects and other types of technical assistance projects in the areas of agriculture, health, education and so on. Rocha, however, contends that while "China's engagement with Africa is producing positive results in the economic dimension of development, it is however clear that this engagement is not yet producing any meaningful impact in the lives of ordinary citizens."[16] This view is supported by the perception that while China has a clear economic policy towards Africa, it does not have a clearly outlined policy targeting poverty alleviation in Africa. As a result of China's strong focus on income generating development projects in which China has stake, few of its programs deliberately tackle the mitigation of poverty in a holistic manner (that is, not only creation of economic opportunities, but also the promotion of sustainable grassroots social and political programs.).

The encouragement of elitism is seen because many of the Chinese business people who emigrate to African countries immediately join the middle class and tend to bolster relationships with local people of similar status, without much regard for the poor. In some countries the Chinese self-segregate and the locals claim they are not respected by the Chinese. In addition to dealing with affluent people, the Chinese often try to lobby African governments to implement policy in their favor. When governments or businesses do not do what the Chinese want, the Chinese have been accused of bribing the necessary people to help them get what they want. Furthermore, the Chinese have also been known to work with whatever regime is in power, regardless of its human rights record in order to achieve their economic interests.

There are several counter arguments to the criticism of China's participation in poverty alleviation in Africa. One is that Africa just as China managed to pull a large portion of its population out of poverty, Africa too should take the lead in the alleviation of its own poverty rather than relying on foreign intervention. Africa should mimic some of the steps that China has taken towards reducing poverty such as liberalizing its economy. "African civil society should bring pressure through the African Union for a parallel civil society forum inclusive of business, labour and consumer groups to be instituted at the biennial meetings of the China-Africa Cooperation Forum"[17]. Additionally, efforts should be made to develop partnerships between Western, African and Chinese civil society groups to communicate Chinese policy towards Africa. Lastly, the onus is on African governments to negotiate more favorable terms in trade contracts with China, Africa should stipulate certain conditions favorable to the alleviation of poverty. For instance, there should be a stipulation that Chinese companies will engage in corporate social responsibility and/or assist the country to attain whatever development goals most affect the industry in which the Chinese business operates. If China fails to comply, Africa could protest Chinese goods, use naming and shaming techniques and request the renegotiation of certain contracts. It should be noted that the same conditions would apply to other non-African trade partners trading in Africa. The problems with these arguments are that the relationship between China and each African country it trades with and

---

[16] John Rocha, "China and African Natural Resources: Developmental Opportunity or Deepening the Resource Curse? In New Impulses from the South: China's Engagement of Africa, Ed Hannah Endinger with Hayley Herman & Johanna Jansson. Stellenbosch, South Africa, center for Chinese Studies, 2008, 64.

[17] Ndibisi, Obiorah "Who's Afraid of China in Africa? Towards an African Civil Society Perspective on China-Africa Relations" African Perspectives on China in Africa ed, Firoze Manji and Stephen Marks, Mkuki na Nyota Publishers, Dar es Salaam, 2005, 52.

the domestic particularities of each African country are different. As a result, it is difficult to create a blanket set of rules for China.

CHINA'S POLICY IN AFRICA: SOCIOPOLITICS, ECONOMICS AND DIPLOMACY

According to Rocha, the emergence of China in Africa raises several questions. One is how China's investments in Africa as well as its geopolitical presence will "impact Africa's weak administrative systems, poor revenue generation system, management and disbursement capacity systems, the absence of rule of law and heavy dependence on national resources, lack of adequately skilled personnel and the general technological divide."[18] As China's diplomatic relations around Africa expand and become more influential, it is essential for not only individual countries, but regional organizations and the African Union at large to formulate policy that's puts Africa's interests first. Lastly, the question must be posed that if Africa does not formulate "pro-African" policy, will Africa ever become self-sustaining?

Five Point Proposal

China's policy towards Africa so far has best been summed up by the Forum on China Africa Cooperation. Its initial "three point proposal" stated China's intention: "to build on the traditional friendship and push for new progress in China-Africa relations; to persist in mutual assistance and mutual benefit and promote common prosperity of China and Africa; and to cooperate even more closely in an effort to safeguard the rights and interests of the developing countries."[19] China's top legislator Wu Bangguo in a speech, entitled "Enhancing Mutual Trust and Promoting Common Development" delivered at the Zambian National Assembly expanded China's three point proposal to a five point proposal to include: "to deepen exchanges in the cultural field and closer consultation and coordination in international affairs."[20] This policy will be hard to put into action because it is too vague. If indeed China's policy is based on the United Nations policy, then China needs to take a less broad and more focused approach to working with Africa not only to improve trade and investment relations, but also to outline how it plans to alleviate poverty and other development issues.

China's policy in Africa should incorporate the United Nation's five-point proposal, which sets out to 'assist' developing countries accelerate development by granting zero-tariff treatment for some exports from the least developed countries, increase aid to the heavily-

---

[18] John Rocha, "A New Frontier in the Exploitation of Africa's Natural Resources: The Emergence of China" African Perspectives on China in Africa ed, Firoze Manji and Stephen Marks, Mkuki na Nyota Publishers, Dar es Salaam, 2005, 28-29.

[19] LUSAKA, Nov. 5 (Xinhuanet) "Top legislator makes 5-point proposal on Sino-African relations" 2004-11-06 http://www.focac.org/eng/zxxx/t169181.htm accessed December 27, 2008.

[20] LUSAKA, Nov. 5 (Xinhuanet) "Top legislator makes 5-point proposal on Sino-African relations" 2004-11-06 http://www.focac.org/eng/zxxx/t169181.htm accessed December 27, 2008.

indebted poor countries and least developed countries and cancel debts contracted by them, provide loans with conditionalities and effective medicine for treating malaria, and training professionals.[21] So far, China has increased aid to HIPCs and LDCs and provided money for medicine and training professionals, however, China's loans, provide similar terms to Western loans. Furthermore, China is yet to cancel debt from such nations or grant zero-tariff treatment for exports. By incorporating the UN five-point proposal, China will help Africa accelerate its development and also poverty alleviation.

China's non-Ideological Footing in Africa: Non-Interference

China's Past Conduct

One aspect of Chinese policy that is not outlined in the five point proposal is its non-interference policy. China's policy of non-interference, whereby it does not seek to interfere with the political, social or other societal structures in the country it trades with, has sparked a controversial debate. On the one hand, China merely seeks to invest and trade therefore it does not find the need to interfere with existing ruling regimes. China's rationale is that being engaged in trade with a country does not make it responsible for the domestic affairs of that country. Additionally, China is supported by opponents of the strict Western ideology of democracy and its correlation to economic success argue that despite China being ruled by a Communist government with no foreign interference it has managed to raise 400 million people out of poverty in over two decades as well as rising as a major economic powerhouse provides encouragement to African dictators. On the other hand, many countries in the international community condemn China's non interference because trading with such regimes gives the impression that China legitimizes such regimes negative actions. The rational is that if a country's leadership is undemocratic or perpetuating human rights violations against its citizens or is disrupting national and/or regional security or any other such practices, then the international community should boycott trade with that country. For instance, in the cases of Sudan and Zimbabwe, China has continued to trade with them despite their bad governance and international condemnation. Continued trade with such countries reflects negatively on China because China is seen to be going against internationally accepted practices. As Africa continues to become more democratic, according to Karumbidza, "China should be wary of losing the political capital and 'credibility' it acquired from supporting African liberation struggles through conniving with dictatorial regimes."[22]

China's non-interference policy cannot be permanent because of the interlinked nature of social, political and economic issues with one another. The spillover effects of political instability are numerous. The Western approach that seeks to punish bad political behavior by reducing and/or cutting off foreign direct investment is a proactive means of demonstrating disagreement with bad leadership. It is inevitable that once China starts to lose money on its

---

[21] Chidaushe, Moreblessings, "China's Grand Re-entrance into Africa- Mirage or Oasis?", African Perspectives on China in Africa ed, Firoze Manji and Stephen Marks, Mkuki na Nyota Publishers, Dar es Salaam, 2005.

investments or is unable to trade due to political instability, destruction of infrastructure, or social issues resulting in the injury or death of the labor force, then China will be left no choice but to become more proactive in promoting peace and democracy. The number of peacekeeping missions that China has participated in, is an indication of China non-interference policy is not sustainable or practical when political instability and domestic strife affects countries in which it has interests. "In 2004, about 1400 Chinese participated in nine UN missions on the continent. The biggest contingent (558 troops) was sent to war-torn Liberia[23] Other accounts of Chinese peacekeepers in UN missions have been recorded in Sudan and the Democratic Republic of Congo.[24] Zhu reports that "since 1990, China has participated in 12 UN peace keeping missions in Africa and that by end of May 2006 she had sent 435 soldiers to Sudan as part of the UN peace keeping efforts."[25] There is a huge difference between assisting with international peace keeping missions versus single-handedly supporting repressive and undemocratic regimes.

The future of China's non interference policy: Absence of Rule of Law in Zimbabwe

A recent case where China has demonstrated its willingness to rethink its non interference policy and take a more proactive approach has been in Zimbabwe. China first became involved in Southern Rhodesia (Zimbabwe) in the 1970s during its fight for independence from Britain. During the Rhodesian Bush War, China assisted Robert Mugabe who was the leader of the Zimbabwe African National Union by supplying him arms. Sino-Zimbabwe relations were formally established when Zimbabwe become an independent country and to this day, China still supplies Zimbabwe with arms. "In return for providing the Mugabe regime with financial aid, machinery, equipment and military supplies, Chinese state-owned enterprises have made substantial investments in some of Zimbabwe's major national assets including hydroelectric power plants and tobacco production facilities." Additionally, "China supplied 12 fighter jets and 100 trucks to Zimbabwe's army even as the country is subject to a Western arms embargo."[26] China's constant refusal to impose sanction on Zimbabwe and its continued association with President Robert Mugabe as the rest of the world continues to cut ties has subjected China to additional criticism.

However, as a result of the extreme economic conditions Zimbabwe is going through (inflation, poverty, loss of currency value), the disease, the expulsion of aid workers, Mugabe's undemocratic regime, the international community has taken several measures to punish Zimbabwe. China was originally reluctant to join such efforts until the international

---

[22] Karumbidza, John Blessing, "Win-win Economic Cooperation: Can China Save Zimbabwe's Economy?", African Perspectives on China in Africa ed, Firoze Manji and Stephen Marks, Mkuki na Nyota Publishers, Dar es Salaam, 2005, 89.

[23] Tull, Denis, "The Political Consequences of China's Return to Africa", Alden, Chris, Daniel Large and Ricardo Soares de Oliveira, China Returns to Africa: A Rising Power and a Continent Embrace, Columbia University Press, New York, 2008, 116.

[24] Garth le Pere, "Prospects for a Coherent African Policy Response: Engaging China" New Impulses from the South: China's Engagement of Africa, Ed Hannah Endinger with Hayley Herman & Johanna Jansson. Stellenbosch, South Africa, center for Chinese Studies, 2008, 19.

[25] Zhiqun Zhu, "China's New Diplomacy in Africa and its Implications." Delivered at the 48th International Studies Association Annual Conference. Chicago, IL. Feb 28-March 3, 2007. http://www.allacademic.com//meta/p_mla_apa_research_citation/1/8/0/6/3/pages180639/p180639-2.php Accessed 08/01/2009.

[26] Ndibisi, Obiorah "Who's Afraid of China in Africa? Towards an African Civil Society Perspective on China-Africa Relations" African Perspectives on China in Africa ed, Firoze Manji and Stephen Marks, Mkuki na Nyota Publishers, Dar es Salaam, 2005, 48.

community put pressure on China. For instance, South Africa refused for a shipment of Chinese weapons to enter its port to be sent to Zimbabwe. "'There is a trend ... of China making decisions that reflect the international perspective more than the narrow Chinese perspective......China is learning on this. They want to be a responsible player' in world affairs, says David Zweig, a professor of Chinese international relations at the Hong Kong University of Science and Technology."[27] Furthermore, China has joined the international community in providing humanitarian aid to Zimbabwe. Chinese Foreign Ministry spokesman Liu Jianchao said, "To help the people of Zimbabwe, China is actively considering providing humanitarian economic aid, including food aid."[28] He also said, "We sincerely hope that all concerned parties in Zimbabwe will truly focus on the interests of the country and its people and soon form a government of national unity."[29] Change of foreign policy takes time. Based on China's involvement in Zimbabwe, there is an indication that China is willing to change. Only time will tell.

China's Non Interference Policy: Sudan's Weak Administrative System

Not only has religious and racial warfare plagued Sudan's past and continues to do so today, but also the strategic arms delivery for the depopulation of the oil regions in order to clear the area for oil extraction has been a modern source of conflict in the region. "China, which buys nearly two-thirds of Sudan's oil exports, has come under fire from rights groups that contend the oil revenues help arm government forces and fuel several conflicts in the country, including a civil was in Darfur that has killed 300,000 people."[30] While the world failed to define the systematic killing of Black Christians in the Darfur genocide, the unsaid agreement became that regardless of the terminology, there was a conflict that was being fueled by foreign investment and trade. The money earned by the Sudanese government ended up fueling the militias that continued the atrocities towards innocent citizens, yet, China continued to buy oil from Sudan.

By supporting the acquisition of conflict resources, the proliferation of small arms, corruption and bribery, by trading with an undemocratic government that is terrorizing its people, China has been seen to encourage a culture of lawlessness and impunity. China has been embroiled in the controversy surrounding the extraction, purchase and use of Sudanese oil. Among other things, China has been accused of assisting local government officials to perpetuate human rights violations against innocent civilians. China's creation of infrastructure and other economic development projects in oil-laden areas is further criticized because of China's willingness to forcibly vacate people from their land with the use of armed forces (both government forces and paid civilian security forces). "The opportunistic nature of Chinese foreign investment, particularly in Sudan, was further exposed when pressures mounted on the Sudanese government to accept peacekeeping forces in Sudan.

---

[27] Scott Baldauf and Peter Ford, "China slammed for arming Zimbabwe's Mugabe" The Christian Science Monitor, April 23, 2008 edition. http://www.csmonitor.com/2008/0423/p07s02-woaf.html
[28] "China Offers Zimbabwe Aid, Urges National Unity" http://www.javno.com/en/world/clanak.php?id=212706.
[29] "China Offers Zimbabwe Aid, Urges National Unity" http://www.javno.com/en/world/clanak.php?id=212706.
[30] The Associated Press, Chinese President Hu pledges support for Sudan, http://www.iht.com/articles/ap/2009/02/04/asia/AS-China-Sudan.php February 4, 2009

China failed to veto any United Nations Security Council Resolutions on Darfur, including the referral of Darfur criminals to the International Criminal Court."[31] All of the above demonstrate China's refusal to interfere with the domestic affairs of another country.

In fact, on February 4, 2009, Chinese President Hu Jintao sent a message to Sudan's president Omar al-Bashir pledging his support for Sudan. "Hu's message, contained in an exchange of greetings marking the 50th anniversary of diplomatic ties, highlights close links between the nations. China "respects Sudan's sovereignty and territorial integrity,... supports the African country's efforts to realize the national reconciliation," Hu was quoted as telling President Omar al-Bashir, according to a report issued by China's official Xinhua News Agency."[32] This statement does not demonstrate China's interest either to stop trading with Sudan or to interfere with Sudan's internal affairs. It is different from China's approach in Zimbabwe where it is condemning Mugabe's actions. China's approach to Sudan differs from its approach to Zimbabwe because despite the war, China remains highly invested in Sudan and did not condemn Al Bashir's government. It was only during the run-up to the 2008 Olympics when China received a lot of negative press with respect to its involvement in Sudan, did China start to discuss how best to mitigate the situation. Nothing was done. It begs the question of whether China indeed plans to eradicate its non interference policy in Africa.

CASE STUDIES

A trait common to many African countries is the heavy dependence on national resources and the undervaluing and undertraining of its human resources. However, as Africa aims to be self sufficient it is critical for Africa to diversify its sources of income generation and maximize all its resources. Additionally, it will be critical for Africa to modernize technology, infrastructure and machinery dealing with trade and production, to improve its management and disbursement capacity systems and to create long term focused plans for political stability and general security. The following cases seek to analyze what China has done in addition to providing aid to address issues that impede Africa's economic development.

Chinese Employers and Labor Relations in Zambia

Introduction

Relations between China and Zambia date back to the 1960s and 1970s. This relationship was influenced by similar ideological beliefs when Zambia under President Kaunda espoused socialist principles. It was during Kaunda's presidency that the Chinese government first supported the construction of the following major infrastructure projects: a railway line, road network and oil pipeline between Zambia and ports in Tanzania. These projects heavily relied

---

[31] Askouri, Ali, "China's Investment in Sudan: Displacing Villages and Destroying Communities", African Perspectives on China in Africa ed, Firoze Manji and Stephen Marks, Mkuki na Nyota Publishers, Dar es Salaam, 2005, 82.

[32] The Associated Press, Chinese President Hu pledges support for Sudan, http://www.iht.com/articles/ap/2009/02/04/asia/AS-China-Sudan.php February 4, 2009

on Chinese loans and technical expertise. The improved infrastructure facilitated Zambian trade at the time when the southern route to the sea was closed. Since then China has been increasing its involvement in other sectors of the Zambian economy such as agriculture, trade, investment, and mining.

Zambia's mining industry and labor laws

China's labor policy in Africa has generally has been a point of contention. First, China's policy of sending Chinese laborers to Africa to work has been a point of contention. Unlike the West that uses Westerners for more skilled project management positions, China sends Chinese workers of all skill sets to work on different projects. By importing Chinese laborers into Africa, it is argued that the Chinese are taking away the jobs from Africans, the same jobs the Chinese claimed they would create. In a continent with high unemployment, taking away existing jobs adversely impacts local communities. Second, as will be seen in the example of Zambia, the Chinese have been accused of being insensitive to workers' rights, disrespecting local labor laws, occupational health and safety standards and failing to adhere to minimum wage structures. Consequently, it is a strong argument that China's labor policies in Africa are contributing to increasing poverty.[33]

Although the Chinese owned mines help Zambians by means of the creation of jobs, the Chinese have gained a very bad reputation of giving low wages, poor working and safety conditions and failure to respect workers' rights. This situation led to several strikes by local workers at Chinese owned mines. There have been many reported incidents, but the government has failed to enforce laws that are being violated by foreign corporate culprits. Some of the reported incidents include the following: in 2005 when fifty-one (51) Zambian miners were killed in a Chinese explosive factory where they were locked up; a 2006 case where 5 miners were shot and killed by police at the Chinese Chambishi mine while lobbying for better conditions of service; a July 2006 incidence when operations of a Chinese coal mine were suspended due to unsafe working conditions, inhuman treatment and lack of respect for workers basic rights as provided for in Zambia Labour Laws; between December 2008 and January 12, 2009, poor safety standards led to three (3) deaths at a Chinese Coal Mine in Sinazongwe, Southern Province[34] and the mine continues to operate and the closure of the largest Chinese Mulungushi Textiles Plant in Kabwe due to poor pay and safety conditions.[35]

In addition to the above, importation of cheap goods has led to the outpricing and eventual closing of local industries. Chinese owned industries have led to closure of local businesses because of the creation of larger stores with cheaper goods and the eradication of small scale manufacturing shops because of cheap Chinese manufactured goods. What is seen as Chinese business protectionism, that is the flooding of the Zambia market with cheap

---

[33] Alison Holder & Rebecca Jackson, "Mutual benefit? The Impact of China's Investment in Africa on Children". New impulses from the South; China's engagement of Africa, ed. Hanna Edinger with Hayley Herman & Johanna Jansson. Stellenbosch, RSA, Center for Chinese Studies, 2008, 71.

[34] Lusaka Times "Chinese Miner Killed in Unsafe Mine in Sinazongwe" Accessed 13/01/2009 from http://www.lusakatimes.com/?p=7262

[35] Glory Mushinge, Labour Day in Zambia "Our workers have been turned into slaves in their own country". The Women's International Perspective (THE WIP) June 12, 2007, http://thewip.net/contributors/2007/06/labor_day_in_zambia_our_worker.html. Retrieved 09/01/2009.

goods, the discouragement of technology transfer and the lack of support for local industries has led to anti-Chinese sentiments. An example of how deep anti-Chinese sentiment ran is in the 2006 national elections, when a leading opposition candidate named Michael Sata ran on the platform of expelling Chinese investors and workers. He was against what he saw as Zambia being turned into an outlying province of China. China retaliated by threatening to remove Chinese investments in Zambia if Sata was elected. Despite Sata's loss, there was resounding agreement with Sata's sentiment that Chinese investors were bringing about more harm to Zambia than good. Despite several Zambia having lax labor laws, China should comply with existing laws. Zambia should revise its labor laws to take into account modern labor issues that affect their citizens. Once laws are in place, Zambia should enforce such laws, which may require the establishment of a special monitoring unit.

Weak Administrative Systems – The West African Timber Industry and the Environment

Introduction

Goal 7 of the MDGs aims to ensure Environmental Sustainability. This paper is especially concerned with Target 2 of Goal 7, which strives to reduce biodiversity loss, achieving, by 2010, a significant reduction in the rate of loss of deforestation slows and more forests are designated for biodiversity conservation is especially relevant to this section. Illegal logging continues to affect West African forests. Due to the lack of tracking infrastructure and enforcement of crimes related to illegal logging, it is difficult for buyers of timber to know whether or not they are buying illegal timber. This situation has been exacerbated by domestic of conflict and spillover effects in some West African countries.

China's purchase of West African timber

China is a major importer of West African timber. "China's imports have risen sharply in recent years, partly to offset reduced domestic production from forest areas affected by logging bans, and partly because of progressive reductions in tariffs and non-tariff trade barriers brought about by China's economy opening to international trade in the late 1980s."[36] "From 1998 to 2003, Chinese log imports have increased from 25% to 42% of all log exports from this region."[37] Some of these imports however, are illegal. Evidence suggests that China imports illegally logged timber from Liberia, Gabon and Cameroon.[38]

The term "conflict timber" arose from the logging and sale of timber during conflict, often for the generation of income to fuel the conflict. The political instability, the lack of

---

[36] Paul Toyne, Cliona O'Brien and Rod Nelson, The timber footprint of the G8 and China: *Making the case for green procurement by government*, June 2002, 12.

[37] Allan Thornton, *CHINESE INVOLVEMENT IN AFRICAN ILLEGAL LOGGING AND TIMBER TRADE,* US House of Representatives Committee on International Relations, Subcommittee on Africa, Global Human Rights and International Operations July 28, 2005

[38] Paul Toyne, Cliona O'Brien and Rod Nelson, The timber footprint of the G8 and China: *Making the case for green procurement by government*, June 2002, 6.

accountability and the general chaos in war torn countries provides opportunistic companies, undemocratic governments and rebels governments the ability to benefit from this trade. One of the most documented instances of conflict timber was the during the civil war in Liberia where, "Rebel leader turned President Charles Taylor relied heavily on timber resources to support his own military efforts and to fund mercenaries in neighboring Sierra Leone and Cote d'Ivoire. Taylor gave Liberian timber companies….unrestricted access to the nation's forests."[39] "In 2003, the United Nations Security Council imposed sanctions on the international trade of round logs and timber products originating in Liberia in an effort to eliminate "conflict timber". At the time, China was Liberia's largest market."[40] Sanctions were a powerful message that the international community did not support Taylor's regime.

China is taking steps to remedy its image of rogue timber trader, however more can be done. From an environmental perspective, it is arguable that civil wars can exert a temporary positive influence in the forestry sector by curtailing logging, and so reducing loss of biodiversity habitat and other forms of costly (and often irremediable) environmental destruction."[41] Thompson and Kanaan further argue that, "Much depends, in fact, on who controls the terrain and how they interpret their interests. If rebel groups opposing the country's government occupy forested areas, they may make it impossible for logging concerns to operate by attacking crews, expropriating equipment, etc."[42] That said, the overall impact of war on a nation is negative. Even though as many forests might not be felled during war, other environmental damage, such as pollution, destruction of other forms of vegetation and wildlife also affect the environment. Control of territory has little impact on environmental degradation during war.

Recommendations for conflict timber exporters and China

China has been accused of not responding to environmental concerns and sustainable use of natural resources especially timber in the case of West Africa. It must be noted that "The government [of China] has set up an informal advisory body for trade and the environment which includes work on forestry, timber and non-timber forest products. China has general procurement policies that relate not only to the life-cycle assessment of products, but also to environmental aspects of imported timber."[43] Criticism of China is that despite having signed several agreements stating its intent to engage in good purchasing practices with respect to timber, none of these agreements have been implemented or enforced.

---

[39] **Allan Thornton, *CHINESE INVOLVEMENT IN AFRICAN ILLEGAL LOGGING AND TIMBER TRADE,* US House of Representatives Committee on International Relations**

[40] Forest Trends , "Helping Liberia Escape Conflict Timber: The Role of the International Community China & Europe", Information Bulletin: China and East Asia, June 2006, Issue 5, 1 http://www.illegal-logging.info/uploads/ForestTrends_Brief_Liberia_English.pdf.

[41] Jamie Thomson and Ramzy Kanaan, **Conflict Timber: Dimensions of the Problem in Asia and Africa Volume I Synthesis Report**

[42] Jamie Thomson and Ramzy Kanaan, **Conflict Timber: Dimensions of the Problem in Asia and Africa Volume I Synthesis Report**
http://www.usaid.gov/our_work/cross-cutting_programs/transition_initiatives/pubs/vol1synth.pdf

[43] Paul Toyne, Cliona O'Brien and Rod Nelson, The timber footprint of the G8 and China: *Making the case for green procurement by government,* June 2002, 23.

Based on the urgent need to eradicate illegal logging, trade of illegal timber and wood-based products and improve forest management in West Africa, China should do the following:

- Enact and enforce the appropriate policies: First, promote bilateral agreements with timber exporters that China will not import illegal logs. Second, China can enact measures similar to those enacted by the G8 countries, committing itself not to import illegal logs. China should enact legislation similar to the Foreign Corrupt Practices Act in the United States that prohibits Unites States businesses to engage in bribery of officials in other countries. This would be aimed at discouraging people from being bribed into mislabeling timber or selling illegal timber. Designate illegal logging and purchase of illegal logs as a criminal offence in both exporting countries and China.[44] Third, China can also conduct environmental assessments before engaging in activities that will have substantial negative impact on the environment. If China decides to continue with a project, China should take responsibility for the consequences, such as cleaning up the environment, paying fines for illegal logging or purchase.
- Make use of existing verification standards: Ensure that the country of origin and legality of timber are correctly recorded. Implement a green procurement policy that includes an enforcement branch that is able to distinguish illegal timber from legal timber. However, it is difficult to track the origin of all imports and exports,[45] especially conflict timber. Nevertheless, "The World Bank-WWF Alliance has developed practical guidelines on the verification of wood sources."[46]
- Create partnerships: China should enter into public-private partnerships by supporting the Global Forest and Trade Network initiative that is committed to improving their management of forests and production so that timber and wood products comply with Forest Stewardship Council (FSC) standards.[47] China should provide aid and technical assistance to timber exporters that have problems with illegal logging.

RECOMMENDATIONS

The following are suggestions on how to improve Sino-Africa relations.

---

[44] Allan Thornton, CHINESE INVOLVEMENT IN AFRICAN ILLEGAL LOGGING AND TIMBER TRADE, US House of Representatives Committee on International Relations, 8.

[45] Paul Toyne, Cliona O'Brien and Rod Nelson, The timber footprint of the G8 and China: *Making the case for green procurement by government, June 2002*, 21.

[46] Paul Toyne, Cliona O'Brien and Rod Nelson, The timber footprint of the G8 and China: *Making the case for green procurement by government, June 2002*, 21.

[47] Paul Toyne, Cliona O'Brien and Rod Nelson, The timber footprint of the G8 and China: *Making the case for green procurement by government, June 2002*, 9.

Corporate Social Responsibility

China can incorporate and enforce at the forefront of its corporate expansion and marketing campaign, corporate social responsibility. China should incorporate and promote corporate social responsibility as a core business function and marketing plan. In doing so, Chinese businesses can work with local stakeholders to assess their needs and tackle especially pressing issues. Therefore, China and Africa should "Combine commercial interests with social interests with particular attention to environmental protection and people's livelihood in the local area."[48]

Public Diplomacy

China should set up a public relations section to its diplomatic core that deals with educating other countries about China and educating Chinese about other countries. This diplomatic section should have the sole job of assisting in bolstering China as a good trade partner as well as a significant contributor aiding its trade partners to achieve the MDGs as well as other development goals. China and Africa should work on "strengthening communications and mutual understanding and conducting dialogues on democracy through multiple channels."[49] Some viable options are through government, civil society and through academia. Further, China can use its diplomatic core to improve its image as a rogue business partner into an ethical business partner that cares for more than the bottom line. There are several countries in which trade with the Chinese is welcomed because of the view that Chinese unlike Westerners act condescendingly and racist towards Africans. The perception is that Chinese treat Africans as equals. China can continue to perpetuate this perception by increasing the number of study abroad programs where African students can study in China and vice-versa. The number of Chinese studies programs in African universities and African studies programs in Chinese universities should be increased. Chinese cultural centers such as Alliance Française for French language and culture, should be set up to help the African public better understand China.

Maintaining Colonial Goodwill

As a Communist country, China can forge strong relationships with its former Cold War allies that it trades with. Many African leaders that understand the importance of the lasting relationship with China are still alive and are likely to continue to support continued interaction with China provided China continues to benefit their countries, not only as a trade partner, but as a development partner too.

---

[48] He, Wenping, "China's Perspective on Contemporary China-Africa Relations", Alden, Chris, Daniel Large and Ricardo Soares de Oliveira, China Returns to Africa: A Rising Power and a Continent Embrace, Columbia University Press, New York, 2008, 159.

[49] He, Wenping, "China's Perspective on Contemporary China-Africa Relations", Alden, Chris, Daniel Large and Ricardo Soares de Oliveira, China Returns to Africa: A Rising Power and a Continent Embrace, Columbia University Press, New York, 2008, 163.

Foreign aid

As is discussed above, interaction with Africa necessitates its partners to take part in the fight against poverty. However, in addition to increased Chinese aid, China should strengthen monitoring and transparency of foreign aid projects.[50] Additionally, "China needs to demonstrate as a donor, what constitutes a responsible transfer of resources and needs to bring to the fore, social, governance, human rights, labour safety and environmental safeguards."[51]

Africa needs to start by "strengthening the African voice, improving the reporting mechanism and monitoring in partner countries, while improving the efficiency in aid management, improving transparency in aid system, engaging African institutions, establishing dialogue and harmonization of partnerships by the Chinese government for Africa to meet the MDGs."[52]

Promotion of Democracy and Human Rights

There are several measures China can take in order to become a better perceived trade partner as well as alleviate poverty in Africa. China should first reduce its trade relations with countries that are ruled by undemocratically elected leaders and democratically elected leaders that violate the human rights of their citizens. In doing so, China will not only change the perception that its non interference policy is unjust and does not care about the human rights situation in the countries it trades with, but it will also promote democratic governance and in effect human rights. China can encourage its trade partners "implement the NEPAD "African renaissance" principles on democracy, stability, good governance, human rights and economic development on the continent."[53] That way, Africa can promote its own development and only look to outside donors for minor assistance rather than to depend on them.

CONCLUSION

There are many competing views on whether or not China's involvement in Africa is helping alleviate poverty. Despite the competing views, it begs the question of whether a trade partner is responsible for helping another country rise out of poverty. Regardless of the answer, it is up to African governments to responsibly utilize and monitor the money and resources that China gives for development aid. Rather than placing a blanket criticism of

---

[50] He, Wenping, "China's Perspective on Contemporary China-Africa Relations", Alden, Chris, Daniel Large and Ricardo Soares de Oliveira, China Returns to Africa: A Rising Power and a Continent Embrace, Columbia University Press, New York, 2008, 162.

[51] Penny Davies " Chinese Development Assistance to Africa: Implications and Challenges." The China Monitor, Issue 28. April 2008, 9.

[52] Hanna Endinger "How China delivers development assistance to Africa." The China Monitor. Issue 28. April 2008, 7.

[53] Ian Taylor, "Unpacking China's Resource Diplomacy in Africa. China in Africa, CURRENT AFRICAN ISSUES NO 33, Compiled by Henning Melber, Nordiska Afrikainstitutet, Uppsala 2007, 21.

China's trade activities in Africa, Africa should use its resources as a bargaining chip not only for increased foreign investment, but also for increased assistance towards achievement of the MDGs and other development goals. Additionally, Africa must work towards creating a more equal partnership with China, one in which Africa makes reasonable decisions without the threat of an abandoned deal with respect to the negotiation and contracting in trade and investment contracts as well as modes of operation in implementing cooperation agreements. Africa should also implement more string labor and environmental laws to protect workers and the environment at large. In addition to implementing new laws, African countries also need to have in place a means a system of enforcing such laws. Thereafter, Africa should not allow any investors, China or otherwise to violate such laws. Africa should also be proactive in setting the agenda for the Sino-Africa relations instead of waiting for China to do it.

BIBIOGRAPHY

Alden, Chris, China in Africa, Zed Books, *New York*, 2007.

Askouri, Ali. "China's Investment in Sudan: Displacing Villages and Destroying Communities", *African Perspectives on China in Africa* ed, Firoze Manji and Stephen Marks, Mkuki na Nyota Publishers, Dar es Salaam, 2005.

Chimangeni, Isabel. China's Growing Presence Met With Resistance Oct 18, 2006. http://*ipsnews.net/news.asp?idnews*=35152 as seen 1/4/09.

Davies, Penny. " Chinese Development Assistance to Africa: Implications and Challenges." *The China Monitor*, Issue 28. April 2008.

Endinger, Hanna. "How China delivers development assistance to Africa." *The China Monitor*. Issue 28. April 2008.

Forest Trends , "Helping Liberia Escape Conflict Timber: The Role of the International Community China & Europe", Information Bulletin: China and *East Asia, June* 2006, Issue 5, 1 http://www.illegal-logging.info/uploads/ForestTrends_Brief_Liberia_ English.pdf.

He, Wenping. "China's Perspective on Contemporary China-Africa Relations", Alden, Chris, Daniel Large and Ricardo Soares de Oliveira, *China Returns to Africa: A Rising Power and a Continent Embrace*, Columbia University Press, New York, 2008.

Holder, Alison & Rebecca Jackson. "Mutual benefit? The Impact of China's Investment in Africa on Children". *New impulses from the South; China's engagement of Africa*, ed. Hanna Edinger with Hayley Herman & Johanna Jansson. Stellenbosch, RSA, Center for Chinese Studies, 2008.

Karumbidza, John Blessing. "Win-win Economic Cooperation: Can China Save Zimbabwe's Economy?", *African Perspectives on China in Africa* ed, Firoze Manji and Stephen Marks, Mkuki na Nyota Publishers, Dar es Salaam, 2005.

Kinfe, Abraham. "Partnership and the Cooperative Framework of NEPAD", China Comes to Africa: The Political Economy and Diplomatic History of China's Relation with Africa.

Kornegay, Francia A. "Africa's Strategic Diplomatic Engagement with China." *New Imulses from the South: China's Engagement of Africa*, edited by Hanna Edinger with Hayley Herman & Johanna Jansson. Stellenbosch, RSA, center for Chinese Studies, 2008.

le Pere, Garth, "Prospects for a Coherent African Policy Response: Engaging China" *New Impulses from the South: China's Engagement of Africa*, Ed Hannah Endinger with Hayley Herman & Johanna Jansson. Stellenbosch, South Africa, center for Chinese Studies, 2008.

Ndibisi, Obiorah. "Who's Afraid of China in Africa? Towards an African Civil Society Perspective on China-Africa Relations" *African Perspectives on China in Africa* ed, Firoze Manji and Stephen Marks, Mkuki na Nyota Publishers, Dar es Salaam, 2005.

Rocha, John. "A New Frontier in the Exploitation of Africa's Natural Resources: The Emergence of China" *African Perspectives on China in Africa* ed, Firoze Manji and Stephen Marks, Mkuki na Nyota Publishers, Dar es Salaam, 2005.

Taylor, Ian, "Unpacking China's Resource Diplomacy in Africa. China in Africa, *Current African Issues* NO 33, Compiled by Henning Melber, Nordiska Afrikainstitutet, Uppsala 2007.

Thomson, Jamie and Ramzy Kanaan, Conflict Timber: Dimensions of the Problem in Asia and Africa *Volume I Synthesis Report.*

Thornton, Allan, *Chinese Involvement In African Illegal Logging And Timber Trade,* US House of Representatives Committee on International Relations, 8.

Toyne, Paul, Cliona O'Brien & Rod Nelson, The timber footprint of the G8 and China: Making the case for green procurement by government, June 2002.

Tull, Denis. "The Political Consequences of China's Return to Africa", Alden, Chris, Daniel Large and Ricardo Soares de Oliveira, *China Returns to Africa: A Rising Power and a Continent Embrace*, Columbia University Press, New York, 2008.

In: Poverty in Africa
Editor: Thomas W. Beasley

ISBN - 978-1-60741- 737-8
© 2009 Nova Science Publishers, Inc.

Chapter 7

THE EVOLUTION AND DYNAMICS OF URBAN POVERTY IN ZAMBIA

Danny Simatele[1] and Munacinga Simatele[2]

[1]University of Manchester School of Environment and Development Global Urban Research Centre Manchester, UK

[2]University of Hertfordshire Business School de Havilland Campus Hatfield,

ABSTRACT

Urban poverty has become a characteristic feature of urban living in Zambia. Statistical evidence suggests that of the 4.3 million people resident in urban areas of Zambia, 34 % live in extreme poverty while 18 % are moderately poor (CSO, 2005). These figures are indicative that more than half (i.e. 53 %) of the urban population in Zambia live in poverty (CSO, 2004, 2005). Despite these high figures in urban poverty, Zambia as a country has not yet developed an explicit policy framework with which to address the increase in urban poverty and vulnerability. Indeed the failure to formulate urban food policies at the national and municipal levels have played a significant role in the increase of contemporary food problems being faced by many urban residents in the country. This chapter reviews the history of urban development and welfare in Zambia and discusses the nature, roots and dynamics of urban poverty and the coping mechanisms employed by urban residents in Zambia. Institutions form a major part of the discussion throughout the chapter.

1. INTRODUCTION

For over two decades, the Zambian economy was dominated by government ownership. The government regulated commodity and food prices and food consumption was heavily subsidised. The mainstay of the economy was mining, and revenue from the export of copper was used not only in financing domestic expenditure, but also to import food in years of shortages. The impact of the world oil crises between 1973 and 1979, falling copper prices and the resulting general economic deterioration, during the same period and in the early

1980s, turned the focus to agriculture as a possible source of growth, export revenue and increased food security.

With no improvements in agriculture and as a way of recovering from the economic problems that the country was experiencing, the government turned to borrowing, both domestically and internationally to meet its domestic budget. This led to the government signing a '*stand-by arrangement*' with the International Monetary Fund (IMF) in 1973. Despite this approach, no significant recovery in either copper revenues or agriculture was achieved. And as result, the balance of payments and fiscal deficits became enormous, and ultimately forcing the country to embark on continued borrowing from the IMF, but with the IMF attaching conditions to the loans in 1976. These conditional loans signalled the birth of the liberalisation process in Zambia, notably Structural Adjustment Programmes (SAP). In 1981, SAP was introduced, although the implementation was surrounded by controversy until 1991, when a fully-fledged reform programme was implemented. At the macro level, the liberalisation process, and in particular SAPs involved the freeing of the exchange rate, trade liberalisation, privatisation, freeing interest rates, removal of subsidies and all forms of price controls, reducing government expenditure and reducing state participation in the economy, including the streamlining of the public service.

These measures, prescribed by the IMF, and having been implemented and performed reasonably well in the Pacific countries (Asian tigers) were meant to stabilise the Zambian economy that had experienced a dramatic decline, arising mainly from the collapse of copper mining in the North of the country, and falling international demand and prices for copper. However, the combined effects resulting from declines in the economy and the reform programmes, have had devastating effects on the standard of living for most of the Zambian people, especially the poor (Bigsten and Mkenda 2001). There has been a general decline in growth of all sectors of the economy and a sharp increase in formal unemployment. This has been manifested through an increase in both rural and urban poverty and a fall in life expectancy from 55 years in 1970, to 35 years in 2000 (CSO 1998, CSO 2004a).

The worst affected from these developments are the urban population, who depend on the money economy and have experienced a tremendous increase in unemployment in the formal sector. Zambia's unemployment rate currently stands at 50% with the agricultural sector employing about 85% of the country's population, industry and services employ 6% and 9% respectively (CIA 2004). The removal of government subsidies on food, transport, health, education and accommodation, which previously where obtained in urban areas before the implementation of SAP, meant that urban residents have to pay for these services without government support. With massive job retrenchments (especially in urban areas), many households were left without a means to pay for these services. This has resulted in a general decline in the well-being of a large sector of the urban population with an estimated 34 % of the 4.3 million urban residents classified as living below the poverty line[1] (CSO, 2008). In fact the Overseas Development Institute (ODI) observes that, "the average percentage of urban household income that is spent on food is rising, indicating that Zambian [urban] households are finding it increasingly difficult to feed themselves" (Overseas Development Institute, 2003:1).

---

[1] Poverty lines in Zambia have been based on the Food-Energy Intake (FEI). These methods attempt to establish a monetary value at which basic needs are met. At present (2008) the monetary value is set at $23 (111,747 Zambian Kwacha).

In view of the above, this chapter attempts to review the history of urban poverty within the context of urban development and welfare in Zambia. The chapter explores the nature, roots and dynamics of urban poverty and the evolution of vulnerability, including some coping mechanism employed by urban residents in Zambia. We end the chapter ends with a discussion on urban agriculture as one of the activities through which urban poverty and urban food security could be attained.

2. URBAN DEVELOPMENT IN ZAMBIA

Urban centres are a recent phenomenon in Zambia's development, and they emerged either as colonial administrative centres, transport networks or depots in the early 1930's. Notably these centres include Kalomo, Zambia's first capital city, Livingstone, Fort Jameson now Chipata and Lusaka the current capital city. The discovery of copper on the Copperbelt Province, and the eventual mining endeavours of the colonial administrators and other mining companies, resulted in the development of a transport and communication network that linked the mining sites (e.g. Katanga Copper mines, Kabwe, Ndola, and kitwe) in Zambia to the exit ports in South Africa, where copper and other products were shipped to the developed West. These emerging urban centres as observed by Williams, (1986), were generally designed to support a limited number of urban residents because of the limited number of economic activities in them. For example, Turok (1989) observes that colonial administrative centres completely depended on taxes from civil servants, shop keepers and miners. Thus, from an initial colonial planning perspective, the new emerging urban centres were not expected to expand and grow into permanent urban settlements. To ensure that these centres did not grow to unmanageable sizes demographically, population movement from rural to urban centres was controlled through the granting or issuing of temporary residence permits by colonial administration. These permits were limited mostly to men who were needed in the mining industries and a few women who worked as domestic servants. Writing on urban agriculture in Lusaka, Simatele (2007) observes that Africans were not permitted to live permanently in town, and were required by law to return to their rural areas after the expiry of their urban residence or work permits.

In view of the planning system embraced by the colonial administration as early as the 1920s, the emerging urban centres in Zambia were deliberately planned and designed to depend on temporary migrant labour from rural areas. But with the introduction of the labour stabilisation policy in 1948, which required, among other things, the granting of long term contracts and residents permits to African workers, and allowing them to bring their families, a new wave of rural – urban movement was introduced. However, the numbers remained low because of the continued issuance of Pass Laws which required every African male to have a permit before seeking urban residence. These colonial measures made it impossible for Africans to live in urban centres and limited the physical growth of urban centres in Zambia. In light of the controlled urban growth, Fallavier et, al. (2005:3), argues that "…municipal authorities concentrated on only delivering urban infrastructure and services to the small urban population in formal housing areas". This development would prove a catastrophe in the post-independence era, as the provision of urban infrastructure and services for housing, sanitation, health and education would be inadequate to cope with the increase in demand for urban services and facilities.

It is important to point out here that urban development in Zambia was also constrained by the lack of a private housing market. Employers were instead required by statutory law, to provide accommodation for their staff, and this resulted in employers developing only a limited number of housing units to meet the needs of their employees. Furthermore, Simatele (2007:57) observes that, "the issuance of temporally urban residence to Africans, reduced the housing capacity as the Africans had no incentive to invest and build their own houses". Thus, the provision of urban housing was considered as a responsibility for the employers and as Fallavier et, al. (2005:7), observes, "there was no room for private developers".

With the increase in global demand for copper in the 1950s, there was a rapid and unprecedented growth in economic growth in the mining and manufacturing industries. This resulted in increased demand for cheap local labour, thereby encouraging labour migration to urban settlements (Turok, 1989). But with an urban system restricting the development of a private housing market, the growth in urban housing could not keep up with the increased demand. The lack of urban housing gave way to the development of informal housing, later classified as squatter or unauthorised settlements which emerged particularly on European farms (which European farmers referred to as Kafir[2] farming) and on the urban fringes (c. Tait, 1997). Rakodi (1988) observes that living conditions in the squatter settlements were harsh because of overcrowding and a general lack of basic services such as piped water and other sanitation services. The urban migrant worker's needs were not considered in the planning policy and were therefore, not entitled to basic urban services and facilities. Tait (1997:153) for example, observes that, "never during the colonial rule was an enfranchisement of Africans living in towns seriously considered" (Tait 1997:153). Furthermore, Freeman (1991:4), is of the view that, "there was no attempt to integrate Africans and their activities into these urban centres. On the contrary, the cities were regarded by the European colonisers as their own exclusive preserves".

At the attainment of independence in 1964, the inadequacy in the provision of urban infrastructure and services, particularly in housing worsened due to increased immigration to urban centre as the travel restriction imposed by the colonial administration were lifted by the new black majority government. Fallavier et, al. (2005) and Tait (1997) argue that due to the shortages of urban housing in the formal settlement, most of the new arrivals from rural areas built temporary houses in the already burgeoning unauthorised settlements. And during the first one and half decades after political independence, one third of the urban population in Zambia was living in the squatter settlements (informal housing) (c. Williams, 1986). And despite the economic deterioration and stagnation arising from the oil crisis of the mid 1970s, and the introduction of structural adjustment programmes in the 1980s, the urban population in Zambia continued to grow. Consequently, demand for informal housing rapidly increased, while the capacity for municipal authorities to provide housing and other essential urban facilities drastically reduced due to lack of financial resources and a weak institutional setup.

Statistical evidence suggests that by 1980, an estimated 40 % of the urban population lived in informal urban settlements, and by 1990, over 50 % lived in the four major cities of Zambia (Livingstone, Kitwe, Lusaka and Ndola) (CSO, 1998). With insufficient resources and an institutional setup designed to meet the needs of a very small number of urban

---

[2] A word in Afrikaans meaning referring to black people).

residents, municipal authorities in Zambia have continued to confine their activities to the maintenance and delivery of urban services in formal settlements. On the contrary, residents in the informal settlements, with limited access to financial resources and other assets, continue to experiment with the self-provision of housing. It is important to note that the initial urban planning and development policy in Zambia laid the foundation for the contemporary urban processes. It could be argued for example that urban poverty and deprivation, is a product of the initial disenfranchisement and marginalisation of the urban poor reflected in the policies implemented to guide urban development. Furthermore, the failure to correct the inequalities and irregularities inherited from the colonial administration is reflective of weak institutions both at the municipal and national levels.

3. URBAN POVERTY IN ZAMBIA

Urban poverty has become a characteristic feature of urban living in Zambia. While its evolution and history is closely linked to poor urban policies, its increase in intensity can, in a large part, be traced to the 1990s when Zambia embarked on a fully-fledged implementation of economic reforms in the form of structural adjustment programmes (SAPs). At the macro level, SAPs involved a number of processes, among which included, the freeing of the exchange rate, privatisation, removal of subsidies, reducing government expenditure, and reducing state participation in the economy, including streamlining of the public service. These measures, prescribed by the IMF and the World Bank were meant to stabilise the Zambian economy that had experienced a dramatic decline arising from the falling demand for copper, and the oil crisis in the 1970s. The combined effects of the economic reforms and an erring economy, especially starting in the 1980s, subjected a large proportion of the Zambian people to high levels of deprivation and poverty. The most affected were urban population who depend on the money economy as their main source of livelihood (c. Milimo et; al. 2002, Simatele and Binns, 2008). The privatisation process and the IMF/World Bank's reform programs which required the government to downsize the civil service and cut its budget by abolishing free social services, such as education and health led to unprecedented levels of poverty as can be seen from the table below. This development, according to Milimo et; al (2002), compromised the ability of many poor and not so poor urban households to access services these key including housing and sanitation facilities.

From the Living Conditions Monitoring Surveys conducted by the Zambian Central Statistics Office (CSO), there is an indication that with the implementation of a fully-fledged reform programme in 1991, Zambia experienced a general decline in growth of all sub-sectors of the economy, and this became manifested in the increase in poverty in both rural and urban areas, 83.1% and 56% respectively (CSO 2005). In fact current statistical evidence suggests that of the 4.3 million people resident in urban areas in Zambia, 34 % live in extreme poverty, while 18 % are moderately poor (CSO, 2005). These figures are indicative of the fact that more than half (i.e. 53 %) of the urban population in Zambia live in poverty (CSO, 2004a, 2005).

Table 1. Incidence of Poverty in Zambia: 1991 – 2006

	1991	1993	1996	1998	2004	2006
Zambia	70	74	69	73	68	64
Rural/urban						
Rural	88	92	82	83	78	80
Urban	49	45	46	56	53	34
Province						
Central	70	81	74	77	76	72
Copperbelt	61	49	56	65	56	42
Eastern	85	91	82	79	70	79
Luapula	84	88	78	82	79	73
Lusaka	31	39	38	53	48	29
Northern	84	86	84	81	74	78
North Western	75	88	80	77	76	72
Southern	79	87	76	75	69	73
Western	84	91	84	89	83	84

Source. CSO (2008a)

Although rural poverty is consistently higher than urban poverty, the trend shows that there is a relative upward trend in urban poverty. This upward trend is clearly more evident in the most urbanised provinces in the country, i.e. Lusaka, Southern and Central Provinces. CSO(2008a) suggests that the increase in these figures would be more visible without the mitigating effect of the decline in rural poverty.

Despite the fluctuations in poverty trends seen in the table, it is apparent that poverty is one of Zambia's development challenges both in rural and urban areas.

The high incidence of poverty in Zambia has drastically lowered the standard of living for many urban residents in Zambia. Access to food in urban areas has declined for many households. A recent study on food production in Lusaka, for example, reveals that a significant number of households have resorted to reducing the number of meals they have per day. The study also shows that there are cases involving household members taking turns to have meals in order to survive. Of the 180 households included in the said study, for example, 32 % revealed that they had one meal a day, 34 % said they had two meals, while 33 % claimed to have all three meals (c. Simatele, 2007, Simatele and Binns, 2008). During one of the interviews, a female respondent remarked;

> "because of hunger and the difficult times in the city, a lot of men are at a 'standstill' and seem not to think anymore. Although in a worse situation, women must think and find food for the family"
>
> (Pers.Com 2006).

The inability to acess food has been attributed to a number of factors, among which include; lack of access to financial resources due to a general lack of employment opportunities in the formal sector, poor health, lack of education and the general stagnation in the economy. With a high dependence on the money economy, urban residents have found it extremely difficult to attain food security and other basic services. In the Lusaka study cited above, only 22 % of the respondents indicated that they were in formal employment, 29 % were employed in the informal sector, and the remaining 44 % were unemployed (c. Simatele and Binns, 2008). Other statistics on the city level reveal that the working population in Lusaka (aged 12 years and above) increased by 13% between 1990 and 2000 from 247,644 in 1990 to 281,397 in 2000. This increase however, is much lower than the increase of 52.9% at the national level (CSO 2004a, 2004b).

Table 2 below shows that the number of self-employed persons as a proportion of the total working population in Lusaka increased from 20.3% in 1990 to 30.0% in 2000. The ratio of self-employed persons by sex also increased between the two intercensal (census) periods. However, the increase in the male self-employed persons (from 17.8% in 1990 to 28.7% in 2000) is considerably greater than the corresponding increase in female self-employed persons (from 27.1% in 1990, to 33.1% in 2000).

Table 2. Changes in employment in Lusaka District between 1990 and 2000

Employment status and gender	Total Lusaka 1990	Total Lusaka 2000	Peri-urban 1990	Peri-urban 2000	Built-up areas 1990	Built-up areas 2000
Total number	247,644	281,397	42,588	49,998	205,056	231,399
Male	181,373	197,476	29,158	33,942	152,215	163,525
Female	66,271	83,930	13,430	16,056	52,841	67,874
Self-employed in %						
Total	20.3	30.0	27.4	30.7	18.8	29.9
Male	17.8	28.7	27.9	33.4	15.9	27.8
Female	27.1	33.1	26.1	25.1	27.3	35.0
Employee in %						
Total	64.8	60.3	37.2	37	70.5	65.3
Male	70.8	64.2	45.8	44.3	75.5	68.3
Female	48.4	51.1	18.5	21.5	56.0	58.1
Employer in %						
Total	2.7	1.1	2.0	0.8	2.9	1.1
Male	3.1	1.2	2.4	0.9	3.2	1.3
Female	1.8	0.7	1.1	0.4	2.1	0.8

Source: CSO (2004a)

Although these figures seem to indicate an upward trend in employment opportunities, a closer look at Table 2 indicates that starting from the 1990s an increasing proportion of males have become self-employed in the informal sector. The considerable increase in self-employment is also noticeable with respect to residence, such that in the built-up area of Lusaka, the proportion of self-employed males increased by a larger margin of 11.9% (from 15.9% to 27.8%), compared with that of females which increased only by 7.7% (from 27.3% to 35.0%). Another striking feature in Table 2 is the decrease in the proportion of the workforce classified as 'employers'. From a total proportion of 2.7% in 1990, this figure was reduced by over 50% to just 1.1% in 2000. Furthermore, the table shows that the proportion of the total population classified as 'employees' decreased from 64.8% in 1990 to 60.3% in 2000. Similarly, the proportion of male employees decreased from 70.8% in 1990 to 64.2% in 2000. On the contrary, however, female employees increased slightly from 48.4% in 1990 to 51% in 2000. The general picture depicted in Table 2 is that Lusaka has experienced a drastic decline in employment opportunities. There is no doubt that the decline in employment trends in urban Zambia has played a significant role in the increase of poverty in urban areas. As stated above the decline in employment opportunities and the deteriorations in other social indicators such as education and health worsened during the period of economic adjustments.

However, the socio-economic reform programmes that Zambia embarked on in the early 1980s, and which were aimed at stimulating the market cannot be exclusively blamed for the increase in urban poverty. A number of studies show that well functioning markets are important in the process of reducing poverty (c. Sjoquist, 2001). However, it is now recognised that markets by themselves are social and political structures composed of people with varying degree of power and influence, and with limited capacity to obtain information they need. In view of this argument, markets in the absence of well functioning institutions cannot reduce poverty. Greeley (2000) for example, observes that in places were poverty reduction has truly been achieved, it has not occurred because of markets alone, but rather because reforms have created opportunities to use assets more productively for the poor.

On the other hand, the nature and effectiveness of any reform programmes is dependent on the type and quality of governance systems and this in turn determines the effectiveness of institutions. In fact proponents of the governance approach to development tend to emphasise the social and political side of people's lives rather than the economic perspective as the most important basis for poverty reduction. The central argument in this approach is that any poverty reduction efforts must seek to enhance individual and community well-being, by promoting capacity building and freedom of choice in an equitable and just society. Thus, social development depends not only on economic growth and getting the fundamentals of macroeconomic policy right, but also on social policy and better distribution of the benefits of growth (UNRISD, 2000). Better distribution of growth and the development of pro-poor social policies are dependent on the institutional setup and their capacities of organising development projects and activities at all levels of society.

It is important to note that the term 'institutions' is here used to refer to, 'the humanly devised constraints that shape human interactions' (North, 1990). In other words, it is being used to refer to *the rules of society*, which can either be formal (e.g. written policies, laws, rules, and regulations) or informal referring to customs, traditions and conventions that constrains, yet makes actors express themselves. It is important to note that, the term 'constraint' must be interpreted in the spirit of *guidelines,* rather then carrying the negative ramifications. Institutional constraints do on one hand, state what is not allowed in a society or community, but on the other identify what is considered normal and appropriate behaviour. According to Eriksson-Skoog (1998), institutions help reduce uncertainty in the individual's daily life, and to structure human activity into lasting or repeated patterns of action. Thus, institutions can limit an individual's action space, but at the same time, they can reduce uncertainty and award proper behaviour, adding a positive implication (North, 1990, Crawfold & Ostrom, 1995).

In light of the arguments above, the link between markets and institutions is paramount in stimulating economic growth and reducing poverty. In other words, institutions are what make a market function well. However, the gap in emphasis placed between economic and institutional reforms, can in part, be argued as one of the factors contributing to the high incidence rate of poverty in urban Zambia. Although Zambia has achieved significant gains in stabilising the economy and attaining some form of balance of payments through the implementation of economic reforms, the neglect in reforming its institutions has compromised the impacts of these gains in poverty reduction and national development (Chisala et; al. 2006). Indeed, institutional reforms in Zambia have lagged behind, and Tordoff and Young (1994:290) observe that "at the present time, the local authorities face what amounts to be a crisis of capacity in the delivery of services". Mukwena (2002), for instance argues that even if funding for the various services councils are expected to provide became available immediately, it is very unlikely that these funds could be applied to the tasks of service provision in a cost-effective manner. This state of affairs must not only be understood as weaknesses in current institutional capabilities in both national and local authorities, but also within the context of the audience that these institutions were meant to serve at their inception.

As stated above, urban institutions were established to serve only a limited number of urban residents in formal settlements. Those in informal settlements were not catered for, but were expected to fend for themselves. And the continued failure to change or modify the colonial institutions to cope with the current new reality by both local and national authorities has implied that these institutions have remained inadequate to incorporate the activities of the urban poor in urban development and planning policy. As during the colonial administration, the urban poor who in most cases are resident in informal settlements continue to be marginalised and have little or no access to basic services such as clean drinking water, health and educational facilities.

The failure to reform both local and national institutions has implied that the informal sector, which plays a significant parallel role to the formal sector, and employs a large section of the urban population in Zambia, has remained underdeveloped and ignored. It is this development that has proved to be catastrophic in poverty reduction efforts in urban Zambia. With increases in job loses, reduced productivity in rural agriculture due to poor rains and cost of agro inputs, including increased mortality rates due to HIV/AIDS and other diseases, the burgeoning urban informal sector has proved to be a life line for many Zambians. However, the neglect in institutional reforms and the inadequate incorporation of the informal sector in policy formulation has had a negative effect on poverty reduction efforts. Furthermore, the neglect of the role played by cultural institutions such as family ties in providing social capital is detrimental not only to the development process but more so to the poverty reduction efforts. The increase in the mortality rates for example, in the face of increased unemployment has meant that households, with only a limited income have had to take on additional family members (orphans), increasing dependence ratios and thereby reducing their standard of living.

It is important to state that urban poverty in Zambia is a result of a combination of factors such as discussed above. However, it is also vital to add that good governance which is a product of well functioning institutions can support poverty reduction, while bad governance and institutions can deprive citizens of income, social services, education, health, and the opportunity to speak and participate in projects and activities that have a direct influence of their lives. In order for Zambia to reduce urban poverty, the country needs to promote values that will facilitate pro-poor growth and empowerment so that poor households are enabled to make choices that allow them to function in the market economy and determine the direction of their lives. Both national and local authorities need to develop a policy framework that will encourage the participation of the poor and *lowers* (e.g women, children and the aged) to ensure equitable growth and poverty reduction. In the absence of well functioning institutions, no approach will reduce urban poverty in Zambia.

4. URBAN AGRICULTURE AS A MEANS OF COPING WITH URBAN POVERTY

The urban poor in Zambia employ a number of livelihood options to wade off poverty. One such option is urban agriculture (UA), which in addition to the more traditional use of large open urban spaces and back yards; it is now being practiced in a much wider variety of situations such as; between railway lines, around industrial areas, along roadsides and in the middle of roundabouts etc. Plot size varies from $5m^2$ to $15m^2$ and crops grown include; maize, cabbage, pumpkin, tomatoes, groundnuts, okra, beans, cucumbers, and sweet potatoes, etc.

Figure 1. A family working a vegetable garden in Garden Compound in Lusaka, Zambia.

Source: author's field work

The underlying motivation for the increased participation in UA is twofold. Firstly, UA has become a major source of food for many urban households, providing both exotic and traditional food stuffs which may be unavailable in shops or markets. Secondly, UA is regarded as a valuable opportunity for income generation through the sale of produce, and even through renting out the land on which it is practiced. There is no doubt that the deterioration in the national economic situation has been a major factor in the flourishing of UA in many urban centres in Zambia. All households have felt the effects of the progressive implementation of a series of reform programmes. These reform programmes, which involved the retreat of the state and widespread privatisation, have led to a significant reduction in opportunities for formal and wage employment, such that formal sector employment in

Zambia as a whole has diminished by over 52% since 1991 (Seshamani, 2006). Such formal sector employment that does exist no longer guarantees the security of lifetime employment with a reliable and adequate income that would ensure continuing household security. A study of UA in three different locations of Lusaka revealed the contribution of this informal activity to food and income.

Table 3. The contribution of UA to food and savings in the three study locations (N=180*).

Characteristics	Survey areas		
	Chilenje	Garden Compound	Seven Miles
Number of respondents	70	70	40
Producer motivation	For h/hold consumption, and savings. Provides 65% leafy vegs. for 30+% of h/holds. 18% of h/holds also report supplying markets with fresh vegs.	For food. Provides 75% of fresh vegs. for 48% of h/holds during the rainy season. Produces mainly local varieties of vegs. not normally sold in shops/markets. Majority are women cultivators.	Full-time production for 96% of households. Provides nearly all domestic food requirements, & for the market. Produces a range of agro-products (vegs., fruits, cereals, dairy, livestock etc)
Economic return	31% women in full-time gardening. Makes an avge. income of $100/month. Equiv. to 1 month civil servant wage/savings	Accounts for 10 –20% of h/hold income during the rainy season. Equiv. to between $15 - $35/month wage savings.	Annual income equiv. to $5000 from sale of cereals or livestock. Also monthly income equiv. to 2 months civil servants wage/per month from sell of vegs. and fruits
Total per cent of all respondents	38.8	38.8	22.2
Average plot size (m^2)	15	5	50 – 300
Distance from city centre (in Km)	5	5	13

* Based on grassroots and focus group interviews.
Source: Authors' field notes, 2005.

It is apparent from the table that UA provided 75% of all vegetable requirements to some 48% of households in Garden Compound during the rainy season, when UA activities are at their peak. Although the income generation aspect of UA is rather limited in Garden Compound, respondents reported that it saves them the equivalent of between $15 and $35 per month. The importance of UA to households in Lusaka was vividly described by a male respondent in Chilenje:

> "Urban agriculture is an important source of food and income for me. Because the law prohibits its practice, I have converted three of my undeveloped residential plots into garden sites. This too is illegal, but it is the only way to beat the system. I have built up security (i.e. wall) fences around them. That way, the Council won't repossess them on the grounds that the land is not developed. Individual cultivators are currently renting these plots for the production of vegetables. They pay me cash and they have reserved a portion of their gardens from where I harvest, although I am not involved in actual cultivation" (Pers. Com, 2005)

Another female respondent involved in urban agriculture commented;

"life in Lusaka has become difficult. Although my husband and I do not own land, growing our own food has helped us a lot because we are now able to feed ourselves and to save a bit of money for other things

(Pers. com, 2005).

Despite the nutritional and economic value of urban agriculture, it is officially prohibited by law, and considered as an illegal activity in Lusaka. Those who practice it, do so in fear of either being prosecuted by the local authority or losing land to other land developers. This is so because of the lack of a legal framework protecting the interests of urban farmers and the urban poor. Many urban farmers and key informants included in the Lusaka study expressed strong views about the marginalization of UA in Lusaka's planning processes. Most responses from professionals for example, shared a common concern, with 68% identifying land as the major constraint facing the future development of urban agriculture in the city.

Table 4. Urban land use in Lusaka City

Land use	Area/hectare	Percentage
Administration	142.03	0.34
Airport	215.17	0.51
Cemetery	247.51	0.58
Central Business District	250.78	0.59
Large/medium-scale and commercial farming	3,979.34	9.50
Industrial	772.59	1.82
Informal settlement	4,442.32	10.49
Institutional	624.87	1.48
Proposed housing project	1,455.17	3.44
Residential	4,818.43	11.38
Small holdings	4,226.42	9.98
Sport & recreation	396.37	0.94
Unutilized land/open spaces	20,765.74	49.05
Total	**42,336.74**	**100.00**

Source: Lusaka City Council, 2000

Key informants, for example, pointed out that urban agriculture requires land, and any available land in the city has already been developed for either residential or business purposes. From a planning perspective, planning authorities argue that

"land is a big problem in the city and people looking for urban land have to buy it from private land owners"

(Pers. com 2005)

However, an examination of the 'Land Use Map of Lusaka' revealed that the city still has huge tracks of land classified as 'unutilised'. Table 3 shows that almost half of the total land surface in Lusaka (c. 49%) is either un-utilized, or lies as open spaces. However, it was revealed by professionals, especially those from the local authority that, although Lusaka has a number of open spaces, these areas have not been linked, from the planning perspective, to possible areas for the future development of urban agriculture. In fact, interviews with senior municipal planners revealed that all existing open spaces in the city have been reserved for either commercial purposes, or are on a 99 year lease to private individuals. Thus, most of Lusaka's urban cultivators are in effect squatters on the land they cultivate. They have no protection in the event that someone decides to develop the land, even when they have crops growing on the land.

It is thus, difficult to envisage how urban poverty in Zambia can be reduced in the absence of well functioning institutions promoting the incorporation of activities of the urban poor into planning policy. Thus, it seems to be the case that weak and inefficient national and local government institutions are responsible for ignoring the significance and potential of small-scale food production initiatives in urban Zambia, which if recognised, would be instrumental in poverty reduction. In Zambia, the Ministry of Agriculture, Food and Fisheries (MAFF), is responsible for any form of agricultural activities. Ideally, MAFF should work in close association with other ministries and organizations, such as the Ministries of Lands and Environment, Local Government and Housing, and the Central Statistics Office (CSO).

However, recent field-based research revealed that there little or no co-ordination and consultation among such organizations concerning both rural and urban food production. This lack of co-ordination and consultation has resulted in a limited comprehension of what urban agriculture actually is, and what are the most appropriate policies to deal with it. A senior official from Lusaka City Council argued that, *"UA should be discussed within the context of the national agricultural policy, which attaches great importance to rural food production. In this way, UA could be included on the urban agenda and contribute to poverty reduction"* (Pers. com 2005). However, interviews with officials from the Lusaka District Agriculture Department revealed that absolutely no effort has been made thus far to document the scale and character of urban agriculture in and around the city. They pointed out that all the food production surveys undertaken in the city have focused on large- and medium-scale commercial farming which is located on the city's urban fringes. When asked to justify why UA in Lusaka has not been documented, an official from MAFF argued that, *"UA is entrenched with negative attitudes which are supported by legislation opposing its practice. It is forbidden by law and no resources are made available to investigate its output"* (Pers. Com 2005). Under these circumstances involving the non recognition of the informal sector, urban poverty in Zambia will remain a permanent feature of the urban landscape. However, with a positive change in the way the informal sector is viewed from a planning perspective, significant gains aimed at reducing urban poverty will be attained.

5. CONCLUSION

It is clear from the discussion in this chapter that poverty in Zambian cities is diverse, dynamic with an upward trend. It is also evident that the relevant authorities have failed to recognise important aspects of its evolution and develop appropriate poverty reduction policies both on the local or national level. These failures must however, be understood within the context of urban development and the development of urban institutions and the purpose for which these establishments were meant to fulfil. With the initial purpose of serving only a limited number of urban residents and the failure to modify or reform them after political independence, urban institutions in Zambia have been overwhelmed and have failed to tap the potential that comes with the process of urbanisation. It has been argued in the discussion that better tapping of this potential would help reduce urban poverty. The inadequacies and weaknesses in urban institutions have resulted in viable coping mechanisms adopted by the urban poor being excluded in urban planning policies. These coping mechanisms, such as UA that the urban poor have developed to face their worsening living conditions, appear as solid blocks upon which to build more prosperous urban futures.

It is important to note that as the role of the state and the local authorities have diminished due to economic stagnation at both the local and the national level, a range of informal coping activities have been developed by the urban poor to deal with the social and economic hardships. However, these informal sector activities alone are not sufficient to propel large numbers of urban residents out of poverty, or even to protect them from the impacts of shocks that might arise from economic or natural events such as climate change. They are however, indispensable foundations upon which any poverty reduction and social protection strategy should build upon, if any local or national efforts to reduce poverty are to succeed. In view of this observation, the comprehension of the nature and dynamics of urban poverty from a planning perspective is paramount. However, the understanding of urban poverty by urban managers in many municipalities in Zambia does not give credit to these informal mechanisms. If anything, urban managers tend to repress local initiatives that could otherwise substantially contribute in poverty reduction. As illustrated in this discussion, the regulatory framework to urban planning concentrate on enforcing a set of physical planning rules remote from the realities obtaining in urban centres, at the expense of promoting and facilitating long term development of local economic and social potentials by supporting local coping mechanisms.

It seems therefore that the way forward is to put in place an efficient and supportive institutional framework recognising the value of the informal sector as an avenue through which the poor can develop coping mechanisms and ways for urban communities in Zambia can work towards poverty reduction. The poor in urban Zambia represent a 'silent majority', who are unable to effectively articulate their economic and social concerns. This is because they lack both protection and adequate representation, which has left them marginalized and vulnerable to exploitation. Their powerless position has left many of them facing difficulties such as forced displacement from the informal activities they engage in such as the land they cultivate by the local authority or powerful land owners. It would prove constructive therefore to encourage a dialogue and to develop greater empathy between the different actors. Future urban planning strategies must be based on this dialogue and the more detailed understanding which it should foster.

In light of the fact that many of the urban poor come from the most disadvantaged groups in economic and social terms, it seems that there would be much to gain from greater collaboration among the urban poor, perhaps through the establishment of a union or an NGO which might be encouraged by the city authorities in a spirit of greater cooperation. With a collective and more articulate message, the urban poor are more likely to be incorporated into debates concerning sustainable urban planning. If properly planned and integrated into sustainable development planning policies, informal sector activities such as urban agriculture could in time actually widen the financial revenue base for Lusaka's local government, through the payment of taxes and rent for use of urban land, and other services such as water. But before this can happen, it is important that everyone is fully aware of the significance of the informal sector for food security, employment and income, and ultimately poverty reduction, at a time when the country is facing economic constraints and post-adjustment pressures.

6. REFERENCES

Bigsten A and Mkenda K (2001). *Impacts of Trade Liberalisation in Zambia: A report for SIDA*, University of Gothenburg.
Central Statistics Office (CSO) (2004a). *Living Conditions Monitoring Survey Report 2002-2003*. CSO, Lusaka, Zambia.
Central Statistics Office (CSO) (2004b). *Zambia, 2000 Census of Population and Housing: Lusaka Province Analytical Report,* Vol 5. CSO, Lusaka, Zambia.
Chisala V, A., Geda, H., Dagdeviren, T., McKinley, A. & Saad-Filho (2006). *Economic Policies for Growth, Employment and Poverty Reduction: Case Study of Zambia.* United Nations Development Programme, Washington DC.
CIA (2004). *The World Factbook 2004.* Washington DC, USA.
Crawford, S. & Ostrom, E. (1995). "A Grammar of Institutions". *American Political Review,* 89(3), Pp. 582-600.
CSO (1998). *Living conditions in Zambia: Preliminary report.* Central Statistic Office, Lusaka.
CSO (2005). *Living Conditions Monitoring Survey Report, 2004.* Government printers, Lusaka.
CSO (2008). *The Monthly.* Vol. 68, Lusaka, Zambia.
CSO (2008a). *Living Conditions* available at http://www.zamstats.gov.zm/lcm.php, accessed 29/12/08
Eriksson-Skoog, G. (1998). *The Soft Budget Constraint. The Emergence, Persistence and Logic of an Institution.* Stockholm, Sweden: The Economic Research Institute at Stockholm School of Economics.
Fallavier, P., Mulenga, C. and Jere, H. (2005). *Livelihoods, poverty and vulnerability in urban Zambia: Assessment of situations, coping mechanisms and constraints.* Draft Paper, the World Bank, Washington DC.
Freeman, D. (1991). *A City of Farmers: Informal Urban Agriculture in the Open Spaces of Nairobi, Kenya.* McGill-Queen's Press, London.
Greeley, M. (2000). *Pro-poor Growth: A Review of Three Issues Informing the Current Policy Agenda.* Paper prepared for the expert consultation on the OECD poverty reduction guidelines, Callantsoog, Netherlands, 13-14September, 2000.
Milimo, J., Shilito, T. & Brock, K. (2002). *Who Would Listen to the Poor? The Poor of Zambia Speak.* PAG Research Reports, Lusaka, Zambia.

Mukwena, R. (2002). *Building the Institutional Capacity of Local Authorities in Zambia in the Third republic: An Assessment.* Lusaka, Zambia.

North, D. C. (1990). *Institutions, Institutional Change and Economic Performance.* London, New York, Cambridge University Press.

Overseas Development Institute. (2003). *Zambia food security issues paper.* Oxford University press. Also published at http:// www.reliefweb.int/w/rwb.nsf. (Date accessed 18.03.04.

Rakodi, C. (1988). *Self Reliance or Survival? Food Production in African Cities with particular reference to Zambia.* University of Wales, Institute of Science and Technology, UK.

Seshamani, V. (2006). 'Privatisation in Zambia', *The Post-Zambia News paper,* Tuesday, 16th of May 2006, Lusaka.

Simatele, D. (2007). *Motivation and Marginalisation of Urban Agriculture in Lusaka, Zambia.* PhD Thesis, University of Sussex, Brighton.

Sjoquist, P. (2001), *Institutions and Poverty Reduction – An introductory explanation.* Capacity Development – SIDA working paper, No. 9.

Tait, J. (1997). *From Self-Help Housing to Sustainable Settlement: Capitalist development and urban planning in Lusaka, Zambia.* Avebury, Aldershot, England.

Tordoff, W. & Young, R. A. (1994). " Decentralisation and Public Sector Reform in Zambia". *Journal of Southern African Studies,* Vol. 20, pp 285-299.

Turok, B. (1989). Mixed Economy in Focus: Zambia. Institute of African Alternatives, London.

UNRISD, (2000). *Visible Hands. Taking Responsibility for Social Development.* Geneva, Switzerland: United Nations Research Institute for Social Development.

Williams, G. (1986). The Physical Growth of Lusaka: Past and Projected. In Williams G (ed) *Lusaka and Its Environs: A geographical Study of a Planned Capital City in Tropical Africa.* Associated Printers Ltd, Lusaka, Pp 138 – 154.

In: Poverty in Africa
Editor: Thomas W. Beasley

ISBN: 978-1-60741-737-8
© 2009 Nova Science Publishers, Inc.

Chapter 8

THE ROLE OF SMALL SCALE SURVIVALIST ENTERPRISES IN GENERATION OF HOUSEHOLD INCOMES IN VHEMBE DISTRICT OF LIMPOPO PROVINCE, SOUTH AFRICA

*[*][1]*Maliwichi, L.L., [2]Oni S.A. and [3]Sifumba, L.*

[1]University of Venda, Department of Family Ecology and Consumer Science,
P/B. X5050, Thohoyandou, 0950, South Africa.
[2]University of Venda, Department of Agriculture Economics,
P/B. X5050, Thohoyandou, 0950, South Africa.
[3]University of Venda, Department of Agriculture Economics,
P/B. X5050, Thohoyandou, 0950, South Africa.

ABSTRACT

Most families in developing countries are resorting to small-scale businesses as a response to economic hardships resulting from inflation and economic changes. The families' role in small scale businesses is carried out under conditions of hardship that include limited economic resources, low levels of technology, lack of adequate knowledge and lack of appropriate skills. Self-employment in South Africa using a variety of skills has become an alternative source of employment for many low income households.

The main purpose of this study was to assess the ability of small scale income generating activities to create employment and generate household income. A total of 85 households were purposely selected using the snow-balling methodology. A set of both closed and open-ended questionnaires was used to collect data on household income generating activities from heads of households.

Results for household income generating activities showed no evidence of employment creation except that the activities were used to generate income and reduce household food insecurity. According to the results a mean income of R873.15 per month was generated by these activities. Although the income was not adequate to support a

---

[*] Corresponding author email: Maliwichi@univen.ac.za

mean number of 8 dependants in a household, the income was higher than the pension grant of R700 which rural people depend on. The main constraints facing household income generating activities were: lack of working capital, lack of management skills, and marketing related problems. Financial support and skills training were identified as necessary strategies to overcome lack of working capital, lack of management skills and marketing constraints.

Keywords: Income-generation, Food Security, Self-employment, Small-scale business enterprises, micro-enterprises

INTRODUCTION

Background to the Study

Economists and policy makers have toyed with the idea of promoting small-scale businesses to nurture economic development, through the creation of jobs for many years. They strongly argued that economic development could be promoted by these businesses. The changes in the 1970s of global economy led to improved prospects about small-scale businesses. These changes included the collapse of the Bretton Woods system of fixed exchange rates, the tripling of oil prices and global liquidity. These changes destabilized the global economy and precipitated two recessions in the 1970s [Vosloo 1994].

Recession is the reduction in the flow of effective demand for capital goods and consumer goods and services. It results in a down spiral of crucial economic activities such as shrinkage of production and employment, diminishing purchasing power of producer and consumers, declining of turn-over and cash flows and rising surplus capacity and lower levels of investment in productive capacity. Small businesses in the United States created two thirds of million jobs during those times of economic difficulties [Vosloo 1994]. Small-scale business is now regarded as an essential element in a successful formula for economic growth, job creation and social progress.

In South Africa the concept of Small Medium and Micro Enterprises (SMMEs) have been receiving a special attention after the 1994 elections, since it is believed to be an important vehicle to address challenges of job creation and economic growth [Department of Trade and Industry 1995].

It is easier to describe small-scale businesses than to define them. Their description can be made in reference to qualitative and quantitative characteristics. Qualitatively, Burns & Dewhurst (1989) described them as those firms that have a small share of the market, managed by their owners and not through formalized management structure. Quantitative measures differ widely, in the economies of Europe, Japan and United States small-scale businesses are those businesses with fewer than 100 employees [Vosloo 1994] compared to African economies whereby small-scale businesses are described as those businesses employing zero (that is the owner does not hire anybody to help him or her) to 50 people [Baud 1993]. The Department of Trade and Industry's white paper on development and promotion of small-scale businesses in South Africa of 1995 described these businesses as those that employ from 5 to 50 employees. These businesses are owned, managed or directly controlled by the community. They are likely to operate from business or industrial premises, be tax registered and meet other formal registration requirements. Classification in terms of assets and turnovers is very difficult because of the wide differences in various business sectors like retailing, manufacturing, professional services and construction. In rural areas of South Africa agribusinesses constitute the bulk of SMMEs hence the focuses on agricultural based small scale businesses.

Survivalist enterprises are those activities carried out by people who are unable to find a paid job or get into economic sector of their choice [Department of Trade and Industry 1995]. Income generated from these activities usually falls far short of even a minimum income standard, with little capital invested and virtually no skills training in the particular field and only limited opportunities for growth into a viable business. Poverty and struggle to survive are the main characteristics of this category of enterprises. This study was designed to analyze the economic contribution of small- scale survivalist enterprises with the hope of highlighting their characteristics and their contribution to household income.

Problem Statement

South African economy like the global economy experienced some economic difficulties in the 1970s and 1980s. There was a slowdown in the growth of both output and employment because of political – uncertainties [Department of Agriculture 1998]. Regardless of this economic slowdown, the population continued to grow at a rate of two percent per year. The real per capita income declined resulting in widespread unemployment which in turn led to widespread poverty.

Poverty has many faces; it is hunger, being sick from drinking unclean water, lack of shelter, being sick and unable to see a doctor, not having a job and fear of the future [Provincial department of agriculture 2001]. Most of the poor people live in rural areas with female-headed households being the poorest. Limpopo province where the study was based has poverty rate of 59% [Poverty and Inequality in South Africa 1998].

One major strategy for alleviating poverty in the Limpopo province is to set up small-scale agribusinesses to promote rural income and employment. The government under the Poverty Alleviation Strategy of 2001 has adopted this strategy. However, one is not sure how far the small-scale businesses have succeeded in promoting rural employment and enhancing rural incomes in the province. This was the rationale for undertaking this study.

OBJECTIVES OF THE STUDY

The objectives of this study were specified as follows:
- To identify agricultural related income-generating activities at household levels in Vhembe district.
- To identify the constraints and problems facing household income generating activities in Vhembe district.
- To identify organizations that are giving support to small scale bussinesses and the type of support that they are providing.
- To establish whether these activities are generating income or not.

Justification of the Study

The research aim was to assess the role of survivalist enterprises as strategies in poverty reduction and also to assess constraints and opportunities offered by small scale business enterprises.

LITERATURE REVIEW

Africa's rural population no longer lives in a closed society, depending on themselves or their clans for their subsistence. The need to meet growing demands for facilities such as schools, health, transport and modern housing make household income-generating activities essential. Rural dwellers boost their income and standard of living through a number of rural activities such as;

- **Agricultural production**, which includes crop production (cereal, cash crops, vegetables); large and small animal raising (poultry, rabbits, pigs); bee keeping and fish culture.
- **Food processing** which involves milling (hands milling), hulling, food preservation (cold storage, juice, jam and bread making) and processing equipment.
- **Agricultural related and non-agricultural activities** such as the manufacture of farm implements, rural construction, wood and metal workshops, masonry welding and motor repair.
- **Art and handicrafts** in the form of weaving, dyeing, basket making, embroidery, shoe making and sewing.
- **Commercial activities** such as selling basic commodities such as salt, sugar, milk, matches and soap.
- **Selling agricultural and related implements** and equipment [Http: www.agnet.org/library/article]

Factors Influencing the Success or Failure of Survivalist Enterprises

People involved in survivalist enterprises have a primary goal of earning income. People do not only want to earn income; they want to get highest (maximum) income from resources at their disposal. According to FAO [2000] three factors need to be considered for maximizing this income namely; technically feasibility, economic profitability and financial feasibility. Basically technical feasibility looks at the individual's ability to know how to perform a certain task. This ability may involve special skills, which can be acquired through special training and from work experience. Liedholm and Chuta [1985] showed this need in their work on small-scale industries of Sierra Leone, whereby there was a positive relationship between owners who had acquired apprenticeship and their levels of profit. In addition to being technically feasible the income generating activity should be profitable that is, it should produce a surplus (profit). Lastly for any business or project to be successful, it must be financially feasible. Capital is needed to acquire other resources like machinery and labour.

The Role of Women in Survivalist Enterprises

As knowledge of small-scale sector increases, it has become apparent that women play a major role in this sector, not just as employees and self-employed participants but also as entrepreneurs [Carr 1993]. Women perform an important role in building the real backbone of the nation's economy through their involvement in the small and medium-scale enterprises as well as cottage industries [Epstein 1990]. Poverty accompanied by lack of income earning opportunities rather than profit incentives motivate a lot of rural women to become petty entrepreneurs. These women are thus pushed out of their conventional setting rather than pulled into entrepreneurship because of the profits it offers. Apart from poverty rural women are attracted to micro businesses because of low barriers to entry and flexible nature of the work, which make it easy to combine gainful employment with domestic responsibilities.

Carr [1993] believed that women are constrained in their ability to make profit by the multiplicity of the roles of their chores at home. This multiplicity is further influenced by the following factors;

i. The lack of Appropriate Domestic Technologies

Lack of appropriate domestic technologies for Third World rural households makes chores such as collecting firewood and water over a long distance extremely labour and time consuming. In addition to performing most of the domestic work, majority of rural women also work on either their farms or are employed as labourers for local larger landowners.

ii. Cultural Beliefs

Child bearing, child caring or minding and looking at physical and emotional well being of the family members usually takes a priority in all women's duties. Marriage influenced by cultural beliefs causes women to be concentrated in low paid jobs and hinders their ability to effectively participate in entrepreneurial activities.

iii. Spatial Mobility

Rural women in many African countries are restricted from moving outside their villages both during the day and at night resulting in dependency on male for both production and marketing stages of an activity. This dependency is motivated by perceived or real inferior physical strength of women.

iv. High illiteracy rate among women

It is estimated that out of 700 million illiterate rate two thirds are females. Lack of time, husband's disapproval, child care, domestic chores and lack of transport severely limit women's ability to participate in non-formal education and life-long education programmes (Epstein : 1990).

In recent years, greater attention has been devoted to gender at both national and international levels, and considerable efforts have been made to improve women's position in society in general and in the legal system in particular. Gender-specific provisions have been adopted to promote gender equality, women empowerment and sustainable development.

Constraints faced by people involved in survivalist enterprises can be summarized as follows:

i. Financial problems

Research from developing countries has proved that many people involved in micro businesses relied heavily on own saving, unorganized markets and on borrowing from friends and relatives. Government financial institutions are often unsympathetic to these people because of a lack of collateral and accounting system. Although governments in Sub-Saharan Africa are trying to correct this, women are often discriminated against as pointed out by Carr [1993]. This discrimination is further strengthened by the fact that women have limited access to resources such as land, training and information.

ii. Marketing problems

In most developing countries marketing channels are underdeveloped as a result of the lack of infrastructure development in rural areas. The smallness of these enterprises scattered over a wide area also contributes to underdeveloped marketing channels. The lack of business skills also presents a serious problem to those involved in survivalist small scale enterprises.

iii. Gender issues

Women's low participation in national and regional policy-making, their invisibility in national statistics and their low participation in extension services (with the exception of home economics programmes) has meant that those issues of most concern to women had been neglected in the design and implementation of many development policies and programmes.

RESEARCH METHODOLOGY

Data Collection Procedures

Vhembe district is made up of four municipalities namely Thulamela, Mutale, Makhado and Musina but the Department of Agriculture in which the study took place is demarcated into Thulamela, Mutale and Makhado contrary to local municipality's demarcation which includes Musina. The study used the Department of Agriculture demarcation since it worked closely with the department.

Sampling Frame

A pre- survey was done to identify households involved in income generating activities in the three municipalities of Vhembe district that is Thulamela, Makhado, and Mutale. This was done through snow- balling, whereby villages in the three municipalities were visited and from those households the researcher was referred to other households involved in income generating activities. On the whole, a total sample of 85 households was purposely selected in the area.

Data Collection Instruments

A set of both closed and open-ended questionnaire was administered to households involved in income generating activities. The designed questionnaire included biographic data of the member of households involved in these activities, details of activities carried by these households and the amount of income generated together with other information on their household activities.

Data Analysis

A gross margin analysis for income generating activities was done to assess the amount of income generated from these activities.

RESEARCH FINDINGS ON SURVIVALIST ENTERPRISES

Characteristics of the People Involved In These Activities

The researcher also wanted to establish the characteristics of people involved in survivalist enterprises. These characteristics include gender, age, marital status, and educational level and lastly the number of dependents.

Gender

Gender can be a major factor influencing survivalist enterprises hence the survey tried to categorize the gender of household heads for the selected areas. Table 1 below represents the results. It can be observed from the table that 79% were females while 21% were males. The results can be related to the history of South Africa whereby men left for cities to look for jobs, leaving their wives and children behind. Some of these men never returned to their families while others sent very little money to supplement household income. The above result is also consistent with studies done on income generating activities in countries like Japan which showed that a lot of people involved in these activities were women. The implication of this result is that any policies geared towards promoting these activities must focus on the gender aspect of the people involved.

Table 1. Gender distribution of people involved in survivalist enterprises in the three municipalities (2003)

Gender	Frequency	Percent
Males	18	21.00
Females	68	79.00
Total	86	100.00

Age

Age was identified as another variable that may influence household activities in the study area. This is because a lot of responsibilities come with age and secondly level of maturity and discipline which is needed in business also comes with age. Table 2 summarises the age distribution among heads of households for the study area.

Table 2. Age distribution among heads of households (2003)

Age	Frequency	Percent
25 – 30	13	15.00
30 – 35	13	15.00
35 – 40	16	19.00
40 – 45	18	21.00
45 – 50	9	10.00
50 – 55	6	7.00
55 – 60	4	5.00
Over 60	7	8.00
Total	86	100.00

Results about age distribution as shown in Table 2 revealed that the age bracket of 40 – 45 year olds had the largest percent of 21%. These are middle - aged people who ideally no longer have children to look after and are able to devote their energy to the different activities such as income generating activities. This group does not qualify for old age grant (pension) provided they are in good health and may be in great need of income to support their children who may be in tertiary education institutions.

Marital Status

Marriage brings about economic opportunities and challenges. Challenges mostly come about when the couples are both unemployed and have to go out and generate some income for their household. The marital status of respondents is presented in Table 3 below:

Table 3. Marital status of the respondents (2003)

Marital Status	Number	Percentage
Single	31	36%
Married	47	55%
Divorced		-
Widowed	8	9%
Total	86	100

The table above revealed that 55% of people involved in survivalist enterprises were married and 36% were single while only 9% were widowed. Literature reviewed indicated that the single headed households are among the most vulnerable section of the population

Table 4. Educational status of the respondents in the 3 municipalities (2003).

Education	Gender	Frequency (N)	Percent (%)
No school	Female	9	10.00
	Male	3	3.00
Primary education	Female	25	29.00
	Male	8	9.00
Secondary education	Female	29	34.00
	Male	5	6.00
Tertiary education	Female	4	5.00
	Male	3	4.00
Other (Adult basic education)	Female	0	0.00
	Male	0	0.00
Total		86	100

Gender and Education

South Africa has a history of imbalances namely racial imbalances and gender imbalances. In the past years the main struggle was to fight racial imbalances while gender imbalances were left unattended. It was a wide belief in black South Africans that educating a girl child was a waste of resources. Table 4 summarises the observed level of education by gender of the respondents.

According to Epstein [1990] women had high illiteracy levels compared to their male counterparts. Table 4 showed that a higher percentage of women had no formal education when compared to men. Both men and women had received no training in business and project management.

Number of Dependants

Dependents of the household may include children, in-laws for married individuals, immediate family and relatives. Black South African households are known of having large numbers of family members. This can be a major source of unpaid labour but it can be problematic when there are high unemployment and food shortages. The study findings revealed that the number of people in the household ranged from two to thirteen (2-13) with a mean of 8 people. This can be a source of labour to assist households in the income generating activities.

Sources of Initial Capital

Sources of initial capital are important determinants of size, structure, growth and expansion patterns of these small scale income generating activities. Assumptions concerning the initial capital are always that if the initial capital is little, the activity or scope will also be small and its chances of growth and expansion will also be limited. Efforts were made in this research to identify the sources of initial capital. Table 5 presents the results.

Table 5. Sources of initial capital (2003)

Sources of initial Capital	Number	Percentage
Own Savings	60	70%
Loan from Relatives	24	28%
Other	2	2%
Total	86	100

Research results showed that seventy percent of the initial capital used to start these activities was from personal savings mostly from piece jobs. This initial capital was often small hence the production was limited, and the output was relatively small.

Ability to Reinvest Profit

The information on people's ability to reinvest was an important question to determine their entrepreneurial skills because business minded people need to make profit. It is easy to determine whether a person has made profit or not based on his ability to reinvest. Reinvestment in this case meant ability to buy another batch of stock from sales generated from previous stock. The research results were quite positive since a large percentage of households claimed that they were able to reinvest the cash made from previous sales to buy new stock as seen below.

Table 6. Reinvestment among Respondents (2003)

Ability to Reinvest Profit	Number	Percentage
Yes	69	80%
No	17	20%
Total	86	100

The results showed that about 80 % of people interviewed were able to reinvest while about 20 % were unable to reinvest the money generated from sales of their products. This is an encouraging aspect as households' ability to reinvest shows some degree of commitment that over a period can translate into the sustainability of the business.

Activities Used for Survivalist Enterprises

Various business activities were carried out by the respondents (Table7).

The results revealed that activities that were used were divided into three categories namely food preparation, crop production and animal production. Food production referred to the prepared food such as atchaar, and fruit juice making; crop production involving primary production and selling of crops and animal production in the form of chicken and pig keeping. Producers grew the vegetables and sold them while hawkers were buying from the producers and selling. These findings shows the high potential of agriculture in the district, and that policies geared towards income generation need to incorporate agricultural policies.

Table 7. categories of activities done by households in survival enterprises (2003)

Categories	Type of activity	Frequency	Percent
Prepared food	Atchaar	5	5.80
	Juice	2	2.30
	Fish	4	4.70
	Home –made bread	1	1.20
Crop production	Fruit	14	16.30
	Mealies	3	3.50
	Seed production	1	1.20
	Pot plants	4	4.70
	Seed production	1	1.20
	Vegetables	6	6.90
	Vegetables & mealies	12	14.00
Animal production	Chicken	4	4.70
	Pig production	5	5.80

Income Generated by Survivalist Enterprises in Rand

The major reason for the existence of these activities is to generate income and for this reason the research had to get some insights on the amount of income that was generated by these activities. Table 8 shows income generated from these activities per month.

Table 8. Income generated from these activities per month (2003)

	Frequency	Percent
Less than R500	27	31.39
R500 – R1000	46	53.49
Between R1000 & R2000	7	8.14
Greater than R2000	6	6.98
Total	86	100

Income Distribution from Survivalist Enterprises

A minimum of –R750 and a maximum of R9000 and a mean of R873.15 income was generated survivalist enterprises. Research results revealed that the labour costs were zero (meaning that hired labour was not used). This revelation is consistent with previous studies which also state that hired labour is not featured in most micro businesses. The R873.15 raised from survivalist enterprises was found to be inadequate to support a household of an average of 8 dependants.

Table 9. Assistance Required (2003)

	Frequency	Percent
Financial help	28	32.60
Marketing	30	34.90
Skill training	28	32.60
Total	86	100.00

Assistance Needed by the People Involved in Survivalist Enterprises

There was a need to find out the type of assistance needed by these households. Table 9 present the findings.

The results showed that these households believed that assistance in marketing could be of great importance for their success and sustainability. Approximately 34.9% of the respondents cited marketing needs while 32.6% cited financial while another 32.6 % cited skills training as their critical needs. These results gave the impression that capital, marketing and skills training were the main constraints facing small scale survivalist enterprises.

Support received from governmental / non- governmental organisation in relation to activities done.

Table 10. Government and non- government support (2003)

	Frequency	Percent
Yes	1	1.16
No	85	98.84
Total	86	100

These households were not receiving any governmental support relating to the activities that they were involved in except for one household that received a loan from a non-governmental organization from former Giyani. It seemed that government was only providing assistance to people that had organized themselves into groups such as agribusiness projects. This approach seems to be unfair as not everyone can be a project member. If this were a government policy then it has to be clearly communicated to people involved in agriculture (primary production) so that they can be encouraged to form organizations to full fill this policy.

Help for Unemployed

The government has been trying to solve the question of unemployment for a long time. Sometimes government tend to impose projects on people, without proper research to identify peoples' needs. There were a variety of answers to this question as shown in Table 10 below.

The results of the study revealed that the people of Vhembe district interviewed believed that unemployment could be reduced by giving them more land to practice agriculture (primary production). This suggestion is very relevant because the district is characterized by very good soils which allow a variety of fruit and vegetables to grow. The idea of promoting farming needs a lot of governmental involvement. People that were involved in primary agriculture production required assistance with agriculture inputs, technical skills and marketing.

Problems Encountered by People Involved in Survivalist Enterprises.

Agricultural business like any business is very risky; there are problems that can hinder production and sustainability. Table 11 presents the respondents' view of the major problems facing their activities.

People involved in survivalist enterprises had several problems as seen above in Table 15 with marketing as a very serious problem. These people believed that the market for their produce was congested in the province. They believed that with the governments' help their produce needed to be sent somewhere. The establishment of marketing cooperatives and a processing plant could help to solve this problem.

Table 10. Suggestions on how to help the unemployed people in the study area (2003).

Type of help	Mutale (15)	Makhado (12)	Thulamela (59)
Given loans to start small businesses	8 9.30%	1 1.20%	21 24.40%
Given food by the state	0 0%	0 0%	0 0%
Given more land to practice agriculture	4 4.56%	7 8.1	32 37.2%
Loans and food	1 1.20%	0 0%	2 2.30%
Land and food	0 0%	0 0%	0 0%
Loan and land	2 2.30%	4 4.56%	4 4.56%

Table 11. Problems cited by the respondents (2003)

Problem type	Frequency	Percent
Lack of working capital	46	53.5
Marketing problems	57	66.3
Financial management	1	1.2

CONCLUSION AND POLICY RECOMMENDATIONS

The results presented in this study show the importance of survivalist enterprises as a poverty reduction strategy and constraints and opportunities that are faced. It is evident that although policy makers may place all Small Medium and Micro Enterprises (SMMEs) into the same category, they are totally different, ranging from management style, size of business, capital invested, final product, income generated and employment generated. Policy makers need to formulate appropriate policies for success and sustainability of SMMEs as poverty eradication strategies.

Coordination between the local departments of agriculture and social development need to be strengthened as the two departments complement each other in the fight against poverty to maintain food security in communities.

The research results showed that people involved in income generating activities can be categorized not only as small scale farmers but also as beginner farmers and proper agricultural policies (including marketing, financial assistance and skills training) are required to improve their productivity.

SUMMARY OF MAJOR FINDINGS

Management style	Survivalist enterprises were geared towards generation of income and creation of self employment. The members of household carrying out the activities carried out all the activities related to the small scale business enterprises. Low education levels sometimes hindered their efficiency in management.
Capital invested	Survivalist enterprises used personal savings as the source of initial capital invested in the projects.
Final products	Survivalist enterprises were more involved in primary production especially crop production.
Income generated	Income generating activities generated a mean profit of Eight Hundred and Twenty Three Rand Fifteen cents (R823.15) per month.
Employment creation	There was no evidence of employment creation but income generated reduced household food insecurities.
Government and non-governmental intervention	There were no financial and skills development support for income generating activities.
Problems experienced	Individuals in income generating activities ranked marketing and working capital as their main problems.

REFERENCES

Albreghts, S. (1987). Policy issues in small enterprise financing. In Neck P. A. & Nelson R. E. (eds.) *Small enterprise development: Policies and Programs*, (203-214). Geneva: International Labor Offices.

Anderson, D. (1982). *Small Industry in Developing Countries:* Some Issues. Washington D.C: World Bank.

Baud, I. S. A. (1993). Gender aspects of small-scale industry and development policy. In Baud, I. S. A. & De Bruijne, G. A. (eds.) *Gender, Small Scale, Industry and Development Policy*, (3-15). London: Intermediate Technology Publication.

Beielein J. G., Schneeberger K.C & Osburn D.D. (1995). *Principles of Agribusiness Management*. IL: Waveland Press.

Burns, P. & Dewhurst, J. (1983). *Small business Management*. Wiltshire: The Macmillan Press Ltd.

Carr, M. (1993). Women in small-scale industry- some lessons from Africa. In Baud, I. S. A. & Debruijne, G. A. (eds.) *Gender, Small-scale Industry and Development policy*. London: I. T. Publications.

Child, F. C. (1977). *Small- scale Rural Industry in Kenya*: Occasional Paper no.17 Los Angeles: African Studies Center, University of California.

Chuta, E. & Liedholm, C. (1985). *Employment and Growth in Small-Scale Industry. Empirical evidence and policy assessment from Sierra Leone.* New York: St Martin's Press.

Department of Agriculture (1994). *White Paper on Agriculture.* Pretoria: African National Congress.

Department of Agriculture (1998). *Poverty and Inequality in South Africa.* Pretoria.

Department of Trade and Industry (1995). *White Paper on National Strategy for the Promotion and Development of Small Scale Businesses in South Africa.* Pretoria.

Epstein, T. S. (1990). Female petty entrepreneurs and their multi roles. In

Food and Agriculture Organization (FAO) (2000). *FAOSTAT Statistics Database.* Rome: Food and Agriculture Organization.

Liedholm, C. & Mead, D. C. (1986). Small-scale industry. In Berg, R. J. &

Management of Rural Income Generating Activities, Village Group Training (FAO) (Online).www.fao.org/AG/ags/subjects/en/ruralfinance/pdf/managingruraliga. Accessed 15/3/2003.

Poverty and Inequality in South Africa [Online]. Http: www.polity.org.za/govdocs/reports/poverty.htlm. Accessed 20/4/2003.

Vyakarnam, S. (ed.). *When Harvest is in* (254). London: Intermediate Technology Publication,

Whitaker, J. S. (Eds.), *Strategies for African Development.* London: University of California Press.

In: Poverty in Africa
Editor: Thomas W. Beasley

ISBN: 978-1-60741-737-8
© 2009 Nova Science Publishers, Inc.

Chapter 9

GENDER INEQUALITY AND POVERTY: THE KENYAN CASE[*]

Tabitha W. Kiriti[†] *and K. C. Roy*
The University of Queensland, Australia

ABSTRACT

Socio-economic conditions in Kenya are deteriorating, and poverty rates are on the rise. This article finds that a significant and rising incidence of absolute poverty exists in Kenya and women suffer from poverty more often than men. This is more pronounced in female-headed households. The high poverty rates among women can be linked to their unequal situation in the labour market, their lack of voice and participation in decision-making in the family/household and other institutions and because gender disparities persist in access and control of human, economic and social reforms.

The female/male ratios in Kenyan decision-making institutions are highly skewed against women and they experience unfavourable enrolment ratios in primary, secondary and tertiary institutions. The share of income earned by women is much lower than men's share. The GDI and GEM, their weaknesses not withstanding, also show that gender inequality exists in Kenya.

INTRODUCTION

Gender inequality involves the denial of opportunities and denial of equal rights on the basis of gender. Enjoyment of opportunities and allocation of resources are based on gender. Gender inequality is generally manifested in unequal rights for women of access to basic social services such as education and health; unequal opportunities for participation in political and economic decision-making, nationally and at the household level; unequal rights for equal

---

[*] This article originally appeared in *Readings in World Development* edited by K.C. Roy and S. Chatterjee, New York: Nova Science Publishers, Inc., 2006, pp. 129-153.
[†] Correspondence to: Tabitha W. Kiriti Email: s805985@student.uq.edu.au, t.kiriti@mailbox.uq.edu.au, or tkiriti@hotmail.com

work; unequal protection under the law; preference for male children; violence against women and so on. Women face constraints in accessing the basic resources needed to participate fully in productive earning opportunities, thereby increasing their probability of falling into poverty or making it difficult for them to get out of poverty.

This paper examines the link between gender inequality and poverty in Kenya. It first examines the various ways that agricultural resources are unequally allocated based on gender, examines the indicators of gender inequality and then provides a link between these and poverty in Kenya.

GENDER INEQUALITY IN THE ALLOCATION OF AGRICULTURAL RESOURCES

Access to critical resources provides an alternative way of conceptualising determinants of women's class position, because it is broader and more flexible than the idea of relationship to means of production, and it applies to class and gender struggle both inside and outside the household (Sorensen, 1990). In her work on the Kipsigis society in Kenya, Sorensen (1990) found that besides satisfying the family's need for food, clean clothes and a nice and tidy home, women's activities include participating in cash crop production, tending cattle, and other income generating activities. Men's responsibility for taking care of the family is primarily fulfilled through provision of cash, mainly through wage labour, and production and sale of cash crops such as tea. The pattern of resource control in this society heavily favours men as they control the major means of production, income and surpluses.

Extension of the market system tends to marginalise rural women economically because males take control of cash and often assume responsibility for activities earning cash (Boserup, 1970; Kennedy and Oniang'o, 1990; Sorensen, 1990; Gross and Underwood, 1971). These authors show that cash cropping has reduced the opportunities for rural women to produce subsistence crops and provide food for their families, especially children. It is not uncommon for women's labour in certain tasks, such as weeding, to increase to a greater extent than men's labour when the agricultural chores associated with cash crops become particularly labour intensive (Spring, 1978). Research on time allocation in Africa by Julin (1993) and Henn (1988) support this view.

Where the structure of agriculture is becoming commercialised, women's roles and thus their economic status are changing. In many regions of the Third world, women are still unremunerated for the long hours they contribute to the tending of commercial crops. As revenue-generating cash cropping rises in importance, the proportion of resources controlled by women tends to diminish. This is largely due to the fact that household resources, such as land and inputs, are transferred away from women's crops in order to promote the production of cash crops (Davison, 1988).

Afonja (1986) shows how women's limited access to land has been a critical factor in explaining gender inequality. She demonstrates how the introduction of cocoa and tenancy in Ile-Ife has led to increased economic differentiation among men, while women are unified in a lower stratum of the peasantry with less control over land, crops and income.

Land adjudication and registration has made women's situations worse because land titles belong to men (Saito, 1992). This makes it difficult to access extension services and formal credit. In any case, credit institutions are situated far away in urban areas. Lack of collateral, transaction costs and long distances, limited education and unfamiliarity with banking procedures, increase the opportunity cost of forgone labour because of their multiple obligations in the household and the farm.

Male out-migration has had a number of adverse consequences for women in terms of time and labour and, less directly on the welfare of their families and on the resource base. Women are constantly making adjustments within a changing set of limitations on their time and labour to provide for the family's subsistence and welfare. They are more bound to the homestead, sometimes waiting for remittances that never come or are too little or too late to purchase fertilizer or hire labour for the agricultural season. Agricultural inputs and training are rarely provided to female farmers. Even efforts to reduce poverty through land reform have been found to reduce female income and economic status because they distribute land titles only to male heads of households (Todaro, 1997). Cultural and social barriers to women's integration into agricultural programs remain strong because in many countries, women's income is perceived as a threat to men's authority. While men are taught new agricultural techniques to increase their productivity, women, if involved at all, are trained to perform low-productivity tasks that are considered compatible with their traditional roles, such as sewing, cooking, or basic hygiene. Women's components of development projects are frequently little more than welfare programs that fail to improve economic well being. Furthermore, these projects tend to depend on the unpaid work of women, while men are remunerated for their efforts (Todaro, 1997).

Households with a male present are 14 times more likely than those headed by a female to have received detailed data on credit and new improved farming practices of all kinds (Spring, 1978; Staudt, 1985). When new agricultural technologies are introduced, women are by-passed in training, credit extension and land reform programs. Extension agents tend to be men who deal with male clients. An increase in family income arising from cash crop production results in a new loss to women as in some societies males take possession of any cash income earned by females, or most of it, and use it for their own ends. Just as Sen (1981) demonstrated that famine could occur in the midst of an increase in aggregate food availability, poverty amongst women and children can increase with rising aggregate family income (Tisdell, 1999).

There is widespread discrimination against women in that few agricultural extension services are directed to them, few women are contacted, female-headed households are less visited and supported by advisers and also members from female-headed households join farmers training centres at a lower rate than members from male-headed households. Most of the males who visit training centres are old retired men who attend because of their high status in society (World Bank, 1989; Bay, 1982). Female-headed households in general have less access to agricultural advice than male-headed ones (Staudt, 1985). Whether the women have large farms, are rich, poor or innovative, the pattern of gender discrimination remains. This may have negative implications for the food production, since women provide most of the food. Women's access to new agricultural technology is limited. Technologies appropriate for household activities, farming objectives, and production conditions for women are lacking. They overlook the requirements of women. The inadequate supply of suitable labour and energy saving farm and household technologies for women's activities impairs women's productivity. This is because technology is mainly male oriented such as heavy machinery, tractors, ploughs and so on. Women use crude implements such as hoes, machetes, cutlasses and so on, which are very slow and labour intensive. Lack of title or secure tenure and access to small dispersed and remote plots are strong disincentives to adopting new agricultural techniques. Diseconomies of scale not only reduce women's yields but cause extension agents to dismiss women as non-adopters of new technologies (Roy and Tisdell, 1993; Saito, 1992; Staudt, 1985).

CULTURE AND ALLOCATION OF RESOURCES

Men's control over labour as a factor of production can translate into claims on women's labour for cultivation of the husband's compound or fields. In effect, the culturally determined rules of access to and control over resources may constrain women as much as external biases in providing access to farm support services (Palmer, 1991). The cultural norms actually may predetermine unequal access to agricultural inputs, marketing services, and farmers' organisations because of the link between farm support services and land title, for which women are rarely eligible (Jiggins, 1989).

In households where women and men have separate accounting unit resources (labour and working capital), household resource use is most efficient when they enjoy equal access to land and other factor markets and in product markets (Palmer, 1991). Unequal access means unequal barter or bargaining capabilities and sub-optimal resource allocations.

The intra-household allocation of resources cannot be disassociated from relations of power within the household and within the community with overlapping livelihoods. The access to and control over productive resources are also a function of social status, which can be ascribed or achieved. The norms and set of values embedded in a particular culture bring with them entitlements or rights ascribed to certain categories of persons to particular shares, often related to basic subsistence needs, such as food and clothing. The way in which domestic groups confer power to some members based on age and gender differences, reflects the norms of distributional justice of the group or society. An individual is, therefore, subject to socially determined valuation that becomes internalised through a socialisation process. The inequality of those valuations is evident between men and women. Male domination, perceived as embedded in cultural norms and institutions, characterises intra-household power relations and resource allocation patterns (Kiriti, et al, 2003b).

Most formal and legal rights to land have been given to men, while women only have user rights to some of the land. This may affect their productivity because of lack of security. Women in Kenya do not inherit land, which means that they depend on their male relatives both when it comes to land distribution and decisions about farming. If a woman chooses to remain unmarried, is divorced or widowed, she does not have any rights to land and will be in a very exposed situation. This lack of security and access to land means that women cannot undertake large investments. An increase in legal rights to land and support could increase overall productivity.

Ethical practices also make it difficult for women to access extension services since most extension officers are men. Information is usually passed on to men who do not pass it on to women. Saito et al. (1994) found that in Kenya, extension positively affected the gross value of output of male farmers but not of female farmers, all other variables being held constant. Male extension agents are generally unaware of the need to communicate differently with women and view women as farmer's wives and not farmers by their own right. Rural women tend to be shy and reluctant to speak up in the presence of male agents from the same village. They lack confidence because they are less educated and have less contact with the outside world. They see men as authority figures whose decisions they are to follow (Roy and Tisdell, 1993; Saito 1992; Kennedy and Peters, 1992).

Where wives head households due to the continued absence of husbands (*de facto*), output may be low because women are not decision-makers. Men, though absent, want to make all the decisions concerning the household and the allocation of resources (Kiriti, et al, 2003a). They control the output, which they sell but do not buy the inputs. Women rely on remittances which come from their husbands and when it comes it is either too little or too late that it can't be used to buy inputs.

ALLOCATION OF RESOURCES AND BARGAINING POWER

The diversity of needs and interests among family members, and the allocation of the scarce resources, are determined by the degree of decision-making power possessed by each negotiating party (Bennett, 1983). Furthermore, not all household members have equal bargaining power to enforce their own definition of utility and therefore not all members benefit equally from the way resources are actually allocated. This view interprets observed inequalities in the distribution of household resources, not as the most efficient reaction to the prevailing wage/price situation or as evidence of the household's maximising behaviour, but as evidence of structural asymmetries in the economic, social, and legal position of men and women, which give the two unequal bargaining power (Bennett, 1983).

Bargaining power or a household member's ability to realise personal allocational priorities, can be influenced by the individual's contribution to the household income and some studies have shown that increases in women's income have given women more decision-making power and control over the distribution of resources within the household. Acharya and Bennett (1983) found that women's involvement in market activities gives them much greater power within the household in terms of their input in all aspects of household and resource allocation decisions. At the same time, confining women's work to the domestic and subsistence sectors reduces their power vis-à-vis men in the household.

Bargaining models often define an individual's "threat points" in terms of his or her market earnings or individual assets. Increasing one's economic valuation improves that individual's bargaining power. The greater a woman's net control of income, the greater her leverage in other household economic and domestic decisions, and the greater her overall "voice and vote" (leadership) in the relationship. Tisdell (1999) identifies five factors that may increase the threat power of a married woman in relation to her husband or partner; (1) her capability of finding independent employment and the level of income earned by her; (2) her ownership of property and ability to transfer, inherit and bequest property; (3) her rights to collective family assets in the event of dissolution of marriage; (4) her ability to institute divorce proceedings, especially if the legal hurdles to divorce are minimal; and (5) contacts with influential networks in a community.

However, legal, institutional, and social factors also affect bargaining power. For example, property rights could easily have a much bigger impact than changes in relative earnings of men and women (Folbre, 1992). The World Bank (1996) says that women and children are more vulnerable because tradition gives them less decision making power and less control over assets than men, while at the same time, their opportunities to engage in remunerative activities, and therefore to acquire their own assets, are more limited.

Compared with men, women are disadvantaged in their access to and control of a wide range of assets. With fewer assets and more precarious claims to assets, women are more risk-averse, more vulnerable, have a weaker bargaining position within the household, and consequently are less in a position to respond to economic opportunities. Access to land is not an end in itself. Access to land and other productive resources are critical in creating wealth and generating growth.

The next section examines the indicators of gender inequality. Some of the indicators, especially the human development index (HDI), gender-related development index (GDI) and the gender empowerment measure (GEM), were introduced by the UNDP in its 1995 and 1997 Human Development Reports.

HUMAN DEVELOPMENT INDEX

The UNDP (1998) defines human development as a process of enlarging people's choices. It tries to measure it by the Human Development Index (HDI). HDI measures the overall achievements in a country in three basic dimensions of human development: longevity, knowledge and a decent standard of living. It is measured by life expectancy, educational attainment (adult literacy and combined primary, secondary and tertiary enrolment) and adjusted per capita income in US$ purchasing power parity (PPP). Longevity and knowledge refer to the formation of human capabilities. Income is a proxy measure for the choices people have in putting their capabilities to use. HDI is the equally weighted sum of deprivation of a country with respect to each of the three components: life expectancy at birth, literacy, and real income per head (UNDP, 1995).

The HDI sets a minimum for each of these components and then shows where each country stands in relation to these scales expressed as a value between 0 and 1. For example, since the minimum adult literacy rate is 0 percent and the maximum is 100 percent, the literacy component of knowledge for a country where the literacy rate is 75 percent would be 0.75. Similarly, the minimum for life expectancy is 25 years and the maximum 85 years, so the longevity component for a country where life expectancy is 55 years would be 0.5. For income, the minimum is $100(Purchasing Power Parity)(PPP) and the maximum is $40000(PPP). Income above the average world income is adjusted using a progressively higher discount rate. The scores for the three dimensions are then averaged in an overall index. The HDI facilitates the determination of priorities for policy intervention and the evaluation of progress over time. It also permits instructive comparisons of the experiences within and between different countries (UNDP, 1995).

The HDI offers an alternative to GNP and GDP for measuring the relative socio-economic progress at national and local levels. Comparing HDI and per capita income ranks of countries, regions or ethnic groups within countries highlights the relationship between their material wealth and income on the one hand and their human development on the other. A negative gap implies the potential of redirecting resources to human development.

Table 1 shows the Human Development Indices for Kenya and Kenya's HDI rank compared to other UN member countries. Compared to other nations, Kenya failed to improve its human development ranking – it was 134th position in 1975 and remained there in 2000.

Table 1: Human Development Indices for Kenya: 1994 – 2000

Year	HDI Rank (among UN member countries)	HDI Value
1975	134	0.443
1980	134	0.489
1985	134	0.512
1990	113	0.533
1994	134	0.463
1995	137	0.523
1997	136	0.519*
1998	138	0.506*
1999	134	0.513*
2000	134	0.513*

* Not comparable with other figures
Source: UNDP: Human Development Reports (various issues)

The table shows that Kenya has not been faring well even when compared with other countries. The lower the HDI value, the worse the state of human development is in a country.

It should be noted that the treatment of the income variable used to calculate HDI from 1997 onwards is different to its treatment in 1994 and 1995. In the two years mentioned, income above the cut-off point of world average per capita income was discounted using a drastic discounting formula. In 1997, the discounting was made more gradual by taking the logarithm of income throughout, as recommended by Kelley (1991). The improvement in methodology and data affect the HDI ranks of almost all countries. Thus, although the HDI of Kenya in 2000 is higher than in 1994, this does not mean that its state of human development has improved. In fact, when individual variables are taken into account, it can be seen that there was a fall in life expectancy and a fall in the real GDP per capita.

CRITICISM OF THE HUMAN DEVELOPMENT INDEX

The HDI has been criticised for some of its choices of components, weights, implicit trade-offs, and aggregation rules (Ravallion, 1997; Kelley, 1991; Srinivasan, 1994; Tisdell, 1999; Tisdell, et al, 2001; Bardhan and Klasen, 1999). These authors argue that the fixed weights used in the calculation of HDI involve value judgements. The variables used may not be independent of each other and the linearity of HDI implies a constant rate of substitution between these variables. They also argue that the HDI is too restrictive in the attributes it takes into account in assessing welfare. For example, it does not take into account such factors as security of income, employment and psychological well-being. It also fails to consider the distributional aspect of its variables. The process of averaging ignores the differences between men and women, rural and urban poor, different ethnic and racial groups and so on.

A country's overall HDI can conceal the fact that different groups within the country have very different levels of human development. This can be improved through disaggregation. Using the data for the HDI components pertaining to each of the groups into which the HDI is disaggregated, treating each group as if it were a separate country arrives at disaggregated Human Development Indices. Such groups may be defined relative to geographical or administrative regions, urban-rural residence, gender and ethnicity.

Using disaggregated Human Development Indices at the national and local levels helps highlight the significant disparities and gaps: among regions, between the sexes, between urban and rural areas and among ethnic groups. This can help guide policy and action to address gaps and inequalities. It can also enable community groups to press for more resources, making the HDI a tool for participatory development.

GENDER RELATED DEVELOPMENT INDEX (GDI)

The GDI involves a variation on HDI. It uses the same variables as the HDI but the GDI adjusts the average achievement of each country in life expectancy, educational attainment and income in accordance with the disparity in achievement between women and men. It incorporates a measure of gender equity into a measure of absolute levels of human development. The GDI methodology imposes a penalty for inequality in that GDI falls when the disparity between achievements of men and women increase. Thus, GDI is simply HDI adjusted for gender inequality. It reflects disparities between gender in health, education and income. For this gender-sensitive adjustment, the UNDP uses a weighting formula that expresses a moderate aversion to inequality, setting the weighting parameter, ϵ, equal to 2. This is the harmonic mean of the male and female values.

In the life expectancy component, it is assumed that, given equal treatment, women would outlive men by an average of five years (UNDP, 1995). If female life expectancy exceeds male life expectancy by less (or more) than five years, a gender gap is held to exist. For example, if female life expectancy is 42 and male life expectancy 40, then a gender gap of two years against females is assumed to exist. The range of possible life expectancies assumed in the HDR is 60 years. The GDI adjusts the maximum and minimum values for life expectancy, to account for the fact that women tend to live longer than men. For women, the maximum value is 87.5 years and the minimum value 27.5 years; for men the corresponding values are 82.5 and 22.5 years.

In the literacy and school enrolment (education) component of the index, women and men are assumed to have the same potential achievement (100 percent literacy and school enrolment) so that any gender differences in literacy rates or school enrolment rates constitute a gap with a maximum possible gap of 100 percent.

To calculate the index for income, the values of real per capita GDP (PPP$) for women and men are calculated from the female share and male share of earned income. These shares, in turn are estimated from the ratio of the female wage to the male wage and the percentage shares of women and men in the economically active population. The estimates of female and male per capita income (PPP$) are treated in the same way as income is treated in the HDI and then used to compute the equally distributed income index. The equally distributed income index is defined as the level of achievement that, if attained equally by women and men, would be judged to be exactly as valuable socially as the actually observed achievement (Anand and Sen, 1995). The equally distributed income index is given by: {[Female population share x (adjusted female per capita PPP$ GDP)$^{-1}$] + [Male population share x (adjusted male per capita PPP$ GDP)$^{-1}$]}$^{-1}$. The indices for life expectancy, educational attainment and income are added together with equal weight to derive the final GDI value.

However, the GDI has been criticised by Tisdell, et al. (2001); Bardhan, and Klasen (1999) for: (1) pre-assigning of a notional value to the sensitive indicator; (2) it is not clear why the same weighting parameter, ϵ, should be applied to the three gaps, particularly since the nature, size, and significance of the gaps differ greatly; (3) allowing the weighting parameter, ϵ, to vary among countries allows for an elastic ruler, which makes the GDI ineffective in international comparisons; (4) GDI may conceal significant gender inequalities since its components are aggregate measures. Thus, for Kenya, female inequality regionally between its tribes, between urban and rural areas, between races and so on may rise considerably without this being reflected in any change in the GDI. Furthermore, (5) GDI ignores the impact of past (and present) pre-natal discrimination in mortality; (6) by concentrating on the life expectancy measure, the overall assessment ends up neglecting the life expectancy measure completely and the education measure largely by giving too small penalties for gaps in these achievements; (7) use of gender disaggregated per capita GDP is a weak indicator of gender inequality because most countries do not report their per capita GDP in terms of men and women. Hence, using GDP per capita disaggregated by gender is unsatisfactory and renders GDI internationally incomparable; (8) because gender-specific attributions of income per head cannot be readily linked to the aggregate GDP per capita in the calculation of GDI, inequalities within the household are difficult to characterise and assess (Anand and Sen, 1995, pp. 12); and (9) using female income shares to calculate GDI does not take into consideration the increased burden of work that women face as their work for paid employment is added onto their other responsibilities of looking after the family and subsistence farming. Also, Kiriti, et al. (2003a) found that access to paid employment is not a sufficient condition for the improvement of the status of women especially at the household level.

Table 2: Kenya's Gender Related Development Index: 1995-2000

Year	GDI
1995	0.459*
1997	0.517
1998	0.508
1999	0.511
2000	0.512

Source: UNDP: Human Development Reports (various issues)
* Not comparable with other GDI values

Table 2 seems to demonstrate an improvement in the status of women in Kenya in the period 1995-2000 as the GDI rose from 0.459 to 0.512 between 1995 and 2000. However, it fell slightly to 0.512 in 2000 compared with 1997 indicating a small deterioration in the status of women. There has been virtually no change in GDI in Kenya since 1997. However, the methodology used in 1995 is different from the 1997 and therefore the two GDI coefficients may not be comparable.

It is possible for gross inequality between females and males to increase and for GDI to remain constant other things being equal. GDI may conceal significant gender inequalities since its components are aggregate measures (Tisdell, et al, 2001). This is because gender inequality only relates to the average situation of males compared to the average for females.

GENDER EMPOWERMENT MEASURE (GEM)

The Gender Empowerment Measure (GEM) measures the extent of gender equity in economic and political power. The GEM uses variables constructed explicitly to measure the relative empowerment of women and men in political and economic spheres of activity. It thus attempts to measure gender equity in participation in governmental and managerial decision-making, professional roles, and economic activities generally.

This is important for several reasons: First, gender equity in access to economic and political opportunities is of intrinsic importance as it determines the status of women in society. Second, it may be that women (and men) are more effective promoters of their own cause. If this is the case, then gender equity in economic and political power may be an effective way to reduce other gender inequalities in society. Third, a society that neglects the economic and political potential of half of its population is likely to perform worse than a society using its talent regardless of gender (Bardhan and Klasen, 1999).

The GEM is calculated in four steps. First, indices for administrative, managerial, professional and technical positions are calculated. This involves calculating male and female shares of administrative, professional, technical and managerial positions. These are broad, loosely defined occupational categories. Because the relevant population for each category is different, a separate index for each is calculated and then added together. Secondly, women and men's percentage shares of parliamentary seats are calculated which reflects political participation and decision-making power. Third, an index for gender relation shares of earned income is calculated. This involves calculation of the male and female shares of earned income similar to that used for the GDI. For all three variables the methodology of population weighted (1-ϵ) averaging to derive an "equally distributed equivalent percentage" (EDEP) for both sexes together is used. Each variable is indexed by dividing the EDEP by 50 percent. Fourth, an income variable is used to reflect power over economic resources. It is calculated in the same way as for the GDI except that unadjusted rather than adjusted real GDP per capita is used. Fifth, the gender empowerment measure is computed which involves adding together the three indices for economic participation and decision making, political participation and decision making, and power over economic resources (UNDP, 1999).

The UNDP does not have a GEM value for Kenya due to non-availability of data and therefore Kenya is not ranked. However, as mentioned earlier, women held only six (3.6 percent) seats out of 202 seats in parliament in 1997, and 17 seats (8.1 percent) in 2002. This was a huge improvement since before the first multi-party elections of 1992 there were no elected women in parliament. There are also an insignificant number of women professionals and technical workers, and very few female administrators and managers.

CRITICISM OF THE GENDER EMPOWERMENT MEASURE

However the GEM has been criticised (Tisdell, et al, 2001) for: (1) its focus on the sources of income but not the users of income since a female may earn cash income but it may be mainly controlled and utilised by her husband. In most African societies, Kenya included, women may earn income but the man controls it or it may be used for the sustenance of the whole family, not solely for the well being of the woman (Kiriti, et al, 2003a); (2) it is questionable how well GEM fully captures economic and political power held by women and their roles in the development process; (3) GEM does not reliably allow for inter-country comparison due to the flexibility of the earnings gap indicator and the weighting and averaging procedures; (4) the choice of representation in parliament ignores the fact that there are some parliaments that do not have any power thereby making it difficult to interpret the share of female political representation. A country may have very high female participation in parliament and hence a high GEM ranking but this does not reflect the actual political power of women; (5) the GEM focuses too much on representation at the national level and in the formal sectors of the economy; (6) the GEM neglects many important aspects of women's economic and political roles that exist outside of national politics and the formal economy, as is the case in many developing countries; and (7) in most developing countries, for example Kenya, where poverty levels are high, most women may not be interested in being members of parliament or even local authorities, let alone being managers. Their interest is, in basic, survival.

EDUCATION AND LITERACY LEVELS

In the developing world's 900 million illiterate people, women outnumber men two to one. And girls constitute the majority of the 130 million children without access to primary school. In sub-Saharan Africa (SSA), the average number of years of schooling for the female adult population in 1960 was only 1.1 years, which was barely half of the schooling achievement by men. Females in SSA experienced the lowest average annual growth of total years of schooling between 1960 and 1990 of all regions (an annual increase of 0.04 years, raising the average years of schooling of the adult female population by only 1.2 years between 1960 and 1990). The female-male ratio in the growth of total years of schooling was only 0.89 meaning that females experienced a slower expansion in educational achievement than males (Blackden and Bhanu, 1998).

Beginning in the early 1990s in Kenya, government expenditure on education, health and other social services decreased due to rising pressure from the World Bank and the IMF to reduce government expenditure. The need to undergo fiscal adjustment because of unsustainable fiscal deficits and mounting payment obligations on its external debt constrained the government's ability to increase the education budget. Attempts to solve the resource shortage by shifting costs to families and communities ran into difficulties.

Extremely low per capita incomes limited the ability of many communities and households to contribute more private funds to the education of their children. The additional burden on low-income households had a negative effect on school enrolment, especially enrolment of girls, as the demand for education is price sensitive in low-income households (Kabubo and Kiriti, 2001).

As can be seen from Table 3, gross enrolment ratios in primary education fell in comparison to 1990. They reached a low of 84.9 per cent in 1995. While the downward trend was reversed as indicated by the 1998 figure, primary school enrolment ratios were still lower in 1998 than in 1991. It is also probable that the quality of education of those in school declined while secondary school ratios also show a decline. This decline halted in the mid-1990s and in fact, in 1998 the secondary education enrolment ratio was higher than in 1991.

Table 3: Gross Enrolment Ratios for Primary and Secondary Levels of Education for Kenya by Gender: 1991-1998

Year	Primary enrolment				Secondary enrolment			
	Total	Male	Female	Gap	Total	Male	Female	Gap
1991	93.0	94.5	91.5	3.0	27.9	31.5	24.4	7.1
1992	91.7	92.9	90.5	2.4	27.3	30.7	23.9	6.8
1993	90.5	91.1	89.8	1.3	25.7	28.5	22.8	5.7
1994	86.9	87.1	86.6	0.5	24.8	27.0	22.6	4.4
1995	84.9	84.9	83.2	1.7	24.8	26.4	22.4	4.0
1998	90.7	91.4	90.0	1.4	29.9	31.5	28.2	3.3

Source: UNESCO Datasets

However, there is no doubt that an increasing number of the poor are missing out on education in Kenya or receiving little education. The distribution of educational opportunity cannot be deciphered from these aggregate statistics. But, they influence UNDP's indices of development such as its Human Development Index (HDI) and its Gender Development Index (GDI). The fact that the secondary enrolment ratio was higher in 1998 than in 1991, but the primary school enrolment ratio was lower in Kenya, suggests that in the 1990s, inequality of income has exerted a rising influence on access to education.

The gender gap in primary school enrolments is measured as the ratio of female to male enrolment at this level times 100. The gender gap in secondary school enrolment is measured as the ratio of female to male enrolment at this level times 100. These two are measures of women's status as far as education in early years is concerned.

Where places in school are limited and resources are scarce, girls are at a particular disadvantage. Parents may prefer to educate sons, both because expected benefits are higher due to better job prospects for sons and dependence on sons in old life (Kiriti and Tisdell, 2003a), and costs are lower because of the low opportunity cost of their time in terms of help in the household (Mincer and Polachek, 1974).

Table 3 shows that the enrolment ratios of females in both primary and secondary schools are lower than that of males. However, the gender gap, though exhibiting a declining trend in both primary and secondary school levels, is much wider in secondary schools. The data indicates that while enrolment levels are high for both girls and boys in primary schools (although enrolment ratios for females are lower than those of males), there is a higher drop-out of female students than of male students and enrolment ratios are much higher for males than for females in secondary school.

The gender gap in adult illiteracy is measured as the percentage of illiterate females in the 25 years and above age group minus the percentage of illiterate males in the same age group. Adult illiteracy rates are largely a reflection of historical trends in primary school enrolment. A higher gender gap is a reflection of women's lower status since literacy is the forerunner to a host of expanded opportunities for women including earning power, control over health and child-bearing, political and legal rights and so on.

As seen from Table 4, in 1970, 74 percent of the adult female population was illiterate compared to 44 percent of adult males. By 1999, 24 percent of the adult female population remained illiterate compared to 11.1 percent of the adult male population. Table 4 demonstrates that there exists a gender gap in adult illiteracy in Kenya although it seems to be declining but at a slow pace between 1990 and 1999. Low enrolment ratios for females in institutions of higher learning and high illiteracy rates means that women cannot participate effectively in decision-making institutions.

Although the data indicate increased access to education for women and a decrease in the gender differences between men and women, it does not take into account the availability of facilities, the quality of education, for example, size of classes and so on. Furthermore, the fact that women in Kenya have access to education does not necessarily lead to their empowerment. Kiriti, et al. (2003a) found that in patriarchal societies, customary conventions play a major role in determining the socio-economic status for women.

Table 4: Adult Illiteracy Rates for Kenya by Gender

Year	Adult Illiteracy			
	Total	Male	Female	Gap
1970	na	44.0	74.0	30.0
1980	na	30.0	57.3	27.3
1990	29.2	19.1	39.2	20.1
1995	23.0	14.7	31.1	16.4
1999	17.6	11.1	24.0	12.9

Source: UNESCO Datasets

FEMALE/MALE RATIOS IN DECISION-MAKING INSTITUTIONS

The effectiveness of Kenya's development efforts and the ability to sustain them are dependent on the full utilisation of all human resources (both men and women). But, socio-economic indicators show that Kenyan women are disadvantaged compared to men in respect of their participation in decision-making. The vast majority of Africa's women find their total livelihood within agriculture and the informal sector. For example, women constitute 95 percent of the agricultural labour force in Lesotho and 54 percent in Tanzania. The UN Economic Commission for Africa (1998) estimates that over 70 percent of Africa's food is produced by women. Women account for 53 percent of all informal sector workers. In Botswana, between 55 percent and 75 percent of all informal sector's businesses are owned and operated by women. In the formal sectors of Africa's economies, women continue to play marginal roles. Their participation rate is less than 30 percent. For example, out of the total in wage employment, women account for 19.9 percent in Angola, 30.7 percent in Botswana, 21.3 percent in Kenya, 14.69 percent in Malawi, 28.8 percent in Swaziland and 16.59 percent in Zimbabwe (Sivard, 1995).

Most women in formal sector employment are concentrated in low-paying semi-skilled and non-skilled jobs. Women's representation in technical and professional fields is still limited. Their representation in major decision-making positions is also extremely limited. There are various reasons accounting for this. First, early socialisation practices emphasise the primary role of women as mothers and wives and influence girls' total expectations for future participation in the labour force and the choice of career paths. Second, women's overall limited educational attainments, as well as the types of curricula used in schools, emphasising stereotypical roles for women, create further barriers. Career guidance and counselling likewise tends to channel girls into traditional female fields such as nursing and home economics. Third, women's multiple responsibilities as mothers, wives, employees and employers create role conflicts that at times could result in compromises in careers. Women's careers tend to be interrupted during their childbearing years, resulting in loss of seniority. In addition, as women are usually expected to move with their husbands, the interrupted career syndrome further compromises their career progression. Fourth, organisational policies and procedures are often influenced by cultural perceptions of women's roles and capabilities. This leads to women being discriminated against in recruitment, and in promotion to senior positions as it is assumed that women lack the qualities essential for successful managerial careers (Mincer and Polachek, 1974).

African culture is a barrier to development because it perpetuates culturally sanctioned biases against women and provides excuses for men. Cultural biases operate at all levels ranging from national institutional level, government policy, community level, household and individual levels (Kiriti, et al, 2003b). In Africa, women's participation at all levels of decision-making is low. In Parliament, the highest level of decision-making, women are under represented. In 1995, at the time of the Beijing Platform for Action, only 10 percent of the members of legislative bodies were women. In 1998, this had increased to 12 percent, still a very low percentage. The UNDP in its Human Development Report of 1995 states that there should be a target of 30 percent of women in all spheres of political and social life for an impact to be felt.

The Beijing Platform for Action (1995) states that women's equal participation in political life plays a pivotal role in the general process of the advancement of women. Without the active participation of women and the incorporation of women's perspectives at all levels of decision-making, the goals of equality, development and peace cannot be achieved. Incorporation would ensure women's equal access to and full participation in power structures and decision-making. It would also increase women's capacity to participate in decision-making and leadership. However, eight years later many of the injunctions in the Beijing Platform for Action still remain agendas for the future and there are even some issues that some governments, for example Kenya, have refused outright to take into account saying that they go against their cultures.

According to the United Nations Division for the Advancement of Women (UNDAW, 1996) the percentage of women in both ministerial and sub-ministerial levels ranges from zero percent (in about 15 countries), to 30 percent in 2 countries. Only 3.5 percent of the world's cabinet ministers are women, and women hold no ministerial positions in 93 countries of the world. In Kenya, most women in high government positions are in such ministries as education, culture, social welfare, women's affairs and so on. Women in Kenya rarely achieve elective office, and are severely under-represented at top positions in political parties. Out of a total of 202 seats in parliament, women occupied only 6 seats after the 1992 first multi-party elections. These increased to 17 in the 2002 elections out of 210 seats. In Kenya, women are under represented in the judiciary, in local authorities and even in government administration. Female lecturers in universities and institutions of higher learning represent only 10 percent of the total teaching staff.

The above statistics show that despite the fact that many governments have adopted and adapted affirmative action measures and the rhetoric of gender equality, women constitute nowhere near half of the personnel in decision-making structures although they are around half of the global population. The threshold of 30 percent advocated by the UNDP Human Development Report (1995), as a prelude to the 50 percent is still a dream for most women.

LIFE EXPECTANCY

Life expectancy is an important human development indicator. Pierre-Yves, et al. (1999) found a strong relationship between national health-care spending and life expectancy. Considering that most African governments have reduced their expenditures on almost all the sectors, due to structural adjustment pressure from the World Bank and the IMF, this suggests that life expectancy in most African countries is going to decline.

Sala-I-Martin and Barro (1995) found a strong and positive relationship between life expectancy and economic growth; a 13-year increase in life expectancy is estimated to raise the annual growth by 1.4 percentage points. Croix and Licandro (1999) argue that there are several channels through which life expectancy affects economic growth directly, for instance, when the probability of dying young is high, the shortened time horizon makes it optimal for people to start working early in their life and not to stay at school for too long. Moreover, when life expectancy is short, the depreciation rate of human capital is high, making its accumulation more difficult. Since the human capital accumulated in school is an important engine of growth, we should thus expect a country's growth rate to depend upon life expectancy.

Development economics literature shows that an increase in economic growth leads to a higher life expectancy due to better nutrition, reduced infant mortality rates and improved medical care. Life expectancy for both men and women in the world's richest countries is about 80 years, which is almost twice that in the world's poorest countries - 45 years (UNDP, 1998). The problem here however, is of deciding what the causal is and what is the dependent factor; a kind of mutual causation problem or "chicken and egg problem" exists.

The average life expectancy for sub-Saharan Africa is 51.1 years, the lowest for all regions in the world. Table 5 shows life expectancy in Kenya for selected years.

It can be seen that when Kenya attained independence in 1963, life expectancy was only 44.7 years. It rose to 50.5 years in 1970, increasing life expectancy coinciding with a growth in GDP of 6.5 percent between 1963-1974 (Republic of Kenya, 1991), and subsequently to 58.3 years in 1990. However, this fell to 47 years in 2001. Kenya started implementing structural adjustment programs in 1994. These reduced government expenditure in such sectors as health, education, transport, social services and so on. This has meant shifting the cost of consultation and drugs to households. Considering their already low per capita incomes, most sick people avoid medical facilities thereby raising morbidity rates and the mortality rate. This has contributed to the decline in the life expectancy for both male and females to less than 50 years. The female life expectancy in 1980 was 57 years compared to 53 years for males. In 2000, it was 47 years for both females and males.

Table 5: Life Expectancy in Kenya in Years: 1963-2001

Year	Life expectancy at birth	Female	Male	Female less male
1963	44.7	na	na	Na
1970	50.5	52	48	6
1980	54.9	57	53	4
1990	58.3	59	55	4
1994	53.6	na	na	na
1995	53.8	53	52	1
1996	49	na	na	na
1997	52	53.0	51.1	1.9
1998	51.3	52.2	50.5	1.7
1999	50.8	48	47	1
2000	47	47	47	0
2001	47	47	46	1

Source: UNDP: Human Development Reports (various issues)

A further reason for declining life expectancy is that Kenya had been relying on donor aid to fund various programs in its health sector. For the last eight years, Kenya has been cut off as a donor aid recipient due to its non-compliance with conditions given by the World Bank, IMF and various bilateral aid agencies. This has resulted in some doctors moving to Southern Africa and to other more developed countries worsening the situation in Kenya.

As mentioned earlier, life expectancy for both men and women in the world's richest countries is almost twice that in the worlds poorest. Much of this differential is due to very high infant mortality rates in low-income countries, which is in turn due to the gap in living standards, particularly nutritional status and medical care. In most of the world, women have a longer life expectancy than men, but differentials are narrower in developing than in developed countries, and in some cases reversed from the norm. In the developed countries, women's life expectancy is on average six to seven years longer than men's. But in most developing countries the gap narrows to three years or less (UNDP, 1995). For example, in Kenya the differential was only four years in 1980 and it fell to one year in 2001. On the whole, the trend in the differential has been downward since 1970 reflecting retrogression in socio-economic conditions in Kenya. The life expectancy gap reflects patterns of discrimination, which give preference to male over female infants and children early in life in nutrition, in medical care, in the mother's scarce time, and so on; discrimination that often continues into adulthood.

Table 6 shows that the child mortality rates for Kenya have been rising since the country started implementing structural adjustment programmes in 1995. In addition, it is found that the child mortality rates for female children rose by 15.2 percent between 1997 and 2000 compared to 9.1 percent for male children. Consequently, in 2000 female mortality rates of children under 5 years exceeded that of males.

Table 6: Child Mortality rates per 1000 live births for Kenya: 1970-2000

Year	Infants 0-1 years	Children under 5 years	Mortality rate (children under 5 years)	
			Male	Female
1970	102	156	na	na
1990	63	97	na	na
1991	62	96	na	na
1995	73	111	na	na
1997	74	112	33	33
1998	76	124	na	na
1999	76	118	na	na
2000	77	120	36	38

Source: World Bank: World Development Indicators, (various issues)

Table 7: People Living with HIV/AIDS in Kenya and sub-Saharan Africa: 1999-2001

Region	Year	Total Adults and Children	Adults (15-49 years)	Women (15-49 years)	Men (15-49 years)	Children (0-14 years)
Sub-Saharan Africa (Millions)	End 1999	24.4	23.4	12.0	11.4	1.0
	End 2001	28.5	25.9	na	na	2.6
Kenya (Millions)	End 1999	2.1	2.0	1.1	0.9	0.078
	End 2001	2.5	2.3	1.4	0.9	0.22

Source: Reports of the Global HIV/AIDS Epidemic and UNAIDS Assessment of the Epidemiological Situation in Kenya, 2002

Furthermore, AIDS-related illnesses in Kenya have taken their toll and contributed to a reduction in life expectancy and an increase in infant and child mortality. The HIV prevalence rate in Kenya for adults aged between 15 and 49 years in 2001 was 15 percent (World Bank, 2002). According to UNAIDS (2002), the majority of those suffering the impact of the epidemic live in the rural areas and are mainly the poor. In 2000, only 20 percent of the HIV-positive population in Kenya lived in the urban areas.

Table 7 provides estimates of people living with HIV/AIDS in Kenya and sub-Saharan Africa between 1999 and 2001. By the end of 2001, about 2.5 million people in Kenya were estimated to be living with HIV/AIDS.

In Kenya 1.4 million women in the age bracket 15-49 years were HIV-positive compared to 0.9 million men in the same category by the end of 2001. Women and girls are more vulnerable to HIV because of their limited access to economic and educational opportunities, and the multiple household and community roles they are responsible for. Also, women and girls are subject to social norms that deny them sexual health knowledge and practices that prevent them from controlling their bodies. The gender division of labour and male urban migration keeps men away from their wives for long periods leading to promiscuity and the spread of HIV. Women in the rural areas may also find themselves discriminated against when trying to access care and support when they are HIV-positive. UNAIDS (2002) reports that in Kenya, women who are HIV-infected are divorced even when their husbands have infected them. Family resources are more likely to be devoted to buying medication and arranging care for ill males than females. Because of lack of hospital facilities in rural areas and lack of income, those in rural areas affected by AIDS may find it difficult if not impossible, to obtain hospital care. Therefore, they mostly have to be cared for at home. Generally this is the burden of females.

As the country loses young productive people to AIDS, the effects have an influence on all sectors of the economy. The loss of income of the breadwinner, increased medical expenses and increased time taking care of the sick persons may lead to reduced agricultural output. Households fall into deeper poverty and women are left bearing even larger burdens as workers, educators, mothers and, ultimately, as caregivers, as the burden of caring for the ill family members rests mostly with women and girls. Of HIV-positive pregnant women in Kenya, 30 percent give birth to HIV-positive babies who are likely to die before 5 years of age, increasing the child mortality rate. UNAIDS (2002) predicts that between 2000 and 2020, 55 million Africans will die earlier than they would have in the absence of AIDS.

The decrease in adult life expectancy, increase in child mortality rates, the narrowing of the difference between female and male life expectancy and the increase in the child mortality rates for female children presents a worrying trend for Kenya.

GDP PER CAPITA LEVELS

GDP is a measure of the value of all the final goods and services newly produced in a country during some period of time. GDP per capita based on purchasing power parity (PPP US$) accounts for price differences between countries and therefore better reflects people's standard of living. In theory, at the PPP rate, 1 PPP dollar has the same purchasing power in the domestic economy as 1 US dollar in the US economy.

Table 8 lists the real GDP per capita for Kenya for a selected number of years, but the data are not disaggregated between men and women. However, taking the share of income earned for females in 1995 (the only available data), women earned only 41.79 percent of total earnings compared to men's 58.22 percent. Yet, this was only in formal paid employment and it does not reflect availability of income to the females in the family.

From Table 8, it is seen that Kenya's GDP per capita peaked in 1995 and thereafter started declining during the implementation of structural adjustments programmes and the withdrawal of donor aid to Kenya. This pattern of decline mirrors the increase in the incidence of poverty and a decline in life expectancy in Kenya during this period. According to the World Bank (1999), Kenya recorded negative real GDP growth rates in 1999. During this time the percentage of the population living on less than a dollar a day was 50.2, implying that they were living in absolute poverty. The World Bank stresses the importance of increased income as a major determinant of wellbeing and poverty reduction. To help raise incomes, the World Bank and other donor agencies have recommended commercialisation of agriculture. However, Kiriti and Tisdell (2003b) found that commercialisation of agriculture has led to gender inequality in families in Kenya. Even when household income goes up, food availability goes down due to male control of household income.

However, GDP per capita only reflects average national income. It does not reveal income distribution. GDP per capita is an aggregate at the national level and so it does not uncover inequalities of access to income within households, for example, the availability of that income to wives. Per capita GDP may show an increasing trend but only benefit the male population who are the main beneficiaries of income-earning assets in Kenya.

Table 8: Kenya's GDP per Capita: 1985-2000

Year	GDP per capita (USPPP$)
1985-88	1010
1990	1058
1991	1350
1992	1400
1993	1400
1994	1404
1995	1438
1996	na
1997	1190
1998	980
1999	1022
2000	1000

Source: UNDP: Human Development Reports (various issues)

POVERTY RATES

Income poverty means the lack of material well-being; lack of income to meet basic needs like food, shelter and clothing. Food poverty is measured by the per capita consumption of the required daily intake of the basic recommended calories per adult equivalent (2250 calories). Several international bodies consider persons to live in absolute poverty when their income is less than a dollar a day to meet food, shelter and other basic needs (FAO, 1984, UNDP, 1995). Fifty four per cent of the people in sub-Saharan Africa live in absolute income poverty on this basis.

Poverty rates in Kenya are substantially lower in urban areas than in rural areas (Republic of Kenya, 1998). In 1992, the absolute urban poverty rate in Kenya was 29.3 percent compared with 46.4 percent in rural areas. In 2000, national incidence of absolute income poverty in Kenya rose to 50 percent but the data are not disaggregated between urban and rural areas. Nevertheless, the incidence remains highest in rural areas.

Of 1.3 billion people in absolute poverty globally, the majority are women who are mainly found in rural areas. Poverty among women has been linked to their unequal situation in the labour market, their poor treatment under social welfare systems and their inferior status and power in the family (UNDP, 1995).

Women bear a significant responsibility for the family's subsistence. In virtually all societies, women are the main carers in a family and they are often willing to sacrifice their own welfare for the benefit of other family members, especially their children (Tisdell, 1999). In many countries, women are also important economic providers for the family giving considerable economic support to their children. But their capacity in some developing countries to fulfil this responsibility has been significantly affected by such factors as unequal sharing of household resources, unequal access to earning opportunities, to agricultural land and by the decline in common property resources and forests (Roy and Tisdell, 1993).

Women and men experience poverty differently, and different aspects of poverty (deprivation, powerlessness, vulnerability, its seasonality) have gender dimensions (World Bank, 1996). Vulnerability reflects the dynamic nature of poverty such as defencelessness, insecurity and exposure to risk. Vulnerability is a function of assets. The more assets people have, the less vulnerable they are. Assets include stores, concrete productive investments, human investments, collective assets and claims on others for assistance. Both absolute and food poverty are associated with lack of physical and human assets (World Bank, 1997). Women and children are more vulnerable because tradition usually gives them less decision-making power over assets than men, while at the same time their opportunities to engage in remunerated activities, and therefore to acquire their own assets, are more limited (World Bank, 1995, 1996; Blackden and Bhanu, 1998). Greer and Thorbecke (1986a, 1986b), Collier and Lal (1980), and Republic of Kenya (1991, 1998), show that food poverty and absolute poverty occur mainly among female-headed households.

Tisdell (2000) found that there is gender imbalance in the formation of Human Resource Capital (HRC) in India and other less developed countries. In many developing countries, females are deprived of HRC compared to men. They have less access to education, and often have less availability of food and medical services. This often results in higher fertility rates and higher population growth reinforcing higher poverty rates.

However, Lipton (1995), Ravallion and Lanjouw (1995) argue that women are not generally over-represented in poor households. Their findings and those of Appleton's (1996) are at odds with the findings by other authors, for example, World Bank (1993) and Quisumbing, Haddad and Pena (2001), who found that women are disproportionately represented among the poor. The World Bank's Participatory Poverty Assessment (1995) for Kenya shows that while 25 percent of the study population was categorised as very poor, there were nearly twice as many female-headed households (44 percent) as male-headed households (21 percent) in that category. The remaining 35 percent represented male-headed with no wife present. Greer and Thorbecke (1986a, 1986b), Collier and Lal (1980), and Republic of Kenya (1991, 1998) also find that female-headed households account for the high proportion of the poor in Kenya. Mwabu, et al. (2000) using the cost of basic needs (CBN) and food energy intake (FEI) approaches in computing poverty rates for Kenya, found that poverty rates were marginally higher in female-headed households (41 percent) than in male-headed households (38 percent) where husband and wife live together.

The World Bank's Participatory Poverty Assessment (1995) for Kenya found that to cope with increased levels of poverty, female heads of households in Kenya consistently limit the number of meals eaten. They found that one third of the female-headed households had only one meal per day while the rest had two meals. Some women resort to begging for food, others rely on brewing alcohol despite being harassed by police.

Apart from lack of physical and human assets, women are generally immobile because of greater responsibilities for childcare, household provisioning, doing household chores and home-based agricultural activities. The cultural norms are such that women find it hard to venture out to look for work or in certain traditions, to mix with men. This prevents them from gathering information on job opportunities. They are cut off from channels of communication, or the information they receive is filtered through the (male) head of household or community leaders.

Poverty rates generally decline as the level of education increases (Mwabu, et al, 2000; Schultz, 1960). Education and training reduce the chances of falling back into poverty. Females in Kenya generally have lower levels of education compared to males. A long-term remedy to alleviate poverty would be to invest in poor people, especially women, particularly in their education and training, and to bring them into the mainstream of development

Women not only suffer from income poverty but also human poverty. Human poverty means that opportunities and choices most basic to human development are denied. Human poverty is more than income poverty. It involves the denial of choices and opportunities most basic to human development to lead a long, healthy, creative life, acquire knowledge, and enjoy a decent standard of living, freedom, dignity, self-esteem and the respect of others (UNDP, 1998a; 1998b).

One way of measuring human poverty, although it is far from adequate, is by using the human poverty index (HPI) introduced by UNDP in the Human Development Report of 1997. The HPI is a composite index of different features of deprivation in the quality of life that helps to judge the extent of poverty in a community. HPI-1 measures human poverty in developing countries. The variables used are: (1) The percentage of people expected to die before age 40; (2) the percentage of adults who are illiterate; and (3) deprivation in overall economic provisioning measured by: (a) the percentage of people without access to health services and safe water and (b) the percentage of underweight children under five. The HPI is constructed by taking a simple average of the three variables.

The trend in the HPI for Kenya between 1997 and 2000 is evident from Table 9. This table shows that the value of the HPI for Kenya has been rising and the poverty ranking of Kenya increased compared to other developing nations.

Table 9 also shows that the percentage of people living below the poverty line rose from 42 percent in 1992 to 50 percent in 2000 implying that half the population in Kenya was living below the poverty line in 2000.

Table 9: Human Poverty Index for Kenya: 1997-2000

Year	Rank among developing countries	Value (%)	Population below absolute national poverty line
1992	Na	Na	42.0
1997	35	27.1	Na
1998	49	28.2	47.0
1999	51	29.5	Na
2000	49	31.9	50.0

Source: UNDP: Human Development Reports (various issues)

However, it is difficult to reflect all dimensions of human poverty in a single quantifiable composite indicator. Lack of political freedom, lack of personal security, inability to participate in the life of a community and threats to sustainability cannot be measured and quantified in a simple aggregate. Also, the HPI does not reflect gender inequality. It also does not show how the increased poverty burden is shared between men and women. It does not reveal who among those who suffer from human poverty are females. It also does not show the disparities in poverty between rural and urban areas or among different ethnic communities.

Conclusion

This paper finds that absolute poverty exists and is rising rapidly in Kenya and that poverty is more pronounced in female-headed households. This can be linked to discrimination in the labour market, in access to education, in decision-making and in access and control of human, economic and social resources.

General indicators have shown declining GDP per capita, increased poverty rates especially for women, reduced life expectancy, a narrowing of the difference in female/male life expectancy rates, increased child mortality rates and an increase in the female child mortality rates. This deterioration results in an increased burden on women who are carers of the family and indicates a deterioration of the status of women. Consequently, there is a need to learn how women and families are coping with growing poverty and the high incidence of AIDS and whether this has led to an increase in gender inequality. This paper advocates the use of household level gender disaggregated data because gender inequality manifests itself not just at the national level but has its roots at the household level where culture plays a very important role in allocation of resources and decision-making.

References

Acharya, M. and Bennet, L, (1983), *"Women and the Subsistence Sector: Economic Participation and Household Decision-Making in Nepal"*, World Bank Staff Working Paper No 526. Washington. D. C.: World Bank.

Afonja, S, (1986), *"Changing Modes of Production and the Sexual Division of Labour Among the Yoruba"*, In Eleanor Leacock and Hellen I. Safa (eds), Women's Work, South Hadley, MA: Bergin and Garvey Publishers, pp. 122-135.

Anand, S. and Sen, A, (1995), *"Gender Inequality in Human Development: Theories and Measurement"*, HDR Office Occasional Paper No. 19, New York: UNDP.

Appleton, S, (1996), *"Women-headed Households and Poverty: An Empirical Decomposition for Uganda"*, Centre for the Study of African Economies Working Paper No. WPS/95-14: Oxford University.

Bay, E. G, (1982), *Women in Africa: Studies in Social and Economic Change*, Stanford, Calif: Stanford University Press.

Bennet, L, (1983), *Dangerous Wives and Sacred Sisters: Social and Symbolic Roles of High Caste Women in Nepal*, New York: Columbia University Press.

Blackden, C. and Bhanu, C, (1998), *Gender, Growth and Poverty Reduction: Special Program of Assistance for Africa, 1998 Status Report on Poverty in sub-Saharan Africa*, World Bank Technical Paper No. 428, Washington, D.C.: World Bank.

Boserup, E, (1970), *Woman's Role in Economic Development*, New York: St. Martin's Press.

Collier, P. and Lal, D, (1980), *Poverty and Growth in Kenya*, Washington D. C.: World Bank Staff Working Paper.

Croix, D. and Licandro, O, (1999), *"Life Expectancy and Endogenous Growth"*, Economics Letters, Vol. 65, No. 2, pp. 255-263.

Davison, J, (1988b), *Agriculture, Women, and Land: The African Experience*, Boulder and London: Westview Press.

FAO, (1984), *"Integrating Nutrition into Agricultural and Rural Development Projects: Six Case Studies"*, Nutrition in Agriculture, No. 2, Rome: FAO.

Folbre, N, (1992), *"Introduction: The Feminist Sphinx"*, In Nancy Folbre, Barbara Bergmann, Bina Agarwal and Maria, Floro (eds), Issues in Contemporary Economics, Vol. 4: Women's Work in the World Economy, Hong Kong: Macmillan Academic and Professional Ltd, pp. 23-30.

Greer, J. and Thorbecke, E, (1986a), *"Food Poverty Profile Applied to Kenyan Smallholders"*, Economic Development and Cultural Change, Vol. 35, No. 1, pp. 115-141.

Greer, J. and Thorbecke, E, (1986b), *"A Methodology for Measuring Food Poverty Applied to Kenya"*, Journal of Development Economics, Vol. 24, pp. 59-74.

Gross, D. and Underwood, B, (1971), "Technological Change and Calorie Costs: Sisal Agriculture in Northern Brazil", American Anthropologist, Vol. 73, pp. 725-740.

Henn, J. H, (1978), *Peasants, Workers and Capital in Cameroon*, Unpublished PhD Thesis, Harvard University.

Jiggins, J, (1989), *"How Poor Women earn Income in sub-Saharan Africa and What Works against Them"*, World Development, Vol. 17, No. 7, pp. 953-963.

Julin, E, (1993), *Structural Change in Rural Kenya*, Unpublished PhD Thesis, University of Gotenborg, Sweden.

Kabubo, J. and Kiriti, T, (2001), *"Macroeconomic Adjustment, Poverty and Economic Growth: An Analysis for Kenya"*, African Journal of Economic Policy, Vol. 8, No. 1, pp. 42-58.

Kelley, A, (1991), *"The Human Development Index: Handle with Care"*, Population and Development Review, Vol. 17, No. 2, pp. 315-324.

Kennedy, E. and Oniang'o, R, (1990), *"Health and Nutrition Effects of Sugarcane Production in Southwestern Kenya"*, Food and Nutrition Bulletin, Vol. 12, pp. 261-167.

Kennedy, E. and Peters, P, (1992), *"Household Food Security and Child Nutrition: The Interaction of Income and Gender of Household Head"*, World Development, Vol. 20, No. 8, pp. 1087-1099.

Kiriti, T. and Tisdell, C, (2003a), *"Family Size, Economics and Child Gender Preference: A Case Study in the Nyeri District of Kenya"*, International Journal of Social Economics [Forthcoming].

Kiriti, T. and Tisdell, C, (2003b), *"Commercialization of Agriculture in Kenya: Case Study of Policy Bias and Food Purchases by Farm Households"*, Quarterly Journal of International Agriculture, Vol. 42, No. 4, pp. 435-453.

Kiriti, T. Tisdell, C. and Roy, K, (2003a), *"Female Participation in Decision-making in Agricultural Households in Kenya: Empirical Findings"*, International Journal of Agricultural Resources, Governance and Ecology, Vol. 2, No. 2, pp. 103-124.

Kiriti, T. Tisdell, C. and Roy, K, (2003b), *"Institutional Deterrents to the Empowerment of Women: Kenya's Experience",* In K. C. Roy (ed), Twentieth Century Development: Some Relevant Issues, New York: Nova Science [Forthcoming].

Lipton, M, (1995), *"Market, Redistributive and Proto-reform: Can Liberalisation Help the Poor?"* Asian Development Review, Vol. 13, No. 1, pp. 1-35.

Mincer, J. and Polachek, S, (1974), *"Family Investment in Human Capital: Earnings of Women",* Journal of Political Economy, Vol. 82, No. 2, pp. S76-S108.

Mwabu, G. et al. (2000), *Poverty in Kenya: Profiles and Determinants,* A Joint Research Project by the Department of Economics, University of Nairobi and the Ministry of Planning and National Development, Nairobi: African Economic Research Consortium (AERC).

Palmer, I, (1991), *Gender and Population in the Adjustment of African Economies: Planning for Change,* Geneva: International Labour Office.

Pierre-Yves, C. Pierre, Q. and Caroline, P, (1999), *"Health Care Spending as Determinants of Health Outcomes",* Health Economics, Vol. 8, No. 7, pp. 627-639.

Quisumbing, A. Haddad, L. and Pena, C, (2001), *"Are Women Over represented among the Poor? Analysis of Poverty in 10 Developing Countries",* Journal of Development Economics, Vol. 66, No.1, pp. 225-269.

Ravallion, M. and Lanjouw, P, (1995), *"Poverty and Household Size",* Economic Journal, Vol. 105, No. 433, pp. 1415-1434.

Republic of Kenya, (1991), *Economic Survey,* Nairobi: Government Printer.

Republic of Kenya, (1998), *National Poverty Eradication Plan; 1999-2015,* Nairobi: Government Printer.

Republic of Kenya, (2002), *Mainstreaming Gender into the Kenya National HIV/AIDS Strategic Plan: 2000-2005.* Nairobi: The Gender and HIV/AIDS Technical sub-Committee of the National AIDS Control Council, November 2002.

Roy, K. C. and Tisdell, C. A, (1993), *"Technological Change, Environment and Poor Women, Especially Tribal Women in India",* Savings and Development, Quarterly Review, Vol. 17, No. 4, pp. 423-439.

Saito, K, (1992), *Raising the Productivity of Women Farmers in sub-Saharan Africa: Overview Report,* World Bank, Women in Development Division, Population and Human Resources Department.

Saito, K, Mekonnen, S, Spurling, D, (1994), *"Raising the Productivity of Women Farmers in sub-Saharan Africa",* Discussion Paper 230 Washington, D.C.: World Bank.

Sala-i-Martin, X and Barro, R. J, (1995), *Economic Growth,* New York: McGraw Hill.

Schultz, T. W, (1960), *"Human Capital Formation by Education",* Journal of Political Economy, Vol. 68, No. 6, pp. 571-583.

Sivard, R. L, (1995), *Women: a World Survey* (2nd Ed.). Washington D.C.: World Priorities.

Sorensen, A, (1990), *"The Differential Effects on Women of Cash Crop Production: The Case of Smallholder Tea Production in Kenya",* CDR Project Paper 90.3.

Spring, A, (1978), *Women in Ritual Symbolic Roles,* New York: Plenum Press.

Srinivasan, T, (1994), *"Human Development: A New Paradigm or Reinvention of the Wheel?"* The American Economic Review, Vol. 84, No. 2, pp. 238-243.

Staudt, K. A, (1985), *Agricultural Policy Implementation: A Case Study from Western Kenya,* West Hartford Conn. Kumarian Press.

Tisdell, C. A, (1999), *"Sen's Theory of Entitlement and Deprivation of Females: An Assessment with Indian Illustrations"*, Social Economics, Policy and Development, Working Paper No. 2, University of Queensland.

Tisdell, C. A, (1999), *"Sen's Theory of Entitlement and Deprivation of Females: An Assessment with Indian Illustrations"*, Social Economics, Policy and Development, Working Paper No. 2, University of Queensland.

Tisdell, C. A, (2000), *"Asset-Poor Women in India and the Relevance of Amartya Sen's Analysis"*, Artha Beekshan: Journal of the Bengal Economic Association, Vol. 9, No. 2, pp. 9-19.

Tisdell, C. A. Roy, K. and Ghose, A, (2001), *"A Critical Note on UNDP's Gender Inequality Indices"*, Journal of Contemporary Asia, Vol. 31, No. 3, pp. 385-399.

Todaro, M. P, (1997), *Economic Development*, Sixth Edition, London and New York: Addison Wesley Longman Limited.

United Nations, (1995), *Beijing Declaration and Platform for Action: Fourth World Conference on Women*, 15th September 1995.

United Nations Development Programme, (1995, 1996, 1997, 1998, 2000), *Human Development Report*, New York: Oxford University Press.

United Nations Development Programme, (1998b), *Overcoming Human Poverty*, New York: Oxford University Press.

United Nations Division for the Advancement of Women, (1996), *Women and Decision-making: Percentage of Women in Government 1996*, Bethesda: United Nations Secretariat.

United Nations Economic Commission for Africa, (1998), *African Women and Economic Development*, Addis Ababa: African Centre for Women.

United Nations Program on AIDS, (2002), *Report on the Global HIV/AIDS Epidemic and UNAIDS Assessment of the Epidemiological Situation in Kenya, 2002.* United Nations Secretariat.

Women Fighting AIDS in Kenya, The Communication Initiative Website, 2001.

World Bank, (1989), *Kenya: The Role of Women in Economic Development. A World Bank Study*, Washington, D.C.: Oxford University Press.

World Bank, (1993), *Kenya: Country Gender Profile*, World Bank, Gender Unit.

World Bank, (1995), *Participatory Poverty Assessment in Kenya*, The World Bank Participation Sourcebook, Washington, D. C.: The World Bank Group.

World Bank, (1996), *The World Bank Annual Report.* Washington, D. C.: The World Bank.

World Bank, (2002), *World Development Indicators.* Washington, D.C.: The World Bank.

In: Poverty in Africa
Editor: Thomas W. Beasley

ISBN: 978-1-60741-737-8
© 2009 Nova Science Publishers, Inc.

Chapter 10

THE GLOBALIZATION-AIDS-POVERTY SYNDROME IN AFRICA[*]

Pádraig Carmody[1] and Glen Elder[2]
[1]Trinity College, The University of Dublin, Dublin 2, Ireland[†];
[2]The University of Vermont, Burlington, Vermont 05405, USA

INTRODUCTION

Geographically speaking, AIDS the usually fatal result of an HIV infection, is primarily instantiated in parts of sub-Saharan Africa, which also contains two-thirds of the world's cases of HIV infection (See Figure 1). There were more than 2.1 million AIDS deaths there in 2006, more than 70% of the world's total from complications related to HIV. Put simply, people live with HIV in most parts of the world but tend to get infected by HIV more often and die more quickly of AIDS in sub-Saharan Africa. A fifteen year old boy in Botswana has over a 90% chance of dying of AIDS (UNAIDS, 2000 cited in Barnett and Whiteside, 2006).[‡] While statistics such as these are well known, what is surprising is that suffering and death on this scale was foreseen and *allowed* to develop (for examples of early warnings pertaining to HIV in sub-Saharan Africa see Seale 1986; Caldwell, Caldwell and Quiggin 1989; Barnett and Blaikie 1992; the links between migrant labor in sub-Saharan Africa and HIV see Jochelson et al., 1991; HIV and gender inequality in sub-Saharan Africa see McFadden 1992). More recent responses from international organizations like the World Health Organization, private foundations like the Bill and Melinda Gates Foundation, and state actors like the European Union and the United States are largely responses to the work of highly organized coalitions of the sick and dying who focussed global attention on the pandemic. The AIDS Coalition to Unleash Power (ACT UP) and the Treatment Action Campaign are

---

[*] We are grateful to the participants of the North Eastern Workshop on Southern Africa, 2007 and Dylan Sutherland for their comments on this paper.

[‡] In spite of these horrifying statistics, however, it is also important to note that 90% of African adults remain uninfected (de Waal, 2005) for now.

two well-known examples. These successes notwithstanding, the depth of the current crisis remains a stark testament to the failure of institutions across multiple scales to respond adequately to treat and halt the virus.

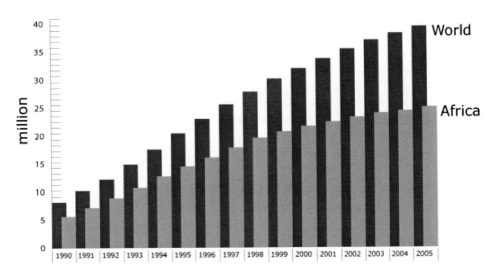

Figure 1. People living with HIV infections (Reproduced by permission: AVERT, 2007).

Our interest here is in the dialectical ways in which the neoliberal globalization has been implemented and the human immonodefiecieny virus has spread producing a Globalization-AIDS-poverty syndrome in sub-Saharan Africa. We are interested in interrogating the multiple forms of agency and scalar processes contained in the verb "acquired" in AIDS. For example, to date biomedical approaches to the prevention of HIV have been premised on the liberal self-determining individual who is "free to choose" health behaviours (Fee and Krieger, 1994 cited in Sember et al., 2003), to the neglect of structural factors. However Fatton (1995 quoted in Howell and Pearce, 2001, p. 189) argues:

> Autonomous agentic individual[s] freed from communal, ethnic and class loyalties [are] nowhere to be found in Africa...By privileging the imaginary 'free, self-determining individuality' of a mythical citizen, it becomes an alien construct forced unto an 'invented' Africa; an intellectual hallucination of a triumphalist liberal *fin de siecle.*'

While the free, self-determining individual has become a convenient and economically efficient construction through which to manage and imagine a global HIV prevention strategy, in sub-Saharan Africa that mythic construction also maps onto bodies that carry the burden of Western gendered fantasies produced during previous rounds of accumulation.

Because the virus can be passed on through sexual contact, albeit an inefficient vector between healthy people, the geographical concentration of the disease, death and dying also maps easily onto post-colonial moralizing fantasies and highly sexualized heteropatriarchal explanations. For example, polygny, promiscuity, and child rape have been highlighted as practices in need of particular attention by many Western observers and HIV prevention specialists. Media representations in the US have been one of the things contributing to making AIDS an "epidemic of significations" (Treichler, 1999 cited in Craddock, 2004).

The spread of HIV has ensured that the Western medical gaze remains actively but ineffectually fixated on an increasingly malnourished but sexually signified "black" African body. The combined result has been that prevention efforts have stalled at that site, privileging sexual behaviour modification almost to the exclusion of any other approach.

Prevention strategies focussed on the body only and inspired by racist and/or homophobic pathologies and neoliberal fantasies about free choice are based on an ontological fallacy – that there is a separate "culture", or patterns of learnt behaviour, which are separate from economy, society and politics. In reality no such separation exists as sexuality and sexual cultural practice are deeply implicated in the economy and politics of society (see Giddens 1992; Castells 1996; D'Emlio and Freedman 1997).

Even recent claims of an "Invisible Cure" for the spread of HIV in Southern Africa by way of an attention to cultural practices put forward by Epstein (2007) have over- dramatized sexual culture (concurrent sexual partnerships) and the potential for behaviour modification (so-called "zero grazing" campaigns) at the expense of economic and cultural empowerment. While concurrent sexual networks are important vectors in the spread of the virus, they should not be de-linked from the ways in which different regions of Africa have been incorporated into the global economy. Thus infection by HIV and the onset of fatal opportunistic infections collectively referred to as AIDS is, in large measure, also a structural condition.

Seeing sexual expression as a cultural and politico-economic transaction, rather than an entirely instinctive and individualised act of self-fulfilment informed only by agency and not structure, is a more appropriate framework for dealing with the pandemic. Thus in examining the epidemiology of HIV it is important to examine how its spread and retreat is informed by multi-scalar co-evolving patterns in "economy", "politics" and "society" – a cultural political economy (Jessop, 2005).

More recently some epidemiologists have recognized the need to revise their epistemological assumptions in light of the frustrating results of previous prevention efforts. Schwartz et al., (1999) argue that epidemiology should not only focus at the level of the body. Instead, they argue that causes of diseases can be distinct at different levels and can be understood through the concept of emergent group properties: that is at each ascending level of organization unique characteristics confined to that level emerge. For geographers, this attention to the different levels at which diseases and their causalities can be discussed easily translates into questions of scale.

Geographers are particularly well-placed to examine the inter-scalar ways in which diseases like HIV spread. For over a decade queer and feminist geographers have shown how human sexuality recursively influences multi-scalar socio-spatial processes from the body to the globe (See Bell and Valentine 1995, Brown 2000, Craddock 2000, Elder 2003, Binnie 2004). Thus HIV/AIDS while a sexually transmitted condition is also a reflection, symptom and a form of globalization (Benetar, 2001): an outcome of particular cultural political economy and operating at a variety of scales. The disease, while partly a virus, is also the result of complex social, cultural and economic webs of affection, transaction and infection – a network disease, in an increasingly networked global society (Castells, 1996, Craddock 2000). Individuals caught up in global networks have differential levels of access to, and forms of, power and therefore the capacity to effect change and modify their behaviour. This recognition flies in the face of almost 20 years of HIV prevention efforts which have sought to bring about changes in personal, and usually sexual, behaviour only.

We seek to extend the framework proposed by Cradock (2000) who has argued that vulnerability to disease must be seen as "historically situated, structured by institutions, households and nations, and shaped by an ever shifting and relentlessly demanding global economy. But it must also be recognized that these structures and economies mesh inextricably with the social ideologies and cultural codes of particular times and places" (p. 164). We are most interested in highlighting how risk is produced through time at multiple scales of analysis that include but also extend way beyond the body and include the household, place, region, nation, and the globe. We argue that neoliberal logics have discounted larger scale processes, privileging sexual agency and so prevention efforts have remained fixated on question of personal responsibility and agency. Our attention to larger scale processes is driven by a desire to intervene in tragically failed HIV prevention efforts that remain fixated on question of individual sexual behavioural modification.

NEOLIBERALIZM AND AIDS IN CONTEXT

Power and globalization are fundamentally linked, as are power and HIV/AIDS (Siplon 2007). Neoliberal globalization is both a class and an inter-state project. At its most basic globalization can be thought of as the global extension of the law of value: the market becomes the predominant method of social coordination, and what is produced and what is not produced depends on profitability. However, the endless drive to accumulate capital does not result in homogenous geographies. Rather places are integrated into the global economy in different ways and spatial differences are a necessary precondition for globalization to occur (Yeung, 2002). Geographical differences in HIV infection rates also reflect this.

The geography of HIV is shaped partly by the nature of the disease but also because of the local conditions surrounding the virus. John Iliffe (2006) argues that the silent and undetected spread of the virus on the continent from the mid 1970's onwards has meant that Africa was worst affected because it has had the first and therefore the longest epidemic. He also goes on to argue that the unique character of the virus – mildly infectious, slow acting, incurable and fatal – decisively shaped both the spread of the epidemic and the human response to it (see also de Waal 2006 on the lack of political response because of the delayed onset of illness). Marmot (2005) argues that on top of the lack of response more recent rounds of structural adjustment programmes have disempowered women and children in Southern Africa and thereby facilitated the spread of the virus into these increasingly economically marginalized groups.

Estimates of prevalence rates within Africa vary, but range from as low as 1% of the adult population in Senegal to almost 40% in Botswana (UNAIDS, 2007). Many divergent explanations have been put forward to explain these differences ranging from religious practice and belief systems in Nigeria and Uganda, higher rates of male circumcision in central and west Africa, isolated island ecologies in Madagascar, to the level of selenium in the soil in Senegal. While these factors provide some analytical purchase, and while being aware that correlation does not equal causation, drawing on the work of Samir Amin (1972) we hope to add a further scale of spatial and temporal complexity by arguing that "AIDS regions" of Africa correspond to colonial macro-regions.

Africa of the trade economy[§] – mostly West Africa, has a relatively low country average prevalence rate of 3.3% of the adult population. Africa of the Concession Owning Companies[**] (Congo River Basin) has intermediate prevalence rates, with an average country rate of 6.8%, which is above the internationally recognized 5% for it to qualify as a pandemic. While the epidemic is at its most severe in Africa of the Labour Reserves[††] (Eastern and Southern Africa), with the highest regional prevalence rate at a country average of 12.5%.

These differences in infection rates are shaped by institutions such as the migrant labour system in Southern Africa; the legacy of the plunder economy in Central Africa, and different types of heteropatriarchal and racialised relations instantiated under different colonial configurations that served to erode male, but particularly female, forms of economic autonomy to varying degrees.

Robson (2004, p. 232) reminds us that "the ways that global processes such as the HIV/AIDS pandemic and economic restructuring intersect with people are uneven and differentiated; often operating through long chains of interaction". Nonetheless, we argue that the relationship between different colonial legacies *and* the current round of globalization are key to understanding differential infection rates "glocally" (Bauman 1998). It is this interaction which is central to the creation of a mutually reinforcing Globalization-AIDS-Poverty Syndrome in parts of the continent.

In order to reflect the view more forcefully, first we draw attention to the history of gender relations in Southern Africa that were adapted during the late nineteenth and twentieth centuries in order to align with the demands of extractive forms of capitalist accumulation. Second, we examine the ways in which more recent policies of economic liberalization have deepened poverty in these now post colonial spaces to produce a population at risk. Third, we draw the links between these phases of accumulation and conclude by offering possible ways forward that will begin to break the globalization-AIDS-poverty (GAP) cycle.

COLONIALISM, GENDER, AND THE GEOGRAPHY OF HIV

Recently Epstein (2007) has argued that sex in some sub-Saharan African regions crosses social boundaries more often than in the West, and that the practice of concurrent partners - simultaneous long-term relationships in which trust undermine regular condom usage – means that one person's infection may spread rapidly through a group. Most studies now suggest that viral load is the chief predictor of transmission, with "no transmission among people with lower serum viral load" (Quinn et al., 2000 cited in Stillwaggon, 2005). People

---

[§] Togo, Ghana, Nigeria, Sierra Leone, Gambia, Liberia, Guinea Bissau, Cameroon, Chad and the Sudan. Figures are calculated from UNAIDS (2005). No data is available for Sudan.

[**] Now the Democratic Republic of Congo, Congo-Brazaville, Gabon and the Central African Republic. The Democratic Republic of Congo has a relatively low rate of 3.2% perhaps because Mobutu left only 10% of the tarmaced road network which the Belgians has put in, thereby impeding movement (Meredith, 2005). Needless to say while Belgian colonialism was noteworthy for certain things, infrastructural investment was not one of them. Also the war there from 1998-2003 had a dialectical effect by promoting migration from war effected regions and encouraging people to stay put, in those regions less affected.

are at their most infectious after they have initially contracted the virus and when they have developed AIDS (de Waal, 2006) and as Epstein (2007) shows, concurrency does increase the chance that sexual partners will interact when they are at their most infectious (right after initial infection). While we are not disputing Epstein's careful analysis, her focus on black African bodies' concurrent sexual practices has done little to disrupt failed prevailing behavioural modification models of disease prevention. Her analysis shifts the gaze from sexual dissidents like prostitutes and "cheating husbands" towards bodies networked through concurrent sexual liaisons. Missing from her analysis, however, is the recognition that concurrent sexual practice is an outcome of structural conditions. Our concern is that her widely disseminated text and its uncritical acceptance has once again drawn attention away from the other scalar influences on the spread of HIV and how place-making produces a landscape of differentiated access to power and thereby levels of risk and vulnerability. Concurrent sex lives are not generalizable cultural practices or an institution *per se*, but represent part of a dynamic sexual political economy that is structured, amongst other things, by the gendered legacy of colonialism and contemporary structural adjustment policies.

Contemporary concurrency rates cannot be uncoupled from the extent to which migrant labour systems throughout Southern Africa facilitate a contemporary polygynous or concurrent sexual outcome. Dynamic sexual economies and economies of affection are not particular to Africa. Heterosexual polygynous households in sub-Saharan Africa are dynamic and widespread social-sexual household responses, as are Western-style heterosexual marriages and serial monogamy for that matter (Castells, 1996). The highly contested definition of marriage as an arrangement between one man and one woman in the United States attests to the fluidity of sexual practices and social response.

It is estimated that 30-50% of women in Sub-Saharan Africa are in polygamous marriages (Hope, 2001 cited in Poku, 2005). A household with multiple wives ensures social reproduction, particularly in areas where agriculture is central to the regional political economy. This argument does not seek to minimize what can be highly oppressive sexual politics within some of these households. These rural households, however, are hamstrung between local demands for domestic and paid and unpaid labour and the incentives produced by a gender segregated labour market that attracts men to seek higher paid formal work which is part of a regional and in some cases international political economy. Gendered assumptions about work and the role of women in rural household reproduction formed during the nineteenth and early twentieth centuries' colonial administrations are not incidental to the shape and form of today's households in Kwazulu-Natal in South Africa, for example, where men move as parts of formal economic chains while women move through informal paid and unpaid economic chains. The resultant political economy, inflected with heteropatriarchal tensions around children, childbearing, child rearing, intimacy, desire and decisions to move from or remain in rural regions produces a highly complex political economic and socio-sexual network, or a political procreational economy (Elder, 2003).

Colleen O'Manique (2004) has shown how the colonial legacy of social disruption in Uganda shaped the epidemic there, as has pre-colonial history. Similarly, in Southern Africa the burdens of social reproduction were placed on women in the reserves (Wolpe, 1980; Bozzoli, 1991; Elder, 2003). Polygyny in parts of Southern Africa changed radically as rural

---

[††] Kenya, Uganda, Tanzania, Rwanda, Burundi, Zambia, Malawi, Angola, Mozambique, Zimbabwe, Botswana, Lesotho and South Africa.

areas were drawn into a regional political economy centred on mining throughout the twentieth century (Moodie et al., 1994; Eprecht 2004). As that sector reorganized in the late 1970's and early 1980's to stall declining rates of profitability resulting from more organized labour, it turned towards increased levels of mechanization and a heavier reliance on foreign labour (Crush, 2001 et al.). With the shift towards regional scale and cross-boundary labour recruitment, the scales of sexual economies shifted too from bonds that linked rural and urban bodies within South Africa to bonds of economy, affection and desire that followed inter regional flows between South Africa and as far away as Malawi.

Interestingly, Oppong (1998 cited in Oppong and Kalipeni, 2004) found that the region with the highest rate of polygny in Ghana had the lowest AIDS rate. However, in the migrant labour system countries of Eastern and Southern Africa the picture is different. One study in Nairobi found that last sex was with a casual partner or commercial sex worker for 26% of men living with a spouse (Ndinya-Achola et al., 1997 cited in Kalipeni, Craddock and Ghosh, 2004). Undoubtedly this is partly because the incidence of absolute poverty there increased from 27 to 50% from 1992 to 1997 (Central Bureau of Statistics, 2000 cited in Zulu et al., 2004), pushing women into sex work and increasing the supply of sex workers. On the Kenya-Uganda highway men are charged as little as £1 sterling for sex ("Killer on the Road", 2001). Thus it is not concurrency which is necessarily the issue in explaining differential rates of infection, but the nature of the sexual network in which people are embedded. As a result of the migrant labour system in Africa of the Labour Reserves, these appear to be more socially and geographically extensive, whereas in Muslim parts of West Africa strict sexual mores may pertain, even though polygny is common.

Gender inequality would appear to be more significant than poverty or the sexual politics of a household *per se* in creating a risk environment, because within those households and as poverty deepened women do not not have the socially defined capabilities to resist unwanted sexual advances by their "partners." As the scale and extent of economic opportunities diminished, the commodification of bodies becomes a viable livelihood strategy.

Kabeer and Whitehead (1999, p. 19 cited in White and Killick, 2000, p.17, but also Marmot 2005 on structural adjustment, economic disempowerment and HIV infection) note in general women in Africa "are less able than men to translate labour into income, income into choice and choice into personal wellbeing". Higher socio-economic classes and genders have greater latitude to alter their behaviour, as risk exposure does not form part of their livelihood strategy. Where large numbers of women are socially excluded by virtue of (colonially enforced) lack of access to material assets, such as land, they may be forced to turn to sex work to support themselves. Practices such as "dry sex", where women insert drying agents into their genitalia to increase friction and male pleasure during sex are indicative of gender inequality. Orphaned girls are particularly susceptible to being pushed into sex work (Marmot 2005). In Kisumu Kenya, 23% of girls between the ages of 15 and 19 were HIV positive in the late 90's versus only 8% of boys (Buvé et al., 1999, cited in Poku, 2002).

THE LIBERALIZATION OF AIDS: GLOBALIZATION AND POVERTY

According to Stillwaggon (2005) unprotected heterosexual intercourse between otherwise healthy adults is a "relatively inefficient mode of HIV transmission". The chances of transmission from an infected man to a woman in this one scenario is about one in five hundred, versus one in a thousand from an infected woman to a man per sexual contact (World Bank, 1997 cited in Stillwaggon, 2005). Thus there must be "intervening variables" for HIV to become a pandemic: gendered poverty being the most important of these.

If African poverty is the outcome of historical processes of extractive globalization from slavery to neoliberalism (Bond, 2006), and HIV is related to a cultural political economy, cycles of impoverishment are deeply implicated in the spread of HIV (Kim et al., 2000 cited in Poku, 2005, also Stillwaggon, 2005). Given these historical and contemporary connections, it is surprising that more attention has not been paid to the material causation of the health crisis.

Globalization is associated with deepening inequality as the "Mathews effect" –"to he who has shall be given" – prevails (Wade, 2004). Average incomes in Africa are 51 times lower than in the rich countries (Poku, 2005). The richest twenty five Americans receive incomes greater than the poorest two billion people on the planet (Kirby, 2006) and the median GDP of a Sub-Saharan African country is equivalent to the output of a town of 60,000 in a rich country (World Bank, 2000). It is little wonder that so many of Africa's health care professionals, trained at public expense, have left for the West, with more Malawian doctors in Birmingham, England than in Malawi (Royal African Society, 2005). In Zambia perhaps up to 85% of the doctors have left (Kelly, 2007).

The current extension of the law of value is perhaps even more pronounced than under colonialism. Associated with this geographical and sectoral extension of the law of value is an increase in risk. Indeed some refer to the development of a global "risk society" (Beck, 1992). However, the distribution of risk is highly uneven across social class and gender geographies. Increased risk for some populations is reflected in the fact that in the early 1990's a child in Sub-Saharan Africa was 19 times more likely to die than in rich countries, whereas by 2003 the figure was 26 times more (UNDP, 2003 cited in Kirby, 2006).

World Bank/International Monetary Fund "structural adjustment programmes" (SAPS) in the 1980's and 1990's which encouraged the introduction of school or "user fees" had the effect of forcing some girls who wanted to stay in school to accept sexual advances in exchange for fees (Stillwaggon, 2005). Vogli and Birbeck (2005) show through an exhaustive review of local and regional epidemiological studies of HIV, more recent round of neoliberal reforms have produced higher rates of vulnerability to HIV/AIDS in sub-Saharan Africa. They argue that the combined effects of currency devaluation and the removal of food subsidies, privatization, financial and trade liberalization, and the charging of user fees for health services and education (all hallmarks of structural adjustment programs implemented in sub-Saharan Africa and since 1981) have come to produce contexts in some parts of the world where the virus spreads more efficiently than others. These economic policies also often fed deindustrialization, which in some cases such as Zimbabwe dramatically lowered incomes (See Carmody, 2001). The economic decline of Zimbabwe was associated with its later intervention in the war in the Democratic Republic of Congo beginning in 1998, in order to distract and reward a restive military leadership (See Carmody 2007). Conflict zones are classic "risk situations" given the family instability which accompany them (Akeroyd, 2004).

War may be thought of as a form of globalisation linking different places together, often preceding economic globalisation (Barkawi, 2006). The linkages between poverty and war are not straightforward, although there does appear to be a correlation (Cramer, 2006). The disruption associated with the impacts of economic globalization on weak economies has fed violent conflict (Kaldor, 2003 cited in Kirby, 2006). However, current "new wars" in Africa involving both state and non-state actors are in reality part of historical continuum of the plunder economy dating back to slavery (Cramer, 2006). While HIV may have crossed species barriers earlier than the 1930's, the upheavals, migration, and infrastructure development of the colonial and immediate post-colonial environments presented a very facilitative environment for the disease to spread (Barnett and Whiteside, 2006).

War is associated with family disruption and mass movements of people which this has occasioned particularly in Africa has created risk environments for the spread of HIV (Barnett and Whiteside, 2006). Refugees often face acute risk environments as traditional sexual norms and social control collapses, poverty is exacerbated and access to condoms is constrained (UN/DESA, 2005 cited in Poku, 2005). However, the impact of war is dialectical, by destroying infrastructure and sometimes locking populations in place it may discourage travel and trade and thereby reduce the potential for HIV infection.

Even where profitability is not possible, partial commodification has often taken place in order to encourage "efficiency". When Kenya introduced user fees at its sexually transmitted disease (STD) clinics of $2.15 attendance fell between 35 and 60% (Poku, 2005). Poverty Reduction Strategy Papers (PRSPs) introduced by the World Bank in 1999 have swung against user fees for primary health care and education, while promoting the commodification of other basic rights, such as water. However, some see this as an attempt to suitor the tattered social fabric resulting from economic crisis and liberalization and to construct a *more competitive* labour market (Cammack, 2004). Thus in a somewhat paradoxical spatial mismatch the law of value is at its most acute in those regions which produce the least value, with "raw accumulation" or "accumulation by dispossession" (Harvey, 2003) to the fore.

Programmes of trade liberalization undermined the fiscal basis of the African state, imposing a cost of US $272 billion on these countries over a twenty year period (Christian Aid 2005 and Dembele 2005 cited in Adésìna, 2006: Although these figures are disputed See Collier, 2007). Trade liberalization within Africa might however, have some beneficial impact on HIV transmission, by reducing the waiting time at borders, often of many days, when truckers often stay with sex workers rather than spend money at hotels (FHI 2003 cited in Stillwaggon, 2005).

The poor quality of African public infrastructure, from health systems to water treatment, is implicated in the fact that 70% of the burden of disease there is from communicable disease, versus only 25% in China (White and Killick, 2000). The inability of many communities to access basic, inexpensive types of medical care and treatment helps to illuminate the ways in which some people get to live, and other are sentenced to death.

A simple illustrative comparison makes the case: in Canada health spending is $2,800 per person per year, versus $14 in Ethiopia, where GDP per capita is $97 a year (African Development Bank, 2003: UNDP, 2004 cited in Stillwaggon, 2005); HIV incidence rates in Canada are 0.3% whereas in Ethiopia they are up to ten times higher at up to 3.5% (UNAIDS, 2006). A central African study in the mid 1980's found that five needles were used to inject up to 400 patients daily at a mission hospital (Seale, 1986 cited in Oppong and Kalipeni, 2004). Undiagnosed sexually transmitted infections make it up to ten times easier to contract HIV (MEDILINKS, 2001 cited in Poku, 2005). Thus the ability to mount an effective public health response was massively different in the "West", compared to African countries, but similarly the political economic conditions in Abidjan and Kinshasa versus those in Toronto also made for the possibility of sky-rocketing infections in some places and not in others. Simply put, economic collapse and attendant political instability in much of the African sub-continent in the 1980's and 1990's increased the risk environment. However, this does not explain why infection rates are up to ten times higher in some of the countries of Southern Africa than they are in Ethiopia, for reasons alluded to earlier.

Poor sanitation infrastructure and undernuitrition also implicated in the spread of the pandemic. The genital lesions associated with schistosomiasis, a common water borne disease in part of Africa, dramatically increase the likelihood of infection, as around Lake Victoria and in the wetter northern and eastern parts of South Africa (Stillwaggon, 2005). In Swaziland, the country now with the highest reported rates of HIV infection in the world at 39% of adults, schistosomiasis in the 1980's ranged from 33 to 60%.

Because Sub-Saharan Africa is in the tropics and sub tropics, it suffers more heavily than other continents from parasitic diseases and poor soil (Stillwaggon, 2005). Selenium deficiency is correlated with mortality in HIV-infected children, again arguing for the importance of nutrition (Campa et al., 1999 cited in Stillwaggon, 2005). Selenium in vitro blocks HIV-1 replication (Kotaro et al., 1997 cited in Foster, 2004), suggesting its importance as a food additive.

These susceptibility factors seem to outweigh or overwhelm behavioural differences in terms of number of sexual contacts (UNAIDS, 1999 cited in Stillwaggon, 2005). One study for the World Health Organization found that "unexpectedly large proportions of men and women reported no sex during the last month, more so in Africa than elsewhere" (Careaël, 1995, p. 104 quoted in Stillwaggon, 2005, p. 20). While behavioural difference are important, they are glocally embedded processes, and require more than a simple "individuated" call for behavioural change.

MAKING THE LINKS: GENDER, DEEPENING POVERTY AND AIDS

As poverty has deepened across much of the continent, some people may choose to heavily discount the future through engagement in risky sexual activity, such as those involved in dangerous activities, like mine workers in South Africa (Campbell, 2003). According to some estimates miners have a one in forty chance of being crushed by falling rock, so HIV seems a remote, and unseen threat (Williams et al., 2000 cited in Poku, 2005). They may also assert their masculinity and power (over women) to offset the disempowerment associated with the harsh labour regime in the mines by insisting on "flesh-to-flesh" sex (Campbell, 2003). In the mining settlement of Carletonville, South Africa, 95% of miners are migrants and there is a is 65% HIV positive rate – the highest in the world.

Others may be forced into Faustian trade-offs of short-term benefits and medium-term risks, such as commercial sex workers, whose choice is often eat today, rather than worrying about dying in years time. In a context of resource scarcity and poverty, sex may become a commodity sold on the market, or bartered for services or goods. Around the shores of Lake Victoria there is a system in operation called "jaboya" where women traders must sleep with fishermen to be allowed to buy their fish. Then they must sleep with truck drivers to bring their fish to market, raising transmission rates (IRIN, 2005). Grinding poverty and disempowerment may encourage a sense of fatalism. In the words of one sixteen year old Ghanaian sex worker "All die be die" – everyone must die sometime (quoted in Awusabo-Asare et al., 1999, p. 134 in Barnett and Whiteside, 2006, p. 22). In this way HIV transmission can be seen as the coal face of the contradiction between literal social reproduction and accumulation. The spread and accumulation of HIV in the body mirrors dispossession and (dis)accumulation in the economy.

AIDS, the death-inducing consequence of untreated HIV infection, is most structurally violent in those areas where "surplus" populations are concentrated, in parts of Africa or Asia. Indeed some go so far as to suggest that poverty and HIV are "instruments for regulating African insecurity" (Amaïzo, 2003). The fact that these people are "disposable" is evidenced by the way in which unethical anti-AIDS drugs trials which also used placebos were conducted in Africa (Craddock, 2004).

In class terms, those people who are neither capital, nor labour and are largely "surplus" to the overall functioning of the global economy. As Jan Pronk puts it:

> Globalization has changed the character of capitalism. There are more people excluded from the system than are exploited in the system. Those who are excluded are being considered dispensable. Neither their labour nor their potential buying power seems to be needed
>
> (Pronk, 2003: 29 quoted in Kirby, 2006: 99).

These people depend for their livelihoods on the unregulated "informal sector" celebrated by neoliberals (e.g. de Soto, 1989). They are petty commodity and service producers merging both capital and labour together in a single class position, characterised by self-exploitation (Chayanov, 1986). Typically petty commodity producers have access to some capital (machinery or commodities) or land to sustain themselves. However, given the extent of primitive accumulation and land dispossession and scarcity in parts of Africa women in particular are sometimes compelled into the sex industry, where the only "capital" – in the conventional definition an asset that yields an income - available is the body. Ironically, it is here too at this "site" that HIV prevention efforts are most intensive, downplaying the multiple points of intervention at other scales. In this formulation HIV is the proxy for "capital depreciation" and the cost of anti-retrovirals (ARVs) and good diet, the costs of capital replacement. In this hyper-competitive market, eating today, versus dying later thus becomes a grim exercise in economic discounting – a truly dismal, and perversely rational science.

In some cases the body is one type of capital used by women traders to agricultural estates who become sex workers at night (Rugelema, 2004). Sex is commodified. This multiple mode of livelihood, and the necessity of "capital switching" from day to night, speaks to the low marginal productivity of labour in the informal sector (Santos, 1979: Mustapha, 1992). These people are neither producers nor consumers of globalised commodities, but they are exposed to commoditized desire through advertising. This may nonetheless produce a kind of cognitive dissonance of unfulfilled desire as even the excluded are exposed to the global ideology of consumerism (Sklair, 2001), which may feed into the commoditisation of sexual relations. Envy of others material possessions, what is called *tamaa* amongst the Chagga people of East Africa, only came with colonialism (Setel, 1999 cited in Barnett and Whiteside, 2006). This was exacerbated during the period of "Acquired Income Deficiency Syndrome" (AIDS?) as the Tanzanian economy declined during the 1970's . The economic structural adjustment programmes (ESAPs) of the World Bank and International Monetary Fund in the 1980's and 1990's arguably further entrenched and deepened poverty. In Zimbabwe its ESAP was known colloquially as the "Extreme Suffering of African People".

In periods of rapid change and disruption, faster turnover of sexual partners may form part of livelihood strategies (Barnett and Whiteside, 2006). In Botswana the proportion of women who had ever been married fell from 63 to 39% from 1971 to 1996 (Barnett and Whiteside, 2006). This was during a period of rapid economic growth and urbanization. Levels of social capital or social capabilities to deal with disease are also likely undermined under such conditions.

As Barnett and Whiteside (2006: 167) put it:

If you put people in circumstances where they cannot maintain stable relationships, where they are mobile, where life is risky and pleasures are few and necessarily cheap, then sexually transmitted disease will be rampant.

This perhaps partly explains why while there is "no evidence of a decrease in HIV infection levels among young people in Mozambique, South Africa or in Zambia" (UNAIDS, 2006, p. 8). A study in Tanzania found respondents who argued that drinking and having sex was more common in the 1990's than in the 1960's because the football clubs and music groups that people used to be involved with have disappeared (Rugelema, 2004). This decline of social capital, mirrors wider capital off-shoring and disaccumulation in the Tanzanian economy. It is estimated that 40% of African private wealth is now held overseas (Commission for Africa, 2004). Indeed the spatial disorder and mutation of global capital flows mirrors the genetic structure of HIV.

Parsing out the national geography of HIV infection at a global scale is revealing. Because while it is clearly understood that HIV infection and AIDS fatalities are outcomes of poverty, those outcomes are in fact most marked in some of the richest countries in Africa South of the Sahara: Botswana and South Africa, for example.

Inequality would appear to be positively correlated with the spread of HIV. It is a feature of neoliberalism, as capital is free to move to where returns are highest, but labour is more spatially restricted (See Saad-Filho and Johnston, 2005). Inequality is associated with poorer health outcomes, as some segments of the population are excluded from accessing public and other health resources (Wilkinson, 1996) and Africa has the highest levels of consumption inequality in the world (World Bank, 2000). South Africa and Botswana have two of the highest Gini coefficients in the world. This high level of inequality is also associated with high levels of absolute poverty, despite these being relatively "rich" countries. In contrast the legacy of "African socialism" in Tanzania means that only 11% of the population there live in absolute (less than one US dollar a day) poverty (IFAD 2001 cited in Moyo, 2006) and the adult prevalence rate there is at around 6.5% (UNAIDS and WHO, 2006). In the countries with some of the highest prevalence rates in the world: South Africa, Zimbabwe, Botswana and Zambia have absolute poverty rates of 24, 41, 35 and 85% respectively. Botswana had the fastest growing economy in the world for much of the latter part of the 20th century (Samatar, 1999), growing an average of 8.5% p.a. from 1975-1990, but per head daily supply of cereals and protein fell 9% during this time and the number of "permanent destitutes" increased dramatically (UNDP, 1998; 2000: Good, 1999 cited in Stillwaggon, 2005). Thus "national" wealth can disguise sub-national poverty.

In Zimbabwe economic liberalization and HIV prevalence growth coincided in the early 1990's . Prior to economic liberalization an estimated three per cent of the population controlled two-thirds of gross national income and income inequality was to worsen after that (Stoneman and Cliff, 1989 cited in Kanyenze, 2003: Bond and Manyanya, 2002). However, Zimbabwe's HIV prevalence has recently declined to 21% of the adult population due to mortality and perhaps behaviour change (UNAIDS 2005b cited in Patterson, 2006).

It is the combination and concatenation of "negative" incentives which results in vulnerability and rapid transmission of the disease (Vogli and Birbeck 2005). Indeed, risk and poverty are the outcomes of intertwined processes, as are safety and affluence. For much of the world's population safety and risk aversion are in fact neoliberal fantasies that are the preserve of very few, and most definitely out of reach for the "global poor". This is interesting because to date most HIV prevention work has focussed, almost exclusively, on behaviour modification, and the assumed power to choose (for example, see Caraël (1995)). This mindset has profound gendered implications. To assume that the best defence poor women have against a global pandemic is to require them to insist that men wear condoms is woefully misogynist and a form of sanctioned domestic violence against poor women of the world. Protecting the vaginal walls of women's bodies from exposure to the virus should be the last possible place where HIV prevention is practiced. This intimate space should not be the first and only site of power struggle. Rather in line with the proven insights of public health theory, the aim should be to eliminate the conditions which allow the virus to flourish, rather than allow a contest between it and the potential host's immune system to be engaged.

Agriculture accounts for about 70% of employment in Africa (Townsend, 2000 cited in Moyo, 2006) and the disease results in a loss of agricultural and other types of labour directly by those who are affected. Satellite photos show that forest is now encroaching in what were once agricultural areas of Uganda and this may be contributing to the recent recorded rise in poverty in that country. One study of small farming areas in Zimbabwe found that the death of an adult member of the household resulted in a 61% reduction in maize output (Kwaramba, 1998 cited in Barnett and Whiteside, 2006). In pastoral communities in Uganda, more than 13% of households with cattle had sold some of them to meet family needs which had resulted from HIV/AIDS, with the figure substantially higher in mixed farming households (Topouzis, 1994 cited in Poku, 2005).

There is also a substantial opportunity cost of forgone incomes as a result of caring for family members who are sick. In Malawi, 43% of people say they are caring for someone with AIDS (Afrobarometer, 2004 cited in Patterson, 2006) and potentially ruinous medical and funeral expenses. AIDS may undermine access to assets, as they are sold to pay for medical expenses and funeral costs and as widows and children are sometimes disinherited on the death of "head of household" (Barnett and Whiteside, 2006). In a rural and urban study of Zambia, when the father in the household died of AIDS average disposable income fell on average by more than 80% (Namposya-Serpell, 2000 cited in Barnett and Whiteside, 2006).

There are reductions in social capital as a result of "hollowing out" of most productive adult members of society in some areas and so the impact on human capital formation has yet to be assessed.

Rates of return on education may decline, as the investment in human capital is lost. Malcolm McPherson (2003 cited in de Waal, 2006) has described this as "running Adam Smith in reverse". Some businesses, such as in the security sector, in Mozambique train two workers for every job in the expectation that one may be lost ("Far Away Up Close", 2006). This raises the cost profile and businesses may substitute capital for labour, reducing overall employment or alternatively may off-shore operations to less affected locations, for tradeable goods and services.

There may also be a loss of capacity to plan on how to combat the disease and to plan the economic growth necessary to generate resources for this. For example, Ministries of Finance, Economic Planning and Development and Public Services and Information are projected to loose 32% of their staff to AIDS in the next decade (Poku, 2005). Declining populations in some of the worst affected countries will shrink local markets, with negative impacts on economic growth.

There are also costs associated with raising orphans: both short and long-term. For example, some project that the inadequate socialization of orphans may lead to higher crime rates in the future and contribute to what psychologists call the talionic impulse, as the sense of abandonment by these children is vented in later life. Although given strong family support systems in much of Africa research suggests that orphaned children do as well, if not better, than their non-orphaned counterparts (Hutchinson, 2006).

Neoliberal globalization has been implicated in worsening poverty in Africa. Poverty in-turn increases vulnerablility to HIV infection for a variety of reasons, which further entrenches poverty. Furthermore, globalization and the increased interconnectedness of some places has facilitated the spread of HIV, yet HIV has also undermined elements of globalization, by discouraging foreign direct investment in some of the worst affected countries, for example. News about AIDS rate may even affect the value of the South African currency (Kaufmann and Weerapana, 2005). Escalating infection rates have also, in turn, created new opportunities for profit maximization. The importance of the potential profits at stake is suggested by the struggle over name brand versus generic anti-retro viral therapies and the "violation" of WTO trading rules on the part of Brazil, India, and South Africa as these countries were forced to bring life-saving therapies to their dying populace (See for example Bond, 1999).

While "surplus" populations are not a market for pharmaceutical companies, who have derived vast profits from patented drugs such as AZT (which was developed using public money through the National Institutes of Health as a treatment for cat's liver problems (Chang, 2003)), Glaxo-Wellcome made $589 million on one AIDS drug in 1999, recouping more than twice its research and development costs in that one year (Médicins Sans Frontière, 2000 cited in Poku, 2002). While globalization is meant to promote competition in the "free" market, many "donor" countries pressure recipients not to import generic ARVs through bilateral trade deals (Patterson, 2006). The severity of the pandemic in-turn has created new global capital flows (pharmaceutical capital flows and foreign aid) to deal with or ameliorate it. Thus, the development of the disease has, like globalization, has been dialectical. Indeed as a global disease, transmitted through global travel, it is a form of globalization.

BREAKING THE GAPS

Behaviour modification is scale specific and class specific and a wholly inadequate path to inhibiting the spread of HIV in Africa. "Although in most countries people are now aware of the causes of HIV infection, their behaviour has not changed because the chief determinants of that behaviour are economic and social, not informational" (Stillwaggon, 2005, p. 81). In fact unprotected sex typically brings a sex worker a higher price (Stillwaggon, 2005). Thus the "education" and responsibilization of the poor (Craig and Porter, 2006), has limits in terms of cutting HIV infection. Prevention programs that assume universal sexual agency across the globe without recognizing that it too has a gendered, sexed, and raced political economy is not prevention at all; it is genocide.

While the director of UNAIDS, Peter Piot (2007) argues that "AIDS is a disease of globalization", and that there is a need to address it core drivers this is cast in terms of a "social change" of diffusionist modernisation agenda. "We cannot wait until the last man or woman and everyone is rich" (Piot, 2007). Rather he argues that the focus should be on things that can be effectively addressed such as rumours in Northern Nigeria that ARVs are designed to kill Muslims or gender-based violence. According to Piot "know your epidemic" and "invest in local solutions". While there is certainly merit in this approach, it has strict limits.

The reversal of the spread of the disease in Africa would appear to be dependent on the development of institutions, incentives and capabilities (Lall, 1992) and the creation of alternative patterns of accumulation and legitimation.

While the prices of anti-retroviral therapies have come down in some parts of the world, they are still expensive, and in many cases in sub-Saharan Africa their cost still exceeds national income per capita (Brown, 2004). This is particularly important because while antiretroviral treatment keeps potential "transmitters" alive it also reduces viral load and thereby should reduce the rate of sexual transmission from those who are infected (Stillwaggon, 2005).

TRIPS (trade related intellectual property rights) in the WTO are symbolic of the structural power of transnational capital. While the WTO acknowledges the right to contravene these in the case of a public health emergence, patents still emerge as a major issue in bilateral aid and trade deals. For example, ARVs bought under the US PEPFAR or by the Bill and Melinda Gates Foundation initially had be in conformity with US patent law, although generics were subsequently approved (Patterson, 2006). In Nigeria 70% of PEPFAR funding goes for the purchase of US goods and contractors. Indeed some have posited that the economic problems which the Bush Administration encountered on assuming office are key in understanding such attempts to tie aid and market access (Soederberg, 2006). Also 90% of PEPFAR "prime partners" are non-governmental, thereby reinvigoration the "by-pass the state" approach of previous aid modalities. Consequently it was only in 2007 that Rwanda became the first country to invoke the exemption and import generic drugs from Canada.

Others have suggested innovations such as recreational facilities on agricultural estates (Rugelema, 2004) and community programmes (Campbell, 2003). Water systems, latrines, and nutritional supplements are vitally important. Undoubtedly behaviour change is important, particularly the issue of concurrency. However, what is important here is the nature of the sexual network (more open or closed) and the contextual conditions, particularly poverty, in which the network is embedded. Behaviour change can be facilitated by empowerment and changing the structure of economies to allow greater opportunities for women in particular, but also by disbanding the migrant labour system.

The nature of globalization also needs to be changed so that it incorporates social and economic rights more generally through minimum or basic income grants to all perhaps funded through national solidarity taxes in richer African countries (Nattrass, 2004) or global ones, such as the recently instituted tax on airplane tickets in France. The recent revival of economic growth on the continent, largely driven by higher oil prices and Chinese demand for minerals, also offers a window of hope, as does recent substantial debt relief (African Development Bank, 2006). Ultimately, however, further power reconstruction and redistribution will take place only through social struggles conducted at multiple scales by progressive social forces.

REFERENCES

African Development Bank (2003) *African Development Report 2003*. Oxford and New York: Oxford University Press.

African Development Bank (2006) *African Development Report 2006: Aid, Debt Relief and Development in Africa*. Oxford and New York: Oxford University Press.

Afrobarometer (2004) Public Opinion and HIV/AIDS: Facing up to the Future? Briefing Paper 12. *http://www.afrobarometer.org/AfrobriefNo1.pfd* Accessed 27 June, 2007.

Akeroyd, A. (2004) Coercion, Constraintss, and Cultural Entrapments: A Further Look at Gendered and Occupational Factors Pertinent to the Transmission of HIV in Africa. In E. Kalipeni, S. Craddock, J. Oppong and J. Ghosh (eds) *HIV and AIDS in Africa: Beyond Epidemiology* (89-103). Malden: Blackwell Publishers.

Amaïzo, Y. E. (2003) Poverty and HIV/AIDS: Instruments for Regulating African Insecurity. In B. Onimode *et al.*, *African Development and Governance Strategies in the 21st Century*. London: Zed.

Amin, S. (1972) Underdevelopment and Dependence in Black Africa: Historical Origin. *Journal of Peace Research*, 9(2): 105-119.

Avert (2007). Available at *http://www.avert.org/worldstats.htm*. Accessed 8th January, 2007.

Awusabo-Asare, K. et al., (1999) All Die be Die": Obstacles to Change in the Face of HIV Infection in Ghana. In J. C. Caldwell et al., (eds) *Resistances to Behavioural Change to Reduce HIV/AIDS Infection*. Canberra: Health Transition Centre, Australian National University.

Barkawi, T. (2006) *Globalization and War*. Lanham, Maryland: Rowman and Littlefield.

Barnett, T. and Blaikie, P. (1992) *AIDS in Africa: It's Present and Future Impact*. New York: Guilford Press.

Barnett, T. & A. Whiteside (2006) *AIDS in the Twenty-First Century: Disease and Globalization*. Basingstoke and New York: Palgrave Macmillan.

Bauman, Zygmunt (1998) On glocalization: or globalization for some, localization for Others: *Thesis Eleven*, No. 54. London: SAGE, 1998.

Beck, U. (1992) *Risk Society*. London: Sage.

Bell, D. & Valentine, G., (1995) *Mapping Desire*. London: Routledge.

Benetar, S. R. (2001) South Africa's Transition in a Globalising World: HIV/AIDS as a Window and Mirror *International Affairs* 77(2): 347-375.
Binnie, J. (2004) *The Globalization of Sexuality.* London: Sage Publications.
Bond, P. (1999) Globalisation, Pharmaceutical Pricing and South African Health Policy: Managing Confrontation with U.S. Firms and Politicians *International Journal of Health Services* 29(4): 765-792.
Bond, P. (2004) *Talk Left, Walk Right: South Africa's Frustrated Global Reforms.* Durban: University of Kwa-Zulu Natal Press.
Bond, P. (2006) *Looting Africa: The Economics of Exploitation.* London: Zed.
Bond, P. & M. Manyanya (2002) *Zimbabwe's Plunge: Exhausted Nationalism, Neoliberalism and the Search for Social Justice.* Scottsville and London: University of Natal Press and Merlin Press.
Bozzoli, B. (1991) *Women of Phokeng: Consciousness, Life Stategy and Migrancy in South Africa, 1900-1983.* Johannesburg: University of Witwatersrand Press.
Brown, L (2004) Economic Growth Rates in Africa: The Potential Impacts of HIV/AIDS. In E. Kalipeni, S. Craddock, J. Oppong and J. Ghosh (eds) *HIV and AIDS in Africa: Beyond Epidemiology.* Malden: Blackwell.
Buvé. A. et al., (1999) *Differences in HIV Spread in Four Sub-Saharan African Cities*, UNAIDS Special Report 12, Lusaka.
Caldwell, J., Caldwell, P. & Quiggan, P. (1989) The social context of AIDS in sub-Saharan Africa. *Population and Development Review* 15: 185-234.
Campbell, C. (2003) *Letting Them Die: Why HIV Prevention Programmes Fail.* Bloomington: Indiana University Press.
Cammack, P. (2004) What the World Bank Means by Poverty Reduction, and Why it Matters. *New Political Economy*, 9(2): 189-211.
Campa, A., G. Shor-Posner, F. Indacochea et al., (1999) Mortality Risk in Selenium-Deficient HIV-Positive Children. *Journal of Acquired Immune Deficiency Syndromes and Human Retrovirology* 20(5): 508-513.
Caraël, M. (1995) "Sexual Behaviour", in J. Cleland and B. Ferry (eds) *Sexual Behaviour and AIDS in the Developing World* (London: Taylor and Francis for the World Health Organization).
Carmody, P. (2001) *Tearing the Social Fabric: Neoliberalism, Deindustrialization and the Crisis of Governance in Zimbabwe.* Portsmouth: Heinemann.
Carmody, P. (2007) *Neoliberalism, Civil Society and Security in Africa.* Basingstoke and New York: Palgrave MacMillan.
Castells, M. (1996) *The Rise of the Network Society.* Malden: Blackwell.
Central Bureau of Statistics (Kenya) (2000) *Economic Survey 2000.* Nairobi: Government Printers.
Chang, H-J. (2003) *Globalisation, Economic Development and the Role of the State.* London: Zed.
Christian Aid. (2005) *The Economics of Failure: The Real Costs of 'Free' Trade.* London: Christian Aid.
Collier, P. (2007) *The Bottom Billion: Why the Poorest Countries are Failing and What Can be Done About it.* Oxford and New York: Oxford University Press.
Commission for Africa. (2004) *An Overview of Evidence*, Secretariat paper presented for the first meeting of the Commission on 4 May 2004 available at

http://www.commissionforafrica.org/english/about/meetings/first/trends_and_evidence.pdf. Accessed 13 September, 2005.

Chayanov, Alexander (1986) *Theory of Peasant Economy*. Madison: University of Wisconsin Press.

Craddock, S., (2000) "Disease, social identity, and risk: rethinking the geography of AIDS", *Transactions of the Institute of British Geographers 25*: 153-168.

Craddock, S. (2004) AIDS and Ethics: Clinical Trials, Pharmaceuticals, and Global Scientific Practice. In E. Kalipeni, S. Craddock, J. Oppong and J. Ghosh (eds) *HIV and AIDS in Africa: Beyond Epidemiology* (240-251). Malden: Blackwell.

Craig, D. & D. Porter (2006) *Development Beyond Neoliberalism: Governance, Poverty Reduction and Political Economy*. London: Routledge.

Cramer, C. (2006) *Civil War is Not a Stupid Thing: Accounting for Violence in Developing Countries*. London: Hurst and Company.

Crush, J. (2001) Undermining Labour: The Social Implications of Sub-Contracting on the South African Gold Mines. *Journal of Southern African Studies* 27(1):5-31 (with Theresa Ulicki, Teke Tseane and Elizabeth Van Veuren).

De Soto, H. (1989) *The Other Path: the Invisible Revolution in the Third World*. New York: Harper Collins.

De Waal, A. (2005) "The Challenge of HIV/AIDS in B. Wisner, C. Toulmin and R. Chitiga (Eds) *Towards a New Map of Africa*. London: Earthscan.

De Waal, A. (2006) *AIDS and Power: Why There is No Political Crisis Yet*. London: Zed.

Dembele, D. M. (2005) Is aid the answer. *Alliance*, 10(3)(September): 57-60.

D'Emilio, J & Freedman, E (1997) *Intimate Matters: A History of Sexuality in America*. Chicago: University of Chicago Press.

Elder, G. (2003) *Hostels, Sexuality and the Apartheid Legacy: Malevolent Geographies*. Athens: Ohio University Press.

Epstein, H. (2007) *The Invisible Cure: Africa, the west and the fight against AIDS*. New York: Faffaf, Straus and Giroux.

Eprecht, M. (2004) *Hungochani: The History Of A Dissident Sexuality In Southern Africa*. Montreal: McGill Queens University Press.

Far Away Up Close: Mozambique (2006) RTE documentary.

Fatton, R. (1995) Africa in the Age of Democratisation: The Civic Limitations of Civil Society. *African Studies Review* 38(2): 67-99.

Fee, E. & Krieger, N. (1994) Understanding AIDS: History and Limits of Biomedical Individualism. In N. Kriger and G. Margo (eds) *AIDS: The Politics of Survival*. Amityville, NY: Baywood.

FHI (Family Health International) (2003) Findings: Chirundu, Zimababwe. Available at *http://www.FHI.org/en/HIV/AIDS/Publications/manualsguidebooks/corrhope/corrfin3.htm* Accessed July 18 2007.

Foster, H. (2004) Halting the AIDS Pandemic. In D. Janelle, B. Warf and K. Hansen (eds) *World Minds: Geographical Perspectives on 100 Problems*, pp. 69-73, Dordrecht: Kluwer Academic.

Giddens, A. (1992) *The Transformation of Intimacy: Sexuality, Love and Eroticism in Modern Societies*. Cambridge: Polity Press.

Good, K. (1999) The State and Extreme Poverty in Botswana: The San and Destitutes *Journal of Modern African Studies* 37(2): 185-205.

Harvey, D. (2003) *The New Imperialism.* (Oxford and New York: Oxford University Press.
Howell J. & Pearce J. (2001) *Civil Society and Development: A Critical Exploration* Boulder, CO: Lynne Rienner.
Hope, K. R. (2001) Africa's HIV/AIDS Crisis in Development Context. *International Relations* 15(6): 15-36.
Hutchinson, E. (2006) Madona's 'adoption' ignores the realities of life in Malawi. *Irish Times*, 18 October, p. 16.
IFAD (International Fund for Agricultural Development) (2001) Assessment of Poverty: Eastern and Southern Africa. New York: Oxford University Press cited in S. Moyo. The Efficacy of the NEPAD Agriculture Strategy. In J. O. Adésínà, Y. Graham and A. Olokushi (eds), *Africa and Development: Challenges in the New Millennium: the NEPAD Debate.* London and New York: Zed.
Iliffe, J. (2006) *The African AIDS Epidemic: A history.* Athens: Ohio University Press.
IRIN (2005) Deadly Catch: Lake Victoria's AIDS Crisis. DVD.
Jessop, B. (2005) Cultural Political Economy, the Knowledge-Based Economy, and the State. In The Techno Economy. London: Routledge. Available at *http://eprints.lancs.ac.uk/191/.* Accessed 8th January, 2007.
Jochelson, K., Mothielei, M., & Leger, J., (1991) Human immunodeficiency virus and migrant labor in South Africa. *Journal of Health Services* 21(1): 157-173.
Kabeer, Naila & Ann Whitehead 1999 "From Uncertainty to Risk: Poverty, Growth and Gender in the Rural African Context" Background paper for 1999 Status of Poverty in Africa Report
Kaldor, M. (2003) *Global Civil Society: An Answer to War.* Cambridge: Polity Press.
Kalipeni, E., S. Craddock & J. Ghosh (2004) Mapping the AIDS Epidemic in Eastern and Southern Africa: A Critical Overview. In E. Kalipeni, S. Craddock, J. Oppong and J. Ghosh (eds) *HIV and AIDS in Africa: Beyond Epidemiology* Malden: Blackwell.
Kanyenze, G. (2003) The Performance of the Zimbabwean Economy, 1980-2000. In S. Darnolf and L. Laakso (eds) *Twenty Years of Independence in Zimbabwe: From Liberation to Authoritarianism,* pp. 34-77, Basingstoke and New York: Palgrave MacMillan.
Kaufmann, K. & A. Weerapana (2005) The Impacts of AIDS-Related News on Exchange Rates in South Africa. Available at *www. wellesley.edu.* Accessed 15th September, 2006.
Kelly, M. (2007) Interview. Lusaka, Zambia, 3rd January.
Killer on the Road (2001), *The Guardian*, 28th December, 2001. Available at *http://society.guardian.co.uk.* Accessed 1st March, 2007.
Kim, J.Y., Millen, J.V. & Irwin, A. (eds) (2000) *Dying for Growth: Global Inequality and the Health of the Poor.* Monroe, ME: Common Courage Press.
Kirby, P. (2006) *Vulnerability and Violence: The Impact of Globalisation.* London: Pluto.
Kwaramba, P. (1998) The Socio-economic Impact of HIV/AIDS on Communal Agricultural Production Systems in Zimbabwe". Working Paper No. 19, Economic Advisory Project. Harare: Friedrich Ebert Stiftung.
Marmot, M. (2005) Social determinants of health inequalities. *The Lancet 365*: 1099-1104.
McFadden, P., (1992) Sex, Sexuality and the Problems of AIDS in Africa. In R. Meena (ed.), *Gender in Southern Africa: Conceptual and Theoretical Issues.* Harare: SAPES, 157-195.

McPherson, M. (2003) *Non-Linear Macro Effects of HIV/AIDS: An Overview*, USAID EGAT/ED/HEW and Centre for Business and Government. JFK School of Government: Harvard, mimeo.

Médicins Sans Frontières (2000) Price of essential drugs for HIV/AIDS, Paper presented at the African Development Forum 2000 conference in Ethiopia.

Meredith, M. (2005) *The State of Africa*, New York: Free Press.

Moodie, D. (1994) *Going for Gold: Men, Mines and Migration.* Berkeley: University of California Press. (with Vivienne Ndatshe).

Moyo, S. (2006) Africa's Agrarian Transformation: The Efficacy of the NEPAD Agriculture Strategy. In J. O. Adésínà, Y. Graham and A. Olokoshi (eds) *Africa and Development: Challenges in the New Millennium: The NEPAD Debate*, pp. 107-139, Pretoria, Dakar and London: UNISA, CODESRIA and Zed.

Mustapha, A. (1992) Structural Adjustment and Multiple Modes of Livelihood in Nigeria. In P. Gibbon, Y. Bangura and A. Ofstad (eds) *Authoritarianism, Democracy and Adjustment: the Politics of Economic Reform in Africa*, pp. 188-216, Uddevalla, Sweden: Scandinavian Institute for African Studies.

Namposya-Serpell, N. (2000) Social and Economic Risk Factors for HIV/AIDS-Affected Families in Zambia. Paper presented at the AIDS and Economics Symposium, IAEN, Durban, 7-8 July, p. 1.

Nattrass, N. (2004) Unemployment and AIDS: The social-democratic challenge in South Africa. In R. Paratian and S. Dasgupta (eds) *Confronting Economic Insecurity in Africa*. Geneva: ILO.

Ndinya-Achola, J.O., Ghee, A. E., Kihara, A.N., Krone, M.R., Plummer, F. A., Fisher, L.D. & Homes, K. K. (1997) High HIV Prevalance, Low Condom Use and Gender Difference in Sexual Behaviour among Patients with STD-Related Complaints at a Nairobi Primary Health Care Clinic, *International Journal of STDs and AIDS*, 8: 506-514.

O'Manique, C. (2004) *Neoliberalism and AIDS Crisis in Sub-Saharan Africa: Globalization's Pandemic*, Palgrave Macmillan International Political Economy Series: Basingstoke and New York.

Oppong, E. (1998) A Vulnerability Interpretation of the Geography of HIV/AIDS in Ghana 1986-1995. *Professional Geographer*, 50(4): 437-448.

Oppong, J. & Kalipeni, E. (2004) Perceptions and Misperceptions of AIDS in Africa. In E. Kalipeni, S. Craddock, J. Oppong and J. Ghosh (eds) *HIV and AIDS in Africa: Beyond Epidemiology*. Malden: Blackwell.

Patterson, A. (2006) *The Politics of AIDS in Africa.* Boulder, CO: Lynne Rienner.

Piot, P. (2007). Irish Aid Seminar on HIV/AIDS, 30th January, Dublin.

Poku, N. (2002) Global Pandemics: HIV/AIDS. In D. Held and A. McGrew (eds) *Governing Globalization: Power, Authority and Global Governance*, pp. 111-125. Oxford: Polity.

Poku, N. (2005) *AIDS in Africa: How the Poor are Dying.* Oxford: Polity.

Pronk, J. (2003) Security and Sustainability. In P. van Seter, B. de Gaay Fortman and A. de Ruijter (eds) *Globalization and Its New Divides: Malcontents, Recipes, and Reform* Amsterdam: Dutch University Press.

Quinn, T., Wawer, M., Sewankambo, N. et al., (2000) Viral Load and Heterosexual Transmission of Human Immunodeficiency Virus Type 1. *New England Journal of Medicine*, 342(13): 921-929.

Robson, E. (2004) Hidden Child Workers: Young Carers in Zimbabwe, *Antipode*, 36(2): 227-248.
Royal African Society (2005) *A Message to World Leaders: What About the Damage We do to Africa?* London: RAS.
Rugalema, G. (2004) Understanding the Africa HIV Pandemic: An Appraisal of the Contexts and Lay Explanation of the HIV/AIDS Pandemic with Examples from Tanzania and Kenya. In E. Kalipeni, S. Craddock, J. Oppong and J. Ghosh (eds) *HIV and AIDS in Africa: Beyond Epidemiology* (191-203). Malden: Blackwell.
Saad-Filho, A. & Johnston, D. (2005) (eds) *Neoliberalism: A Critical Reader*. London: Pluto.
Samatar, A. (1999) *An African Miracle: State and Class Leadership, and Colonial Legacy in Botswana Development*. Portsmouth, New Hampshire: Heinemann.
Santos, M. (1979) *The Shared Space: The Two Circuits of the Urban Economy in Underdeveloped Countries*. New York: Methuen.
Schwartz, S. Susser, E. & Susser, M. (1999) "A future for epidemiology", *Annual Review of Public Health*, 20: 15-33.
Seale, J. (1986) "Infectious AIDS", *Nature*, 320: 391.
Sember, R., Gscholossman, S. & Moses, J. (2003) Global and Local: Living within the Epidemic. Available at *http://www.ssrc.org* Accessed 20 April 2007.
Setel, P. (1999) *A Plague of Paradoxes: AIDS, Culture and Demography in Northern Tanzania*. Chicago: University of Chicago Press.
Siplon, Patricia (2007) Power and the Politics of HIV/AIDS. In P. Harris and S. Siplon (eds) *The Global Politics of AIDS* (pp 17-34). Boulder, CO: Lynne Rienner Publishers.
Sklair, L. (2001) *The Transnational Capitalist Class*. Malden: Blackwell.
Soederberg, S. (2006) *Global Governance in Question: Empire, Class and the New Common Sense in Managing North-South Relations*. London: Pluto.
Stillwaggon, E. (2005) *AIDS and the Ecology of Poverty*. Oxford: Oxford University Press.
Stoneman, C. & L. Cliffe (1989) *Zimbabwe: Politics, Economics and Society*. London and New York: Pinter.
Topouzis, D. (1994) *Uganda – The Socio-Economic Impact of HIV/AIDS on Rural Families with an Emphasis on Youth*. Rome: FAO.
Townsend, R (2000) *African Agricultural Research and Development: Increasing Effectiveness and Financial Sustainability*. Washington, D.C.: European Commission and World Bank.
Treichleer, P. (1999) *How to Theory in an Epidemic: Cultural Chronicles of AIDS*. Durham: Duke University Press.
Tripp, A. M. (2003) Forging Developmental Synergies Between States and Associations. In N. Van de Walle, N. Ball and V. Ramachandran (eds) *Beyond Structural Adjustment in Africa: the Institutional Context of Development*, pp. 131-158. Basingstoke and New York: Palgrave MacMillan.
UN/DESA (2005) *World Population Prospects. The 2004 Revision. Highlights*. United Nations: New York.
UNAIDS (1999) *Listen, Learn, Live: Challenges for Latin America and the Caribbean*. Geneva: UNAIDS.
UNAIDS (2000) *Report on the Global HIV/AIDS Epidemic* (June). Geneva: UNAIDS.
UNAIDS (2005a) Map of Country Prevalence Rates. Available at *www.unaids.org*.

UNAIDS (2005b) "AIDS in Africa: Three Scenarios to 2025. Available at *www.unaids.org*. Accessed 8th January, 2007.
UNAIDS (2007). *www.unaids.org*. Accessed 8th January, 2007.
UNAIDS and WHO (2006) *AIDS epidemic update*. Geneva: UNAIDS.
UNDP (United Nations Development Programme) (2003) *Human Development Report*. New York: Oxford University Press.
UNDP (United Nations Development Programme) (2004) *Human Development Report*. New York: Oxford University Press.
Vogli, R. & Birbeck, G. (2004) Potential impacts of adjustment policies on vulnerability of women and children to HIV?AIDS in sub-Saharan Africa. *Journal of Health Population and Nutrition* 23: 105-20.
Wade, R. (2004) On the causes of widening world income inequality, or why the Matthew Effect prevails. *New Political Economy*, April.
White, H. & Killick T. in collaboration with Kayizzi-Mugerwa, S. and Savane, M-A.(2000) *African Poverty at the Millennium*. New York: Oxford University Press.
Wilkinson, R. (1996) *Unhealthy Societies: The Afflictions of Inequality*. London: Routledge.
Williams, B. G., Gilgen, D., Campbell, C. M., Jaljaard, D. & MacPhail, C. (2000) *The Natural History of HIV/AIDS in South Africa: A Biomedical and Social Survey in Carletonville*. Johannesburg: Centre for Scientific and Industrial Research.
Wolpe, H. (ed.) (1980) *The Articulation of Modes of Production*. London: Routledge.
World Bank (1997) *Confronting AIDS: Public Priorities in a Global Epidemic*. Oxford: Oxford University Press.
World Bank (2000) *Can Africa Claim the 21st Century?*(New York: Oxford University Press.
Yeung, H. (2002) The limits to globalization theory: a geographic perspective on global economic change. *Economic Geography 78*: 285–305.
Zulu, E. M., Nii-Amoo Dodoo, F. & Ezeh, A. C. (2004) Urbanization, Poverty, and Sex: Roots of Risky Sexual Behaviours in Slum Settlements in Nairobi, Kenya. In E. Kalipeni, S. Craddock, J. Oppong and J. Ghosh (eds) *HIV and AIDS in Africa: Beyond Epidemiology* (89-103). Malden: Blackwell Publishers.

INDEX

A

abortion, 106
absolute poverty, xii, 209, 226, 227, 228, 230
access, xii, 209, 210, 211, 212, 214, 217, 218, 219, 220, 221, 222, 225, 227, 228, 229, 230, 237, 240, 241, 243, 245, 247
accessibility, 14, 22, 86, 108, 115, 118
accidents, viii, 10, 41, 45, 55, 69
accommodation, 178, 180
accountability, 32, 171
accounting, 29, 198, 212, 222
accumulation, 223
achievement, 6, 45, 62, 66, 162, 175, 216, 217, 219
acid, 138, 139, 140, 153
Acquired Immune Deficiency Syndrome (AIDS), vi, vii, 73, 127, 135, 155, 225, 226, 230, 232, 233, 235, 236, 237, 238, 239, 240, 241, 242, 244, 245, 246, 247, 248, 249, 250, 251, 252, 253, 254, 255, 256
activities, 210, 211, 213, 214, 218, 228
acute, 243
additives, 143, 144
adhesion, 137
adjudication, 210
adjustment, 79, 143, 191, 216, 219, 223, 224, 238, 240, 241, 242, 246, 256
administration, 92, 131, 139, 162, 179, 180, 181, 185, 223
administrative, 6, 89, 164, 179, 216, 218
administrators, 179, 219
adolescents, 72
adult, 80, 214, 219, 221, 226, 227, 238, 239, 246, 247, 248
adult literacy, 214
adult population, 219, 238, 239, 247
adulthood, 224
adults, 66, 80, 225, 229, 235, 242, 244

advertising, 245
advisory body, 171
aerobic, 142
affect, 212, 213, 215
affirmative action, 34, 223
African continent, vii, xi, 4, 157
African culture, 138, 222
African National Congress, 208
African Union, 6, 33, 161, 163, 164
Afrikaans, 180
agar, 140
age, 10, 47, 48, 56, 87, 91, 93, 117, 134, 187, 199, 200, 212, 221, 225, 226, 229, 250, 251
agents, 99, 137, 161, 211, 212, 241
aggregation, 99, 215
agrarian, ix, 75, 76, 81, 82, 85, 87, 94, 95, 98, 100
agricultural, ix, x, 13, 14, 15, 16, 18, 19, 20, 21, 76, 77, 78, 79, 81, 82, 83, 84, 88, 89, 91, 92, 93, 94, 98, 99, 100, 133, 134, 135, 136, 142, 143, 150, 152, 178, 189, 195, 196, 203, 206, 210, 211, 212, 221, 226, 228, 245, 247, 249
agricultural residue, 152
agricultural sector, 83, 99, 178
agriculture, vii, ix, 16, 18, 34, 72, 75, 79, 81, 82, 85, 88, 93, 98, 100, 134, 135, 138, 144, 163, 169, 178, 179, 185, 186, 187, 188, 189, 191, 195, 203, 205, 206, 210, 221, 226, 240
agroindustrial, 153
aid, 11, 43, 114, 117, 158, 159, 160, 161, 162, 163, 164, 166, 168, 172, 174, 224, 226, 248, 249, 252
aiding, 173
air, 140, 142, 143, 145, 151
alcohol, 228
Algeria, 4, 35, 37
alien, 236
alienation, 135
allies, 173
alternative, xi, 52, 85, 88, 193, 210, 214, 249
alternatives, 145

ambiguity, 69
ambulance, 116, 119
ambulances, 7, 116
amino, x, 134, 138
amino acid, x, 134, 138
amino acids, x, 134, 138
ammonium, 146
Amsterdam, 103, 254
anaemia, 45, 106, 107, 128
anaerobic, 145
anaerobic digesters, 145
analytical framework, 85
androgen, 154
anger, 55
Angola, vii, 222, 240
animal diseases, 78
animals, 53, 55, 63, 88, 90, 92, 95, 97
Animals, 44
anti-cancer, 137, 138
anti-HIV, 139
anti-inflammatory agents, 137
antimalarial drugs, 114
antioxidant, 137
antiretroviral, 249
antitumor, 138, 139, 154, 155
antiviral, 139, 154
apartheid, 43, 81, 87
apoptosis, 139
application, 10, 84, 89, 153
argument, xi, 65, 157, 169, 184, 240
arid, 78, 88, 93
armed forces, 167
articulation, 84
ascorbic, 138
ascorbic acid, 138
ash, 88, 139
Asia, 5, 7, 8, 9, 11, 39, 40, 82, 83, 96, 101, 103, 171, 175, 176, 233, 245
Asian, 20, 21, 28, 37, 38, 39, 40, 178, 232
Asian countries, 28
assessment, 76, 99, 171, 208, 217
assets, ix, 22, 33, 75, 76, 82, 84, 85, 86, 91, 92, 93, 94, 95, 98, 100, 135, 166, 181, 184, 195, 213, 214, 227, 228, 241, 247
assumptions, 69, 237, 240
asthma, 137
Athens, 252, 253
atrocities, 167
attacks, 43
attention, xii, 235, 236, 237, 238, 239, 240, 242
attitudes, 63, 85
Australia, 209
authority, 188, 189, 190, 211, 213

Autonomous, 236
autonomy, 239
availability, 13, 22, 93, 100, 136, 138, 145, 152, 211, 218, 221, 226, 227, 228
averaging, 11, 216, 218, 219
aversion, 216, 247
avoidance, 45, 63
awareness, 61, 107

B

babies, 55, 60, 117, 120, 122, 123, 226
bacillus, 117, 124
bacteria, 44, 56, 61, 139, 140, 144, 152
bacterial, 154
balance of payments, 178, 184
bananas, 139
banking, 211
bargaining, 175, 212, 213, 214
barrier, 222
barriers, 33, 67, 95, 96, 170, 197, 211, 222, 243
barriers to entry, 197
barter, 212
basic needs, ix, 105, 158, 178, 227, 228
basic rights, 169, 243
basic services, 180, 182, 185
basic trust, 86
BCG, 117
beating, 125
beer, 144, 155
behavio(u)r, 158, 165, 213
behaviours, 46, 47, 63, 68, 236
Beijing, 222, 233
belief systems, 238
beliefs, 65, 71, 72, 168, 197
benefits, 9, 12, 13, 14, 16, 18, 19, 20, 22, 33, 34, 39, 66, 100, 150, 154, 184, 220, 244
beta-carotene, 138
bible, 58, 61
bifurcation, 83
bilateral, 248, 249
bilateral aid, 11, 224, 249
bilateral trade, 159, 248
binding, 100
bioconversion, 154
biodegradation, 153
biodiversity, 138, 170, 171
biogas, 142, 153
biomedical, 236
bioremediation, 136
biosphere, 136
biotechnology, 155
biotin, 138

birds, 53, 108
birth, ix, 105, 106, 107, 117, 118, 120, 121, 123, 124, 128, 129, 131, 178, 214, 224, 226
births, ix, 105, 107, 225
black, 237, 240
blame, 129
blocks, 190, 244
blood, 44, 125, 127, 137, 139
blood pressure, 127, 139
boiling, 146, 151, 152
bonds, 241
borrowing, 178, 198
Boston, 73
Botswana, 22, 35, 221, 235, 238, 240, 246, 252, 255
bottlenecks, 14
boys, 44, 57, 220, 241
Brazil, 71, 153, 231, 248
breakdown, 127
breeding, 44, 57, 59
Bretton Woods, 194
Bretton Woods system, 194
bribery, 167, 172
bribing, 163
Britain, 166
British, 252
buildings, 59
bureaucracy, 116, 129
Burkina Faso, 35
burn, 88
burning, 92, 136, 142
Burundi, vii, 35, 240
buses, 7
Bush Administration, 249

C

cabbage, 186
calcium, x, 134
California, 254
calorie, 135
Cameroon, 35, 170, 231, 239
campaigns, 237
Canada, 243, 249
canals, 45
Canberra, 250
cancer, 155
cancer cells, 137, 139
cancer treatment, 155
capacity, 237, 248
capacity building, 184
Cape Town, 72, 75, 101, 102
capital, 212, 223, 228, 231, 232, 238, 245, 246, 248, 249
capital flows, 246, 248
capital goods, 98, 194
capital intensive, 140
capitalism, 97, 245
capitalist, 84, 96, 239
carbohydrates, x, 134, 138, 139
carbon, 136, 141, 143
carbon dioxide, 141, 143
carcinoma, 139
caregivers, 226
Caribbean, 5, 7, 9, 11, 255
case study, 71, 72
cash crops, 80, 196, 210
cash flow, 194
cast, 249
category b, 225
Catholic, 113, 114
Catholic Church, 114
cattle, 44, 89, 90, 92, 96, 153, 210, 247
causality, 29
causation, 223, 238, 242
CD8+, 139
CDR, 232
cell, 136, 137, 139, 144
cell adhesion, 137
cellulose, 143
cellulosic, x, 133, 153
cement, 142, 145
Census, 191
Central African Republic, 239
Central Asia, 5, 7, 9
cereals, 187, 247
Chad, 10, 239
Change, 230, 231, 232
changing environment, 97
channels, 13, 14, 16, 20, 173, 198, 223, 228
chaos, 125, 171
charcoal, 89, 90, 92, 93, 96
cheating, 240
Chicago, 252, 255
chicken, 117, 150, 203, 223
chickens, 55
child mortality, 106, 107, 224, 225, 226, 230
child rearing, 240
childbearing, 107, 222, 240
childbirth, 106, 107
childcare, 228
children, vii, viii, 14, 34, 35, 41, 42, 44, 46, 48, 54, 55, 56, 57, 59, 61, 62, 63, 66, 72, 73, 107, 115, 118, 119, 129, 134, 137, 145, 150, 185, 200, 202, 210, 211, 214, 219, 220, 224, 225, 226, 227, 228, 229, 238, 240, 244, 247, 248, 256

Index

China, xi, 5, 9, 11, 17, 19, 20, 21, 22, 23, 38, 39, 40, 157, 158, 159, 160, 161, 162, 163, 164, 165, 166, 167, 168, 169, 170, 171, 172, 173, 174, 175, 176, 243
Chinese, 250
Chinese goods, 163
cholera, 42, 44, 55, 63, 72
cholesterol, 137, 138
cholesterol lowering agents, 137
chopping, 144, 146
Christianity, 58, 65
Christians, 63, 167
CIA, 178, 191
circulation, 142, 145, 152
circumcision, 238
citizens, xi, 87, 157, 160, 161, 163, 165, 167, 170, 174, 185
civil servant, 43, 96, 179, 187
civil servants, 179, 187
civil service, 181
civil society, 46, 86, 161, 162, 163, 173
civil war, 43, 44, 171, 252
civilian, 167
classes, 221, 241
classification, 112
clay, 52
cleaning, 45, 50, 55, 56, 57, 62, 69, 72, 91, 172
clients, 119, 122, 123, 211
climate change, 136, 190
clinics, 114, 115, 117, 119, 122, 128, 129, 243
closure, 169
cluster analysis, 91
clusters, 91, 92, 93, 94, 95
Co, 72, 73, 116, 117, 123, 163, 164, 166, 175
coal, 52, 54, 55, 169, 245
coal mine, 169
coalitions, 235
cocoa, 210
codes, xii, 51, 238
coffee, 143
cognitive, 246
cognitive dissonance, 246
cohesion, 13
Cold War, 173
colds, 137
collaboration, 124, 125, 126, 129, 190, 256
Collaboration, 124
collateral, 198, 211
collectivism, 83
colon, 139
colon cancer, 139
colonial, 236, 239, 240, 243
colonial power, 43, 160

colonial rule, 43, 84, 180
colonialism, 78, 87, 98, 159, 239, 240, 242, 246
Columbia, 166, 173, 174, 175, 176, 230
Columbia University, 166, 173, 174, 175, 176, 230
combat, 248
combined effect, 178, 181, 242
combustion, 7
commercial, 210, 241, 244
commercialization, 16
commodities, 245
commodity, 84, 177, 245
commodity producers, 245
common rule, 58
communication, 12, 14, 19, 68, 179, 229
Communism, 158
communities, ix, 18, 76, 77, 89, 91, 99, 111, 115, 116, 118, 129, 136, 145, 150, 169, 190, 206, 219, 230, 243, 247
community, viii, 6, 14, 41, 44, 47, 48, 51, 56, 60, 62, 64, 66, 71, 73, 77, 78, 83, 86, 89, 91, 92, 93, 94, 95, 97, 98, 100, 107, 119, 126, 127, 135, 138, 150, 165, 166, 171, 184, 194, 212, 213, 216, 222, 225, 229, 249
compensation, 36
competition, 25, 33, 248
competitiveness, vii, 1, 2, 12, 16
competitor, 159
complement, 21, 125, 206
complexity, 82, 239
compliance, 224
complications, 107, 235
components, 139, 143, 211, 214, 215, 216, 217, 218
composition, 86, 153
compost, 141
composting, 143
compounds, 135, 136, 137, 139, 143
comprehension, 189, 190
computing, 228
concentration, 236
conceptual model, 70
concrete, 48, 52, 56, 61, 62, 77, 142, 145, 228
concurrency, 240, 241, 249
condensation, 142
condom, 239
condoms, 243, 247
confidence, 119, 161, 213
confidentiality, 51, 67
conflict, vii, 67, 135, 167, 170, 171, 172, 243
conformity, viii, 2, 31, 249
Congress, iv
connectivity, 7
consensus, 33, 162
consent, 51, 67

conservation, 81, 92, 170
constant rate, 215
constipation, 46
constraints, xi, 46, 64, 106, 107, 116, 117, 123, 184, 191, 194, 195, 196, 204, 206, 210
construction, x, 10, 14, 21, 52, 54, 57, 58, 61, 62, 63, 65, 69, 133, 140, 141, 145, 168, 195, 196, 236
consumer goods, 79, 194
consumer price index, 25
consumerism, 246
consumers, 6, 10, 79, 194, 245
consumption, x, 13, 15, 17, 19, 22, 78, 85, 88, 93, 106, 127, 135, 177, 187, 227, 246
consumption patterns, 78, 88
contamination, 141, 145
content analysis, 51, 71
contractions, 127
contractors, 52, 249
contracts, 163, 175, 179
control, viii, xii, 24, 26, 41, 56, 59, 63, 64, 68, 69, 142, 160, 209, 210, 212, 213, 214, 221, 226, 230, 243
controlled, 247
conversion, 138, 155
cooking, 52, 55, 56, 63, 72, 211
coordination, 238
coping, 186, 230
copper, 154, 177, 178, 179, 180, 181
corporate governance, 161
corporate responsibility, 162
corporate social responsibility, 158, 160, 163, 173
corporations, 162
correlation, 165, 238, 243
corridors, 34
corruption, 167
cost-effective, 86, 185
costs, vii, 1, 2, 6, 10, 11, 14, 16, 18, 21, 22, 23, 33, 39, 79, 86, 89, 115, 118, 124, 141, 150, 152, 204, 211, 219, 220, 245, 247, 248
cotton, 53
cough, 117, 124
country of origin, 172
couples, 201
CPI, 36
credibility, 68, 69, 165
credit, 16, 20, 85, 190, 211
crime, 248
crimes, 170
criminals, 168
critical value, 30
criticism, 163, 166, 174
crop production, 196, 203, 207, 210, 211
crops, x, 45, 78, 92, 96, 133, 186, 189, 203, 210

cross-border, 13, 33
cross-country, 23
Cuba, 43
cultivation, x, 89, 133, 136, 137, 139, 140, 141, 142, 143, 145, 150, 151, 152, 153, 154, 155, 187, 212
cultural, xii, 212, 222, 228, 237, 238, 240, 242
cultural beliefs, 197
cultural clash, 68
cultural norms, 212, 228
cultural perspective, 71
cultural practices, 237, 240
cultural values, 57
culture, 42, 46, 58, 65, 128, 138, 140, 143, 167, 173, 196, 212, 222, 223, 230, 237
currency, 166, 242, 248
customers, 120
cycles, 242
cyclists, 10
Cytotoxic, 154
cytotoxicity, 139

D

dairy, 90, 187
data collection, 131
data set, vii, 1, 2, 4, 5, 32
database, 22, 25, 36
dating, 243
death, 106, 107, 123, 128, 131, 166, 235, 236, 243, 245, 247
death rate, 131
deaths, ix, x, 10, 105, 106, 107, 127, 169, 235
debt, 165, 219, 250
debts, 165
decay, 151
decision makers, 44, 63, 69
decision-making, xii, 46, 58, 209, 213, 214, 218, 221, 222, 223, 228, 230
decisions, 16, 59, 99, 167, 175, 212, 213, 240
decomposition, 20
defecation, 45, 56, 57, 58, 62, 64
deficiency, 244
deficit, vii, 1, 2
deficits, 178, 219
definition, 64, 84, 85, 137, 153, 154, 213, 240, 245
deforestation, 170
degradation, 80, 81, 88, 99, 123, 171
dehydration, 45, 46
delivery, x, 14, 16, 22, 106, 107, 108, 111, 114, 115, 116, 117, 118, 119, 120, 121, 122, 123, 124, 125, 127, 129, 130, 167, 181, 184
demand, 220, 250
democracy, 43, 87, 165, 166, 173, 174

Index

Democratic Republic of Congo, 166, 239, 242
denial, 209, 229
density, 8, 9, 19, 22, 82
Department of Agriculture, 193, 195, 198, 208
dependent, 221, 223
dependent variable, viii, 2, 24, 28, 31
depreciation, 223, 245
deprivation, 181, 214, 228, 229
desiccation, 141
desire, xii, 238, 240, 241, 245
destruction, 162, 166, 171
detergents, 44, 52, 54, 58
detritus, x, 133
devaluation, 242
developed countries, 8, 11, 164, 224, 228
developing countries, x, xi, 11, 12, 32, 81, 106, 133, 137, 164, 193, 198, 219, 224, 228, 229
developing nations, 229
developing world, 219
development, 211, 214, 215, 216, 217, 219, 220, 221, 222, 223, 224, 225, 227, 229, 230, 231, 232, 233
development assistance, 10, 11, 158, 174, 175
development policy, 181, 207
diarrh(o)ea, 42, 44, 45, 56, 125
Diaspora, 70
dichotomy, 83, 98, 99
diet, 47, 135, 245
dietary, 137, 138, 139
differential rates, 241
differentiation, ix, 75, 76, 77, 78, 81, 82, 83, 84, 85, 86, 87, 89, 91, 93, 94, 95, 96, 97, 98, 99, 100, 210
digestibility, 138, 142
dignity, viii, 41, 46, 229
direct foreign investment, 159
direct investment, 248
disabled, 68
disbursement, 164, 168
discipline, 200
discomfort, viii, 41, 69
discount rate, 214
discounting, 215, 245
discounts, 160
discourse, 159, 162
discrimination, 69, 198, 211, 217, 224, 230
diseases, ix, 42, 44, 45, 55, 61, 63, 65, 66, 105, 108, 113, 118, 125, 127, 129, 144, 237, 244
disorder, 246
displacement, 190
disposable income, 247
distress, 87
distribution, 13, 15, 19, 24, 25, 34, 66, 135, 152, 154, 184, 200, 212, 213, 220, 226, 242

divergence, 82
diversification, ix, 16, 75, 76, 77, 81, 82, 83, 84, 85, 86, 87, 88, 89, 91, 93, 94, 96, 98, 99, 100
diversity, 68, 77, 91, 95, 99, 100, 213
division, 46, 57, 58, 61, 76, 78, 82, 98, 225
division of labour, 225
divorce, 213
doctors, 56, 61, 63, 107, 113, 124, 125, 126, 129, 224, 242
Doha, 34
domestic chores, 198
domestic economy, 226
domestic laws, 158
domestic resources, 161
domestic tasks, 96
domestic violence, 247
dominance, 159
donations, 119
donor, xi, 6, 32, 59, 157, 158, 174, 224, 226, 248
donors, 13, 32, 65, 174
doors, 63
downsizing, 83
drainage, 7, 62, 65, 72, 142
dream, 223
drinking, 19, 44, 45, 185, 195, 246
drinking water, 12, 19, 45, 185
drought, 89, 96, 135
droughts, 151
drowsiness, 125, 127
drugs, ix, 105, 106, 114, 115, 128, 224, 245, 248, 249, 254
drugs [medicines], 224
drugs [narcotics], 224
dry, 241
drying, 43, 151, 241
duration, 141
dust, 55, 154
duties, 58, 63, 72, 123, 197
DVD, 253
dyeing, 196

E

early warning, 235
earning power, 221
earnings, 23, 81, 92, 145, 213, 214, 219, 226
earnings gap, 219
earth, 142
East Asia, 5, 7, 9, 11, 40, 171, 175
Eastern Europe, 5, 11
eating, 54, 55, 63, 245
ecological, ix, 47, 61, 76, 78, 89, 92, 93, 136

economic, xii, 209, 210, 211, 213, 214, 218, 219, 221, 223, 224, 225, 227, 229, 230, 237, 239, 240, 241, 242, 243, 244, 245, 246, 247, 248, 249, 250, 253, 256
economic activity, 14, 19
economic change, xi, 193, 256
economic crisis, 243
economic development, 6, 13, 34, 82, 83, 161, 167, 168, 174, 194
economic globalisation, 243
economic growth, vii, ix, 1, 2, 6, 10, 11, 15, 16, 19, 20, 21, 24, 25, 87, 105, 135, 180, 184, 194, 223, 246, 248, 250
economic hardships, xi, 137, 190, 193
economic indicator, 79, 221
economic liberalization, 239, 247
economic policy, 163
economic problem, 178, 249
economic reform, 18, 181, 184
economic reforms, 18, 181, 184
economic resources, xi, 134, 193, 218
economic status, 210, 211, 221
economic welfare, 15, 20
economics, 75, 198, 222, 223
economies, xii, 238, 240, 241, 243, 250
economies of scale, 6
economy, 237, 239, 240, 241, 242, 243, 245, 246, 247, 249
ecosystem, 136
Ecuador, 118
education, 26, 27, 29, 30, 31, 95, 201, 209, 211, 216, 217, 219, 220, 221, 223, 228, 229, 230, 232, 242, 243, 248, 249
educational attainment, 82, 95, 135, 214, 216, 217, 222
educational institutions, 87
educators, 226
egg, 223
Egypt, 4, 35
elasticity, 19, 22, 24
elderly, 44
electricity, vii, 1, 2, 7, 10, 23, 44, 48
elementary (primary) school, 219, 220, 221
email, 105, 133, 193
emancipation, 43
embargo, 166
emergency relief, 22
emigration, 42
emotional, 197
emotions, 42
empathy, 190
Empirical, 230, 231
employee compensation, 36

employees, 55, 115, 116, 180, 183, 194, 197, 222
employers, 1, 180, 183, 222
employment, xi, 6, 13, 14, 15, 19, 20, 21, 22, 23, 34, 43, 48, 65, 73, 81, 87, 90, 95, 96, 98, 182, 183, 186, 191, 193, 194, 195, 197, 206, 207, 213, 215, 217, 222, 226, 247, 248
employment growth, 81
empowerment, 14, 20, 46, 185, 198, 214, 218, 219, 221, 232, 237, 250
encouragement, 163, 165
endogeneity, 22, 31
energy, vii, 1, 2, 12, 16, 18, 23, 142, 200, 211, 228
engagement, 138, 162, 163, 169, 175, 244
England, 192, 242, 254
enterprise, 6, 207
entrepreneurs, 197, 208
entrepreneurship, 197
environment, 45, 56, 77, 78, 86, 124, 129, 136, 140, 141, 142, 151, 157, 158, 171, 172, 175, 232, 241, 243, 244
environmental conditions, 62, 141
environmental control, 142
environmental degradation, 80, 81, 88, 99, 123, 171
environmental factors, 47
environmental protection, 173
environmental standards, 158
enzymatic, 141
enzymes, x, 134, 136, 141
epidemic, 42, 107, 225, 237, 238, 239, 240, 249, 256
epidemiological, 242
epidemiology, 237, 255
epilepsy, 118
epistemological, 237
equality, 24, 42, 65, 158, 222, 223
equity, viii, 33, 41, 46, 66, 70, 216, 218
ERD, 37, 40
ergosterol, 138
Eritrea, 70
erosion, 135
error estimation, 22
estates, 108, 114, 115, 116, 245, 249
estimating, 29
ethical principles, 67
ethics, 67, 130
Ethiopia, 17, 18, 35, 158, 243, 254
ethnic groups, 214, 216
ethnicity, 216
Eurocentric, 71
Europe, 7, 9, 65, 171, 175, 194
European, 235, 255
European Commission, 255
European Union, 235
Europeans, 81

evaluation, 214
evening, 149
evidence, 213, 246, 252
evolution, 179, 181, 190
examinations, 91
exchange rate, 178, 181
exchange rates, 194
exclusion, 237
excrements, 51, 55
excuse, 222
execution, 131
exercise, 47, 245
expectations, 222
expenditure on, 219
expenditures, 10, 34, 223
expertise, 107, 169
exploitation, 89, 97, 190, 245
exporter, 18
exports, 12, 26, 36, 81, 164, 167, 170, 172
exposure, 62, 76, 77, 78, 82, 83, 84, 86, 96, 98, 99, 100, 138, 228, 241, 247
expulsion, 166
external shocks, 97
extraction, 167
extreme poverty, vii, ix, xi, 4, 105, 157, 160, 177, 181

F

fabric, 243
factor market, 20, 76, 82, 99, 212
failure, xi, 45, 78, 106, 127, 134, 158, 169, 177, 181, 185, 190, 236
faith, 97
family, viii, xii, 41, 44, 47, 48, 52, 53, 55, 56, 57, 58, 59, 62, 63, 64, 65, 66, 70, 72, 78, 85, 86, 91, 93, 96, 97, 115, 116, 134, 152, 182, 185, 186, 197, 202, 209, 210, 211, 213, 217, 219, 226, 227, 230, 231, 232, 243, 247, 248
family income, 211
family members, viii, 41, 86, 91, 93, 96, 116, 185, 197, 202, 213, 226, 227, 247
family planning, 115
family support, 248
famine, 211
FAO, 134, 153, 196, 208, 227, 231, 255
farmers, x, 9, 13, 20, 22, 69, 78, 82, 89, 133, 134, 135, 137, 140, 141, 143, 145, 146, 150, 151, 152, 180, 188, 206, 211, 212
farming, ix, 43, 44, 76, 77, 78, 79, 80, 81, 82, 83, 87, 88, 89, 90, 92, 93, 94, 95, 96, 97, 98, 100, 123, 124, 136, 138, 180, 188, 189, 205, 211, 212, 217, 247

farms, 79, 80, 97, 134, 155, 160, 180, 197, 211
fat, 138, 139, 140
fatalism, 245
fatalities, 246
fats, 139
fatty acid, 140
FDI, vii, 1, 2
fear, 188, 195
fears, 55, 124
February, 167, 168
fee, 59
feedback, 118
feeding, 142, 153
feelings, 69
fees, ix, 79, 105, 106, 120, 123, 242, 243
feet, 52, 64
female, xii, 209, 211, 212, 216, 217, 218, 219, 220, 221, 222, 224, 226, 228, 230
females, 118, 183, 198, 200, 211, 216, 218, 219, 220, 221, 224, 226, 228, 230
feminism, 70
feminist, 71, 237
fertility, 107, 228
fertility rate, 107, 228
fertilizer, 211
fertilizers, 146
fever, 44, 137
FID, 130
field crops, x, 133
financial aid, 166
financial capital, 94, 100
financial institution, 34, 198
financial institutions, 34, 198
financial problems, 124
financial resources, 180, 181, 182
financial support, 33
financing, 11, 32, 34, 177, 207
fines, 172
fire, 7, 108, 146, 167
firewood, 53, 90, 91, 96, 151, 197
firms, 16, 194
first aid, 114, 117
fiscal deficit, 178, 219
fish, 196, 245
fishing, 44
fixed exchange rates, 194
flavonoids, 137
flexibility, 219
flooding, 169
flow, vii, 1, 2, 10, 194
fluctuations, 85, 182
focus group, 19, 112, 113, 117, 131, 187
focusing, 100

folklore, 138
food, vii, x, xi, 13, 16, 43, 52, 53, 54, 55, 56, 62, 63, 78, 80, 88, 93, 123, 133, 134, 135, 136, 137, 138, 144, 150, 152, 154, 167, 177, 178, 179, 182, 186, 187, 188, 189, 191, 192, 193, 196, 202, 203, 206, 207, 210, 211, 212, 221, 226, 227, 228, 242, 244
food aid, 167
food production, vii, 43, 135, 182, 189, 211
football, 246
Ford, 167
foreign aid, 174, 248
Foreign Corrupt Practices Act, 172
foreign direct investment, vii, 1, 2, 165, 248
foreign exchange, 108
foreign investment, 167, 175
foreign policy, 167
forest management, 172
forestry, 131, 171
forests, 88, 89, 93, 160, 170, 171, 172, 228
forgetting, 67
formal education, 198, 201
formal sector, 178, 182, 185, 186, 219, 221, 222
fragmentation, 135
France, 16, 250
free choice, 237
free radical, x, 134
free radical scavenger, x, 134
freedom, 51, 57, 184, 229
freedom of choice, 57, 184
freezing, 151
freight, 7, 14
friction, 241
Friday, 122
friendship, 164
fruit juice, 203
fruits, 54, 89, 92, 96, 97, 187
fuel, 167, 170
funding, 11, 33, 59, 114, 163, 185, 249
funds, 185, 220
fungal, 137
fungi, x, 133, 136, 140, 141, 145, 154
fungus, 141
futures, 190

G

G8, 170, 171, 172, 176
Gabon, 170, 239
gas, 7
Gaza, 43
GDP, 9, 10, 11, 13, 18, 19, 21, 24, 25, 26, 27, 29, 30, 31, 32, 36, 81, 134, 214, 215, 216, 217, 218, 223, 226, 227, 230, 242, 243

GDP per capita, 215, 217, 218, 226, 227, 230, 243
gender, viii, xii, 41, 42, 44, 46, 48, 57, 61, 65, 66, 67, 71, 72, 82, 118, 183, 198, 199, 201, 209, 210, 211, 212, 214, 216, 217, 218, 220, 221, 223, 225, 226, 228, 229, 230, 235, 239, 240, 241, 242, 249
gender differences, 46, 212, 216, 221
gender equality, 44, 57, 61, 65, 66, 72, 198, 223
gender equity, 216, 218
gender gap, 216, 220, 221
gender inequality, xii, 65, 66, 209, 210, 214, 216, 217, 218, 226, 229, 230, 235, 241
gender-sensitive, 216
gene, 206
generation, 135, 137, 164, 168, 170, 186, 187, 194, 203, 207
generic drug, 249
generic drugs, 249
generics, 249
genes, 47
genetic, 246
Geneva, 72, 130, 192, 207, 232, 254, 255, 256
genocide, 167, 249
geography, 76, 238, 246, 252
gestation, 122
Gini coefficients, 246
girls, 14, 44, 57, 59, 219, 220, 222, 225, 226, 241, 242
global demand, 180
global economy, vii, xii, 1, 2, 79, 81, 83, 85, 86, 96, 98, 99, 194, 195, 237, 238, 245
global networks, 237
globalization, vi, 33, 37, 101, 102, 235, 236, 237, 238, 239, 242, 243, 245, 248, 249, 250, 251, 254, 256
gloves, 120
GNP, 10, 214
goals, 33, 44, 88, 106, 158, 161, 162, 163, 173, 175, 222
God, 57, 58, 113
gold, 80
gonorrhea, 125
goods and services, 6, 46, 226, 248
governance, ix, 34, 76, 89, 90, 94, 98, 162, 165, 174, 184, 185
government, iv, ix, xi, 6, 11, 19, 32, 34, 35, 42, 43, 45, 65, 78, 79, 80, 87, 88, 105, 106, 107, 115, 116, 117, 118, 124, 129, 152, 154, 157, 158, 159, 161, 162, 163, 165, 167, 168, 169, 170, 171, 172, 173, 174, 176, 177, 178, 180, 181, 189, 191, 195, 198, 205, 219, 222, 223, 232, 233
government budget, 33
government expenditure, 19, 178, 181, 219, 223
government policy, 205, 222

grades, 44
grain, 90, 140, 155
grains, 13, 16, 144
grants, 97, 250
grass, 96, 120, 143, 144, 145, 150
grasslands, 108
grassroots, 64, 70, 163, 187
gravity, 22
grazing, 78, 88, 93, 237
greening, 81
groundwater, 45
groups, 33, 42, 47, 60, 61, 63, 64, 86, 89, 95, 96, 107, 136, 137, 163, 167, 171, 190, 205, 212, 214, 216, 238, 246
growth, vii, ix, 1, 2, 6, 10, 11, 12, 13, 14, 15, 16, 17, 18, 19, 20, 21, 22, 23, 24, 25, 32, 39, 79, 81, 82, 87, 88, 90, 98, 105, 134, 135, 139, 140, 141, 142, 146, 154, 178, 179, 180, 181, 184, 185, 194, 195, 202, 214, 219, 223, 226, 228, 230, 231, 232, 246, 247, 248, 250
growth rate, 223, 226
growth rates, 226
growth time, 142
guardian, 253
guidance, 75, 222
guidelines, 67, 172, 184, 191
Guinea, 38, 239

H

habitat, 171
handling, 69, 72, 119
hands, 45, 52, 54, 63, 196
harm, 170
harmonization, 161, 174
Harvard, 231, 254
harvest, 81, 187
harvesting, 149, 151
hazards, 47
HDI, see human development index, 214, 215, 216, 217, 220
head, 247
headache, 125
healing, 123
health, viii, ix, x, 11, 12, 13, 14, 20, 21, 23, 34, 41, 42, 43, 44, 45, 46, 47, 55, 57, 61, 63, 64, 66, 69, 70, 71, 72, 73, 79, 85, 105, 106, 107, 108, 114, 115, 116, 117, 118, 119, 122, 123, 125, 129, 130, 131, 134, 135, 136, 137, 162, 163, 178, 180, 181, 182, 183, 185, 196, 200, 209, 216, 219, 221, 223, 224, 225, 229, 236, 242, 243, 246, 247, 249, 253
health care professionals, 242
health clinics, 43

health problems, 107, 114
health services, 20, 79, 107, 117, 229, 242
health status, 85, 106, 107
healthcare, x, 22, 23, 47, 106, 107, 108, 111, 113, 114, 115, 117, 123, 124, 125, 129, 130, 134, 135, 242, 243
heart, 127
heat, 143
heating, 144
helium, 155
hepatoma, 139
herbal, 137
herbal medicine, 137
heterogeneity, 95, 100
heterogeneous, ix, 76, 77, 83, 84, 85, 87, 88, 89, 91, 99, 100
high blood pressure, 125, 137
high risk, 107
higher education, 86
highlands, 81, 88, 89
high-value products, 136
hip, 18, 26
hiring, 66, 116
historical trends, 221
HIV, xi, xii, 34, 55, 59, 60, 69, 71, 73, 107, 124, 127, 134, 135, 137, 138, 139, 185, 225, 226, 232, 233, 235, 236, 237, 238, 239, 240, 241, 242, 243, 244, 245, 246, 247, 248, 249, 250, 251, 252, 253, 254, 255, 256
HIV infection, 235, 236, 238, 241, 243, 244, 245, 246, 248, 249
HIV/AIDS, xi, 34, 71, 73, 107, 124, 134, 135, 137, 138, 185, 225, 232, 233, 237, 238, 239, 242, 247, 250, 251, 252, 253, 254, 255, 256
HIV-1, 244
holistic, 47, 48, 51, 67, 163
homogenous, 48, 89, 238
Hong Kong, 167, 231
horizon, 223
hospital, 44, 48, 56, 59, 60, 61, 64, 70, 73, 108, 111, 114, 115, 116, 117, 118, 122, 126, 127, 128, 129, 226, 244
hospital care, 73, 226
hospitalized, 72
hospitals, ix, x, 43, 105, 106, 114, 115, 117, 118, 123, 124, 125, 126, 127, 129, 133, 150
host, 3, 68, 136, 221, 247
hot water, 139, 143, 145
hotels, x, 133, 243
House, 55, 170, 171, 172, 176
household, ix, xi, xii, 17, 18, 19, 22, 24, 43, 46, 48, 50, 52, 54, 55, 56, 57, 58, 60, 61, 62, 63, 64, 65, 66, 68, 69, 71, 72, 75, 78, 79, 81, 82, 84, 85, 86,

87, 88, 89, 90, 91, 94, 95, 96, 97, 100, 178, 182, 187, 193, 195, 196, 199, 200, 201, 202, 204, 205, 207, 209, 210, 211, 212, 213, 214, 217, 220, 222, 225, 226, 228, 230, 238, 240, 241, 247
household income, xi, 17, 79, 86, 87, 178, 193, 195, 196, 200, 213, 226
households, viii, ix, xi, xii, 16, 18, 19, 22, 23, 34, 41, 43, 44, 46, 48, 50, 51, 52, 55, 56, 58, 59, 60, 61, 62, 63, 64, 65, 68, 70, 71, 75, 77, 78, 80, 81, 82, 83, 84, 85, 86, 87, 88, 89, 91, 92, 93, 94, 95, 96, 97, 99, 100, 145, 152, 178, 181, 182, 185, 186, 187, 193, 195, 197, 199, 200, 201, 202, 203, 204, 205, 209, 211, 212, 213, 220, 224, 227, 228, 230, 238, 240, 241, 247
housing, 72, 179, 180, 181, 188, 196
human, viii, xi, xii, 17, 22, 23, 25, 32, 33, 34, 35, 41, 42, 43, 44, 55, 72, 73, 85, 94, 95, 100, 139, 154, 157, 158, 160, 162, 163, 165, 167, 168, 174, 184, 209, 214, 215, 216, 221, 223, 228, 229, 230, 236, 237, 238, 248
human actions, 73
human activity, 184
human capital, 22, 25, 32, 35, 44, 95, 100, 223, 248
human development, 72, 214, 215, 216, 223, 229
human development index (HDI), 214, 215, 216, 217, 220, 231
Human Development Report, 214, 215, 217, 222, 223, 224, 227, 229, 233, 256
human interactions, 184
Human Poverty Index, 229
human resource development, 33
human resources, 23, 43, 168, 221
human rights, xi, 72, 157, 158, 160, 162, 163, 165, 167, 174
humanitarian, 167
humanitarian aid, 167
humans, 44, 58, 73
humidity, 140, 141, 145, 149, 151
husband, 57, 59, 66, 115, 188, 198, 212, 213, 219, 228
hybrid, 69
hydroelectric power, 166
hydrogen, 136
hydroxide, 143
hygiene, 45, 46, 48, 50, 56, 57, 61, 62, 63, 64, 68, 69, 72, 123, 211
hygienic, 42, 44, 54, 56, 65, 126
hypertensive, 137
hypothesis, 24, 30

I

ICT, vii, 1, 2
id, 63, 66, 153, 167
identification, 77, 79, 83, 131
identity, 252
ideology, 165, 246
illiteracy, 67, 198, 201, 221
ILO, 254
images, 131
imbalances, 201
IMF, see International Monetary Fund, 11, 37, 38, 178, 181, 219, 223, 224
immigration, 90, 180
immune response, 135, 139
immune system, x, 134, 137, 247
immunity, 127, 139
immunocompromised, x, 134
immunodeficiency, 253
immunomodulation, 155
immunomodulatory, 139
immunostimulatory, 139
implementation, 178, 181, 184, 186, 198, 226
importer, 170
imports, 26, 36, 81, 170, 172
in vitro, 137, 139, 244
in vivo, 139
incentive, 100, 180
incentives, 82, 89, 91, 96, 160, 197, 240, 247, 249
incidence, viii, xii, 2, 19, 20, 21, 23, 24, 25, 30, 32, 33, 43, 162, 169, 182, 184, 209, 226, 227, 230, 241, 243
inclusion, 25
income distribution, 13, 15, 24, 25, 34, 135, 226
income inequality, viii, 2, 19, 24, 31, 32, 82, 247, 256
incomes, ix, 12, 18, 19, 22, 23, 48, 75, 79, 80, 81, 82, 83, 89, 91, 92, 93, 95, 96, 135, 195, 220, 224, 226, 242, 247
increased access, 221
incubation, 142
incubation period, 142
incurable, 238
independence, 42, 43, 44, 65, 78, 88, 166, 179, 180, 190, 223
India, 5, 9, 17, 20, 21, 22, 38, 228, 232, 233, 248
Indian, 23, 38, 42, 233
Indian Ocean, 42
Indiana, 251
indication, 159, 166, 167, 181
indicators, 6, 22, 36, 82, 135, 210, 214, 221, 225, 230, 233
indices, 24, 217, 218, 220
indigenous, 77, 78, 88, 89, 90, 93, 97, 143
indirect effect, 20
individualism, 83

individuality, 236
Indonesia, 19, 20, 21, 37, 39
industrial, 14, 88, 90, 93, 97, 142, 143, 144, 152, 186, 194
industrial wastes, 142, 143, 144, 152
industrialisation, 80
industry, 34, 80, 137, 152, 158, 163, 169, 178, 207, 208, 245
inequality, viii, xii, 2, 4, 19, 21, 22, 24, 25, 28, 31, 33, 34, 38, 209, 210, 212, 214, 216, 217, 218, 220, 226, 229, 230, 235, 241, 242, 246, 247, 256
inequity, 48
infant mortality, 223, 224
infant mortality rate, 223, 224
infants, 224, 225
infection, 66, 117, 135, 235, 237, 238, 239, 241, 243, 244, 245, 246, 248, 249
infections, 44, 46, 69, 236, 237, 244
infectious, 238, 240
infertility, 127
infestations, 120
inflammatory, 137, 138
inflation, viii, xi, 2, 24, 25, 28, 31, 32, 79, 137, 166, 193
influence, 220, 222, 226
informal sector, 182, 183, 185, 189, 190, 191, 221, 245
Information, 212
information and communication technology, 19
informed consent, 67
infrastructure, vii, viii, x, 1, 2, 3, 4, 5, 6, 7, 8, 9, 10, 11, 12, 13, 14, 15, 16, 17, 18, 19, 20, 21, 22, 23, 24, 25, 26, 28, 30, 32, 33, 34, 38, 39, 43, 59, 61, 62, 64, 77, 81, 85, 94, 119, 120, 133, 134, 166, 167, 168, 170, 179, 180, 198, 243, 244
inherited, 181
inhibitory, 139, 143
inhibitory effect, 139
inhuman, 169
injuries, 9
injury, iv, 166
injustice, 66
innovation, 34
inoculation, 141
inoculum, 140
inorganic, 146
input, 213
inputs, 210, 211, 212, 213
insects, 55, 142, 152
insecurity, xi, 135, 154, 193, 228, 245
insertion, 81
insight, 70, 76, 99
inspiration, 11

instability, 166, 243, 244
institutional reforms, 20, 34, 184, 185
institutionalisation, 77
institutions, xii, 17, 33, 34, 60, 61, 62, 64, 65, 76, 77, 85, 86, 87, 161, 174, 181, 184, 185, 189, 190, 200, 209, 211, 212, 221, 223, 236, 238, 239, 249
instruments, 30, 83, 245
insulation, 72
insurance, 12
integration, vii, 1, 2, 7, 34, 92, 135, 211
integrity, 168
intellectual property, 249
intellectual property rights, 249
intentions, 160
interaction, 51, 173, 174, 239
interactions, 76, 82, 83, 99, 184
interdependence, 83, 84, 86, 96, 97, 99
interest, 219
interest rates, 178
interference, 160, 162, 165, 166, 168, 174
intergenerational, 34
internal combustion, 7
internalised, 83, 212
international, 235, 240
International Criminal Court, 168
International Labour Office, 232
international markets, 85
International Monetary Fund (IMF), 37, 38, 178, 219, 223, 224, 242, 246
international relations, 167
international trade, vii, 1, 2, 6, 17, 170, 171
intervention, 15, 116, 163, 207, 214, 242, 245
interview, 67
interviews, ix, 19, 50, 51, 65, 68, 71, 89, 105, 112, 118, 123, 131, 182, 187, 189
intimacy, 240
intrinsic, 47, 218
intrusions, 98
invasive, 137, 144, 152
investment, vii, ix, x, 1, 2, 5, 6, 8, 9, 10, 11, 13, 14, 15, 19, 20, 21, 23, 32, 33, 34, 35, 39, 76, 77, 79, 81, 82, 86, 87, 98, 105, 106, 117, 133, 134, 136, 150, 152, 158, 159, 162, 164, 165, 167, 169, 175, 194, 232, 239, 248
investors, 170, 175
Ireland, 235
iron, x, 122, 134, 139
irrigation, 19, 23
island, 65, 238
issues, 215, 217, 222, 224, 225, 227, 229

J

January, 250, 253, 254, 256
Japan, 11, 194, 200
job creation, 194
job loses, 185
job loss, 80
jobs, 34, 124, 145, 162, 169, 194, 197, 200, 202, 222
joints, 142
judge, 229
judiciary, 223
just society, 184
justice, 212

K

Kenya, v, ix, xii, 35, 75, 76, 77, 79, 80, 81, 88, 89, 91, 95, 96, 97, 98, 99, 100, 101, 102, 103, 130, 135, 191, 207, 209, 210, 212, 215, 217, 218, 219, 220, 221, 222, 223, 224, 225, 226, 227, 228, 229, 230, 231, 232, 233, 240, 241, 243, 251, 255, 256
key indicators, 82
killing, 167
knowledge, 214, 225, 229

L

labor force, 166
labor markets, 20
labor productivity, 18, 25
labor relations, 162
labo(u)r, xi, xii, 18, 20, 21, 25, 34, 38, 43, 46, 76, 78, 79, 82, 84, 85, 86, 87, 89, 92, 95, 96, 97, 98, 99, 107, 116, 117, 120, 126, 127, 128, 135, 136, 145, 152, 157, 158, 162, 163, 166, 169, 170, 174, 175, 179, 180, 197, 202, 204, 209, 210, 211, 212, 221, 222, 225, 227, 230, 235, 239, 240, 241, 243, 244, 245, 246, 247, 248, 250, 253
labour force, 43, 221, 222
labour market, xii, 43, 46, 82, 87, 96, 98, 209, 227, 230, 240, 243
LAC, 7
land, x, 7, 9, 10, 34, 51, 55, 78, 79, 80, 82, 85, 87, 88, 91, 95, 96, 97, 98, 116, 133, 134, 136, 138, 167, 186, 187, 188, 189, 190, 191, 198, 205, 206, 210, 211, 212, 214, 228, 231, 241, 245
land tenure, 78
land use, 138, 188
landlocked countries, 6, 10, 12, 18
language, 42, 50, 67, 69, 107, 113, 173
language barrier, 67
language skills, 69

large-scale, 80
later life, 248
Latin America, 5, 7, 9, 11, 84, 96, 101, 103, 255
laughing, 65
law, 158, 164, 179, 180, 187, 188, 189, 210, 238, 242, 243, 249
laws, xi, 47, 59, 157, 158, 169, 170, 175, 184, 202
LDCs, vii, 1, 2, 165
lead, 221, 226, 229, 248
leadership, 48, 161, 165, 213, 222, 243
learning, 64, 167, 221, 223
legal, 212, 213, 221
legality, 172
legislation, 172, 189
lesions, 244
Less Developed Countries, vii, 1, 2
leucine, 138
leukemia, 139
liberal, 79, 236
liberalization, 17, 25, 32, 33, 34, 178, 232, 239, 242, 243, 247
liberation, 43, 165
Liberia, 166, 170, 171, 175, 239
Libya, 4
lice, 120
life cycle, 140, 141
life expectancy, 106, 178, 214, 215, 216, 217, 223, 224, 225, 226, 230
life-cycle, 171
lifestyle, 42, 47, 62, 63, 66, 78
lifestyle changes, 78
lifestyle perspective, 63
lifetime, 45, 107, 187
lignin, 143
likelihood, 160, 244
limitations, 68, 160, 211
Limpopo, v, 101, 193, 195
links, 13, 14, 15, 16, 17, 168, 235, 239
linoleic acid, 140
liquidity, 194
liquids, 54
literacy, 214, 216, 221
literacy rates, 216
literature, 223
liver, 137, 248
livestock, 78, 82, 87, 88, 89, 90, 91, 92, 93, 94, 95, 96, 97, 103, 142, 187
living conditions, 6, 42, 64, 66, 135, 180, 190
living standard, 224
living standards, 224
loans, 43, 165, 169, 178, 206
lobby, 163
lobbying, 169

local authorities, 184, 185, 190, 219, 223
local community, 47
local government, 167, 189, 191
localization, 250
logging, 108, 170, 171, 172, 175
London, 38, 70, 101, 102, 130, 191, 192, 207, 208, 231, 233, 250, 251, 252, 253, 254, 255, 256
long distance, 116, 124, 129, 151, 197, 211
long period, 141, 225
longevity, 214
long-term, 239, 248
Lorenz curve, 24
Los Angeles, 102, 207
loss of control, 68
low temperatures, 141
low-income, viii, 9, 41, 42, 44, 67, 73, 85, 220, 224
lysine, 138

M

machinery, 166, 168, 197, 211, 245
machines, 85
Mackintosh, 120
macroeconomic, 17, 22, 184
macroeconomic policy, 184
macronutrients, 143
macrophages, 139
Madison, 252
magazines, 52
magnetic, iv
main line, 11
mainstream, 229
maintenance, 6, 9, 10, 11, 13, 14, 16, 33, 43, 46, 52, 181
maize, 53, 54, 87, 88, 89, 90, 91, 92, 96, 136, 145, 146, 186, 247
major cities, 180
malaria, 55, 107, 125, 127, 165
Malaysia, 11
male, xii, 209, 210, 211, 212, 216, 218, 219, 220, 221, 224, 225, 226, 227, 228, 229, 230
males, 80, 81, 118, 183, 200, 210, 211, 218, 219, 220, 221, 224, 225, 226, 229
malnutrition, vii, 44, 134, 135
management, xi, 89, 91, 93, 96, 100, 107, 111, 158, 164, 168, 169, 172, 174, 194, 202, 206, 207
manganese, 143, 144, 154
manners, 48
manufactured goods, 169
manufacturing, 169, 180, 195
manure, 149, 150
marginal product, 245
marginalisation, 181, 188, 192

marital status, 112, 199, 201
market, xii, 6, 8, 14, 16, 17, 18, 20, 22, 23, 33, 34, 39, 43, 76, 77, 81, 82, 83, 84, 87, 88, 94, 98, 135, 150, 152, 159, 162, 169, 171, 180, 184, 185, 187, 194, 205, 209, 210, 213, 227, 230, 238, 240, 243, 245, 248, 249
market access, 8, 22, 88, 249
market economy, 23, 98, 159, 185
market failure, 14
market penetration, 77
marketing, xi, 13, 158, 173, 194, 197, 198, 204, 205, 206, 207, 212
markets, 6, 16, 17, 18, 20, 34, 39, 77, 79, 80, 81, 85, 97, 98, 99, 135, 184, 186, 187, 198, 212, 248
marriage, 213, 240
marriages, 46, 240
Maryland, 250
masculinity, 244
masonry, 196
maternal, ix, x, 14, 105, 106, 107, 108, 111, 113, 114, 117, 118, 123, 126, 127, 128, 129, 130, 131
Mauritania, 36
Mauritius, 4, 22, 39
meals, 53, 54, 182, 228
measles, 117
measurement, 24
measures, viii, 2, 24, 25, 26, 28, 30, 31, 32, 61, 69, 81, 92, 158, 166, 172, 174, 178, 179, 181, 194, 214, 217, 218, 220, 223, 229
meat, x, 133, 138
media, 140
median, 18, 242
medical care, ix, 105, 107, 135, 223, 224, 243
medical services, 115, 116, 228
medication, 128, 226
medicinal plants, ix, x, 105, 106, 107, 108, 123, 125, 126, 127, 128, 129, 130
medicine, 61, 62, 118, 123, 125, 126, 130, 165
men, viii, xii, 41, 43, 44, 45, 46, 56, 57, 58, 61, 62, 63, 65, 66, 67, 69, 78, 87, 118, 145, 179, 182, 200, 202, 209, 210, 211, 212, 213, 214, 216, 217, 218, 219, 221, 222, 223, 224, 225, 226, 228, 229, 240, 241, 244, 247
menstruation, 46, 53, 55, 57, 63, 127
mental disorder, 118
metabolic, 141
metastatic, 139
methane, 139, 142
methodological implications, 91
methodological individualism, 83
methodology, 215, 216, 218
Mexico, 39
mice, 139

microbial, 137, 155
micronutrients, 135, 143, 144
microorganisms, 143, 151
middle class, 163
Middle East, 5, 7, 9, 11
middle income, 11
migraine, 125
migraine headache, 125
migrant, 36, 66, 79, 86, 87, 92, 96, 97, 179, 180, 235, 239, 240, 241, 250, 253
migrant workers, 66, 87
migrants, 244
migration, 13, 77, 82, 96, 98, 135, 137, 180, 211, 225, 239, 243
military, 166, 171, 243
militias, 167
milk, 138, 196
Millennium, vii, xi, 3, 6, 13, 16, 134, 157, 160, 253, 254, 256
Millennium Development Goals, 3, 6, 16, 134, 160
Millennium Project, 13
minerals, x, 134, 136, 139, 250
mines, 79, 80, 160, 169, 179, 244
minimum wage, 169
mining, 80, 87, 169, 177, 178, 179, 180, 241, 244
minority, 97
miscarriage, 120, 128
missions, 166
MNA, 7
mobility, 6, 83, 95
modalities, 249
models, 83, 98, 100, 213, 240
modernisation, 249
moisture, 141, 145, 152
molecules, 136
money, 11, 12, 34, 59, 65, 68, 87, 107, 115, 116, 117, 123, 129, 136, 145, 165, 167, 174, 178, 181, 182, 188, 200, 203, 243, 248
monopoly, 25
Monroe, 253
morality, 45
morbidity, 107, 224
morning, 55, 149
Morocco, 4, 36
mortality, ix, 10, 14, 105, 106, 107, 108, 126, 127, 129, 130, 160, 185, 217, 223, 224, 225, 226, 230, 244, 247
mortality rate, ix, 14, 105, 107, 108, 129, 185, 223, 224, 226, 230
mortality rates, 224, 226, 230
mosquito nets, 61
mosquitoes, 55, 57, 59
mothers, 60, 64, 107, 118, 119, 222, 226

motivation, 69, 186, 187
motorcycles, 7
movement, 6, 33, 34, 65, 83, 179, 239
Mozambique, v, vii, viii, 36, 41, 42, 43, 44, 48, 65, 66, 69, 70, 71, 72, 73, 108, 117, 124, 240, 246, 248, 252
multilateral, 11, 32, 161
multiples, 11
multiplicity, 197
multiplier, 33
multiplier effect, 33
mushrooms, x, 133, 136, 137, 138, 139, 140, 141, 142, 143, 144, 145, 149, 150, 151, 153, 155
music, 246
Muslim, 241
Muslims, 249
mutagenic, 139
mutation, 246
mycelium, 140, 141

N

Namibia, 35, 152
naming, 163
NAS, 101, 102
NASA, 108, 131
nation, xii, 43, 44, 47, 64, 171, 197, 238
national, 214, 216, 219, 222, 223, 226, 227, 229, 230, 246, 247, 249, 250
National Academy of Sciences, 101, 102
national economies, 81, 98, 99
national income, 72, 226, 247, 249
National Institutes of Health, 248
National Strategy, 208
natural, xi, 17, 22, 43, 83, 85, 89, 90, 93, 97, 99, 100, 134, 137, 138, 140, 141, 157, 171, 190
natural capital, 100
natural disasters, 22, 134
natural habitats, 138
natural resources, xi, 17, 89, 93, 97, 99, 100, 157, 171
needles, 144, 243
needs, 213, 227, 228
negative attitudes, 189
negative relation, 18, 26
neglect, 184, 185, 236
negotiating, 162, 213
negotiation, 175
neoliberal, xii, 236, 237, 238, 242, 247, 248
neoliberalism, 242, 246
NEPAD, 33, 161, 174, 175, 253, 254
Nepal, 19, 230
Netherlands, 130, 191

network, 7, 22, 62, 116, 168, 179, 237, 239, 240, 241, 249
networks, 213
New England, 254
New Frontier, 161, 164, 176
New York, iii, iv, 71, 102, 153, 159, 160, 162, 166, 173, 174, 175, 176, 192, 208, 209, 230, 232, 233, 250, 251, 252, 253, 254, 255, 256
NGO, 190
NGOs, 90, 96, 162
niacin, x, 134, 138
Nielsen, 71
Niger, 35
Nigeria, 1, 35, 37, 130, 139, 153, 154, 238, 239, 249, 254
nitrate, 146
nitrogen, 136, 143, 146
nodules, 139
normal, 67, 115, 127, 184
norms, 99, 158, 212, 225, 228, 243
North Africa, vii, viii, 1, 2, 3, 4, 5, 7, 9, 11, 26, 28, 32
Northeast, 153, 155
nucleic acid, 139
nudity, 63
null hypothesis, 30
nurse, 114, 118
nurses, 61, 72, 114, 118, 119, 131
nursing, 73, 222
nutraceutical, 137, 152
nutraceuticals, 153
nutrient, 139, 143
nutrients, 135, 136, 137, 141, 144, 153
nutrition, 13, 34, 106, 138, 139, 141, 142, 145, 223, 224, 244
nutritional supplements, 137, 249

O

oat, 92
objectives, 211
objectivity, 67
obligations, 211, 219
observations, 25, 50, 51, 63, 68
obsolete, 89, 93, 96
occupational, 79, 169, 218
occupational health, 169
OECD, 8, 9, 11, 12, 14, 17, 37, 38, 39, 191
Ohio, 252, 253
oil, 154, 167, 168, 177, 180, 181, 194, 250
oil revenues, 167
oils, 136
oilseed, 144

old age, 200
omega-6, 140
online, 131
open space, 188, 189
open spaces, 188, 189
openness, viii, 2, 24, 25, 26, 28, 31, 32, 34, 36, 41, 63, 79, 81, 83, 85, 86, 96, 98, 99
opposition, 170
oppression, 46
optimal resource allocation, 212
oral, 114, 138
ORC, 131
organic, 137, 142
organic food, 137
organization, 237
organizations, 235
orthodox, 76, 107
outpatients, 115
output, 212, 213, 226
ownership, 145, 161, 177, 213
oxidants, x, 134
oxygen, 141, 143
oyster, x, 133, 134, 136, 139, 140, 141, 142, 143, 144, 152, 153, 154

P

Pacific, 5, 7, 11, 39, 63, 178
packaging, 146, 148
packets, 120
pain, 55, 114
Pakistan, 10, 154, 155
pandemic, 135, 137, 235, 237, 239, 242, 244, 247, 248
paper, 235, 250, 251, 253, 254
Papua New Guinea, 38
paradoxical, 243
parameter, 216, 217
parasites, 44, 135
parasitic diseases, 244
parents, 55, 59, 72
Paris, 37, 39
Parliament, 222
participant observation, 89
participation, xii, 209, 218, 219, 221, 222, 230, 231, 233
partnership, 161, 175
partnerships, 159, 160, 161, 163, 172, 174, 237
passenger, 7, 14
pastoral, 77, 89, 92, 99, 247
patents, 249
pathogenic, 72
pathogens, 44, 45, 46

pathways, 15
patients, 44, 115, 116, 123, 124, 125, 126, 138, 244
pay off, 98
payroll, 123
peacekeeping, 166, 167
peacekeeping forces, 167
pectin, 143
pedestrians, 10
pediatric, 72
penalties, 217
penalty, 216
pension, xi, 87, 88, 91, 92, 94, 96, 97, 194, 200
pension system, 87
pensions, 87, 93
people living with HIV/AIDS, xi, 134, 225
PEPFAR, 249
per capita, vii, viii, 2, 18, 19, 22, 24, 25, 28, 31, 32, 72, 195, 214, 215, 216, 217, 218, 220, 224, 226, 227, 230, 243, 249
per capita income, viii, 2, 18, 24, 25, 28, 31, 195, 214, 215, 217, 220, 224
perception, 58, 158, 159, 162, 163, 173, 174
perceptions, viii, 41, 42, 68, 160, 222
periodic, 43
peri-urban, 32
permit, 179
personal, xii, 238, 241
personal hygiene, 45, 50
personal responsibility, xii, 238
Peru, 38
pesticide, 136
pests, 142, 145
pH, 141, 143
pharmaceutical, 248
pharmaceutical companies, 248
phenolic, 137
phenolic compounds, 137
Philippines, 19, 37
phosphate, 146
phosphorus, x, 134
photographs, 150
phototrophic, 141
physiological, viii, 41, 64, 69
pig, 203
pigs, 55, 196
pilot studies, 145
pilot study, 145
placenta, 107, 119
planning, 14, 115, 179, 180, 181, 185, 188, 189, 190, 191, 192
plants, ix, x, 105, 106, 107, 108, 123, 125, 126, 127, 128, 129, 130, 136, 154, 166, 203
plastic, 48, 52, 54, 142, 146

play, 22, 32, 45, 56, 63, 114, 117, 118, 135, 197, 221
pleasure, 241
Pleurotus ostreatus, 138, 153, 154, 155
ploughing, 93, 96
pneumonia, 125
police, 7, 169, 228
policies, 222
policy, 214, 216, 231, 232, 233
policy choice, 21
policy instruments, 34, 82
policy levels, 47
policy makers, 34, 85, 99, 194, 206
political, 237, 238, 240, 241, 242, 244, 249
political instability, 135, 165, 170, 244
political participation, 135, 218
political parties, 223
political power, 25, 49, 218, 219
political stability, 160, 168
politics, 46, 67, 159, 219, 237, 240, 241
pollution, 142, 162, 171
polygamous marriages, 240
polysaccharide, 139
polysaccharides, 139, 155
polythene, 145
polyunsaturated fat, 140
polyunsaturated fatty acid, 140
polyunsaturated fatty acids, 140
poor, vii, viii, ix, x, xi, 1, 2, 6, 9, 11, 12, 13, 14, 15, 16, 18, 19, 20, 21, 22, 24, 25, 28, 30, 32, 33, 34, 38, 39, 41, 42, 76, 77, 78, 83, 84, 85, 86, 87, 89, 93, 95, 97, 100, 105, 106, 107, 108, 116, 117, 128, 129, 133, 134, 135, 140, 141, 143, 145, 150, 151, 163, 164, 165, 169, 177, 178, 181, 182, 184, 185, 186, 188, 189, 190, 191, 195, 211, 216, 220, 225, 227, 228, 229, 243, 244, 247, 249
poor health, 182
population, ix, xi, 8, 10, 16, 18, 25, 34, 42, 44, 60, 64, 78, 81, 82, 88, 90, 98, 105, 106, 107, 108, 118, 134, 160, 163, 177, 178, 179, 180, 181, 183, 185, 195, 196, 201, 216, 218, 219, 221, 223, 225, 226, 227, 228, 229, 231, 232, 238, 239, 246, 247
population density, 82, 88, 98
population growth, 88, 90, 228
portfolios, ix, 75, 77, 88, 96, 97, 100
ports, 168, 179
Portugal, 42, 137, 139, 153
positive relation, 196, 223
positive relationship, 196, 223
postpartum, 107
potatoes, 186
poultry, 196
poverty alleviation, xi, 6, 20, 21, 152, 157, 161, 162, 163, 165

Index

poverty eradication, 32, 34, 206
poverty line, 4, 20, 21, 24, 25, 28, 106, 134, 178, 229
poverty rate, xii, 195, 209, 227, 228, 230, 247
poverty reduction, vii, viii, 1, 2, 3, 5, 6, 12, 13, 14, 15, 16, 17, 18, 19, 20, 21, 22, 23, 24, 25, 28, 32, 33, 34, 79, 162, 184, 185, 189, 190, 191, 196, 206, 226
poverty threshold, 24
poverty trap, 13, 34
power, 21, 25, 42, 43, 46, 49, 58, 60, 65, 67, 70, 135, 163, 166, 184, 194, 212, 213, 214, 218, 219, 221, 222, 226, 227, 228, 237, 238, 240, 244, 245, 247, 249, 250
power plant, 166
power relations, 212
PPP, 11, 25, 214, 216, 226
pre-existing, 135
preference, 210, 224
pregnancy, 107, 117, 137
pregnant, ix, 105, 107, 113, 114, 116, 117, 119, 121, 122, 123, 125, 127, 128, 129, 226
pregnant women, ix, 105, 107, 113, 114, 116, 117, 119, 121, 122, 123, 125, 127, 128, 129, 226
premium, 12
presidency, 168
president, 168
pressure, 53, 78, 81, 82, 88, 98, 125, 127, 137, 139, 163, 167, 219, 223, 248
prestige, 45
Pretoria, 208, 254
prevention, xii, 34, 61, 117, 137, 236, 237, 238, 240, 245, 247, 249
prices, 4, 6, 13, 15, 16, 20, 80, 177, 178, 194, 249, 250
primary, xii, 209, 214, 219, 220, 221, 222
primary school, 219, 220, 221
primary schools, 220
priorities, 213, 214
privacy, 42, 46, 52, 64
private, vii, ix, 1, 2, 6, 7, 11, 14, 32, 33, 35, 39, 45, 46, 52, 53, 55, 63, 70, 79, 83, 97, 99, 105, 106, 114, 115, 116, 118, 129, 161, 172, 180, 188, 189, 220, 235, 246
private investment, 6, 8, 14, 33
private sector, vii, 1, 2, 6, 32, 34, 35, 39, 97, 114, 161
private sector investment, 32, 39
privatisation, 178, 181, 186
privatization, 242
proactive, 165, 166, 175
probability, 18, 19, 22, 66, 210, 223
procedures, 211, 219, 222
producers, 84, 85, 143, 203, 245

product market, 14, 212
production, x, 6, 14, 16, 18, 82, 84, 85, 88, 89, 90, 96, 98, 133, 134, 135, 136, 137, 141, 142, 143, 144, 150, 151, 152, 153, 155, 166, 168, 170, 172, 187, 189, 194, 196, 197, 202, 203, 205, 207, 210, 211, 212, 230, 231, 232
production costs, 152
production technology, 153
productive capacity, 194
productivity, 6, 13, 14, 15, 16, 18, 19, 20, 25, 34, 134, 160, 185, 206, 211, 212, 232, 245
profit, 196, 197, 202, 207, 248
profitability, 100, 196, 238, 241, 243
profits, 197, 248
program, 34, 73
programs, 211, 223, 224
progressive, 250
proliferation, 167
promote, 210, 248
property, iv, 34, 98, 213, 228, 249
property rights, 34, 98, 213, 249
prosperity, 164
prostate, 137, 154
prostate cancer, 137, 154
protected area, 108
protection, 137, 173, 189, 190, 210
protectionism, 169
protein, x, 133, 135, 138, 139, 142, 247
proteins, 139
proteoglycans, 139
prototype, 145, 150
proxy, 25, 86, 214, 245
psychological well-being, 215
psychologists, 248
public, 242, 243, 244, 246, 247, 248, 249
public goods, 33
public health, viii, 41, 42, 44, 47, 48, 58, 70, 73, 124, 244, 247, 249
public investment, 13, 21, 23
public money, 248
public relations, 173
public sector, 78
public service, 178, 181
public-private partnerships, 172
pulps, 143
punitive, 158
purchasing power, 135, 194, 214, 226
purchasing power parity (PPP), 214, 226
pure water, 44
P-value, 30

Q

qualitative research, 67, 71
quality of life, 229
quality of service, 33
questionnaire, ix, 105, 112, 113, 118, 131, 199
questionnaires, xi, 112, 113, 193

R

racial groups, 216
radioactive waste, 136
radius, 106
rain, 52, 53, 248
rainfall, 140
range, x, 7, 21, 22, 34, 45, 76, 84, 114, 133, 141, 143, 152, 187, 190, 214, 216, 238
ranking, 215, 219, 229
rape, 236
RAS, 255
rats, 55
raw material, 155
reading, 131
real income, 15, 214
reality, 43, 46, 57, 62, 66, 67, 96, 185, 237, 243
rebel, 171
reception, x, 105, 117, 129
recession, 87
recessions, 83, 194
recognition, ix, 42, 75, 189, 238, 240
reconciliation, 168
reconstruction, 250
recovery, 178
recreation, 188
recreational, 249
redistribution, 13, 34, 80, 250
reduction, 225, 226, 247
refining, ix, 75
reflection, 221, 237
reforms, xii, 17, 18, 34, 82, 181, 184, 209, 242
regional, 239, 240, 241, 242
regional cooperation, 33
regional policy, 198
regional public goods, 33
regression, 26
regular, 34, 81, 82, 84, 86, 87, 89, 90, 91, 92, 93, 95, 96, 97, 100, 116, 120, 239
regulation, 10, 33, 34, 39
regulations, 184
regulatory framework, 190
rehabilitation, 11, 19, 22
rehydration, 114

relationship, xi, 5, 18, 23, 25, 26, 136, 154, 157, 159, 160, 163, 168, 173, 196, 210, 213, 214, 223, 239
relationships, 26, 48, 69, 98, 163, 173, 239, 246
relative prices, 83
relatives, 44, 123, 198, 202, 212
relevance, 64
religion, 45, 112, 118
religious, 238
remittances, 23, 24, 25, 28, 29, 30, 31, 34, 36, 80, 82, 87, 89, 92, 96, 97, 211, 213
rent, 191
repair, 13, 196
replication, 244
report, 217
reproduction, 85, 240, 245
reputation, 169
research, 248
Research and Development, 152, 248, 255
research design, 68
reservation, 196
reserves, 78, 79, 240
residence permits, 179
residential, 187, 188
residues, 136, 142, 152, 153, 155
resistance, 118, 154
resource allocation, 212, 213
resource management, 89, 91, 96, 100
resources, xi, 8, 16, 17, 23, 43, 65, 83, 86, 89, 93, 97, 98, 99, 100, 117, 120, 123, 125, 129, 134, 140, 157, 158, 161, 164, 167, 168, 171, 174, 180, 182, 189, 193, 196, 198, 201, 209, 210, 212, 213, 214, 216, 218, 220, 221, 226, 228, 230, 231, 232, 246, 248
responsibility, 210, 227
restaurant, 13
restructuring, 80, 239
retention, 145
returns, 21, 78, 79, 81, 89, 91, 96, 150, 246
revenue, 164, 177, 191, 210
reverse transcriptase, 139
rhetoric, 223
riboflavin, x, 134, 138
rice, 139, 143, 144, 154, 155
rights, 209, 212, 213, 221
risk, viii, xii, 14, 41, 42, 44, 45, 46, 56, 64, 66, 67, 69, 83, 85, 98, 99, 100, 106, 107, 214, 228, 238, 239, 240, 241, 242, 243, 244, 247, 252
risk aversion, 247
risk management, 100
risk society, 242
risks, 22, 44, 56, 65, 69, 77, 78, 83, 84, 85, 86, 88, 94, 98, 99, 100, 107, 244
road safety, 10

Roads, 7, 9, 10, 11, 20, 26, 27, 29, 30, 31, 36, 37, 38, 40
rodents, 55
role conflict, 222
rolling, 108
Rome, 43, 208, 231, 255
rule of law, 164
ruminant, 142, 153
rural, vii, viii, ix, x, xi, 8, 9, 13, 14, 15, 16, 18, 19, 20, 21, 22, 23, 33, 34, 39, 41, 42, 44, 45, 48, 58, 64, 66, 71, 72, 73, 75, 76, 77, 78, 79, 80, 81, 82, 83, 84, 85, 86, 87, 88, 89, 91, 92, 93, 94, 95, 96, 97, 98, 99, 100, 105, 106, 107, 108, 116, 117, 118, 123, 129, 133, 134, 138, 150, 153, 178, 179, 180, 181, 182, 185, 189, 194, 195, 196, 197, 198, 210, 216, 217, 225, 227, 230, 240, 247
rural areas, vii, ix, 9, 16, 19, 21, 33, 58, 64, 77, 81, 94, 105, 106, 107, 123, 129, 134, 150, 179, 180, 195, 198, 216, 217, 225, 227, 241
rural communities, 44, 77, 86, 97
rural development, ix, 45, 75, 76, 77, 82, 84, 92, 97, 99, 100, 153
rural people, vii, xi, 93, 116, 129, 194
rural population, x, 8, 78, 79, 133, 138, 196
rural poverty, ix, 13, 14, 18, 19, 20, 21, 23, 75, 76, 77, 82, 83, 85, 96, 99, 100, 182
rural women, 108, 118, 197, 210
Rwanda, 35, 240, 249

S

sacrifice, 227
safe drinking water, 12
safeguard, 164
safeguards, 174
safety, 10, 34, 45, 64, 123, 169, 174, 247
salaries, 43, 87, 96
sales, 87, 150, 202, 203
salt, 196
salts, 114
sample, 20, 26, 31, 48, 199
sample mean, 31
sampling, 48, 68
sanctions, 162, 171
sand, 44, 52, 55, 145, 149
sanitation, vii, viii, 1, 2, 10, 12, 16, 19, 23, 41, 42, 44, 45, 46, 48, 50, 55, 56, 57, 58, 59, 60, 61, 62, 63, 64, 65, 66, 68, 69, 70, 71, 72, 107, 180, 181, 244
SAP, 79, 178
SAPs, 178, 181, 246
SAPS, 242
SAR, 7

saving, 211
savings, 19, 33, 85, 187, 202, 207, 232
sawdust, 143, 144, 154
scalar, 236, 237, 240
scarce resources, 213
scarcity, 123, 245
scatter, 26
scatter plot, 26
schistosomiasis, 244
scholarship, 71
school, x, 14, 25, 35, 43, 44, 52, 61, 70, 78, 83, 95, 96, 124, 126, 133, 134, 150, 160, 196, 201, 216, 219, 220, 221, 222, 223, 242
schooling, 19, 94, 219
science, 245
scores, 214
sea level, 108
search, ix, 48, 75, 85, 88, 98, 99, 135
searching, 100
seasonality, 228
secondary, xii, 209, 214, 220
secondary education, 14, 220
secondary schools, 220
security, 20, 43, 87, 135, 165, 167, 168, 178, 179, 182, 187, 191, 192, 206, 212, 215, 229, 248
Security Council, 168, 171
seed, 154
selenium, 238
Self, xi, 183, 192, 193, 194, 229
self employment, 207
self-confidence, 69
self-employed, 183, 197
self-employment, 96, 183
self-esteem, 229
semi-arid, 77, 78, 88, 89, 93
Senegal, 35, 71, 238
sensitivity, 59
sentences, 51
separation, 44, 73, 237
septic tank, 44, 45, 48, 52, 56, 66, 69
serum, 239
service provider, 113, 117
services, iv, ix, x, 6, 7, 12, 13, 14, 16, 20, 21, 23, 32, 33, 34, 46, 47, 78, 79, 89, 105, 106, 107, 108, 114, 115, 116, 117, 118, 119, 120, 124, 125, 126, 128, 129, 178, 179, 180, 181, 182, 184, 185, 191, 194, 195, 198, 209, 210, 211, 212, 219, 223, 226, 228, 229, 242, 245, 248
settlements, 7, 44, 179, 180, 185
settlers, 79
severity, viii, 2, 24, 25, 26, 28, 31, 248
sewage, 45, 64

sex, 47, 56, 58, 66, 71, 119, 183, 239, 241, 243, 244, 245, 246, 249
sexual activity, 244
sexual assault, 45
sexual assaults, 45
sexual behaviour, xii, 237, 238
sexual contact, 236, 242, 244
sexual health, 225
sexuality, 237
sexually transmitted disease, 243, 246
sexually transmitted infections, 244
shame, 60
shape, 141, 184, 240
shares, 212, 216, 217, 218
sharing, 34, 64, 100, 228
sheep, 92
shelter, 46, 195, 227
shocks, 84, 97, 99, 190
shores, 245
short run, 34
shortage, 219
short-term, 159, 244
shy, 213
Sierra Leone, 171, 196, 208, 239
sites, 145, 146, 151, 179, 187
skewness, 66
skilled personnel, 164
skills, x, xi, 69, 81, 84, 86, 100, 134, 193, 194, 195, 196, 198, 202, 204, 205, 206, 207
skills training, xii, 194, 195, 204, 206
slavery, 242, 243
slaves, 169
sleep, 67, 120, 121, 245
smallpox, 137
small-scale business, xi, 193, 194, 195
SMMEs, 194, 195, 206
smoke, 97
smoking, 47
snakes, 55, 57
social, xii, 237, 238, 239, 240, 242, 243, 245, 246, 248, 249, 250, 251, 252, 254
social capital, 85, 86, 100, 185, 246, 248
social change, ix, 75, 77, 83, 87, 88, 94, 100, 249
social class, 242
social cohesion, 13
social construct, 46, 65
social context, 251
social control, 243
social development, 18, 184
social exclusion, 86
social fabric, 243
social factors, 213
social group, 95

social identity, 252
social indicator, 183
social interests, 173
social life, 222
social network, 85
social norms, 99, 158, 225
social policy, 184
social relations, 48, 77, 83, 84, 85, 86, 91, 96, 98, 99
social resources, 230
social responsibility, 116, 158, 160, 163, 173
social security, 43, 87
social services, 21, 181, 185, 209, 219, 223
social status, 212
social structure, 73, 83, 98
social support, 47
social transition, ix, 76, 87, 91
social welfare, 223, 227
socialism, 246
socialist, 168
socialization, 85, 212, 222, 248
socially, 241
society, 237, 248, 253
socioeconomic, 62
socio-economic status, 221
sociological, ix, 75, 84
sociologists, 83
sociology, 84
sodium, 151
soil, 64, 78, 80, 81, 92, 136, 238, 244
soil erosion, 80
soils, 88, 205
solid tumors, 139
solid waste, 55
solidarity, 250
solutions, 249
soot, 54
South Africa, 2, v, ix, xi, 3, 22, 35, 42, 43, 44, 75, 76, 77, 79, 80, 81, 87, 88, 89, 91, 92, 93, 94, 95, 96, 97, 98, 99, 100, 101, 102, 105, 133, 138, 163, 166, 167, 176, 179, 193, 194, 195, 200, 201, 202, 208, 240, 241, 244, 246, 248, 251, 252, 253, 254, 256
South Asia, 5, 7, 8, 9, 11, 82
South Korea, 11
Southeast Asia, 82
sovereignty, 160, 168
spatial, 22, 79, 237, 238, 239, 243, 246
spawning, 143, 146, 149
specialisation, 78, 88, 92, 100
specialists, 237
species, x, 105, 108, 113, 127, 128, 129, 134, 137, 138, 139, 140, 141, 142, 143, 151, 152, 153, 154, 243

speech, 164
speed, 35
spelling, 33
spheres, 6, 218, 222
spillover effects, 165, 170
sporadic, 43
spouse, 241
springs, 161
SPSS, 113
squatter, 180
Sri Lanka, 10, 125
stability, 56, 57, 141, 160, 168, 174
stabilize, 52
staff, 223
stages, 86, 140, 197
stakeholders, 173
standard of living, 134, 178, 182, 185, 196, 214, 226, 229
standards, 42, 158, 169, 172, 224
starch, 143
state intervention, 77
state welfare, 80, 87, 96
state-owned, 166
state-owned enterprises, 166
statistics, 30, 43, 113, 130, 160, 183, 198, 220, 223, 235
statutory, 180
STD, 243, 254
stereotypical, 222
sterile, 119
sterilization, 145
stimulus, 83
stock, 25, 65, 89, 202
stomach, 128, 137
storage, 135, 141, 196
strategies, xii, 34, 47, 70, 76, 77, 82, 84, 85, 86, 87, 89, 91, 94, 95, 96, 97, 100, 107, 125, 190, 194, 196, 206, 237, 246
stratification, 82
strength, 47, 68, 197
stress, 76, 100
strikes, 169
structural adjustment, 180, 181, 223, 224, 226, 238, 240, 241, 242, 246
structural adjustment programmes, 180, 181, 224, 238, 242, 246
structural unemployment, 81, 89, 97
students, 152, 173, 221
study, 228
subjective, 48
Sub-Sahara Africa, 9
Sub-Saharan Africa, viii, 2, 5, 8, 9, 10, 11, 13, 26, 28, 29, 30, 31, 37, 76, 103, 134, 135, 160, 198, 219, 223, 225, 227, 230, 231, 232, 235, 239, 240, 242, 244, 249, 251, 254, 256
subsidies, 79, 178, 181, 242
subsistence, 78, 84, 87, 89, 91, 92, 93, 96, 97, 99, 123, 124, 135, 196, 210, 211, 212, 213, 217, 227, 230
subsistence farming, 87, 93, 96, 97, 123, 124, 217
subsistence production, 84
substances, 72, 154
substitution, 215
substrates, 136, 139, 140, 143, 144, 145, 150, 152, 154
Sudan, 158, 165, 166, 167, 168, 175, 239
suffering, 134, 225, 235
sugar, 120, 144, 153, 196
sugarcane, 152
summer, x, 134, 146
supplements, 137, 249
supply, 15, 20, 72, 126, 135, 142, 150, 151, 211, 241, 247
support services, 212
surgeries, 115
surplus, 150, 194, 196, 245, 248
Survey, 232
survival, 77, 78, 97, 203, 219
susceptibility, 135, 244
sustainability, 76, 203, 204, 205, 206, 229
sustainable development, 71, 191, 198
Sweden, 41, 70, 71, 72, 73, 191, 231, 254
switching, 245
Switzerland, 72, 192
symbolic, 249
symptom, 237
symptoms, 113
synchronization, 161
syndrome, 222, 236
systems, 227, 240, 243, 248, 249

T

tactics, 162
Taiwan, 11
talent, 218
tangible, 63
Tanzania, 35, 42, 102, 168, 221, 240, 246, 255
targets, 4, 6, 134
tariff, 81, 164, 170
tariffs, 18, 170
taste, x, 134
taxes, 47, 78, 179, 191, 250
taxis, 7
tea, 53, 54, 108, 114, 210, 232
teaching, 59, 60, 64, 96, 223

technical assistance, 119, 163, 172
technical change, 25
technological change, 161
technology, 211
technology transfer, 170
telecommunication, vii, 1, 2
telecommunications, 7, 16, 23
temperature, 140, 141, 143, 149
temporal, 96, 239
tenure, 212
term plans, 160
terraces, 81
territorial, 168
territory, 171
tertiary, xii, 209, 214
tertiary education, 200
Tetanus, 117
Thailand, 10, 21, 144, 155
Theories, 230
theory, 247, 256
therapy, 125, 155
thiamin, x, 134
Third World, 197, 252
Thomson, 171, 176
threat, 175, 211, 213, 244
threatened, 88
threatening, 90, 170
threats, 229
threshold, 24, 223
timber, xi, 108, 145, 157, 158, 162, 170, 171, 172, 176
time, xii, 210, 211, 213, 214, 220, 222, 223, 224, 226, 228, 238, 243, 245, 247
time allocation, 210
time consuming, 46, 197
time series, 21
timing, 151
tin, 54
TIPS, 102
tissue, 136, 140
title, 63, 162, 212
tobacco, 108, 166
Togo, 239
Tokyo, 75
tomato, 186
top-down, 64, 125
tracking, 170
trade, vii, viii, xi, 1, 2, 6, 9, 12, 13, 17, 18, 22, 25, 28, 31, 32, 33, 34, 79, 157, 158, 159, 161, 162, 163, 164, 165, 166, 167, 168, 169, 170, 171, 172, 173, 174, 178, 215, 239, 242, 243, 244, 248, 249
trade costs, 33
trade liberalization, 25, 32, 34, 79, 178, 242, 243

trade policies, 13
trade-off, 215, 244
trading, xi, 157, 158, 159, 162, 163, 165, 167, 168, 248
tradition, 57, 128, 214, 228
traditional healers, 117, 118, 123, 124, 125, 128
traditional medicines, 128
traditions, 228
traffic, 9, 10
training, xii, 34, 93, 106, 115, 119, 124, 150, 152, 165, 194, 195, 196, 198, 202, 204, 206, 211, 229
trans, 237
transaction costs, vii, 1, 2, 9, 14, 18, 22, 39, 86, 211
transcriptase, 139
transcripts, 51, 69
transfer, 34, 80, 135, 158, 170, 174, 213
transformation, 26, 83, 84, 98, 99
transition, 43, 87, 171
translation, 50, 51, 68, 69, 72, 73
transmission, 239, 242, 243, 245, 247, 249
transnational, 249
transparency, 158, 162, 174
transparent, 34
transport, vii, 1, 2, 6, 7, 8, 10, 12, 14, 16, 17, 18, 21, 22, 23, 32, 33, 43, 81, 114, 116, 122, 123, 124, 178, 179, 196, 198, 223
transport costs, 6, 18, 23, 33, 124
transportation, 6, 9, 13, 16, 23
transportation infrastructure, 9, 23
travel, 12, 18, 21, 116, 180, 243, 248
treatment, 215, 216, 227
trees, 52, 90, 97, 136
trend, 220, 224, 226, 227, 229
tribes, 137, 217
TRIPS, 249
trucks, 166
trust, 61, 86, 98, 239
tuberculosis, 55
tumor, 139
tumors, 137, 139
Tunisia, 1, 4, 35, 37
turnover, 246
twins, 119

U

Uganda, vii, 17, 18, 23, 35, 38, 40, 135, 230, 238, 240, 241, 247, 255
ultraviolet, 138
umbilical cord, 120
UN, 13, 37, 43, 134, 135, 165, 166, 215, 221, 243, 255
uncertainty, 32, 184

UNDP, 44, 69, 214, 215, 216, 217, 218, 220, 222, 223, 224, 227, 229, 230, 233, 242, 243, 247, 256
unemployment, ix, 76, 81, 83, 87, 89, 97, 169, 178, 185, 195, 202, 205
unemployment rate, 87, 178
UNESCO, 130, 131, 220, 221
United Kingdom, 40, 71
United Nations, vii, xi, 44, 71, 72, 131, 142, 157, 160, 164, 168, 171, 191, 192, 222, 233, 255, 256
United Nations Development Program(me), 44, 72, 160, 191, 233, 256
United Nations Environment Program, 160
United States (US), 43, 101, 102, 172, 194, 214, 226, 235, 240
units of analysis, 51
universities, 135, 173, 223
urban, 241, 247
urban areas, xi, 177, 178, 181, 182, 183, 211, 225, 227, 230
urban centres, 179, 180, 186, 190
urban population, xi, 177, 178, 179, 180, 181, 185
urban settlement, 179, 180
urbanisation, 190, 246
urinary, 44, 46
urinary tract, 44, 46
urinary tract infection, 44, 46
urine, 42, 44, 45
US dollar, 246
US, see United States, 214, 226
USAID, 135, 254
uterus, 107, 126

V

vaccination, 117
vaccine, 122
vacuum, 17
vagina, 125
vaginal, 247
validity, 30, 71
value added tax, 10
values, 14, 57, 69, 88, 91, 96, 139, 152, 185, 212, 216, 217
variable, 215, 218
variables, 20, 24, 25, 26, 29, 30, 32, 94, 212, 215, 216, 218, 229, 242
variation, 135, 216
vector, 236
vegetables, 87, 136, 138, 149, 187, 196, 203, 205
vegetation, 78, 88, 108, 171
vehicles, 7
vein, viii, 2
ventilation, 72, 121, 145

venue, 131
Vermont, 235
Victoria, 244, 245, 253
Vietnam, 18, 22, 28, 38, 39
village, viii, 18, 41, 42, 43, 44, 48, 50, 51, 55, 56, 57, 58, 59, 60, 61, 62, 64, 65, 68, 69, 71, 72, 79, 85, 86, 96, 119, 145, 213
violence, 210, 247, 249
violent, 243, 245
viral, 239, 248, 249
virus, 44, 236, 237, 238, 240, 242, 247, 253
visible, 43, 54, 182
vision, 18, 34, 64, 161
vitamin C, 138
vitamin D, 138
vitamins, x, 133, 138, 139
voice, xii, 160, 174, 209, 213
vulnerability, xi, xii, 14, 84, 97, 99, 134, 135, 177, 179, 191, 228, 238, 240, 242, 247, 256

W

wage rate, 21
wages, 13, 14, 15, 19, 20, 21, 25, 87, 169
Wales, 192
walking, 55
war, 65, 134, 166, 168, 171, 239, 242, 243
warfare, vii, 43, 158, 167
Washington, 255
waste disposal, 44
waste products, x, 46, 133
wastes, 136, 142, 143, 144, 152, 153, 155
water, vii, 1, 2, 7, 10, 12, 16, 19, 23, 43, 44, 45, 46, 47, 48, 52, 53, 54, 55, 56, 57, 59, 60, 61, 62, 63, 64, 65, 66, 71, 72, 90, 107, 125, 139, 141, 142, 143, 145, 146, 149, 151, 152, 180, 185, 191, 195, 197, 229, 243, 244
water evaporation, 141
water-holding capacity, 143
water-soluble, 139
wealth, 6, 45, 83, 87, 91, 92, 95, 96, 107, 214, 246, 247
weapons, 167
wear, 247
welding, 196
welfare, xi, 16, 19, 28, 80, 85, 87, 88, 96, 97, 177, 179, 211, 215, 223, 227
welfare system, 80, 87, 96, 227
wellbeing, 15, 25, 64, 71, 178, 184, 215, 226, 227, 241
wells, 44
West Africa, 158, 170, 171, 172, 239, 241
Western aid, 162

Index

Western-style, 240
wetlands, 144
wheat, 140, 142, 144, 153, 154, 155
wildlife, 171
windows, 121, 142, 145, 149
Wisconsin, 252
witchcraft, 127
withdrawal, 226
wives, 200, 213, 222, 225, 227, 240
wood, x, 52, 53, 133, 136, 142, 146, 172, 196
wood products, 172
wool, 120
work, 210, 211, 213, 217, 228, 230, 231
workers, 19, 25, 42, 66, 81, 87, 93, 97, 123, 166, 169, 170, 175, 179, 219, 221, 226, 241, 243, 244, 245, 248
workforce, 183
working conditions, 62, 64, 169
working population, 183
workload, 57
World Bank, 7, 8, 9, 11, 13, 19, 20, 22, 25, 36, 37, 38, 39, 40, 43, 72, 73, 86, 160, 172, 181, 191, 207, 211, 214, 219, 223, 224, 225, 226, 228, 230, 231, 232, 233, 242, 243, 246, 251, 255, 256
World Health Organization (WHO), 42, 46, 72, 130, 235, 244, 246, 251, 256
World Resources Institute, 160

World Trade Organization (WTO), 159, 248, 249
World War, 42
World War I, 42
World War II, 42
worms, 42, 44
worry, 55, 56, 64
wound healing, 140

X

Xinhua News Agency, 168

Y

yield, 21, 81, 141, 143, 144, 145, 149, 154
young women, 61, 62
yuan, 19, 21

Z

Zimbabwe, x, 10, 35, 42, 43, 72, 133, 135, 138, 141, 142, 145, 151, 152, 158, 165, 166, 167, 168, 175, 222, 240, 242, 246, 247, 251, 253, 255
zinc, 48